Sustainable Retrofit and Facilities Management

Sustainable Retrofit and Facilities Management is a comprehensive guide for anyone involved in the refurbishment and management of existing buildings. It sets out ways to minimize carbon emissions, water consumption and waste, as well as to enhance the long-term sustainability of a building.

The book provides practical advice on how to improve the efficiency of existing buildings through both good management and refurbishment. It considers the building as part of a wider network, looking at the collaborative relationship between building refurbishment, facilities management and community infrastructure.

Illustrated throughout with case studies and examples of best practice, this is a must-have handbook for engineers, architects, developers, contractors and facility managers.

Paul Appleby advises design and masterplanning teams on the integrated sustainable design of buildings and communities. He has recently been appointed as a CABE Built Environment Expert for the Design Council and has worked in the construction industry as a consultant, lecturer and researcher for over 40 years, working on award-winning projects with some of the world's leading architects. As well as writing key guidance published by CIBSE, his book *Integrated Sustainable Design of Buildings* appeared in a list of Cambridge University's 'Top 40 Sustainability Books of 2010'. He has spoken at numerous conferences and seminars worldwide. He was listed as a 'Green Hero' in a list published by *Property Week*.

'Excellent and accessible for both the technical and lay reader. A comprehensive cradle-to-grave account for improving sustainability in and around the built environment.'

Justin Snoxall, British Land

'Spanning global and local policy, Paul's book is an essential guide to the challenges and strategies to save energy, and improve on efficiencies in our existing building stock. With so much of it still in use, and in desperate need of refurbishment and retrofitting, there could be no better guide, nor this, a better instruction manual.'

Andrew Daws, Director, Andrew Daws Projects Ltd

Praise for Paul Appleby's *Integrated Sustainable Design of Buildings*:

'Paul Appleby succeeds in doing the seemingly impossible: explaining all the main aspects of sustainable building in only approximately 400 pages. His writing is concise, succinct and knowledgeable . . . What is most astonishing, given the large scope of the subject, is that Appleby never loses sight of the essential . . . The book combines two things in one: a well structured and comprehensive introduction to the design and construction of sustainable buildings and a powerful search-engine in the form of a book.'

Detail, Issue 2, 2011

Sustainable Retrofit and Facilities Management

Paul Appleby

Routledge
Taylor & Francis Group

LONDON AND NEW YORK

earthscan
from Routledge

First published 2013
by Routledge
2 Park Square, Milton Park, Abingdon, Oxon, OX14 4RN

Simultaneously published in the USA and Canada
by Routledge
711 Third Avenue, New York, NY 10017

Routledge is an imprint of the Taylor & Francis Group, an informa business

British Library Cataloguing in Publication Data
A catalogue record for this book is available from the British Library

Library of Congress Cataloging-in-Publication Data
Appleby, Paul.
  Sustainable retrofit and facilities management / Paul Appleby.
    p. cm.
  Includes bibliographical references and index.
  1. Buildings—Repair and reconstruction. 2. Sustainable buildings.
  3. Buildings—Energy conservation. 4. Architecture and energy conservation. I. Title.
  TH3401.A67 2013
  658.2'02—dc23   2012026853

ISBN13: 978–0–415–53109–2 (hbk)
ISBN13: 978–0–203–07573–9 (ebk)

Typeset in Helvetica and Sabon by
Keystroke, Station Road, Codsall, Wolverhampton

Printed in Italy by Printer Trento S.r.l.

To Liz, for your endless patience

The greater danger for most of us is not that our aim is too high and we miss it, but that it is too low and we reach it.

Michelangelo Di Lodovico Buonarroti Simoni, 1475–1564

Contents

Figures

Tables

Boxes

Acknowledgements

I would like to thank the following for their invaluable assistance and support:

- Tatiana Bosteels, Head of Responsible Property Investment, Hermes Real Estate for the Crystal Peaks case history in Chapter 4.10;
- Justin Snoxall of British Land for the York House case history in Chapter 4.10;
- Sarah Stickland of Davis Langdon – an AECOM Company – for the Project INSPIRE case history in Chapter 2.3.

I would also like to thank the many others who have provided permission to use the images in this book.

In particular, I would like to thank Nicki Dennis and Alice Aldous of Earthscan/Routledge for putting faith in my original ideas and supporting me through the process.

Abbreviations

ach^{-1}	air changes per hour
AC	alternating current
ACGIH	American Conference of Governmental Industrial Hygienists
ACP	alternative compliance path
ACPO	Association of Chief Police Officers
ADT	air-dried tonne
AECB	Association of Energy-Conscious Builders
AIHA	American Industrial Hygiene Association
AMR	automatic meter reading
AOX	adsorbable organic halogenated compound
ARRA	American Recovery and Reinvestment Act
ASHRAE	American Society of Heating, Refrigeration and Air-Conditioning Engineers
ASID	American Society of Interior Designers
BAP	Biodiversity Action Plan
BARS	Biodiversity Action Reporting System
BAT	best available technique
BBP	Better Buildings Partnership
BCIS	Building Cost Information Service
BEMS	building energy management system
BFRC	British Fenestration Rating Council
BHC	Building Health Consultants Ltd
BIFM	British Institute of Facilities Managers
BMI	body mass index
BMS	building management system
BPA	British Parking Association
BREEAM	Building Research Establishment Assessment Method
BS&EA	Building Services and Engineering Association
BSRIA	Building Services Research and Information Association
BTP	Building Technologies Program
BUG	bicycle user group
CAFM	computer-aided facilities management
capex	capital expenditure
CARMA	Carbon Monitoring for Action
CBM	condition-based maintenance
CBE	Center for the Built Environment
CCHP	combined cooling heat and power
CCS	carbon capture and storage
CDC	Centers for Disease Control and Prevention
CERT	carbon emission reduction target
CESP	Community Energy-Saving Programme
CEWT	condenser entering water temperature
CFL	compact fluorescent lamp
CHP	combined heat and power
CIBSE	Chartered Institution of Building Services Engineers

CIEB	continual improvement assessment for existing buildings
CIGA	Cavity Insulation Guarantee Agency
CLG	Communities & Local Government
CMMS	computerized maintenance management system
CoP	coefficient of performance
COSHH	Control of Substances Hazardous to Health Regulations
CPSL	Cambridge Programme for Sustainability Leadership
CRI	Carpet and Rug Institute
CSE	Centre for Sustainable Energy
CSH	Code for Sustainable Homes
CSR	corporate sustainability reporting
CSR	corporate social responsibility
dB	decibel
DCLG	Department for Communities & Local Government
DEC	Display Energy Certificate
DECC	Department of Energy and Climate Change
DEFRA	Department for Environment, Food and Rural Affairs
DGS	Department of General Services
DHW	domestic hot water
DQM	Design Quality Method
DTI	Department for Trade and Industry
DTS	Distributor Take-Back Scheme
EA	Electricity Association
EA	Environmental Agency
EAD	Energy Action Devon
ECA	Empty Homes Agency
ECA	enhanced capital allowance
ECF	elemental chlorine free
ECO	Energy Company Obligation
EEI	energy efficiency index
EEV	electronic expansion valve
ELV	emission limit value
EMAS	Eco-Management and Audit Scheme
EMS	environmental management system
EPA	Environmental Protection Agency
EPACT	Energy Policy Act
EPBD	Energy Performance of Buildings Directive
EPC	Energy Performance Certificate
EPC	energy performance contracting
EPDM	ethylene propolene diene monomer
EPI	Environmental Performance Indicator
EPS	expanded polystyrene
ESCO	energy service company
ESD	Energy Services Directive
ESPC	energy-saving performance contract
EWC	European Waste Catalogue
FEMP	Federal Energy Management Program
FIT	feed-in tariff
FM	facilities management

FPE	facility performance evaluation
FSC	Forest Stewardship Council
GA	Green Associate
GBC	Green Building Council
GBI	Green Build Initiative
GBMG	Green Building Management Group
GCHP	ground-coupled heat pump
GEM	Global Environmental Method
GHG	greenhouse gas
GIFA	gross internal floor area
GIRS	Gas Industry Registration Scheme
GISP	Global Invasive Species Programme
GPG	good practice guide
GPP	green public procurement
GRI	Global Reporting Initiative
GRO	Green Roof Organization
GSA	General Services Administration
GWP	global warming potential
HAWT	horizontal axis wind turbine
HFC	hydrofluorocarbon
HHSRS	Housing Health & Safety Rating System
HIU	hydraulic interface unit
HTP	human toxicity potential
HUD	Housing and Urban Development
HVAC	heating, ventilation and air conditioning
HVCA	Heating and Ventilation Contractors Association
IAQ	indoor air quality
ICC	International Chamber of Commerce
IEA	International Energy Agency
IEQ	indoor environmental quality
IPPC	Integrated Pollution Prevention Control
ISO	International Organization for Standardization
JRC	Joint Research Centre
kWp	kilowatt peak
LCBA	Low-Carbon Buildings Accelerator
LCC	life cycle costs
LED	light-emitting diodes
LEED	Leadership in Energy and Environmental Design
LLF	light loss factor
LIST	Low-Impact Shopfitting Tool
LTP	Local Transport Plan
LZC	low or zero carbon
MILCON	military construction
MCA	motor circuit analysis
MORE	maintenance and operations recommender
MRT	mean radiant temperature
MSHA	Mine Safety and Health Administration
M&T	monitoring and targeting
MUSCO	multi-utility service company

MVHR	mechanical ventilation heat recovery
NAAQS	National Ambient Air Quality Standards
NADCA	National Air Duct Cleaners Association
NAPM	National Association of Paper Manufacturers
NECPA	National Energy Conservation Policy Act
NERS	National Electricity Registration Scheme
NFC	near field communication
NIA	National Insulation Association
NIOSH	National Institute of Occupational Safety & Health
NOFA	Northeast Organic Farming Association
NO_x	oxides of nitrogen
NPPF	National Planning Policy Framework
NSPP	National Sustainable Public Procurement Programme
OEL	occupational exposure limit
OGC	Office of Government Commerce
OMB	Office of Management & Budget
OSH	Occupational Health & Safety
OSHA	Occupational Safety & Health Administration
PAS	Publicly Available Specification
PCF	process chlorine free
PCM	phase change material
PEFC	Programme for the Endorsement of Forest Certification
PEL	permissible exposure limit
PF	power factor
PFC	perfluorocarbon
PHPP	Passivhaus Planning Package
PIR	passive infra-red
PMV	predicted mean vote
POE	post-occupancy evaluation
PPD	predicted percentage dissatisfied
PRSV	pre-rinse spray valve
PV	photovoltaic
PWM	pulse width modulation
RCM	reliability-centred maintenance
RCRA	Resource Conservation & Recovery Act
REL	recommended exposure limit
RHI	Renewable Heat Incentive
RHPP	Renewable Heat Premium Payment
RICS	Royal Institution of Chartered Surveyors
rms	root mean square
RoI	return on investment
RSL	registered social landlord
SAP	Standard Assessment Procedure
SBEM	Simplified Building Energy Model
SBS	sick building syndrome
SCC	Southampton City Council
SF_6	sulphur hexafluoride
SMART	simple, measurable, achievable, relevant and time-based
SMEs	small and medium-sized enterprise

SPT	Strathclyde Partnership for Transport
SSSI	sites of special scientific interest
SUDS	sustainable urban drainage system
SWMP	site waste management plan
TDS	total dissolved solid
TFT	thin-film transistor
TIEMS	tenant interface for energy and maintenance system
TIFM	total integrated facilities management
TLV	threshold limit value
TRV	thermostatic radiator valve
TVC	total viable count
UESC	utility energy services contract
UF	utilization factor
UNEP	United Nations Environment Programme
USGBC	US Green Building Council
VAV	variable air volume
VAWT	vertical axis wind turbine
VIP	vacuum insulation panel
VOC	volatile organic compound
VVVF	variable voltage, variable frequency
WEEE	waste electrical and electronic equipment
WEEL	workplace environmental exposure limit
WER	Window Energy Rating
WGBC	World Green Building Council
WIRS	Water Industry Registration Scheme
WLC	whole-life costs
WRAP	Waste & Resources Action Programme

Part 1

Background

1.1

Introduction and scope

The title of this book is *Sustainable Retrofit and Facilities Management*, but it could just have well have been 'Sustainable Refurbishment and Property Management' or even 'Sustainable Rehabilitation and Building Management'. However, in the UK at least, the term 'retrofit' has largely replaced 'refurbishment' in the context of improving existing buildings. 'Property management', on the other hand, is widely applied to a residential estate, while 'facilities management' applies primarily to non-residential buildings. This book looks at sustainable principles and methods that can be applied to the management of existing buildings, estates and communities and when considering retrofit (or refurbishment).

Of course, many of the same challenges arise in retrofit as in the design and construction of new buildings and developments. These are dealt with in more detail in the sister book to this one: *Integrated Sustainable Design of Buildings* (Appleby, 2011a). This book focuses specifically on those issues that should be addressed by designers, owners and operators who want to improve the performance of existing buildings across the full range of sustainability criteria.

It has been widely reported that, in the United Kingdom at least, between 72 and 75 per cent of the buildings that will exist in 2050 have already been built (Low-Carbon Construction Innovation and Growth Team, 2010). For example, in 2010, there were around 27 million homes, of which between 25 and 26 million will remain standing in 2050. UK Government predictions of future demand for homes indicate that around 250,000 should be built per annum, resulting in 10 million additional homes being constructed between 2010 and 2050. As it happens, only 150,000 dwellings were completed in 2010, and if this rate continued, there would be between 31 and 32 million homes in existence in 2050. Projections of the future demand for homes assume that there will be a growing population, and the Office of National Statistics estimates a population increase of 10.2 million between 2008 and 2033.[1]

Similarly, the majority of non-residential buildings that are standing today will remain with us through the middle part of the twenty-first century. The Low-Carbon Construction IGT boldly states that the majority of these buildings must have their energy efficiency improved if carbon targets are to be met, corresponding to approximately one building per minute until 2050. In 2010, the average CO_2 emissions associated with a British home were 5.4 tonnes/annum, while a home built to comply with 2006 Part L Building Regulations targets creates emissions of 3.2 tonnes/annum on average and, when built to meet 2010 targets, creates 2.4 tonnes/annum. The UK Government is committed to further step reductions in carbon targets so that, by 2016, the requirement will be zero regulated emissions. This has been diluted from the previous government's commitment to making the target truly zero carbon, taking into account all operational emissions, including all plugged-in appliances such as white goods, televisions and computers, which are not included in the list of 'regulated' emissions. It is important to realize the contribution of 'unregulated' emissions and embodied carbon to the carbon footprint of a home. On average, plug-in items constitute a further 2 to 3 tonnes of carbon dioxide per annum, while embodied emissions might be around 50 tonnes, or 1 tonne/annum for a life expectancy of 50 years. Similar improvements in Building Regulations are being introduced across the European Union through the Recast EC Directive on Energy Performance of Buildings (EC, 2010).

In parallel with this, an ambitious programme of decarbonization of the electricity grid is planned. In Europe, there is a large variation in the carbon intensity of electricity generation, varying from around 0.09 $kgCO_2/kWh$ in France to 1.0 $kgCO_2/kWh$ in Poland, demonstrating the difference between reliance on nuclear and coal-fired power stations. France produces around 78 per cent of its electricity from nuclear power and Poland generates 96 per cent from coal. This might explain why in June 2011 Poland was the only EU member to veto the EU 2050 Roadmap,[2] which would have committed them to a massive programme of renewable energy and carbon capture and storage. The UK has produced its own 2050 Pathway Analysis[3] which postulates a number of alternative pathways for achieving the 80 per cent carbon reduction required by 2050, as mandated by the 2008 Climate Change Act. These include decarbonization strategies based on some combination of renewable, nuclear power and fossil fuel with carbon capture and storage (CCS). By 2050, all existing nuclear plants would be decommissioned and it is predicted that, unless these are replaced, in excess of 500 TWh/year of electricity would be required from renewable sources and 220 from fossil fuels with CCS. However, this strategy requires a corresponding drop in the carbon emissions associated with buildings, including unregulated emissions and embodied carbon, with a greater reduction in those buildings that rely primarily on electricity to meet their energy demands.

Across Europe, there are national schemes, extant or proposed, that have been designed to address the energy efficiency of existing buildings. Historically in the UK there have been grants available through energy companies or the Department of Energy and Climate Change (DECC), such as the Warm Front scheme for those on income-related benefits or who live in homes that are poorly insulated or that have inadequate heating. In late 2012 the Energy Company Obligation (ECO) replaced these schemes, while the Green Deal was established to provide loans to individual households for energy efficiency measures that meet the so-called 'Golden Rule' – i.e. that the annual saving in energy bills is equal to or greater than the annual repayment cost within a specified pay-back period or the lifetime of the product.

However, the picture is complicated by the proliferation of sub-standard and empty dwellings across the UK. The Decent Homes Programme, introduced in the UK in 2000, aimed to refurbish all social sector homes to a minimum standard between 2000 and 2010. By 2008, the percentage of council housing that had reached the government's decency standard was 69 per cent. This compared with 49 per cent of private rented and 65 per cent of owner-occupied, although housing association social housing had reached 77 per cent.[4]

In parallel with the Decent Homes Programme, the New Deal for Communities scheme, run by the Department of Communities & Local Government (DCLG) Neighbourhood Renewal Unit, was launched in 1998 and provided funding to improve 39 deprived neighbourhoods in England. One of the early projects in Newcastle upon Tyne's West End has resulted in an impressive 21 per cent fall in recorded crime between 2000 and 2010.

Between 30 and 35 per cent of households in Britain cannot be considered decent homes by currently accepted standards. The collateral damage from this is not only socio-economic but runs into billions of pounds per year, much of which is a burden on the taxpayer. Although there has been a steady improvement in social housing, the private sector has always been more difficult to reach. Although the Green Deal and ECO are intended to pay for energy efficiency improvements, for those homes that remain below the decency threshold, this can be compared with applying greenwash to a wall with rising damp.

Of course, poor housing is not a problem that is restricted to the UK. Globally it has been estimated by the UN that some 1.6 billion people live in sub-standard accommodation, out of a world population approaching 7 billion; with some 1.5 billion not having access to electricity (International Energy Agency, 2009). In the United States, following the sub-prime mortgage disaster, the number of people reported to be suffering from housing problems is around 94 million, or one third of the population.

The churn rate for buildings in the USA is significantly greater than for the UK and much of Europe. A UNEP report on green buildings finance states that 'at least half [of current buildings in the USA] will still be standing by 2050'.[5]

Of the homes that are standing today, a significant number remain empty. In England, for example, more than 740,000 homes were empty in 2010 (3.4 per cent of the total stock), of which some 300,000 had been empty for more than 6 months. In the USA, the number of empty homes has reached epidemic proportions, the figure having reached 11.4 per cent of the total stock by March 2011, corresponding to around 15 million homes.

The Obama Administration launched its 'Recovery through Retrofit' initiative in 2009, which 'lays the groundwork for a self-sustaining and robust home energy efficiency industry'.[6] It is supported by federally insured low-interest 'PowerSaver' loans from private lenders, which can be paid back over a term of up to 20 years. All work carried out with this money must comply with the Federal Housing Agency Home Energy Efficient Improvement Standards.[7]

Of course, sustainable retrofit and facilities management are not only about energy efficiency and carbon management, and this book tackles the full range of issues that must be addressed if our existing building stock is to be made more sustainable.

With much of the world experiencing severe economic turndown while facing potential environmental catastrophe, the relationship between sustainability, economics and poverty has been brought into focus. Strategies for the management and refurbishment of existing buildings play a significant role in the transition to a green economy. During 2011 strategies were set out for this transition by the United Nations Environment Programme (UNEP), the European Union and the UK Government. UNEP defines a green economy as 'one that results in improved human well-being and social equity, while significantly reducing environmental risks and ecological scarcities'. The EU and UK Government focus on sustainable development with economic growth.

Overview of the book

The following chapters provide the tools for developing a strategy for sustainable retrofit (used here interchangeably with the term refurbishment) and facility (or property) management. Chapter 1.2 expands on the above by examining the history of relevant policies and legislation worldwide relating to retrofit and facilities management, as well as those aspects of transport and infrastructure that impact on existing buildings. Chapter 1.3 reviews tools designed for assessing the environmental impact of the retrofit process and for existing buildings.

Part 2 looks at a range of strategies for maximizing the sustainability of retrofitting existing buildings, managing existing buildings and deciding on whether to retrofit or demolish an existing building. Part 3 looks at specific elements of retrofitting, such as the building fabric, building services, air quality, indoor environment, water, waste, materials, ecology and transport; and Part 4 sets out the principles of sustainable facility and property management. The strategies, examples and case histories are applicable to residential and commercial building types.

1.2
Policy and legislation

It is not intended here to provide a comprehensive overview of policy and legislation relating to sustainable design and development. For this, it is suggested the reader goes to Chapter 1.2 of the sister book to this one: *Integrated Sustainable Design of Buildings* (Appleby, 2011a). Instead it is intended to explore policies and legislation worldwide that relate to both sustainable retrofit and facilities management, including those aspects of transport and infrastructure that impact on existing buildings.

International overview and historical perspective

Some form of sustainable management and improvement of existing buildings has been practised since humans first built shelters from the materials they found around them. Of course, across much of the planet, humans all but wiped out the forests by using wood for constructing buildings and ships, as a fuel for heating and cooking, as well as clearing them for growing crops.

In ancient Greece, the importance of the orientation of buildings and streets in relation to the trajectory of the sun and prevailing winds was understood. The Hippocratic treatise on *Air, Water and Places* stated that 'There is a need to orient streets and buildings in such a way as to avoid the summer sun and take advantage of cooling winds, to build away from mosquito-infested areas and unhealthy places and have sources of clean water.' The application of this principle can be seen in towns and cities across the Mediterranean, many of which have lasted for centuries with minimal use of natural resources.

It could be argued that the Industrial Revolution and the exploration and availability of large stocks of, first, coal and then oil and gas, as well as iron ore and other minerals, led to profligacy in the use of natural resources. In the developed world there has been erosion in the skills and culture associated with sustainable living. Following the Second World War, large parts of the developed world had to deal with devastation on a massive scale, and hence there was a rapid building programme, without much thought to quality, longevity or sustainability. However, in the early 1970s, the oil bubble burst and the concept of energy conservation was born, leading to a new breed of energy managers, enhanced building standards and significant investment in energy efficiency improvements.

In modern times sustainability in the context of existing buildings has primarily focused on the conservation of resources. This was predicated by the Club of Rome in the Epilogue to their Second Report (Mesarovic and Pestel, 1975) setting out a 'New Global Ethic' that included: 'a new ethic in the use of material resources [that] will require a new technology of production based on minimal use of resources and longevity of products'. Also the United Nations Conference on the Human Environment set out a series of Principles in 1972, known as the Stockholm Declaration, that referred to the safeguarding of natural resources, the wise management of wildlife and its habitat, the prevention of the future exhaustion of non-renewable resources and minimizing pollutant emissions to air and water.

In 1987, the World Commission on Environment and Development delivered its final report (World Commission on Environment and Development, 1987) (the Brundtland Report). Apart from providing the seminal definition for sustainable development, the report commented on many of the same issues that were highlighted in the Stockholm Declaration. For example, with regard to energy policies it stated: 'Energy efficiency policies must be the cutting edge of national energy strategies for sustainable development, and there is much scope for improvement in this direction.'

Paragraph 30.10 of Agenda 21 of the Rio Declaration (UN, 1992) states:

> Business and industry, including transnational corporations, should be encouraged:
> a   To report annually on their environmental records, as well as on their use of energy and natural resources.
> b   To adopt and report on the implementation of codes of conduct promoting the best environmental practice, such as the Business Charter on Sustainable Development of the International Chamber of Commerce (ICC) and the chemical industry's responsible care initiative.

This resulted, in part, in the development of the suite of voluntary international environmental management standards: ISO 14000, including ISO 14001: 2006, which provides a specification and guidance for environmental management systems (EMS); and ISO 14031: 1999, which provides guidelines for evaluation of environmental performance. Refer to Chapter 1.3 for more details on the application of these and parallel European and British standards.

Agenda 21 also refers to 'rehabilitation' of older buildings, historic precincts, degraded land, water resources and power systems, although most of the landmark sustainable development and climate change conferences, protocols and declarations were concerned with the environmental impact of new development and signing up to carbon reduction targets. Originally adopted in 1997, Article 2 of the Kyoto Protocol requires signatories to implement measures for the 'enhancement of energy efficiency in relevant sectors of the national economy', which includes both new and existing buildings.[1]

More recently, the United Nations set out its *Medium Term Strategy 2010–13*,[2] including a statement that:

> [The] United Nations Environment Programme (UNEP) will support countries to make a transition towards societies based on more efficient use of energy, energy conservation and utilization of cleaner energy sources, with a focus on renewable energy, and on improved land management.

In the Conclusions to the chapter dealing with Buildings in the 2011 UNEP publication *Towards a Green Economy*, the authors state that:

For developed countries, which account for most of the existing building stock, the priority is to put in place measures and incentives that will enable large-scale investments in retrofitting programmes. Those will come not only with the benefits of energy savings but also a high potential of net job creation.

The International Energy Agency (IEA) produces an authoritative *World Energy Outlook* annually, including an analysis of global energy-related carbon dioxide emissions. In 2010, it extended this work to produce a set of 'scenarios and strategies to 2050' (IEA, 2010). This extends the projections developed for the so-called 'IEA 450 Scenario' which were developed in 2008 based on the pledges proposed for the Copenhagen Accord, setting out a technologically-based strategy to stabilize long-term atmospheric CO_{2eq} (greenhouse gas) concentrations to 450 ppm, equivalent to a global temperature rise of 2°C. The IEA BLUE Map scenario targets a reduction in energy-related emissions of 50 per cent by 2050 compared with 2005, i.e. 14 Gt CO_2 compared with 28 Gt, and a 75 per cent reduction compared with a 'business as usual' baseline of 57 Gt by 2050 (see Figure 1.2.1).

It is important to note that this scenario depends not only on the carbon intensity of energy generation falling by 64 per cent, with 48 per cent of electricity generation from renewables, 24 per cent from nuclear power and 17 per cent from fossil fuel with carbon capture and storage (CCS), but also a 66 per cent reduction in CO_2 emissions associated with buildings. It can be seen in Figure 1.2.1 that 'end use' measures represent 53 per cent of the total carbon savings required to meet the IEA target for 2050. Bearing in mind globally that more than 50 per cent of the buildings that are currently standing will still exist in 2050, it can be concluded that energy management and improvements for existing buildings are critical in meeting this target.

With this in mind, the IEA funded a programme of 37 demonstration projects in OECD countries that resulted in an average energy saving of 75 per cent for the houses refurbished (see Chapter 2.4 for more details).

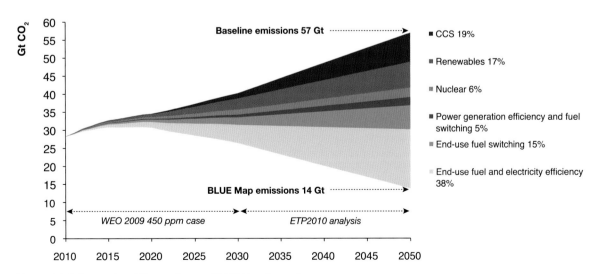

Figure 1.2.1 *International Energy Agency BLUE Map Scenario*
Source: Energy Technology Perspectives © OECD/IEA, 2010.

The World Energy Council[3] has produced an important report on energy efficiency including strong recommendations to policy-makers globally that:

> Energy efficiency policies and programmes should give long-term signals to market players. They should rely on a sustainable regulatory framework that can provide a long-lasting context for energy efficiency policies and avoid the negative effect of stop and go actions.
>
> (WEC, 2010)

The International Organization for Standardization (ISO) published a standard for energy management systems in July 2011 (ISO 50001, 2011) that sets out procedures based on the ISO's established 'Plan, Do, Check, Act' methodology. These provide standardized procedures based on proven energy management techniques (see Chapter 4.1).

Globally the Green Building Councils (GBC) are influencing policy in the individual countries in which they have a presence, which currently number 89. They produce guidance, provide training and information and lobby governments on policy and legislation. The World Green Building Council (WGBC),[4] which has a mission 'to facilitate the global transformation of the building industry towards sustainability through market driven mechanisms' is the umbrella organization providing support to the national organizations and help in establishing new ones. The GBCs evolved from the US Green Building Council (USGBC) which was formed in 1993. Shortly after its formation, the Leadership in Energy and Environmental Design (LEED) scheme[5] was launched. Although initially developed for assessing the environmental impact of new buildings, along with the UK Building Research Establishment Assessment Method (BREEAM), it now provides protocols that can be used to rate the environmental performance of existing buildings. The LEED Existing Buildings Operation & Maintenance scheme has been provided with an 'alternative compliance path' (ACP) for projects outside the USA.[6] For more details on this and other national and international assessment schemes, refer to Chapter 1.3.

European Union policy and directives

The EU Parliament, the Council of Ministers and the Commission of the European Union have provided a series of directives, roadmaps, plans and strategies over the years that have directed Member States towards achieving standards and targets across a range of issues that relate to sustainable retrofit and facilities management.

The Lisbon Treaty was agreed by the 27 Member States in 2007 and 'clearly sets out the European Union's aims and values of peace, democracy, respect for human rights, justice, equality, rule of law and sustainability'. It includes a pledge that the EU will 'work for the sustainable development of Europe based on balanced economic growth and price stability, a highly competitive social market economy, aiming at full employment and social progress, with a high level of protection of the environment'. It also 'affirms the EU's commitment to a united European policy on sustainable energy'.[7]

The Commission launched an overarching Sustainable Development Strategy in 2001, reviewed in 2009 (EC, 2009a), across seven 'key challenges and cross-cutting themes', under the headings of:

- Climate change and clean energy
- Sustainable transport
- Sustainable consumption and production
- Conservation and management of natural resources
- Public health
- Social inclusion, demography and migration
- Global poverty and sustainable development challenges
- Education and training
- Research and development
- Financing and economic instruments.

The overall performance of the EU in achieving a series of sustainable development targets is reported on by Eurostat on a biennial basis in a *Monitoring Report of the EU Sustainable Development Strategy*.[8] This includes statistics for issues under 11 headline indicators that relate to the headings above, including such factors as 'greenhouse gas emissions' and 'consumption of renewables' within which existing and refurbished buildings play their part, of course.

Energy and climate change

When it comes to the EU's priorities for sustainable retrofit and facilities management, the emphasis is on energy policy and the mitigation of and adaptation to climate change, as exemplified by the EU Climate Change Programme[9] and the *White Paper: Adapting to Climate Change* (EC, 2009b). The European Retrofit Network focuses on energy efficiency measures and job creation from the retrofit markets created. Key directives include the Energy Services Directive (ESD) from 2006 (EC, 2006) and the Energy Performance of Buildings Directive (EPBD), first published in 2002 and recast in 2010 (EC, 2010).

The ESD requires that: 'The public sector in each Member State should . . . set a good example regarding investments, maintenance and other expenditure on energy-using equipment, energy services and other energy efficiency improvement measures'; and that:

> Member States shall ensure the availability of efficient, high-quality energy audit schemes which are designed to identify potential energy efficiency improvement measures and which are carried out in an independent manner, to all final consumers, including smaller domestic, commercial and small and medium-sized industrial customers.

The original version of the EPBD set the framework by which Member States were required to shape their individual energy performance legislation for buildings. The Recast EPBD from 2010 states that:

> Major renovations of existing buildings, regardless of their size, provide an opportunity to take cost-effective measures to enhance energy performance. For

> reasons of cost-effectiveness, it should be possible to limit the minimum energy performance requirements to the renovated parts that are most relevant for the energy performance of the building.
>
> (EC, 2010b)

Paragraph 8 also states:

> Measures to improve further the energy performance of buildings should take into account climatic and local conditions as well as indoor climate environment and cost-effectiveness. These measures should not affect other requirements concerning buildings such as accessibility, safety and the intended use of the building.

Paragraph 29 states:

> Installers and builders are critical for the successful implementation of this Directive. Therefore, an adequate number of installers and builders should, through training and other measures, have the appropriate level of competence for the installation and integration of the energy-efficient and renewable energy technology required.

The EPBD requires that energy performance certificates are issued for the following buildings:

- buildings that are constructed, sold or rented out to a new tenant;
- buildings where a total useful floor area over 500 m² (250 m² from 2015) is occupied by a public authority and frequently visited by the public.

The EPBD also states that 'an independent assessment of the entire heating and air-conditioning system should occur at regular intervals'.

The European Commission published its Energy Efficiency Plan in March 2011 (EC, 2011) stating that:

> The greatest energy-saving potential lies in buildings. The plan focuses on instruments to trigger the renovation process in public and private buildings and to improve the energy performance of the components and appliances used in them. It promotes the exemplary role of the public sector, proposing to accelerate the refurbishment rate of public buildings through a binding target and to introduce energy efficiency criteria in public spending. It also foresees obligations for utilities to enable their customers to cut their energy consumption.

It also states that: 'A large energy-saving potential remains untapped. Techniques exist to cut existing buildings' consumption by half or three quarters and to halve the energy consumption of typical appliances.'

In September 2011, the Commission produced its *Roadmap to a Resource Efficient Europe*, one Milestone from which requires that 'by 2020 the renovation and construction of buildings and infrastructure will be made to high resource efficiency levels'. The Annex refers to 'increasing the renovation rate of existing buildings'.

Each Member State has incorporated the requirements of EC Energy Directives (see the next section for the UK approach), but their approaches to improving the sustainability and energy efficiency of existing building stock vary considerably.

The German KfW Energy-Efficient Construction and Rehabilitation Programme targets all dwellings built prior to 1984, with a view to bringing them up to current energy performance standards. Subsidized loans are available through the German Development Loan Bank (KfW *Bankengruppe*). This is similar to the UK's 'Green Deal' described below. A comprehensive summary of the progress of all 27 Member States, as well as Norway and Croatia, in implementing the EPBD is provided in a report from the Concerted Action EPB forum published in 2011 (Concerted Action EPB, 2011). The first of these 'books of Country Reports' was published in 2009, with another scheduled for 2013.

Other financial mechanisms designed to promote the uptake of renewable energy in Europe, such as feed-in tariffs (FITs), are discussed in Chapter 2.5.

Other policy issues

EU directives and legislation cover numerous other issues that relate to the sustainable retrofit and management of buildings, such as water, waste, pollution, air quality, health and safety, and biodiversity.

The Drinking Water Directive 98/83/EC deals primarily with the quality of water in public supplies and delivered for public consumption, setting standards for the most common substances found in water intended for supply.

At the time of writing, the Commission has within its work programme the development of a directive on the 'water performance of buildings', based on its view that 'binding rules could be envisaged to promote water savings in public and private buildings'.[10]

The Urban Waste Water Directive 91/271/EEC, amended by Directive 98/15/EC, was introduced in order to protect the water environment from the adverse effects of discharges of urban waste water and from certain industrial discharges.

The Waste Framework Directive 2008/98/EC repeals and consolidates a number of earlier directives, providing a rationale based on a waste hierarchy and the drawing up of waste management plans, while the Waste Electrical and Electronic Equipment (WEEE) Directive 2002/96/EC, being recast at the time of writing, sets out collection, recycling and recovery targets for all types of electrical and electronic goods.

The Integrated Pollution Prevention Control (IPPC) Directive 2008/1/EC introduces a permitting requirement with the aim of minimizing industrial pollution to air, land and water, covering the generation of waste, use of raw materials, energy efficiency, noise and accident prevention. It sets emission limit values (ELVs) and defines best available techniques (BATs) as the appropriate use of technology to achieve the required ELVs.

The Air Quality Directive 2008/50/EC consolidates earlier directives requiring Member States to establish air quality plans, harmonize ambient air quality standards and methods of assessment, and share information, while introducing Air Quality Objectives for particulate matter finer than 2.5 microns ($PM_{2.5}$).

Directive 89/391/EEC was a landmark directive in the context of health and safety legislation in Europe, introducing the requirement for risk assessment and prevention, stressing the importance of safety and health management as part of general management processes. Sometimes referred to as the Occupational Health & Safety (OSH) Framework Directive, its full title was, more prosaically, 'the Directive on the introduction of measures to encourage improvement in the safety and health of workers at work'. In the UK, this led to the 1992 Management of Health & Safety at Work Regulations and associated 'six pack' of regulations (see below). For more details on European health and safety legislation and links to relevant pdf files, refer to the European Agency of Safety and Health at Work website.[11]

The Habitats Directive 92/43/EEC, together with the Birds Directive 2009/147/EC, forms the cornerstone of Europe's nature conservation policy.[12] It is built on the Natura 2000 network of protected sites and a strict system of species protection. The Directive protects over 1000 animals and plant species and over 200 'habitat types', including designated types of forest, meadow, wetland, etc., which are of European importance.

There is also an EC Regulation that allows for voluntary participation in an Eco-Management and Audit Scheme (EMAS):

> Its aim is to recognize and reward those organisations that go beyond minimum legal compliance and continuously improve their environmental performance. In addition, it is a requirement of the scheme that participating organisations regularly produce a public environmental statement that reports on their environmental performance.[13]

The most recent version (EMAS III Regulation 1221/2009) was published in 2009: see Chapter 1.3 for more details.

UK policy and legislation

An extensive review of the history of UK policy and legislation relating to sustainable buildings and development is provided in *Integrated Sustainable Design of Buildings* (Appleby, 2011a). This includes reference to an array of policy and legislative devices, much of which is applicable to existing buildings, as well as planning law and policy relevant to major refurbishments. As well as providing for the regulation of new building standards, the Building Act 1984 allowed for regulations to be made with respect to 'alterations and extensions of buildings and of services, fittings and equipment in or in connection with buildings'. This has resulted, for example, in Part L of Building Regulations being divided into requirements for new and for existing buildings (Part L1b for dwellings and Part L2b for buildings other than dwellings). Part G (Sanitation, hot water safety and water efficiency) applies to change of use as well as new buildings, while Part M2 (Access to extensions to buildings other than dwellings) and Part B (Fire safety) can also be applied to extensions and change of use within defined constraints.

Energy and climate change

Energy Performance Certificates (EPCs) and Display Energy Certificates (DECs) were introduced in England and Wales in 2008 through the Energy Performance of Buildings (Certificates and Inspections) (England & Wales) (Amendment) Regulations 2007. The requirement from the EC EPBD was divided into separate types of certificate based on a prediction of energy performance (the EPC) and actual metered energy performance (the DEC). The former is not only a requirement for all new buildings, but also all buildings (or parts thereof) offered for sale or to rent. The latter is currently only required for existing buildings 'occupied by a public authority and frequently visited by the public' (see European policy and directives above).

2008 saw the enactment of both the Climate Change Act and a revised Energy Act. Prior to this, UK energy legislation had been divided principally between generation and infrastructure (Energy Act 2004, Utilities Act 2000, Coal Industry Act 1994, Electricity Act 1989, and Gas Act 1986) and buildings (Building Act 1984, as amended by the Sustainable & Secure Buildings Act 2004, Housing Act 2004, Home Energy Conservation Act 1995). However, in 2006, the Electricity and Gas Acts were modified by the Climate Change and Sustainable Energy Act to require the energy companies to meet a carbon emission reduction target (CERT) and in 2009 the Community Energy-Saving Programme (CESP) was introduced to oblige energy companies to fund energy efficiency improvements in partnership with Local Authorities and community groups.

As well as long-term commitments to greenhouse gas and CO_2 emission targets, the Climate Change Act 2008 included obligations on government to report on progress in improving the sustainability and efficiency of the UK civil estate and to introduce measures to promote corporate greenhouse gas emission reporting. The Energy Act 2008 saw provisions for the introduction of feed-in tariffs for small-scale renewable electricity generation, the roll-out of smart metering and incentives for renewable heat installations.

The Energy Act 2011 brought together and modified many of these provisions and introduced the Green Deal and Energy Company Obligation as a replacement for CERT and CESP (see Box 1.2.1).

Box 1.2.1 The UK Energy Act 2011

Through the UK Green Deal scheme, the Act does the following:

- creates pay-as-you-save financing framework for energy efficiency measures;
- limits access through the 'Golden Rule';
- invests obligation to fund Green Deal with energy companies;
- enables energy companies and Green Deal Providers to operate outside the Consumer Credit Act;
- requires dwellings in England to meet appropriate targets in achieving the 2020 carbon budget;

- requires the Secretary of State to report on contributions made by the Green Deal and the Energy Company Obligation (ECO) in achieving carbon budgets.

For the private rented sector, the Act does the following:

- forces residential landlords to consent to request for energy efficiency improvements from tenants (from April 2016);
- affirms that landlords of all property types ensure properties they lease achieve an EPC rating of at least E (from April 2018).

In the Act, the Energy Company Obligation (ECO) does the following:

- replaces the CESP and CERT from December 2012;
- targets households that require additional support.

Additional measures in the Act are:

- roll-out of smart meters cut-off date confirmed as 2018;
- restrictions of access to EPC data removed;
- Secretary of State given powers to require energy companies to publicize cheapest tariffs;
- measures to improve energy security;
- measures to enable low-carbon technologies;
- amendments to existing legislation to facilitate offshore electricity transmission regime, nuclear decommissioning and carbon capture and storage (CCS);
- extension of Renewable Heat Incentive (RHI) to Northern Ireland.

The UK therefore has developed a suite of discrete but inter-dependent legislative and financial devices to provide leverage for the improvement of the energy efficiency of existing buildings, namely:

- the Green Deal and the ECO
- the feed-in tariff
- the Renewable Heat Incentive
- smart meters.

The Green Deal and Energy Company Obligation

Like elsewhere in Europe, the UK is introducing a combination of 'pay as you save' loans and grants in order to drive the retrofit of existing buildings to improve energy efficiency. At the time of writing, the UK Government's proposals are out for consultation, with a launch date of October 2012 proposed. The Green Deal will be offered by Green Deal Providers through a 'value chain' that can be supplied by a single organization or separately as appropriate. Figure 1.2.2 is extracted from the DECC consultation document published in November 2011 (DECC, 2011a).

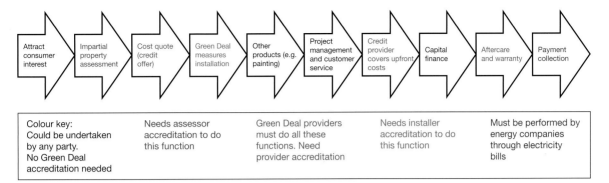

Figure 1.2.2 *The Green Deal value chain*

The accreditation requirements for Assessors and Installers are set out in the Green Deal Code of Practice (DECC, 2011b) which also specifies what is expected of Green Deal Providers, the contents of a Green Deal Plan, the terms of reference for a Green Deal Oversight Body and the application of a Green Deal Quality Mark.

A separate piece of legislation will be published, setting out the 'Specified Energy Efficiency Improvements and Qualifying Energy Improvements' as referred to in the Energy Act 2011. These include what might be considered most of the commonly installed renewable technologies, insulation measures and technical fixes (see Box 1.2.2).

Box 1.2.2 Qualifying energy improvements for the Green Deal and the Energy Company Obligation

According to a working draft for the Green Deal (Specified Energy Efficiency Improvements and Qualifying Energy Improvements) Order, the following energy improvements will be valid:

- air-source heat pumps
- biomass boilers
- biomass room heaters with radiators
- cavity wall insulation
- high-efficiency gas-fired condensing boilers
- oil-fired condensing boilers
- cylinder thermostats
- draught proofing
- energy-efficient glazing
- external wall insulation
- fan-assisted replacement storage heaters
- flue gas heat recovery devices
- ground-source heat pumps
- heating controls (for wet central heating systems and warm air systems)
- high-efficiency replacement warm air units

- high thermal performance external doors
- hot water cylinder insulation
- internal wall insulation
- lighting systems, fittings and controls
- loft or rafter insulation
- mechanical ventilation with heat recovery
- micro combined heat and power
- micro wind generation
- photovoltaics
- roof insulation
- room in roof insulation
- solar water heating
- underfloor heating
- underfloor insulation or
- waste water heat recovery devices attached to showers.

The Green Deal comprises a low-interest long-term loan repaid through the electricity bill, while the Energy Company Obligation will be a grant available to those on benefits or for 'hard to treat' properties. Qualification for a loan will be assessed by calculation using modified versions of the Standard Assessment Procedure (SAP) for dwellings and Simplified Building Energy Model (SBEM) for non-residential buildings. Predicted payback periods for the various measures proposed by the assessor will be compared with the life expectancy of the measures. If the payback is longer, then the 'Golden Rule' is not met and the measures could be assessed for an Energy Company Obligation grant. This is most likely to be relevant for solid wall dwellings requiring either internal or external insulation. The aim is that repayments for the first year do not exceed the saving in energy costs due to the measures installed.

A Publicly Available Specification (PAS 2030) sets out a Specification for Installation Process Management and Service Provision to support the Green Deal, including a framework for accreditation of installers (BSI, 2012a), with the certification process set out in a separate PAS (BSI, 2012b).

Feed-in tariff (FIT)

The UK version of the feed-in tariff was introduced through the Feed-in Tariffs (Specified Maximum Capacity and Functions) Order 2010 exercising authority set out in the 2008 Energy Act. This Order was subject to several amendments during 2011 which drastically reduced the subsidy offered for solar photovoltaics. For a more detailed analysis and comparison with similar mechanisms developed in other countries, refer to Chapter 2.5.

Renewable Heat Incentive (RHI)

The RHI scheme was introduced for non-domestic renewable heat installations through the Renewable Heat Incentive Regulations 2011 to provide a long-term (20-year) subsidy for qualifying technologies. The second phase of the scheme, for domestic installations, will coincide with the launch of the Green Deal towards the end of 2012.

For non-domestic installations, the RHI is paid quarterly, based on readings obtained from a heat meter conforming with EN 1434 Class 2 (European standard). This includes district energy schemes serving residential accommodation. For domestic installations serving individual homes the consultation document proposed that a fixed annual compensation rate could be adopted 'by paying the tariff not on the basis of a metered number of kWh generated, but instead on a "deemed" number of kWh, namely the reasonable heat requirement (or heat load) that the installation is intended to serve', based on a SAP calculation (DECC, 2010).

The domestic RHI is likely to follow a similar requirement to amendments to the FIT from April 2012 in binding qualification for the highest tariff to a certain level of energy efficiency or insulation level. This approach has been used in vetting applications for the Renewable Heat Premium Payments (RHPPs) which provided a one-off payment for solar thermal, biomass, air-source and ground-source heat pumps with a cut-off date of 31 March 2012. Qualifying homes required 250 mm of loft insulation and cavity wall insulation where appropriate.

RHPP and RHI both require technologies and installers to be certified under the Microgeneration Certification Scheme for installations rated at less than 45 kWth.[14] The technologies that are eligible for the RHI are listed in Table 1.2.1, which also gives the tariff at the launch date of 28 November 2011.

The tiers applied to small and medium biomass in Table 1.2.1 refer to the percentage load factor at which the plant operates. For example, the Tier 1 tariff is paid for the first 1314 hours of operation in the year, which is equivalent to the plant operating at 15 per cent of maximum load for the whole year. The Tier 2 tariff is paid for any remaining kWh in the same year. Qualifying plant that was installed and first commissioned after 15 July 2009 is eligible for the RHI. See also Chapter 2.5.

Table 1.2.1 *Technologies that are eligible for the Renewable Heat Incentive*

Tariff name	Eligible technology	Eligible sizes	Tariff rate (pence/kWh)
Small biomass	Solid biomass; Municipal Solid Waste (incl. Combined Heat and Power)	Less than 200 kWth	Tier 1: **7. 9** Tier 2: **2.0**
Medium biomass		200 kWth to (but not including) 1,000 kWth	Tier 1: **4. 9** Tier 2: **2.0**
Large biomass		1,000 kWth and above	**1**
Small heat pumps	Ground-source heat pumps; Water-source heat pumps; Geothermal	Less than 100 kWth	**4.5**
Large heat pumps		100 kWth and above	**3.2**
Solar thermal	Solar thermal	Less than 200 kWth	**8.5**
Biomethane	Biomethane injection and biogas combustion, except from landfill gas	Biomethane all scales, biogas combustion <200 kWth	**6.8**

Source: www.ofgem.gov.uk/e-serve/RHI/Document1/RHL per cent20leaflet.pdf.

Smart meters

The UK Government set out a programme to roll out the installation of free smart meters for all households between 2014 and 2018. These will combine two-way communication of gas and electricity data between the consumer and a newly established Data and Communications Company and provide feedback on consumption to the customer via an in-home display. As well as allowing consumers to understand how their behaviour impacts on energy consumption and providing automated billing, these allow the energy company some degree of control over consumers' connected load, including demand management and remote disablement of supply. The arrangements for non-domestic consumers are more complex and will depend on their existing arrangements.

The mechanisms by which smart metering has been enabled were incorporated into the Energy Act 2008, with time scales extended in the 2011 Act. The earlier Act incorporated appropriate modifications to the Electricity Act 1989, the Gas Act 1986 and the Utilities Act 2000. At the time of writing, regulations to enable implementation of the roll out are being developed by four Smart Meter Working Groups.

More discussion is provided on the use of energy data from building energy management systems (BEMSs) in Chapter 4.1.

Water and waste

The Water Supply (Water Fittings) Regulations 1999 cover the design of water installations to prevent leakage, excessive consumption, contamination, etc., and apply to work carried out on retrofitting or extending existing buildings as well as to new installations. Part G (Sanitation, hot water safety and water efficiency) of the Building Regulations 2000 and the associated Approved Document have established a maximum water consumption per person of 125 litres/day which applies to change of use of existing buildings as well as to new buildings.

The Green Deal will cover measures that reduce the energy consumption associated with heating hot water, such as solar water heating, and may also include water-/energy-efficient taps and showers.

Discharges of solid, liquid and airborne waste and pollutants are governed by the Environmental Permitting (England and Wales) Regulations 2010 which have produced a single regulatory framework by streamlining and integrating:

- waste management licensing;
- pollution prevention and control;
- water discharge consenting;
- groundwater authorizations;
- radioactive substances regulation.

The framework also transposes relevant parts of the EU Integrated Pollution Prevention and Control Directive, Waste Framework Directive, Landfill Directive, Asbestos Directive, Mining Waste Directive and Batteries Directive. These complex regulations are policed by the Environment Agency and permitting of discharges is required for 'Regulated Facilities'. These are generally large-scale industrial plants ranging from mining operations and nuclear facilities to raw food processing and paper manufacture. Detailed guidance is provided on the Environment Agency's website.[15]

The Environment Agency is also responsible for the 2011 Waste (England & Wales) Regulations. These set out requirements for the development of waste prevention programmes and waste management plans, including a mandate for at least 50 per cent of household waste to be either 'prepared for re-use or recycled' by 2020. 'Appropriate authorities', such as the Secretary of State at DEFRA, are to establish suitable 'waste prevention programmes' by 12 December 2013. Para 12 -(1) of Part 5 of the draft Regulations states:

> An establishment or undertaking which imports, produces, collects, transports, recovers or disposes of waste, or which as a dealer or broker has control of waste, must, on the transfer of waste, take all such measures available to it as are reasonable in the circumstances to apply the following waste hierarchy as a priority order:
> a   Prevention
> b   Preparing for re-use
> c   Recycling
> d   Other recovery (for e.g. energy recovery)
> e   Disposal.

Evidence that this hierarchy has been adopted will have to appear on waste transfer notes (or consignment notes for hazardous waste).

The Waste Electrical and Electronic Equipment (WEEE) Regulations 2006 were introduced to implement the EC Directive of the same name (see above and Chapter 4.3).

Pollution and air quality

External air quality is the responsibility of the government and as such is regulated by the Air Quality Standards Regulations, the most recent version of which was published in 2010. Emissions to the atmosphere by major polluters have to go through a permitting process managed by the Environment Agency and regulated by the Environmental Permitting (England and Wales) Regulations 2010 referred to above.

The Clean Air Act 1993 is still current and gives powers to local councils to control domestic and industrial smoke to improve local air quality and meet EU air quality standards for sulphur dioxide and particulates. It enables local councils to create 'smoke control areas' and order the use of cleaner fuels in these areas.

Planning, biodiversity and land use

At the time of writing, planning policy is going through a major review process, with the UK Government proposing the scrapping of a panoply of Planning Policy Statements and Guidance and replacing them with a more concise National Planning Policy Framework (NPPF) (CLG, 2011). The consultative document for this Framework replaces a commitment for 60 per cent of housing development to be on previously developed (brownfield) land and that 'the priority for development should be previously developed land, in particular, vacant and derelict sites and buildings' with statements that 'allocations of land should prefer land of lesser value' and that 'plans should allocate land with the least environmental or amenity value where practical'.

In contrast, the 2011 version of the London Plan actively promotes sustainable retrofit through Policy 5.4 which includes the statement that:

> The environmental impact of existing urban areas should be reduced through policies and programmes that bring existing buildings up to the Mayor's standards on sustainable design and construction. In particular, programmes should reduce carbon dioxide emissions, improve the efficiency of resource use (such as water) and minimize the generation of pollution and waste from existing building stock.

Similarly, PPS 9 Biodiversity and Geological Conservation of 2006 states: 'where [brownfield sites] have significant biodiversity or geological interest of recognized local importance, local planning authorities, together with developers, should aim to retain this interest or incorporate it into any development of the site'.

The draft NPPF requires that:

> The planning system should aim to conserve and enhance the natural and local environment by:
> * protecting valued landscapes;
> * minimizing impacts on biodiversity and providing net gains in biodiversity, where possible; and
> * preventing both new and existing development from contributing to or being put at unacceptable risk from, or being adversely affected by unacceptable levels of land, air, water or noise pollution or land instability.

Management of biodiversity and ecological value on existing landscaped areas is not covered by any current legislation, but we will be addressing assessment of these issues in Chapter 1.3 and the processes involved in Chapter 3.9 and Chapter 4.9.

Environmental impact: noise, light and wind

Some major refurbishments will have significant impacts and may fall under Environmental Impact Assessment legislation (see Chapter 1.4 of Appleby, 2011a) or the Right to Light Act 1959.

Health and safety, hygiene and legionellosis

Workplace legislation in the UK has a history dating back to 1802 when the Factories Act first appeared on the statute book and the Factories Inspectorate was created in 1833. The main purpose was to limit the hours worked by children, requiring factory owners to provide schooling, and pay attention to infectious disease. Workrooms were to be well ventilated and whitewashed twice a year. Over the years the Act evolved until in 1961 it included provisions covering most aspects of health, safety and welfare, most of which have been subsequently incorporated into the Health & Safety at Work etc. Act 1974 and its daughter regulations such as the Control of Substances Hazardous to Health Regulations (COSHH) and the 'Six Pack', first published in 1992 and including the Management of Health & Safety at Work Regulations 1999, the Workplace (Health, Safety & Welfare) Regulations 1992, and the Health & Safety (Display Screen Equipment) Regulations (amended 2002).

Exposure to legionella bacteria and other airborne pathogens is covered by the COSSH Regulations, which mandate a series of preventative measures, including risk assessment, institution of control measures, preparation of written procedures, operation and monitoring of maintenance regimes and the provision of information, instruction and training for employees. The Notification of Cooling Towers and Evaporative Condensers Regulations 1992 require the Local Authority to be formally notified of such equipment when installed and again on removal.

Asbestos is a substance that is so harmful that it has been provided with its very own legislation, the Control of Asbestos Regulations 2012, which in 2006 was formed by the consolidation of separate legislation covering prohibition, control at work and licensing. Further amendments were made to these regulations in 2012, responding to a legal challenge from the EU.

In parallel with the development of building and health and safety legislation, public health legislation was introduced through the Public Health Act in 1848, which also paradoxically led to the system of local government and associated planning law and building control that we have today. It had its genesis in the cholera outbreaks that arose from poor sanitation in the rapidly growing towns and cities, and placed the supply of water, sewerage, cleansing and paving under local control, with oversight from a General Board of Health. The Local Government Act of 1858 replaced the Board of Health with a Local Government Board, leading to a broadening of the remit of local boards to cover duties that had previously been covered by the Town Police Clauses Act of 1847 including a range of public safety measures, such as removal of obstructions in streets and of dangerous buildings, and the prevention and fighting of fire. The Public Health Act continued to provide a mandate for local authorities, and, in a landmark version enacted in 1875, gave them power to regulate sizes of rooms, space around houses and street width.

Both of the acts have evolved over the years with the most recent incarnation of the Local Government Act coming into force in 2000, while following the 2006 Strong and Prosperous Communities White Paper (CLG, 2006) it evolved into the Local Government and Public Involvement in Health Act 2007.

The health and safety of people in their homes, where the homes are owned and maintained by a public authority, or an entity acting on its behalf (social landlords), are protected to some extent by Section 9 of Part 1 of the Housing Act 2004. This provided a vehicle for the implementation of the Housing Health & Safety Rating System (HHSRS) Act 2006 (HMG, 2005),[16] which sets out a checklist of minimum standards that a home is expected to meet in order to be considered to be safe and healthy for occupants and visitors. This replaced the Housing Fitness Standard which was introduced in an amendment to the 1985 Housing Act by the 1989 Local Government and Housing Act. The HHSRS hazard profile headings are similar to those that might be considered for the workplace and are listed in Box 1.2.3.

The HHSRS and its predecessor are key components of the government's ongoing Decent Homes Programme (CLG, 2006). This demands that a home fulfil the following criteria:

- does not present one or more hazards assessed as serious (Category 1) under the HHSRS assessment protocol;
- is in a reasonable state of repair;
- has 'reasonably modern' facilities and services;
- provides a reasonable degree of thermal comfort.

Box 1.2.3 Housing Health & Safety Rating System (HHSRS)

Annex D (ODPM, 2006) sets out the issues covered by the HHSRS assessment process:

- damp and mould growth
- excess cold
- excess heat
- asbestos and man-made mineral fibres
- biocides
- carbon monoxide and fuel combustion products
- lead
- radiation
- uncombusted fuel gas
- volatile organic compounds
- crowding and space
- entry by intruders
- lighting
- noise
- domestic hygiene, pests and refuse
- food safety
- personal hygiene, sanitation and drainage
- water supply
- falls associated with baths, etc.
- falling on level surfaces, etc.
- falling on stairs, etc.
- falling between levels
- electrical hazards
- fire
- flames, hot surfaces, etc.
- collision and entrapment
- explosions
- position and operability of amenities, etc.
- structural collapse and falling elements.

Detailed guidance on the definitions of 'reasonable' for each of the above is provided in the CLG guidance.

Noise at work

Occupational exposure to noise is regulated by the Control of Noise at Work Regulations 2005, which set limits to exposure above which employers must provide hearing protection (85 decibels) and dictates when employers must assess risk and provide information and training (80 decibels). The music and entertainment sector was given an additional two years to prepare for their enforcement in 2008 and the HSE has established a 'Sound Advice' website to address the specific issues found in this sector.[17]

US policy and legislation

An overview and history of US environmental and green buildings policy and legislation are provided in Chapter 1.2 of Appleby, 2011a (pp. 40–8). Historically, the focus of federal US policy and legislation in relation to the sustainability of existing buildings has been on energy and water conservation. For example, President Carter's National Energy Conservation Policy Act (NECPA) of 1978 required utilities to provide residential consumers with energy conservation advice. This Act has been regularly updated and amended and, together with the 2005 Energy Policy Act (EPACT) and the 2007 Energy Independence and Security Act, formed the basis for a Federal Energy Management Program[18] which includes requirements for:

- federal buildings to reduce their energy intensity by 2 per cent per annum, with a cumulative saving of 20 per cent by 2020;
- federal agencies to introduce 'advanced metering' by October 2012;
- executive agencies to purchase products designated by the Energy Star[19] and Federal Energy Management Programs (FEMPs);[20]
- federal agencies to use energy performance contracts until 2016;
- the Secretary of Energy to enter into voluntary agreements with energy-intensive industries for a 2.5 per cent reduction in energy annually between 2007 and 2016;
- energy-efficient management of buildings and vehicles associated with federal lands;
- introduction of a low-income energy assistance programme;
- funding of State energy programmes and community groups;
- consumer education and information programmes;
- energy efficiency standards for rehabilitation of public housing.

In 2008, the Energy Improvement and Extension Act extended energy efficiency tax deductions for commercial buildings and home improvement to the end of 2013, including a new tax credit for energy-efficient biomass 'stoves'.

In 2009, under the Obama Administration, a raft of legislation was considered by both the House and the Senate, including the ambitious Climate Change Bill and the American Clean Energy and Security Act along with some 13 Acts addressing energy efficiency, clean energy and associated tax breaks and funding devices. Only the American Recovery and Reinvestment Act (ARRA), or Recovery Act, as it is more widely termed, and the Federal Personnel Training Act 2010 have made it into law, while the School Buildings Fairness Act and the Livable Communities Act are being considered by relevant committees at the time of writing.

The Federal Personnel Training Act provides funding for training of federal personnel in the operation of buildings at peak efficiency. The School Buildings Fairness Act provides funding to local educational agencies for school repair, renovation and construction with a requirement to apply green building standards. The Livable Communities Act provides grants to incentivize integrated community planning and the implementation of sustainable projects.

In February 2011, President Obama launched the Better Buildings Program,[21] using funding from the Recovery Act. This is administered under the Department of Energy Building Technologies Program (BTP) with a stated ambition of stimulating a ten-fold increase in commercial retrofits, while making commercial buildings 20 per cent more energy efficient by 2020, using tax incentives to leverage investment from the private sector.

In parallel with this, the White House is promoting a 'Recovery through Retrofit' programme which has used the 2010 Consolidated Appropriations Act to enable the US Department of Housing and Urban Development (HUD) to launch an 'efficient mortgage innovation pilot' which has been branded as PowerSaver.[22] This works in a similar manner to the UK Green Deal referred to above, providing 20-year low-cost federally insured loans. Eligible improvements are specified which include enhancing insulation, retrofitting double glazing, replacement of a heating, hot water or air-conditioning system with an Energy Star-rated option[23] and the appropriate use of renewable technologies.

Emissions to air and water have been regulated for decades through the Clean Air Act 1990 and Clean Water Act 1972, amended by various administrations. These Acts are administered by the US Environmental Protection Agency (EPA). The Clean Air Act was used to introduce National Ambient Air Quality Standards (NAAQS) and, in 1990, systems for emissions trading and permitting.

The EPA also produces standards and guidance for indoor pollutants, addressing such issues as sick building syndrome,[24] and achieving safe and healthy indoor environments following home energy retrofits (EPA, 2011).

Under the Clean Water Act, the EPA has implemented pollution control programmes such as setting wastewater standards for industry, setting water quality standards for all contaminants in surface waters and introducing a permit requirement for emissions into navigable waters.

The EPA also administers the Resource Conservation & Recovery Act (RCRA) 1976, which sets national goals for:

- protecting human health and the environment from the potential hazards of waste disposal;
- conserving energy and natural resources;
- reducing the amount of waste generated;
- ensuring that wastes are managed in an environmentally sound manner.

This remains as the primary legislation for the reduction and management of waste in the USA, with separate programmes for solid waste and hazardous waste, although it has been amended through other provisions in 1984, 1992 and 1996.[25]

US health and safety law is enshrined in the overarching Occupational Safety & Health Act 1970 under the Department of Labor, which produces an array of subsidiary acts, regulations and standards. Nuclear safety is the exception, which is under the Department of Energy, Office of Health, Safety and Security, which draws up legislation specific to this sector. Health and safety law is overseen by a number of 'administrations' within the Department of Labor, including the Occupational Safety and Health Administration (OSHA) and the Mine Safety and Health Administration (MSHA), as well as another 27 or so bureaux, offices, divisions, etc., covering everything from pension benefits to statistics.

OSHA oversees the legal framework for limiting occupational exposure to airborne contaminants in the workplace, including occupational exposure to noise and asbestos. It publishes schedules of enforceable permissible exposure limits (PELs),[26] along with background data for each substance. There are a number of competing guideline values developed by others including the widely used threshold limit values (TLVs), published by the American Conference of Governmental Industrial Hygienists (ACGIH), the recommended exposure limits (RELs), published by the National Institute of Occupational Safety & Health (NIOSH), and the workplace environmental exposure limits (WEELs), produced by the American Industrial Hygiene Association (AIHA).

1.3
Assessment tools

Introduction

There are numerous tools for assessing the environmental performance of new building projects, many of which, such as the Building Research Establishment Environmental Assessment Method (BREEAM), have also been used to assess major refurbishments. Most cover the core impacts under headings such as Energy/CO_2 Emissions, Water, Materials, Waste, Pollution, Health & Wellbeing, Transport and Ecology. The residential schemes, such as the Code for Sustainable Homes (CSH) and BREEAM Domestic Refurbishment, deal with transport issues indirectly, by including provision for cyclists and home offices within the Energy criteria. The assessment schemes developed by BRE mostly require a formal assessment carried out by a qualified assessor with a rating determined by rewarding scores for estimated performance against a series of criteria compared either against legislative requirements or best practice. Scores are weighted according to the importance assigned by BRE to the individual issue, and a total percentage is calculated, which is converted to a rating from Unclassified to Outstanding, via Pass, Good, Very Good and Excellent.

With attention turning to improvement of the existing building stock, BRE has developed BREEAM Domestic Refurbishment, which was piloted during 2011,[1] and it is also developing a protocol for the assessment of non-residential refurbishment and fit-out projects. BRE also developed Office Scorer under contract from the UK Department for Trade and Industry (DTI) in 2002. This used the Ecopoint system to compare the environmental impact of refurbishment and new build options for office development (see Chapter 2.1). The Ecopoint system was developed by BRE primarily to rate the environmental impact of building materials, where 100 Ecopoints is the environmental impact of an average European person, based on a lifecycle assessment of climate change impact, water consumption, fossil fuel and mineral depletion, toxicity to air and water, waste generated, acid deposition, ecotoxicity, and eutrophication (excess of nutrients in water) (BRE, 2000).

The Royal Institution of Chartered Surveyors (RICS) launched the Ska Rating scheme in 2009,[2] extensively revised in 2011, as a competitor to BREEAM specifically in the office fit-out sector. A version for retail fit-outs is in the pipeline at the time of writing. Meanwhile, BRE has launched its Low-Impact Shopfitting Tool (LIST), a web-based tool which is intended to rate environmental impact from concept through to use, using CO_2 equivalent (greenhouse gas) emissions and Ecopoints-based benchmarks.[3]

The US version of BREEAM is Leadership in Energy and Environmental Design (LEED), which is adaptable for use in refurbishment projects, while the North American Green Globes® Fit-Up scheme is specifically designed for fit-out of office buildings (new or existing). The US Green Building Council has collaborated with the American Society of Interior Designers (ASID) in the development of REGREEN,[4] which is not an assessment scheme, but provides guidelines to homeowners and designers on sustainable renovation of homes.

Since its early days in the 1990s, there have been different versions of BREEAM that are applicable to existing buildings, adding operation and maintenance issues to the topics covered, although for offices the process was absorbed into the protocol for new buildings in 1998 as a Management and Operation option. However, the take-up was very low and BRE re-launched the existing offices protocol as BREEAM In-Use in 2009.[5] LEED did not launch a protocol for existing buildings until 2003, the most recent version of which evolved in 2008 into LEED Existing Buildings Operation & Maintenance.[6] The Green Build Initiative (GBI) Green Globes® Continual Improvement Assessment for Existing Buildings (CIEB) scheme[7] covers similar ground to LEED. The Green Globes® brand, which originated when BREEAM was adapted for use in Canada in 1996, has also been adopted for the Global Environmental Method (GEM),[8] which was originally sponsored by the RICS Foundation and the (seemingly defunct) Global Alliance for Building Sustainability. Like other Green Globes® schemes, this is an on-line assessment tool, similar to BREEAM and LEED, but designed for self-administration and allowing benchmarking against similar buildings.

For large operations and especially those that have significant environmental emissions and impacts, a voluntary environmental management system is likely to provide the most appropriate vehicle for ongoing evaluation and assessment. BREEAM and LEED are designed to assess primarily building-related impacts, so for an industrial organization or medium to large business, one of the standardized voluntary environmental management systems (EMS) is likely to be appropriate in order to manage, evaluate and report on their environmental emissions and impacts.[9] The International Organization for Standardization's (ISO) suite of environmental management standards provides requirements and guidelines that can be applied to most applications, including ISO 14031: 1999, which provides a framework for environmental performance evaluation (ISO, 1999), while ISO 14044: 2006 provides a standard for life cycle assessment (ISO, 2006).

The European Eco-Management and Audit Scheme (EMAS) provides a vehicle for registration and scrutiny across Europe, including an 'Ecomapping' toolkit for use by small and medium-sized enterprises (SMEs), that incorporates a template for reporting on performance against environmental indicators.[10] BS 8555: 2003 also includes procedures for environmental performance evaluation (BSI, 2003a).

The main difference between all of these schemes and BREEAM, LEED, etc., is that the method of assessing environmental performance has to be tailored to the individual business, process or factory. Whereas BREEAM and LEED use generic benchmarks which are based on legislative criteria or analysis of typical applications (offices, homes, schools, etc.), this would be very difficult to do for the multiplicity of industrial processes covered by the ISOs, EMAS and the BS.

However, tools that convert impacts into a common parameter, such as carbon emissions or equivalent land use, allow a wide variety of applications to be evaluated. For example, ecological and carbon footprinting are assessment schemes that can equally be applied to countries and individuals as well as to businesses, buildings and developments.

Although there are almost as many definitions of ecological footprint as there are tools professing to calculate it, the principle behind most of them involves a calculation of the land area in 'global hectares' required to feed, provide resources for, produce energy and absorb pollution and waste from the supply chains feeding the activities and structures:

> Ecological footprint analysis compares human demand on nature with the biosphere's ability to regenerate resources and provide services. It does this by assessing the biologically productive land and marine area required to produce the resources a population consumes and absorb the corresponding waste, using prevailing technology.[11]

A global hectare represents the average bio-capacity of the entire planet, where the bio-capacity is 'the area of productive land and water available to produce resources or absorb CO_2 given current management practices'.[12]

Most ecological footprint calculators are designed to estimate individual footprints in terms of the land area required to support a person's lifestyle compared with the land use that is sustainable for 'one-planet living'.[13] The Global Footprint Network has developed Ecological Footprint Standards[14] which provide methodologies for determining footprints for sub-national communities, organizations and products.

Similarly, carbon footprinting is used to indicate greenhouse gas emissions, from the personal to the national. Typically a carbon footprint estimates the total greenhouse gas emissions caused directly and indirectly by a person, organization, event or product. The footprint gives the total equivalent carbon dioxide emissions for all six of the Kyoto Protocol greenhouse gases: carbon dioxide (CO_2), methane (CH_4), nitrous oxide (N_2O), hydrofluorocarbons (HFCs), perfluorocarbons (PFCs) and sulphur hexafluoride (SF_6).

The Carbon Trust defines a carbon footprint thus:

> A carbon footprint is measured in tonnes of carbon dioxide equivalent (tCO_{2eq}). The carbon dioxide equivalent (CO_{2eq}) allows the different greenhouse gases to be compared on a like-for-like basis relative to one unit of CO_2. CO_{2eq} is calculated by multiplying the emissions of each of the six greenhouse gases by its 100 year global warming potential (GWP).[15]

The Carbon Trust website provides a calculator tool to estimate the carbon footprint for an organization. Similarly, the Envirowise Indicator[16] provides estimated carbon footprint and running costs for a number of sectors, including offices, retail, food and drink, manufacturing, chemical processing and construction, based on an on-line tool that allows the input of data from energy metering, raw material consumption, etc.

Assessment schemes for refurbishment and fit-out

BREEAM

The BREEAM Domestic Refurbishment scheme was piloted in 2011. The protocol is based on the Code for Sustainable Homes (CSH), which in turn is based on its predecessor EcoHomes. The weighting for each of the headings is the same as for the CSH and the main differences lie in what is being assessed under each heading, which has been adapted to cater for what can be influenced by the refurbishment process (see Table 1.3.1).

The 2011 version of BREEAM New Construction can only be used for a 'major refurbishment', where

> major refurbishment is defined as construction that results in the fundamental remodelling or adaptation of existing elements of the building envelope, structure and renewal of key building services. And where, on completion of the works, such remodelling / renewal will materially impact on the performance of the building.[17]

The New Construction protocol can also be used for extensions to existing buildings. Projects that do not comply with these definitions can use the appropriate version of BREEAM 2008.

At the time of writing, BRE is developing a protocol for refurbishment and fit-out of commercial buildings.

The Ska Rating scheme

The Ska Rating scheme[18] uses broadly the same headings as the BREEAM 2011 New Construction protocol, although there are some important differences which may impact on the choice of which to use:

- Ska omits Land Use and Ecology, which may be important where significant effort and investment are being made to improve the ecological value of the landscaping.
- In general, Ska is more detailed in its approach to assessing performance under each heading, for example, instead of assessing the predicted total in the reduction of CO_2 emissions, the Energy credits are assessed using 22 credits, including: reducing lighting and small-power energy; using energy-efficient lighting, lamps, heat pumps, HVAC, boilers, domestic hot water and hand dryers; daylighting and lighting controls.
- Energy credits are weighted in order of importance so that, for example, reducing lighting energy is ranked as the single most important measure in refurbishing an office: indeed, making improvements to the lighting specification contributes to around one third of the energy credits.
- Under the Pollution heading, there is no credit assessing NO_x emissions, hence there would be no penalty for using biomass boilers, for example.
- The Materials credits are partly based on the BRE's *Green Guide to Specification* and Green Book Live ratings,[19] assessing each component separately, with timber requirements specifying Forest Stewardship Council

Table 1.3.1 *Comparison between Code for Sustainable Homes (CSH) and BREEAM Domestic Refurbishment*

Heading/weighting (%)	CSH	BREEAM Domestic Refurbishment
Energy & CO_2 Emissions (36.4)	Dwelling emission rate	% reduction in CO_2
		CO_2 emissions post refurbishment
	Fabric energy efficiency	
	Energy display devices	
	Drying space	
	Energy-labelled white goods	
	External lighting	
	Low- & zero-carbon technologies	Renewables
	Cycle storage	
	Home office	
Water (9)	Indoor water use	
	External water use	
Materials (7.2)	Environmental impact	
	Responsible sourcing – basic building elements	
	Responsible sourcing – finishing elements	
		Insulation
Surface Water Run-Off (2.2)	Management	
	Flood risk	
Waste (6.4)	Storage	Recycling facilities
	Construction site waste management	
	Composting	
Pollution (2.8)	Global warming potential of insulants	
	NO_x emissions	
Health & Wellbeing (14)	Daylighting	
	Sound insulation	
	Private space	Inclusive design
	Lifetime homes	Volatile organic compound emissions
		Thermal comfort
Management (10)	Home user guide	
	Considerate Constructor Scheme	
	Construction site impacts	
	Security	
		Fire safety
Ecology (12)	Ecological value of site	
	Ecological enhancement	
	Protection of ecological features	
	Change in ecological value of site	

certification, among others (see Chapter 3.8). BREEAM, on the other hand, uses BRE's on-line calculator (only accessible by licensed BREEAM/CSH assessors) and also includes an assessment of 'Responsible sourcing of materials', not covered in the Ska Rating scheme.

- The Ska Rating scheme assesses the avoidance of sending 11 separate waste elements to landfill, including furniture, carpets, ceilings and partitions. This is covered by a single credit in BREEAM under the heading 'Diversion of resources from landfill' (see Chapter 3.6).
- The Ska Rating includes a number of specific credits under Wellbeing, such as cleaning ductwork that is to be retained, providing extract ventilation from printing/photocopying rooms and filter specification, that should be captured by BREEAM under the heading of Indoor Air Quality (see Chapter 3.4).
- The Ska Rating does not cover the safety and security measures included in BREEAM under Health & Wellbeing, covering such issues as safe access, Secured by Design and the Safer Parking Scheme (see Chapter 3.7).
- The Ska Transport credits are limited to the provision of facilities for cyclists, whereas BREEAM includes issues around access to public transport, car parking and travel plans.

Of course, it must be remembered that BRE do not recommend BREEAM for anything other than major refurbishments and extensions (see above) whereas the Ska Rating should be suitable for small-scale refurbishments, as well as fit-outs.

LEED

As the title implies, LEED 2009 New Construction and Major Renovations (LEED 2009 NC)[20] is intended for use in the assessment of major renovation or refurbishment of existing buildings as well as new construction projects. However, as with BREEAM New Construction, some credits will not be suitable and some adaptation will be required. LEED 2009 NC uses slightly different headings to BREEAM, namely Sustainable Sites, Water Efficiency, Energy & Atmosphere, Materials and Resources, Indoor Environmental Quality and Innovation in Design. Although most credits will be directly applicable to major renovations, those under the Sustainable Sites heading will need some interpretation.

The Sustainable Sites criteria are cross-cutting, in that they include construction issues, site selection, brownfield use, development density, proximity to dwellings and transport nodes, facilities for cyclists and low-emission vehicles, limiting car parking, open and vegetated spaces, storm water control, and heat island and light pollution mitigation. Some of these will not be under the influence of the designer of a renovation/refurbishment project and hence scores will be predestined. If in doubt, assessors will need to contact USGBC to obtain an adjudication on their interpretation of specific credits.

LEED 2009 NC is a flexible scheme that not only can be used for a number of different building types, but also incorporates credits that allow for regional priorities and innovations, and can be adapted for use outside the USA.

Green Globes® Fit-Up

The Green Globes® Fit-Up[21] is a freely available on-line assessment scheme that is designed specifically for 'fit-ups' (fit-outs), and allows many aspects of retrofit and refurbishment, including modifications to the building fabric and environmental services. Comparing the weightings with those used for LEED 2009 NC, Green Globes® Fit-Up allocates a much lower weighting to Energy (18 per cent against 32 per cent) and higher weightings for Indoor Environmental Quality (29 per cent against 14 per cent) and Materials & Resources (27 per cent against 13 per cent). Although the credits under comparable headings are slightly different, this probably recognizes the potential influence that the fit-out designer has on the latter two factors compared with energy.

The Green Globes® Fit-Up is a much simpler scheme than LEED and does not require the detailed guidance and evidence that are inherent in the latter. This is likely to lead to greater scope for interpretation but allows a faster and lower-cost process.

Assessment schemes for existing buildings and operations

BREEAM In-Use

This is an on-line assessment tool that can be completed by anyone who has successfully completed the on-line training scheme and paid the necessary fees to BRE for training and asset registration. Certification, if required, must be carried out by a licensed BREEAM In-Use Auditor, triggering further fees.

The scheme can be undertaken in three parts (BRE, 2009): (1) Part 1 Asset Rating; (2) Part 2 Building Management Rating; and (3) Part 3 Organizational Rating.

The Asset Rating 'provides a quality measure of a building's inherent performance characteristics based on its built form, construction and services' (ibid.). The Building Management Rating assesses policies, procedures and practices related to building operation, actual resource consumption and other environmental impacts and mitigation. The Organizational Rating 'provides a framework for the assessment and evaluation of management policies, practices and procedures related to the activities that an organization is carrying out in the building being assessed' (ibid.). It can be carried out independently from a Part 1 or 2 assessment. Table 1.3.2 shows the headings for each Part and the weightings used for each heading.

It can be seen from Table 1.3.2 that by excluding travel, ecology, land use and waste issues that a Part 2 assessment has a more limited scope than Parts 1 and 3. This is because it is intended to cover management of the building alone, although the exclusion of waste management may be considered to be an omission.

The main application for BREEAM In-Use is as a tool for identifying methods by which building and facility managers can improve the environmental performance of existing buildings. It also provides a benchmark against which improvements can be measured.

Table 1.3.2 *BREEAM In-Use scope and weightings*

Heading	Part 1 Asset Rating (%)	Part 2 Building Management Rating (%)	Part 3 Organizational Rating (%)
Energy	CO_2 emissions, sub-metering, integral LZC energy (26.5)	CO_2 emissions, maintenance & management: audit, monitoring, reporting, information (31.5)	Management & purchasing policies, measuring, recording, targeting, monitoring, training, carbon footprinting (19.5)
Water	Consumption, metering, leak detection, recycling (8)	Maintenance, monitoring (5.5)	Environmental & purchasing policies, measuring, recording, targeting, monitoring, training (3.5)
Materials	Robustness, maintenance standard, security, fire protection (8.5)	Hazardous materials, security survey & remote monitoring, fire protection & emergency plan (7.5)	Purchasing policies, measuring, recording, targeting, monitoring, hazardous materials, security, fire protection, resilience (4.5)
Waste	Recyclables storage (5)		Policies, measuring, recording, targeting, monitoring, training management plan (11.5)
Health & Wellbeing	Daylighting, lighting, IAQ, thermal control, acoustics, drinking water, outdoor space (17)	Policies dealing with refurbishment, VOC emissions & cleaning, occupant satisfaction surveys, lighting levels (15)	Stakeholder engagement, staff development & feedback, targeting, monitoring, management training (15)
Pollution	Emissions to air, ground & water control, flood risk, SUDS, refrigerants, land contamination (14)	Management of: air, ground, water emissions & light pollution controls, flood risk, refrigerant leakage, land contamination (13)	Management of: air, ground, water emissions, flood risk, hazardous chemicals, land contamination (10.5)
Transport	Proximity to amenities & transport nodes, cyclist facilities, pedestrian/cyclist safety (11.5)		Green travel plan, transport surveys & mitigation, policies & procedures, car sharing, deliveries management, public transport access (18.5)
Land Use & Ecology	Ecological value (9.5)		Biodiversity survey & action plan (5)
Management		Building user guide, operating manuals, environmental policy & EMS including purchasing, designated staff, occupant satisfaction feedback, condition surveys, user liaison & transport impact, planned maintenance, refurbishment policy (15)	Building user liaison & education, EMS, environmental policy & staff responsibility, business continuity plans (12)

BREEAM EcoHomes XB

The BREAM EcoHomes XB[22] scheme dates from 2006 and was designed by BRE to assess the environmental management of portfolios of dwellings. It has been designed for purpose-built or converted flats, bungalows and terraced, semi-detached or detached houses. It covers similar ground to BREEAM In-Use, i.e. Management, Energy, Transport, Pollution, Water, Health and Waste, but does not result in a rating. It has been developed to allow existing housing stock to be assessed and monitored. This facilitates the tracking of improvements made during routine maintenance and minor refurbishment.

LEED Existing Buildings

The LEED 2009 Existing Buildings: Operations & Maintenance Project protocol is divided into the same headings as LEED 2009 NC (see above), although with slightly different weightings. Obviously the credits are given a management slant and points are awarded if the building was LEED certified during the design and construction stages. Unlike BREEAM In-Use, LEED Existing Buildings does not differentiate between inherent core building performance issues, management or organization, hence the process is similar to a post-construction phase assessment for new constructions, but with a greater emphasis on operation and maintenance issues. The assessment is carried out over a defined 'performance period' since some credits are based on performance monitored over a discrete period of time. Buildings can be re-assessed a minimum of one year after the initial assessment and some owners or facility managers may wish to use the scheme to monitor performance periodically. Table 1.3.3 summarizes the issues covered by the protocol.

LEED also offers an Alternative Compliance Path for projects outside the USA. Where credits are dependent upon national or local factors, then alternative means of benchmarking are provided.

There is also a LEED Volume Program[23] that enables organizations that are managing portfolios or multiple buildings on a campus, for example, to benefit from economies of scale and avoid duplication of effort.

Table 1.3.3 *LEED 2009 Existing Buildings issues and weightings*

Heading/weighting (%)	Issues covered
Sustainable Sites (24)	LEED certified design and construction, low-impact procedures for exterior fabric and hard landscape maintenance; environmentally friendly pest control, chemical use, erosion control and landscape waste disposal; reducing commuting; maintain or enhance biodiversity; storm water control; heat island and light pollution reduction
Water Efficiency (13)	Water-efficient fittings and landscaping; metering or monitoring; cooling tower management
Energy & Atmosphere (32)	Good practice energy management; metered energy performance meeting good/best practice benchmark; CFC refrigerant replacement or elimination; energy audit, re-commissioning and enhancement; automation/BEMS and sub-metering; on/off-site renewable; emissions reporting
Materials & Resources (9)	Sustainable purchasing of consumables, electrical equipment, furniture, alterations, lamps, and food; solid waste management policy and audit
Indoor Environmental Quality (14)	IAQ performance and best management practices, ETS control, low-emission cleaning products, occupant satisfaction survey, thermal monitoring, lighting control, daylight and views
Innovation in Operations (5)	Including enhanced performance paths, using a LEED Approved Professional to support the project and tracking sustainable performance costs
Regional Priority (3)	Address geographically specific environmental priorities

Green Build Initiative Green Globes®

The Green Globes® for Continual Improvement of Existing Buildings (CIEB) scheme[24] is an on-line protocol with similar scope to LEED 2009 Existing Buildings, but with slightly different categories (see Table 1.3.4).

Building projects that have completed the on-line CIEB questionnaires and scored a minimum threshold of 35 per cent of the 1000 available points are eligible for a detailed third-party review of documentation and an on-site walk-through that will lead to a formal Green Globes® rating/certification. Buildings that successfully complete a third-party assessment are assigned a Green Globes® rating of one to four 'Green Globes'.

EMS-based systems

There are a number of routes by which organizations can gain certification for their environmental management systems (EMSs). In Europe, certification may be through either the Eco-Management and Audit Scheme (EMAS) or ISO 14001, while elsewhere the ISO is the primary scheme adopted. In achieving certification it will be necessary to establish a system for the ongoing evaluation and reporting of environmental performance. For large polluting industries this can be through the ISO 14031 framework for environmental performance evaluation, while for SMEs it may be more appropriate to use the EMAS Ecomapping toolkit,[25] Envirowise Indicator or the processes set out in BS 8555.

Annex IV of EMAS[26] sets out the requirement for reporting of Environmental Performance Indicators (EPIs) comprising the core indicators of energy efficiency, material efficiency, water, waste, biodiversity and emissions, with a graphical representation of annual input or impact, annual output and the ratio of the two. Where there are specific environmental impacts associated with the operations being reported, then further indicators must be developed.

Many companies will want to incorporate EMSs into their corporate social responsibility (CSR) reporting, while the Global Reporting Initiative (GRI) has developed Sustainability Reporting Guidelines[27] that incorporate a framework of economic, environmental and social indicators. Unlike BREEAM and its rivals, there are no benchmarks built into this system, hence performance has to be either compared against similar businesses or tracked over time, although BREEAM In-Use or similar may be used to report on the performance of buildings, of course.

Table 1.3.4 *Green Globes® CIEB scheme weightings*

Heading/weighting (%)	Issues covered
Energy (35)	Performance, efficiency, management, CO_2, transportation
Indoor Environment (18.5)	Air quality, lighting, noise
Emissions & Effluents (17.5)	Boilers, water effluents, hazmat (hazardous material)
Resources (11)	Waste reduction, recycling
Environmental Management (10)	EMS documentation, purchasing, environmental awareness
Water (8)	Performance, conservation, management

GRI's Economic Performance Indicators include such factors as direct economic value generated, costs of adapting to and mitigating against climate change, and dependence on government financial assistance.

GRI's Environmental Performance Indicators follow similar headings to those found in ISO 14034, EMAS (Annex IV) and BREEAM, covering materials, energy, water, biodiversity, emissions, effluents, waste, transport, products (mitigation initiatives and reclamation opportunities) and costs of compliance and environmental protection.

GRI Social Performance Indicators include employment profile, labour relations, occupational health and safety, training opportunities, diversity and equality.

The GRI reporting protocol also includes sections dealing with human rights, society impacts and product responsibility. These include such issues as employment policies to avoid discrimination, child and forced labour, corruption and anti-competitive behaviour. Indicators also question community engagement, public policy and what measures are taken to ensure customer health, safety and privacy.

Ecological footprinting

There are numerous on-line tools for estimating an individual's ecological footprint, but for an organization there is less choice. One of the best established tools has been developed by Best Foot Forward, a UK-based sustainability consultancy.[28] The methodology relies on being able to convert resource use, such as that arising from energy consumption, product manufacture, food production and preparation, travel, etc., to a single metric, expressed as 'global hectares' (see above).

Carbon footprinting

Footprinting tools more commonly use CO_{2eq} emissions as the core metric. Many of the processes that occur in a building or factory can be converted to greenhouse gas (GHG) or CO_{2eq} emissions. This requires drilling down into the lifecycle of each component's supply chain to raw material extraction, distribution, processing, retail, consumption and disposal.

At the time of writing, the International Organization for Standardization is developing ISO/DIS 14067, setting out requirements and guidelines for the quantification and communication of carbon footprints for products, along with ISO/WD TR 14069 on the quantification and reporting of GHG emissions for organizations (i.e. carbon footprinting). This will apply the lifecycle assessment methodologies set out in ISO 14064-1: 2006.

In the UK, a Publicly Available Specification PAS 2050 (BSi 2011) is available that provides a methodology and certification process for establishing 'lifecycle greenhouse gas emissions of goods and services'. The Carbon Trust uses this in its Footprint Expert™ protocol[29] which provides 'a common set of pre-configured templates that a user works through in order to construct a product carbon footprint'.

The carbon footprint of a building or infrastructure is the total amount of carbon dioxide (CO_2) and other greenhouse gases emitted over the lifecycle of that building, expressed as kilograms of CO_{2eq}. This includes all greenhouse gases generated in the manufacture of the raw materials, construction of the building, transport of materials to the construction site, operation of the building, periodic refurbishment and replacement of materials, and end-of-life disposal of the building materials. Because different countries have different carbon intensities for energy generation and transport fuels, the footprinting tools available tend to be country-specific. One such tool available for US buildings has been developed by CleanMetric[TM][30] based on an extensive lifecycle inventory database. Another major provider of tools and databases is the international Greenhouse Gas Protocol,[31] which has developed 'toolsets' for a wide range of industrial sectors as well as service sector organizations and infrastructure.

The embodied carbon, greenhouse gas emissions and other impacts associated with building materials are covered in more detail in Chapter 3.12 of *Integrated Sustainable Design of Buildings* (Appleby, 2011a). Also in this book, later, in Chapter 2.4 and Chapter 3.8, we will look specifically at strategies for reducing carbon footprints in the management and refurbishment of existing buildings.

Part 2

Strategy

2.1
Reasons to retrofit
Refurbishment versus new build

There is an enormous stock of buildings in the world, many of which fall below modern standards in energy performance, sustainability, condition or accommodation. It is interesting to note that in England, for example, the 2007 English Housing Condition Survey found some 7.7 million homes fell below government decency standards.[1] This represented 35 per cent of housing at the time. Apart from the need to improve the energy efficiency of the existing building stock, it is clear that many buildings – commercial and residential – are in need of improvement. This chapter looks at the issues involved in deciding whether to refurbish an existing building or to build a replacement, either by demolishing the existing one or building on an empty site elsewhere. Clearly there are many criteria involved in making this decision and the nature of the decision-making process will vary between residential and non-residential, privately and publicly owned, greenfield and urban location, while also having to take into account plot size, structural condition, budgetary constraints, planning constraints, accommodation needs and other objectives of the building owner/developer.

One of the key challenges impacting on this decision, and one that we will be returning to frequently during the course of this book, is that older buildings tend not to have been designed to be sustainable. Frequently the most sustainable feature of an existing building is the fact that there are existing components that can be re-used, including the site itself. Obviously the greater the volume of building materials that can be retained, the lower the impact of the new materials required for refurbishment. Where a refurbishment involves demolition and removal of most of the fabric and structure with retention of one significant façade, for example, then the impacts are not much lower than demolition and re-build.

In its 2009 report, *UK Offices: Refurbishment vs Development*, GVA Grimley sets out some of the issues relating to costs and risks associated with refurbishment as follows:

- It is unlikely that the Local Authority will require Section 106 (Planning Act) or Section 278 (Highways Act) contributions for a refurbishment that does not significantly increase the accommodation provided.
- Construction impacts are reduced – especially avoiding demolition, site clearance, pile driving, etc.
- Material costs and embodied impacts will be lower.
- Phased refurbishment allows for continuity of use and income.

- Refurbishment will normally be achievable within shorter programme times.
- Tax benefits of up to 100 per cent can be obtained in the UK where the building is in a 'disadvantaged' area that qualifies for Business Premises Renovation Allowances.
- Flexibility may be limited by existing floor-to-ceiling heights, limited services routes, plant room sizes, and scope for enhancing insulation, daylighting or natural ventilation.
- Older buildings may contain asbestos or other hazardous materials which in some cases may not be discovered during a survey.
- Refurbishment avoids uncertainties involved in site condition but contingencies to budget and programme may be required to allow for problems that might be uncovered during refurbishment.
- Not all contractors can handle refurbishments and a premium may have to be paid to a specialist.[2]

A key differentiator between refurbishment and demolition/new build is the amount of solid waste material generated. A BRE report from 2006 states that some 26 million tonnes of waste arise from demolition annually, 81 per cent of which was hardcore materials such as concrete, bricks, block, glass, etc.; 12 per cent is reclaimable waste; and 6.5 per cent is non-reclaimable materials such as plastics that go to landfill.[3]

Although much of this waste can be crushed and recycled as aggregate, there are significant environmental impacts associated with crushing, including noise and air pollution. Refer to Chapter 3.6 and Chapter 3.8.

In a project for the Department of Trade and Industry that was published in 2002, BRE used its 'Office Scorer' tool to compare the environmental impact and lifecycle costs of refurbishing and redeveloping offices (see Chapter 1.3 for more details).

The Part 1 report (Anderson and Mills, 2002a) provides a useful set of categories covering the options available to those considering significant changes to their office accommodation:

- major refurbishment – replacement of major plant and services, suspended ceilings, floor finishes, raised floors and internal walls;
- complete refurbishment – only substructure, superstructure and floor structure retained;
- redevelopment with retained façade;
- complete redevelopment.

For complex sites such as shopping centres or university campuses, redevelopment may include some combination of refurbishment, new build and relocation.

The Office Scorer methodology assigned Ecopoints to the environmental impact of the refurbishment and construction processes, where 100 Ecopoints is the environmental impact of an average European person. Ecopoints have since been used as a parameter in the environmental profiling of construction products as published in the *BRE Green Guide to Specification*[4] (see Chapters 1.3 and 3.9).

BRE used the Office Scorer tool and Ecopoints metric to compare the impacts and whole-life costs for 17 different office buildings of different sizes and servicing strategies. Table 2.1.1 summarizes the average impacts for the three main options examined: major refurbishment, complete refurbishment and redevelopment, demonstrating the importance of ventilation strategy in the resultant Ecopoints score.

Table 2.1.2 shows a sample of results from a series of case histories published in Part 2 of the BRE report (Anderson and Mills, 2002b) and Figure 2.1.1 shows a typical graphical output from Office Scorer.

The results in Tables 2.1.1 and 2.1.2 illustrate that, perhaps unsurprisingly, the environmental impact of refurbishment is generally lower than for redevelopment. Although Case History 3 demonstrates that, with attention paid to designing a low-energy building, the additional impact from the embodied impacts of materials can be offset by a reduction in environmental impact associated with 'ventilation', albeit this building started with relatively inefficient air conditioning installed by some of the tenants.

Figure 2.1.1 is perhaps more typical in that the environmental impact of the redevelopment option is some 40 per cent greater than refurbishment, mostly due to the embodied impact of materials.

What these case histories do not reveal is the difference in quality of the accommodation between the options presented. For example, refurbishing a

Table 2.1.1 *Summary of environmental impacts (Ecopoints/m^2) of ventilation strategies of a 60-year building life*

Ventilation strategy	Major refurbishment	Complete refurbishment	Redevelopment
Natural ventilation	19.5	20.5	24
Displacement ventilation	21.5	22.5	26
Air conditioning with night cooling (by natural ventilation)	25.5	26.5	30
Air conditioning	27	28	32

Source: Anderson and Mills, 2001a.

Table 2.1.2 *Refurbishment versus redevelopment case histories: results from Office Scorer tool*

Case history	Gross floor area (m^2)	Ecopoints /m^2	Capital cost (£)	Whole-life cost (60y)	Rental value (£)	Energy cost (£/yr m^2)
1 Stockport Borough Council offices						
Refurb with nat vent mn	4,030	15.27	693	2,239	N/A	170.89
Redev with air con mn	4,030	29.98	1,230	2,863	N/A	283.01
2 Shepherds Bush offices						
Refurb with nat vent & night cooling	17,109	19.3	678	2,497	N/A	248.51
Redev with air con & night cooling	15,559	26.81	1,145	3,028	N/A	313.45
3 Offices in London W1						
Refurb with mixed mode	12,500	28.81	837	2,720	400	325.13
Redev with air con inc demolition	15,000	35.07	1,145	3,028	500	499.00
Redev with air con & night cooling inc demolition	15,000	28.53	1,145	3,028	500	341.00

Note: The Office Scorer website has been discontinued.
Source: Anderson and Mills, 2002b.

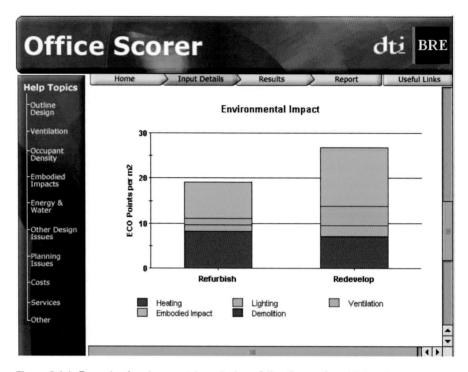

Figure 2.1.1 *Example of environmental results from Office Scorer Case History 2*

Source: Anderson and Mills, 2002b. Copyright BRE, reproduced from BRE IP 9/02 Part 2 with permission.

naturally ventilated office building that opens onto a busy street and conse-quently suffers from excessive noise and air quality problems may not work without major changes to the fabric and ventilation strategy. BRE's research did point out, however, that occupancy density was a key factor in the success of a naturally ventilated refurbishment, with densities greater than 1 person per 10 m² generally presenting an overheating risk.

Some organizations outgrow their existing accommodation. For example, some existing schools and further and higher education establishments find that their buildings are no longer fit for purpose and cannot accommodate modern methods of education and corresponding technological developments.[5]

Baker points out in Chapter 1 of his *Handbook of Sustainable Refurbishment* (Baker, 2009) that there are socio-economic differences between refurbishment and redevelopment in that 'generally, refurbishment carries a higher proportion of labour cost than new build'. In other words, typically there will be a greater contribution to employment from a refurbishment project.

The arguments for refurbishment are even stronger in the retail shopping centre sector. A recent article on German retail investment[6] reported that 40 per cent of Germany's total retail stock is currently in need of refurbishment and that:

Medium-sized developers, private owners and investors are becoming far more interested in the possibilities of renovation within the majority part of the retail market in Germany. The obvious financial advantage for refurbishment as opposed to new build is that construction duration is approximately halved. Automatically the cash flow is far more attractive. With shorter timescales for the turnaround of renovation work, new or existing tenants can move into retail space far quicker. It is also possible that in larger retail premises the conversion for floor levels can be phased to allow even more efficient rental use of retail areas.

There are no equivalent modelling studies to Office Scorer available for dwellings; however, a paper prepared by Anne Power of the London School of Economics for the Sustainable Development Commission on the demolition or refurbishment of homes concludes that:

> The evidence we have uncovered counters the suggestion that large-scale and accelerated demolition would either help us meet our energy and climate change targets or respond to our social needs. Many arguments remain unclear, but the overall balance of evidence suggests that refurbishment most often makes sense on the basis of time, cost, community impact, prevention of sprawl, reuse of existing infrastructure and protection of existing communities. It can also lead to reduced energy use in buildings in both the short and long term.
>
> (Power, 2008)

However, in a paper presented to a conference in Hong Kong in 2007, Waters *et al.* (2007) stated:

> A key rationale for the demolition of large areas of existing housing in some parts of the UK is their poor environmental performance, non-compliance with modern building regulations and the absence of demand for its continued ownership or occupation, coupled with evidence of huge costs involved in refurbishment. While developers are able to reclaim value-added tax (VAT) on expenditure on new build, they are unable to reclaim the 17.5% VAT on refurbishment projects – this additional cost can be make or break for the financial viability of a proposed scheme. Thus, the UK tax system discriminates against refurbishment and in favour of demolition and new build.

A limited study by the Empty Homes Agency (ECA) dating from 2008, comparing three newly built houses with three refurbished ones found that the 'lifetime CO_2 emissions' per unit floor area, calculated over 50 years, were little different across the board.[7] However, the critical factor in this case is the operational carbon and the investment in carbon reduction measures made during refurbishment. Clearly, once the UK Building Regulations set a target of zero carbon, it will be more difficult for a refurbished dwelling to compete, even when factoring the whole-life embedded carbon difference.

There have been some notable attempts to minimize carbon emissions through refurbishment. One example reported on the BSRIA website in February 2010[8] is a Victorian terraced house in Hackney. Through using Passivhaus principles,[9] this has achieved a 75 per cent reduction in CO_2 emissions (see Table 2.1.3).

This was a major refurbishment that retained the front elevation (see Figure 2.1.2) but an internal frame was constructed within to support rebuilt floors,

Table 2.1.3 *House in Hackney, London N1: CO$_2$ emissions before and after refurbishment*

Energy end use	Prior to refurb CO$_2$kg/y	After refurb CO$_2$kg/y	Cut in CO$_2$kg/y	Percentage reduction	Energy
Space heating gas	4683	419	4264	91	
Water heating gas	765	742	23	3	
Pumps and fans electricity	74	124	−50	−68	Regulated
Lighting electricity	387	228	159	41	
Other electricity	633	633	0	0	Unregulated
Total regulated (excluding PV)	5909	1513	4396	74	
Total (excluding PV)	654	2146	4396	67	
Contribution from photovoltaics and the effect on total emissions					
Photovoltaics (PV)		−516	516		
Total regulated energy use including PV	5909	997	4912	83	
Total including PV	6542	1630	4912	75	

Source: www.bsria.co.uk/news/low-carbon-refurb.

Figure 2.1.2 *House in Hackney: front and rear elevations after refurbishment*
Source: Kilian O'Sullivan.

eliminate thermal bridges and allow 140 mm of insulation to be applied to the front wall with double-glazed sash windows, incorporating four draught seals per sash. The new rear wall contained 200 mm of insulation and triple glazing, while the ground floor was given an extra 100 mm of insulation and the roof another 180 mm. A high standard of air tightness was achieved, with 1.1 air changes per hour measured for the house before plastering. Because of this, a mechanical ventilation unit was installed with heat recovery (MVHR).

For non-residential buildings, a similar picture emerges. The Carbon Trust's Low-Carbon Buildings Accelerator (LCBA) programme examined ten buildings through the design and refurbishment process and found that it was not uncommon for CO_2 emissions associated with building services to increase by 20 per cent in absolute terms following refurbishment, mainly because of the higher specification required by the occupier.[10] However, where a low-carbon specification of environmental services was used, the increase was only around 10 per cent higher than before refurbishment.

We will be examining the strategies and technologies involved in low-carbon and sustainable refurbishment of both residential and non-residential buildings in Chapter 2.4 and in Part 3.

2.2
Post-occupancy evaluation

Introduction

Post-occupancy evaluation (POE) is thought to have evolved in the United States in the 1960s from one-off case history evaluations through a more systematic approach in the 1970s and 1980s. Wolfgang Preisner coined a definition in 1988 as 'the process of evaluating buildings in a systematic and rigorous manner after they have been built and occupied for some time' (Federal Facilities Council, 2001).

In the UK, they evolved from a growing concern about the effect that office buildings were having on their occupants through surveys that were designed to investigate the causes of and cures for 'sick building syndrome' or building sickness (see Chapter 3.4 and Chapter 4.4).

POEs take various forms and are known by a number of different names including 'building performance studies', 'facility performance evaluations' and 'Building Health Checks'.

Drivers for POE

The final stage of the Royal Institute of British Architects (RIBA) 2007 Plan of Work Stages, which runs from A to L, headed 'Post Practical Completion', includes Stage L3: 'review of project performance in use'. This stage is best achieved through some form of POE, although historically it has not always been implemented. However, some public sector funding bodies, such as the Scottish Funding Council, are insisting on POE before final instalments will be paid. Similarly, UK public auditing bodies such as the Audit Commission use the Design Quality Method (DQM) to assess the quality and value for money of large educational and health projects in the UK.[1] Table 2.2.1 summarizes the composition of a DQM assessment.

BREEAM New Construction 2011(see Chapter 1.3) includes a Management credit (Man 04 Stakeholder Participation) for undertaking POE one year after occupation. At the design stage the credit is awarded if:

> The client makes a commitment to carry out a Post-Occupancy Evaluation (POE) one year after building occupation, to gain building performance feedback. The POE should be carried out by an independent third party and should cover:
> * A review of the design and construction process (review of design, procurement, construction and handover processes).

Table 2.2.1 *Design Quality Method scope*

Architecture	Including the more functional qualities of specification, site and space planning, as well as the relatively subjective area of aesthetic merit
Environment Engineering	Including objective and scientifically measurable aspects such as lighting, noise, temperature, and air pollution levels
User Comfort	Internal comfort conditions are scientifically measurable and links between them and productivity are increasingly evident
Whole-Life Costs	Including occupancy costs and the whole-life performance of building fabric, components and services. Assessment of the balance between capital and running costs that affect future building performance
Detailed Design	Including assessment of the maintenance and occupancy costs arising from aspects of detailed design and specification
User Satisfaction	Building occupants are asked to rate their satisfaction with their building by responding to structured questions

Source: www.aude.ac.uk/info-centre/goodpractice/AUDE_POE_guide.

- Feedback from a wide range of building users including Facilities Management on the design and environmental conditions of the building covering:
  - Internal environmental conditions (light, noise, temperature, air quality);
  - Control, operation and maintenance;
  - Facilities and amenities;
  - Access and layout;
  - Other relevant issues.
- Sustainability performance (energy/water consumption, performance of any sustainable features or technologies, e.g. materials, renewable energy, rainwater harvesting, etc.).

For the credit to be awarded, the client has to make 'a commitment to carry out the appropriate dissemination of information on the building's post-occupancy performance in order to share any good practice and lessons learned'.

LEED Existing Buildings 2007, on the other hand, incorporates a more limited credit under the Indoor Environmental Quality (IEQ) heading: Credit 2.1 Occupant Comfort – Occupant Survey. This requires the implementation of

an occupant comfort survey and complaint response system to collect anonymous responses about thermal comfort, acoustics, IAQ (indoor air quality), lighting levels, building cleanliness and other occupant comfort issues. The survey must be collected from a representative sample of building occupants making up at least 30% of the total occupants, and it must include an assessment of overall satisfaction with building performance and identification of any comfort-related problems.

The British approach

In 1987, a Building Use Studies report produced evidence from surveys of 4373 office workers across 47 office sites in the UK, based on purpose-designed questionnaires and observations of the buildings and their environmental services (Wilson and Hedge, 1987). The methodology used in these surveys was adapted by Leaman and others for a series of 'Probe' (post-occupancy review of buildings and their engineering) (Leaman *et al.*, 2010) reports, published in the *Building Services Journal* between 1995 and 2002.[2] The methodology was extended to include:

- site visits including:
  - interviews with key staff;
  - review of drawings , specifications, operation and maintenance records, commissioning records, meter readings, building management system (BMS) outputs and office equipment inventories;
  - spot checks of illuminance levels, temperatures, humidities, air velocities, room air movement, electrical demand;
- occupant feedback survey;
- energy assessment;
- pressure test to determine air leakage rate.

Probe was a unique third-party assessment of office buildings that had been occupied for between one and five years and was intended to provide construction professionals with quite detailed feedback on the performance of buildings, compared with typical and good practice benchmarks. For example, energy assessment was carried out using techniques published by the Chartered Institution of Building Services Engineers (CIBSE) in their Technical Memorandum TM22: *Energy Assessment & Reporting Methodology* (EARM), now in its second edition (CIBSE, 2006) and using benchmarks from Energy Consumption Guide 19 (DETR, 1999). Air leakage results were compared with results from the BRE/BSRIA database.

The Probe team also developed its own benchmarks for occupant satisfaction based on responses to questionnaires grouped under the headings of 'Overall satisfaction and comfort' and 'Overall satisfaction with health & perceived control over the environment'. Under the comfort heading, the occupants were asked to report their perceptions of summer and winter temperature and air quality, lighting and noise. The second group asked for occupants to report levels of satisfaction with their health and the controllability of heating, cooling, ventilation, lighting and noise.

Since 2008, the Probe methodology has been owned by Arup and known as the 'Arup Appraise' (Leaman, 2010).

Figures 2.2.1 and 2.2.2 show some results for one of the buildings studied by Leaman, comparing questionnaire responses in 1999 and 2009, showing the breakdown of questions used to assess occupant perceptions of thermal, ventilation and visual environments. It is interesting to note how little the study building has changed in ten years.

Also evolving from the work of Wilson and Hedge, and Building Use Studies, 'Building Health Checks' were developed in the UK in the 1990s as a

Scale: 1 = Unsatisfactory 7 = Satisfactory

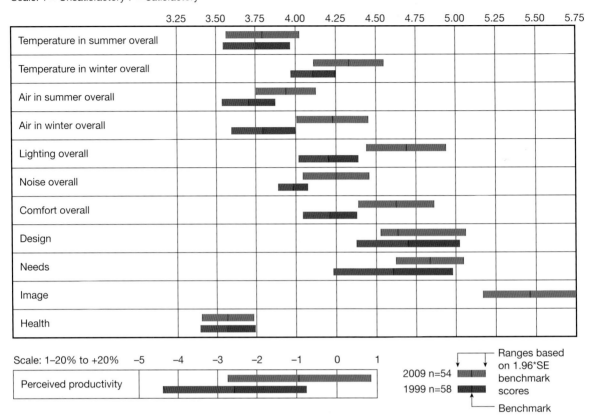

Figure 2.2.1 *Typical representation of questionnaire results from the Arup Appraise study*
Source: Arup.

service provided by a team led by the author at Building Health Consultants Ltd (BHC). In a collaboration between CIBSE, BRE, BHC and the Building Services Research & Information Association (BSRIA), a standard protocol was developed in 1998 (BSRIA, 1998). The Building Health Check comprises a series of surveys and inspections that form the diagnostic component of a preventative maintenance regime in order to do the following:

- Minimize the risk of sick building syndrome.
- Reduce the incidence of environment and services-related problems.
- Improve productivity and reduce the risk of sickness absenteeism.
- Check the effectiveness of operating and maintenance regimes.

The protocol sets out a stepwise approach as follows:

- Step 1 – obtain preliminary information.
- Step 2 – carry out walk-through survey.
- Step 3 – self-administered questionnaire survey.

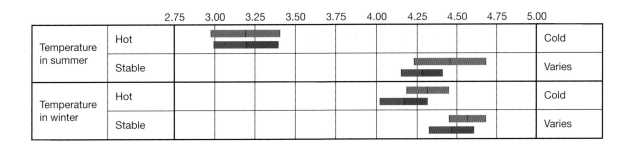

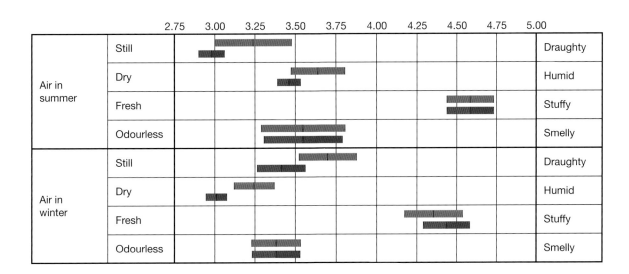

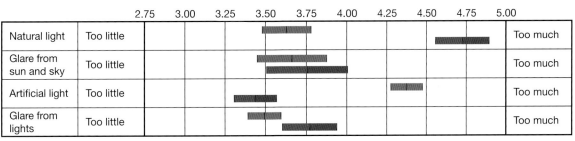

Scale: 1=Unsatisfactory 7=Satisfactory

Figure 2.2.2 *Breakdown of key environmental parameters from the Arup Appraise questionnaire*
Source: Arup.

- Step 4 – carry out preliminary analysis to identify clusters of symptoms and complaints and help design physical surveys.
- Step 5 – physical surveys, including thermal environment and air movement, air quality and ventilation, light, noise, electric and magnetic fields and inspection of environmental services.
- Step 6 – report.

At the heart of a Building Health Check is the questionnaire. For anyone wishing to design their own or adopt one from elsewhere, it is worth noting that a questionnaire must ask the right questions that in no way lead or coach the respondent, while ensuring that the information gleaned can be related to measurements and observations made during the physical surveys and walk-throughs. It is also important to maximize the response rate by ensuring the questionnaire is not too onerous or open to interpretation. It must not be alarmist, avoiding references to 'sick buildings' or 'building-related illness' for example.

The preamble to a questionnaire should include background on what the intention of the survey is, emphasizing the confidential nature of the survey. It should seek information on the location of the respondent's workstation, perhaps on a suitable floor plan, or where they spend the majority of their working day.

Most questionnaires separate health and comfort issues, for example, using headings such as 'Personal Well-being' to seek information on the severity and frequency of symptoms and 'Environmental Comfort' to obtain feedback on environmental conditions.

Personal Well-being might include questions relating to:

- dryness of the eyes;
- itchy or watery eyes;
- blocked or stuffy nose;
- runny nose;
- dry throat;
- lethargy and/or tiredness;
- headache;
- dry, itching or irritated skin.

It is useful to include a question under each heading that determines whether the symptom is better on days away from the office.

Some questionnaires seek information on comfort conditions experienced at the time of the survey, so that a direct correlation can be made with measurements taken during the site visit. Others, such as that used by Wilson and Hedge and BSRIA, attempt to glean information in both summer and winter, hoping to identify performance issues that may occur under extreme external conditions. Under the heading of 'Environmental Comfort' the following information may be sought:

- temperature: between too hot and too cold, stable or variable;
- air movement: from still to draughty;

- air quality: covering humidity, fresh or stuffy conditions and odourless to smelly;
- light or visual environment: fit for purpose or too dim, or distracting glare;
- noise and vibration.

It may also be useful to include questions on controllability of temperature, ventilation and lighting, along with privacy, layout, décor, cleanliness and maintenance response times.

Questionnaires can be designed to be completed on-line provided that confidentiality and security issues are addressed. On-line questionnaires can be linked to software that enables rapid analysis of the results.

A case history for a Building Health Check carried out by the BHC team for the European Commission in Brussels is provided at the end of this chapter. This illustrates the procedure in the early stages of evolution of the Building Health Check and the kind of information that can be gleaned from the process.

The North American experience

Facility performance evaluation (FPE) has been developed in the USA as an extension to POE that establishes a continuous process of systematically evaluating the performance and effectiveness of one or more aspects of buildings in relation to issues such as sustainability, productivity, safety, security, functionality, accessibility, cost-effectiveness and aesthetics.[3] It is being used extensively by federal and state agencies as a management tool for existing buildings as well as providing feedback to the design team, or as an extension to the commissioning process for new buildings.

The California Department of General Services (DGS) has introduced an FPE programme for educational establishments[4] which serves as a model for other programmes in the USA. The goals of the programme are to do the following:

- Define facility performance criteria based on the local school district's priorities.
- Evaluate these performance criteria with user feedback, professional investigation, and standardized benchmarks.
- Interpret evaluation results as guidelines for future improvement.
- Create a centralized databank of current design, construction, and operations practices and their respective evaluations.
- Disseminate evaluation results to a wide audience of decision-makers, and in language and format accessible to all.

The DGS has a stated aim of learning from the operation of its existing estate in the design of new schools.

FPEs typically assess the performance of a number of aspects of buildings and their services. Techniques commonly used to collect data on the building–user relationships are similar to those referred to above for the Probe studies. They include questionnaires, interviews, field observations, walk-throughs, workshop sessions, photographic surveys, recordings of the use of time, and looking at the physical evidence of use. An FPE normally goes beyond a standard POE in that it not only assesses technical performance but also covers economic and organizational issues.

The US General Services Administration (GSA) launched the Workplace 20.20 Program in 2002 with the aim of improving the workplace for public sector workers, focusing specifically on organizational aspects of existing offices. Its 2009 report, *The New Federal Workplace*[5] includes analysis of six of the buildings in the programme. A questionnaire was used to determine whether 'users' of the buildings rated the workplaces better, worse or the same as their old workplaces. Although only a small percentage (5–10 per cent) reported that their workplace was worse, there was a bigger variation among those reporting an improvement, ranging from 51 per cent who reported an improvement in their 'ability to get timely answers to questions' to 66 per cent who reported an improvement in sharing information.

Modifications were made to workspace design, fenestration and environmental services resulting in significant improvements in satisfaction with buildings, workspaces, lighting, daylight, view out, visual quality, air quality and temperature.

The GSA has also carried out a Workplace Performance Study[6] which comprised surveys involving

> [more than] 6,000 federal workers and measuring environmental conditions at 624 workstations in 43 workplaces in 22 separate buildings. The sample chosen [was] representative of the building ages, workplace types, and climate zones in GSA's national portfolio. The study evaluated everything from the technical attributes of building systems to acoustical, air quality, lighting, and thermal conditions; from workplace ergonomics to end user satisfaction.

The study employed an on-line questionnaire, posing similar questions to that used in the Probe, Arup Appraise and BSRIA questionnaires referred to above. A standard rig was developed for measuring environmental conditions locally (see Table 2.2.2) and measured conditions were compared against questionnaire responses. The Standards/Thresholds column states the US reference standard used as the basis for comparing measured results (refer also to Chapter 4.4.

Case history: Building Health Check for Charlemagne building, Brussels[7]

Introduction

Passive smoking and draught were identified as common causes of complaint among ambassadors and staff in the recently refurbished meeting rooms on the 15th floor of the Charlemagne building, the headquarters of the Council of Ministers of the European Commission in Brussels.

These problems were identified by a multi-disciplinary team, comprising specialists from the South Bank Polytechnic, the London School of Hygiene & Tropical Medicine and Bruel & Kjaer, brought together by London-based Brian Colquhoun and Partners.[8]

Table 2.2.2 *GSA Workplace Performance Study: environmental conditions measured*

Measurements Taken at Each Workstation*	Standards/Thresholds
Temperature at 4 feet (*spot & 24 hr continuous*) Temperature at 2 feet Temperature at floor level Horizontal and vertical radiant temperature difference	ASHRAE 55-2004 cooling and heating season
Relative humidity (*spot & 24 hr continuous*) Air flow rate of floor and 4 foot level CO_2 concentration (*spot & 24 hr continuous*) CO concentration (*spot & 24 hr continuous*) Small and large particulates (*24 hr continuous*) TVOC index, Ozone, Radon, (*24 hr continuous*)	ASHRAE 62-2004 ASHRAE 55-2004 ASHRAE 62-2004, EPA IAQ specs EPA IAQ specifications HPSH based on EPA IAQ specs EPA IAQ specifications

Light level:
  on primary work surface (*w/task light off*)
  on keyboard (*w/task light off*)
  on monitor (*w/task light off*)
  on primary work surface (*w/task light on*)
  on keyboard (*w/task light on*)
  on monitor (*w/task light on*)
Calculate luminance/brightness contrast ratio
	IESNA RA-1-04

Background noise level (RC) and noise quality (QAI)	ASHRAE Applications Handbook 2003
Partition noise reduction (dBA) Privacy Index (PI) Calculated: Predicted Occupancy Dissatisfaction	ASTM E1130-02

Source: www.gsa.gov/portal/content/103975.
* spot measurements unless noted

As well as indoor air quality problems, the team found uneven illumination, with glare and low lighting levels in the meeting rooms, which suffered from contrasting surface brightness and a lack of decorative embellishment.

The team carried out their investigation in a number of stages: starting with an inspection of the rooms and plant, along with discussions with occupants and maintenance personnel, followed by the distribution of tailor-made question-naires, surveys of thermal, visual and aural environments and observations of air movement, work patterns and smoking habits. Further targeted surveys were carried out after analysis of the questionnaires.

Despite there being nominally adequate rates of outdoor air drawn into the central air-handling plant for dilution of tobacco odours in the meeting rooms, observations indicated that the air leaving the diffusers was creating noticeable air movement in the occupied zone and tobacco smoke was tending to travel with very little dilution into the faces of non-smokers. It was concluded that this excessive air movement, combined with convection and radiant cooling from the very large single-glazed windows, would account for the draught.

The investigating team suggested a number of optional remedial measures, graded by cost. These included reducing air movement without reducing outdoor air supply rate or, at greater cost, replacing the existing supply air terminals with a system creating buoyancy-assisted displacement ventilation.

Recommendations also included alterations to the lighting to create more even illumination and reducing glare, draught and thermal loads by modifying the fenestration.

The building and services

At the time of the survey, in April 1989, the Charlemagne building incorporated large areas of single glazing, mostly openable, and a floor plan which was too deep for satisfactory penetration of daylight. It was not designed to be air conditioned and most of the building was naturally ventilated and heated by radiators.

The 15th floor had been adapted for meetings of the Council of Ministers. There were three large meeting rooms, with seating for 80–100 people at inner and outer tables, and a smaller 60-seat room which was used intermittently. The larger meeting rooms were bordered by interpreters' cabins to three sides.

The original environmental services serving the 15th floor were replaced in 1985, except for supply air distribution ductwork above a false ceiling and circular diffusers served from the ductwork.

The meeting rooms and their interpreters' cabins were fully air conditioned, each meeting room being supplied with treated air from its own separately controlled air-handling unit, the supply air comprising a variable proportion of room and outdoor air. A nominal minimum outdoor air supply rate of 14 litres/s per person was drawn into the plant and adjusted according to a CO_2 return air sensor as an indicator of occupancy level. Each set of cabins was supplied with 100 per cent outdoor air conditioned in central plant and reheated as necessary to meet comfort conditions.

Initial observations

The complaints received by management had been non-specific, indicative of a general level of dissatisfaction with the working environment. Random questioning of occupants and observations made during meetings indicated that a number of problems with the indoor environment required investigation.

The questionnaire was designed to elicit information from the occupants on factors relating to their work which might exert stress on them, to obtain their qualitative views on their working environment and to ascertain the incidence of symptoms that might indicate some level of 'building sickness'. The questionnaire included questions about age and gender, nature of work, journey mode and duration, working hours, smoking habits, use of contact lenses, work-related likes and dislikes, perceptions of thermal comfort, air quality, noise, visual environment, furniture, physical comfort and health.

The questions concerning health referred to symptoms that disappear when occupants leave their place of work, i.e. the 15th floor. These covered the classic building sickness symptoms of headaches, nausea, dizziness, irritation of the eyes, nose and throat, shortness of breath, tightness of chest, skin rashes, itching or dryness of skin, joint and muscle aches, flu-like symptoms and general malaise. The incidence of other potentially stress-related symptoms, such as irritability, depression, anxiety and frustration associated with work, was also ascertained. Further questions were designed to determine the proportion of occupants who suffered from respiratory ailments and allergies.

Building sickness scores refer to the average number of workplace-related health symptoms reported per occupant. The survey by Wilson and Hedge (referred to above) reported scores of between 1.25 and 5.25 on a 7-point scale, where 1 is good and 7 is bad (Wilson and Hedge, 1987). For air-conditioned buildings they found an average score of 3.05 among private sector buildings and 4.29 in the public sector. Using a similar questionnaire and a 7-point scale, the 15th floor of the Charlemagne building scored 2.9 overall from 127 regular users of the floor, which represents a below-average building sickness score for public sector occupants.

Occupants' ratings of their environment, however, largely supported the initial observations of the investigating team. More than half of the respondents who regularly use the meeting rooms thought them stale or smoky, while inner table users in particular thought them draughty. Around half also reported that the rooms were too hot, and about the same number too noisy. Around one third of inner table users complained of glare and excessive illuminance, while nearly the same proportion of outer table users had similar complaints, although some 20 per cent thought it too dim.

Room air conditioning

Despite the number of complaints that the rooms were too hot, measurements taken over a one-week period indicated that the thermal environment was relatively comfortable and stable, fluctuating between 20 and 22°C, even with the air-handling plant shut down overnight and at weekends (Figure 2.2.3). Radiant temperatures did not vary greatly from room air temperatures. Air velocities, however, varied greatly, and in many instances exceeded the maximum values recommended in ISO 7730 for comfort at the operational temperatures experienced (ISO, 1984).

Figure 2.2.3 *Charlemagne building, Brussels: thermal environment survey rig set up in 15th-floor meeting room*

Source: Appleby, 1989.

This may explain why some occupants complained of draught, particularly those seated under the region where airstreams from two neighbouring diffusers met and were deflected downwards into the occupied zone. Smoke tests confirmed this phenomenon and also indicated that cold windows exacerbated this by cooling the already downward moving air which moved with increasing momentum into the occupied zone. Convectors located under the tall single-glazed windows only had the effect of deflecting this downward moving airstream into the room.

Smoke tests and other observations also indicated that there was considerable horizontal air movement within the occupied zone, leading to tobacco smoke being conveyed with little dilution between smokers and others. This was exacerbated by the observed short circuiting of 15 per cent of the supply air straight back into the extract air system.

It can be concluded from these fairly rudimentary observations that, in general terms, the provision of outdoor air as recommended in the (then) national standards did not guarantee an acceptable purity of inhaled air. (This has since been recognized in most countries by the prohibition of tobacco smoking in the workplace and public spaces in general.) It is essential that the method of air supply is capable of diluting contaminants to an acceptable level everywhere in the occupied zone or displacing them away from breathing zones of the occupants. (For a more extension discussion of air quality and ventilation issues, see Chapter 3.4.)

The visual environment

As analysis of the responses to the questionnaire had indicated, an illumination survey proved that light distribution was uneven – with the highest illuminance values being measured at the inner tables, with levels being daylight-dependent close to the window walls and inadequate along those internal walls furthest from the windows. It was observed that the glare was caused in part by artificial sources and partly by natural light.

The warm white fluorescent lamps were mounted in diffusers having dark perspex baffles at right angles to the tube axis, hence reducing the sideways light emission along its axis. Illuminance directly below these lamps and close to the windows was measured as high as 1800 lux, even on an overcast day. At the same time, levels measured at outer desks furthest from the windows were nearer 500 lux, not a low value in absolute terms, but low compared with elsewhere in the rooms.

The large area of unobstructed sky seen through the windows represented a particular glare problem, even with the net curtains drawn. While providing a source of natural light and a link with the outside world, the link is tenuous since it is uncluttered with scenery; the daylight providing a greater illuminance than necessary close to the windows and distracting glare for those facing the windows.

The team recommended that the baffles be removed from the luminaires and that whiter lamps be installed. It was also suggested that the window area be reduced to 40 per cent of the total wall area and insulation improved through the installation of double glazing and insulated infill panels.

Conclusions

The investigation was a good example of the effective application of questionnaires and targeted measurements and observations. It is thought that the main causes of complaint were identified without having to resort to lengthy and costly ventilation and contaminant surveys. For investigations that reveal higher-than-average building sickness scores with less obvious causes of complaint, further studies may be necessary. In this case, no follow-up survey was possible; however, it is strongly recommended that, where possible, further studies be carried out once recommendations have been implemented and bedded in.

2.3
The cost of sustainable refurbishment and management

Introduction

Historically, sustainability has generally been considered to add to the bottom line of construction projects and building facilities management. The main drivers were framed in terms of meeting legislative requirements, obtaining planning consent or ticking corporate sustainability reporting (CSR) boxes. Ideally, all cost modelling and option studies should be based on life cycle cost models. The biggest problem in applying life cycle costing, however, has always been where a developer or landlord does not benefit from the reduction in running costs that accrue from a reduction in energy or water use. This tends to be less of an issue for refurbishment and retrofitting where the capital expenditure (capex) is frequently borne by those benefiting from reduced running costs.

In this chapter we look at the issues that impact on capex and life cycle costs, how these are modelled and the funding vehicles that are available for those considering refurbishment or wishing to improve the sustainability of an existing building.

Cost models for sustainable refurbishment

A cost model can provide unit rates for individual components of a clearly defined scenario or marginal costs for options compared with a defined baseline. Cost models need to use the same basis for comparison: for example, any comparison of energy-saving techniques, including renewable technologies, should quote costs on a per kWh and $kgCO_2$ per annum basis. The latter is particularly important as it enables the carbon intensity of energy sources to be accounted for. This sort of cost model is most useful if it provides marginal costs, that is, costs that are extra to a defined baseline, such as solar hot water collectors compared with the equivalent boiler capacity.

For the refurbishment or retrofitting of buildings, there are numerous variables, and hence a model must be found that is as close as possible to the proposed scenario. As well as operational energy, water and waste costs, these should factor in the cost, durability, life expectancy and replacement cost of alternative materials and products. The purpose of the cost model needs to be defined, as well as the margins of error that can be accommodated. Cost models can be used to assess and monitor budgets for a project or provide a benchmark for options analysis. Cost models have been published for different building types, both new build and refurbishment, and for technologies such as renewables and lighting. In the UK, *Building Magazine* has published the former on a bi-monthly basis for a number of years.[1] Davis Langdon has been responsible for most of these,[2] while their subsidiary Davis Langdon Mott Green Wall have published similar articles for the *Building Services Journal* (the predecessor to the *CIBSE Journal*) dealing with the technologies.

In 2004, the London Energy Partnership produced the 'Renewables toolkit' (LEP, 2004) which provided a series of 'References tables' providing capital costs for various renewable technologies, location and building type scenarios, such as photovoltaic panels for a 'town centre prestige office development'. Estimated marginal costs are provided on a treated floor area and installed kW basis, with estimates provided for annual carbon savings, enabling marginal costs per unit of CO_2 saved to be estimated. Unfortunately this tool has not been updated since publication and hence any pro-rata costs that are taken from the tables in Section 4.12 thereof would have to be updated using factors that reflect the difference in costs between the present day and 2004.

Davis Langdon has also been responsible for the *Spon's Architects' and Builders' Price Book* (Davis Langdon, 2012) which is updated annually and includes cost models for 'sustainable office refurbishment' and 'school refurbishment'.

Funding

In its *Low-Carbon Retrofit Toolkit*, the Better Buildings Partnership considers funding as a key issue in the success of low-carbon retrofit and states that it is necessary to do the following:

> Agree financing arrangements between owner and occupier typically via the service charge using an exceptional expenditure clause to repay costs through the Hard Services portion (e.g. building services management component of service charge) or through a sinking fund. Whichever option is considered, transparency is crucial to gain occupier buy-in. For high-cost projects third-party finance may be sought or performance contract options through an ESCO model.
>
> (BBP, 2010a)

The energy services company (ESCO) model

The ESCO model was developed in mainland Europe more than 100 years ago.[3] Modern-day versions take various forms and offer a wide variety of energy-related services including the design, financing, installation, commissioning, operation and maintenance of energy-generating plant and equipment, energy audit, monitoring and management. See also Chapter 2.5.

Most ESCOs offer some or all of the following:

- A guarantee of energy savings or carbon reduction or the provision of the same level of energy service at a lower cost through the implementation of agreed energy efficiency measures. A performance guarantee can take several forms: it can relate to actual energy/carbon savings; it can stipulate that the energy savings will be sufficient to repay monthly debt service costs for the measures installed; or that the same level of energy service will be provided for less money, based on predicted savings in running cost.

- The remuneration of ESCOs is directly tied to the energy savings achieved.
- ESCOs typically either finance, or assist in arranging financing for, the installation of an energy project with guaranteed savings through an Energy Performance Certificate (EPC).
- ESCOs retain an on-going operational role in measuring and verifying the savings over the financing term.

'Pay-as-you-save' vehicles

As we saw in Chapter 1.1, funding and financing vehicles are seen by some national governments as key mechanisms for driving energy efficiency and other sustainability improvements, using some combination of tax incentives, subsidy and efficient loans. A number of countries are introducing 'pay-as-you-save' schemes, such as the Green Deal in the UK.

In an Interim Working Group report from 2009, the Housing Forum stated:

> In the social housing sector, the landlord's capital investment saves the residents' utility costs but they have no formal facility to increase rental values to correspond with this utility cost reduction and thereby recover capital expenditure. (Within the private sector the opportunity exists to gain market advantage or increase rents from improved building performance.) A mechanism should be introduced to allow social housing providers to recover capital expenditure through the utility bill benefits of the occupier which could jointly address carbon reduction and fuel poverty issues.
>
> (Housing Forum, 2009)

The Green Deal and Energy Company Obligation (ECO) provide an opportunity for energy efficiency measures for multi-tenanted buildings to be financed by some combination of adjustments to electricity bills (Green Deal) and grant funding via the energy company (ECO).

Cost of sustainable facilities management

It is clear from the above that there is significant overlap between operating a building sustainably and sustainable refurbishment. The issues involved are the same but cover a broader range of scales: from decisions about lamp replacement and stationary procurement, for example, through to retrofit of building services and whether to demolish and rebuild, or renovate (see Chapter 2.1).

There will, of course, be cost implications associated with most of the decisions made in sustainable facility and property management. Most will have both capital and life cycle cost impacts that need to be factored into the management and procurement strategies.

Energy and water management tend to be dealt with separately, perhaps by a specialized individual or team, depending on the scale of an operation. These will be dealt with in more detail in Chapter 2.4, Chapter 4.1 and Chapter 4.2. Other procurement issues are dealt with in Chapter 4.8.

Procedures and terminology for life cycle costing are defined in BS ISO 15686-5 (ISO, 2008) supported by a 'Standardized method of life cycle costing for construction procurement', developed for use in the UK by the Building Cost Information Service (BCIS) and the British Standards Institute (BSI, 2008). These define whole-life costs (WLC) as those associated with payroll costs, business operational costs and soft facilities management, as well as life cycle costs (LCC) for the building, while LCC comprise the cost of constructing, operating and maintaining the building (hard facilities management), as well as 'end-of-life' costs.

The European Commission has also produced *A Common European Methodology for Life Cycle Costing (LCC)*,[4] which is based on ISO 15686-5. It 'provides a general framework for the common and consistent application of LCC across the EU without replacing country-specific decision models and approaches'. Extracts from a case history that includes a refurbished building provided in the Guidance to this methodology are given at the end of this chapter.

The EU document referred to above provides a useful summary of the benefits of life cycle costing as follows:

- transparency of future operational costs;
- ability to plan for future expenditure (e.g. through the establishment of sinking funds);
- improved awareness of total costs;
- ability to manipulate and optimize future costs at the design stages;
- achieving and demonstrating better value for money in projects;
- compliance with public sector procurement requirements;
- evaluation of competing options, either for entire assets or parts thereof;
- performance trade-offs against cost (e.g. environmental performance).

Life cycle costing techniques are a fundamental part of sustainable facility/property and energy management. A strategy based on capital expenditure (capex) alone would only ever deal with the 'low-hanging fruit' or items requiring little or no investment.

Considering the life cycle of a typical office building, more than 80 per cent of costs are associated with operation and maintenance. Decisions made during the design of the building clearly impact on running costs and a good design team should have used life cycle costing to support the design process.

There is, however, a significant problem with the reliability of the data on which life cycle cost predictions are made, for example, dealing with contingencies and breakdowns requires statistically based probability techniques, with inevitable margins for error.

The BCIS provides a regularly updated subscription on-line database of rates for building products and materials, along with running cost indices,[5] that can be used in LCC calculations.

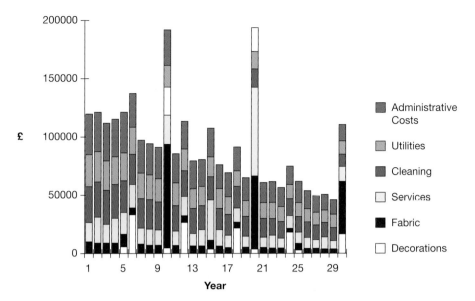

Figure 2.3.1 *Histogram showing typical life cycle costs over 30 years*

Source: BCIS Running Costs Online Service, Building Costs Information Service, www.bcis.co.uk.

Figure 2.3.1 shows a graphical representation for a typical LCC analysis showing costs-in-use expressed as present value (PV): in this case, for a primary school based on a 30-year life cycle. This indicates peaks in expenditure when it is anticipated that major work will have to be carried out on fabric and services.

Life cycle costing is an important tool for energy and water management in existing buildings. In the USA, the Federal Energy Management Program (FEMP)[6] provides support documentation and computer software for calculating LCC for Federal buildings. A Building Life-Cycle Cost Program is available on-line which includes capacity for computing LCC for different types of public sector contracts, including energy-saving performance contracts (ESPCs), utility energy services contracts (UESCs), Office of Management & Budget (OMB) analysis (for over-sight by the President's office), and military construction (MILCON) projects.

Case history: Project INSPIRE life cycle costing[7]

Project INSPIRE was a project for the Defence Science & Technology Laboratory, completed in 2009, and comprising refurbishment of existing buildings and construction of new technical buildings, along with a 15-year facilities management contract.

This case history considers two of the buildings – a refurbished office block and new build having a combined gross internal floor area (GIFA) of 20,390 m^2.

All costs were itemized and costed using the BCIS classification system. The cost data was derived from BCIS databases [the UK's Building Cost Information Service], Davis Langdon's [the cost consultants] internal databases, the contractor's databases and other available published data. The main exercise was carried out for two options of HVAC solutions. At the time of calculations, the capital costs that fed into the Model were in cost plan form only [contractor's MPTC – maximum plan target cost – figures], thus with only generic information on the works being undertaken, assumptions were made as to the quality of the materials and workmanship.

Values of financial parameters were identified as follows: discount rate of 3 per cent [real – as advised by *Treasury Green Book*] and no inflation. This allowed for the fact that the opportunity cost of money meant that monies spent in the future were worth less in present day terms (i.e. present value).

The model was indexed to reflect any inflation between the date of the costs and the start date of the model. The source prices included an allowance for indexation up to and through the Construction period. To allow us to present 2005 prices for the Maintenance and Asset Replacement cost streams, a deflator has been used for the annual costs, which was published by the BCIS and typically used for these types of calculations.

Replacement timings for the assets were assessed using a combination of Davis Langdon's own database and published information on the likely life expectancy of various assets. Refinement of this was made by adjustment of the percentage of the capital cost which was allowed at each replacement cycle. For instance, on average, windows may be expected to last around 20–35 years, dependent on quality of materials and workmanship. However, the likelihood was that many will last considerably longer, while some may fail early. Two mechanisms were used to account for this. First, a percentage of the capital cost was allowed at the earlier published life expectancy, and second, the expenditure was spread over more than one year, allowing some money to be drawn down early, should it be necessary. The desired redecoration cycle for the facilities was carefully considered. Another asset that required consideration was loose furniture, as this could add considerably to the cost of a facility over time. The 'norms' used on other office accommodation projects at Davis Langdon were used.

Different types of obsolescence were of importance in assessing asset lives. For instance, while office fit-out components might not become physically obsolete for 20 or more years, if carefully maintained, it was commonly understood that they might become functionally or aesthetically obsolete within a much shorter timescale. Thus a realistic assessment of life cycle costs had to take into account these aspects in addition to the physical durability.

Cost add-ons which were listed included certain costs associated with the replacement work, all necessary scaffolding, temporary access and temporary works, as well as removal of the components to be replaced and testing/ commissioning of plant and equipment. Exclusions which were listed broadly included the following: contingencies, VAT and other relevant financing charges and rates, certain management fees, business interruption costs/unavailability, backlog charges, hard and soft FM services, relocations and insurances. Approach to sensitivity comprised identification of maximum and minimum values published or used as common practice and calculating 'the middle' value of selected parameters, which were: selected cost data and selected financial parameters.

2.4
Carbon reduction strategy

Introduction

There are many reasons for refurbishing existing buildings and many ways of reducing carbon emissions without refurbishment. In this chapter we start from the assumption that a decision has been made to reduce carbon emissions through refurbishment/retrofit and that a strategy is required to optimize the process. In Chapter 4.1 we will be looking at the energy management of existing buildings through audit and ongoing monitoring and data analysis, the output from which may include a programme of retrofitting, as well as adjustments to housekeeping, operation and maintenance. Historically energy management has been combined with water management (see Chapter 4.2) and has focused on operational energy and water consumption.

In this chapter we will look at strategies for reducing total greenhouse gas (CO_2 equivalent) emissions, comprising operational and embodied carbon, nitrous oxide (N_2O) and fluorinated hydrocarbons, while in Chapters 3.1, 3.2 and 3.3 we will be looking in detail at options for renovation of building fabric, retrofitting of building services and retrofitting of renewable technologies respectively.

Framework for low-carbon refurbishment

The shape and complexity of the framework will vary depending on the type and scope of the refurbishment project. The Carbon Trust has produced guidance on low-carbon refurbishment of non-domestic buildings that, commenting on the reasons to refurbish, reckons that:

> despite the increasing legislative and market drivers for low-carbon buildings, the principal drivers for the decision to refurbish a building are still primarily to update the brand format, improve the quality of the building for the occupants or attract higher rental values and new tenants, rather than reducing carbon emissions.
>
> (Carbon Trust, 2008)

However, once the decision is made to refurbish, there are persuasive reasons to use the opportunity to reduce the carbon and greenhouse gas emissions, such as:

- lower running costs associated with lower energy use;
- limiting exposure to future energy price rises and supply uncertainty;

- potentially improved comfort conditions and associated occupant satisfaction and productivity;
- reducing environmental impacts and global warming potential;
- demonstrating corporate responsibility, with consequent kudos resulting in benefits in staff retention and recruitment and company image.

Opportunities for carbon savings will depend on the extent of refurbishment as illustrated in Figure 2.4.1. In most instances the options further up the list will include at least some elements of the options below them. The figure refers to non-residential buildings; however a similar hierarchy applies to multi-residential buildings and even individual dwellings.

The Better Buildings Partnership (BBP) has published a 'retrofit toolkit', designed primarily for those who manage estates of office buildings, although the same principles can be applied to other scenarios. BBP's *Low-Carbon Retrofit Toolkit* (BBP, 2010a) recommends that organizations do the following:

- Set clear corporate retrofit goals to include energy saving and carbon reductions, introduction of new technologies and accelerated replacement of inefficient services equipment. These goals should be clearly articulated and in line with broader organizational emissions reduction targets.
- Designate roles and define processes to ensure that a dedicated individual within the organization is given the responsibility and authority to assess retrofit opportunities across the property portfolio. Develop a clearly defined internal approvals process specific to low-carbon retrofit projects.
- Prioritize buildings most suitable for retrofit by analyzing portfolios against key selection criteria.

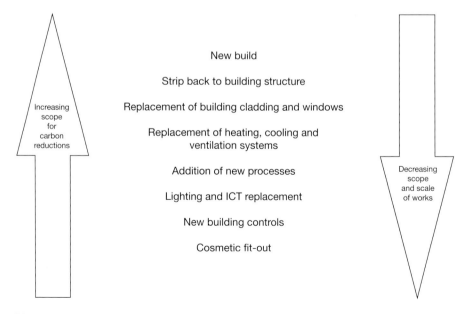

Figure 2.4.1 *Relationship between refurbishment scope and ability to influence carbon emissions*
Source: Carbon Trust, 2008.

- Engage occupiers to determine common goals, identify barriers and formulate solutions.
- Agree financing arrangements between owner and occupier.
- Select appropriate technology best suited to the constraints of the building and which minimizes the level of disruption to the occupiers.
- Deliver using a trusted supply chain with a performance guarantee.
- Evaluate performance in-use to inform future internal retrofit projects as well as the wider market.

The Carbon Trust has also developed a framework for low-carbon refurbishment that relates to RIBA Work Stages (RIBA, 2007) under the headings of Prepare, Design, Construct and Use (Carbon Trust, 2008). These headings are used below in an outline of the key stages of a carbon reduction strategy for a significant refurbishment project. This is intended as a framework that can be adapted for any kind of refurbishment or retrofit, although smaller projects may not have a design team or follow RIBA Work Stages.

It is important to note that types of refurbishment that are towards the top of the hierarchy shown in Figure 2.4.1 can be treated in a similar manner to new build projects, for which the reader should refer to Chapter 2.6 of *Integrated Sustainable Design of Buildings* (Appleby, 2011a).

Preparation

The preparation for refurbishment of an existing building differs significantly from a new build in that there is an opportunity to learn from its performance and the views of the occupants. Hence the following tasks will differentiate the process from new build:

- Using any existing drawings, specifications and technical records, undertake a full survey of fabric, services and processes that impact on carbon/ greenhouse gas (GHG) emissions and refurbishment strategy.
- Identify sources and establish the magnitude of carbon and GHG emissions for the existing building.
- Decide on targets for carbon and other GHG emissions for the refurbished building, including lifetime and running costs. The implications of setting ambitious targets, such as 'zero carbon' or designing to Passivhaus retrofit standards such as EnerPHit must be established at this stage (see Chapter 3.1).
- Undertake a questionnaire survey of existing occupants, tailored to establish their views on the refurbished building, including those issues that will impact on carbon emissions and are designed to be followed up by a post-occupancy evaluation (see Chapter 2.2).

Establishing existing operational carbon emissions will require metered energy data, either from energy company bills, smart metering or building energy management systems (BEMSs). The level of detail will depend on the sophistication of metering available. If there is an energy management regime already in place, then there may be a wealth of information that can be used to provide baseline information by which the carbon reduction from specific measures can be determined post refurbishment.

Ideally the refurbishment should include retrofit or upgrade of the BEMS and metering to enable an accurate assessment of the improved carbon performance of the building (see Chapter 3.2).

For a sustainable and low-carbon refurbishment, there must be a commitment to the process from the building owner and occupiers, or the developer, and the agreed targets and this must be enshrined in a compact involving all parties. The process will be more complex for a building that is to retain some or all of the existing occupiers; even more so if there are multiple tenancies. Accurate prediction of the cost benefits of the carbon reduction strategy to the occupiers is important since reductions in energy bills can represent at least partial compensation for the disruption associated with refurbishment.

Pre-refurbishment questionnaire surveys may be more difficult to arrange where there are multiple tenancies, for buildings that are primarily for short-term public use, such as stadia or railway stations, or for residential accommodation. However, some level of engagement with all occupants exposed to internal conditions for long periods will be extremely valuable.

Depending on the scale of the refurbishment and the availability of energy/carbon specialists in the owner organization, it may be appropriate for at least some of the design team to be appointed to carry out the studies described above. Indeed, it may be appropriate to employ an energy/sustainability specialist to establish the baseline carbon/GHG footprint for the existing building, survey the building and services, carry out questionnaire surveys, establish targets, prepare low-carbon vision statements, carry out computer simulation, and support the owner on the appointment of suitably experienced designers.

Design

The scale of the design process and the constituency of the design team will depend on the type and scale of refurbishment proposed. For example, a fit-out will be dominated by the interior designer, a building services retrofit will be dominated by the building services engineer, while a major refurbishment with demolition back to the structure will require a more conventional architect-led design team, with strong input from the structural engineer.

A renewables retrofit project, on the other hand, may be led by a specialist contractor. Table 2.4.1 indicates the key tasks as identified by the Carbon Trust in their *Power Play* booklet on applying renewable energy technologies to existing buildings (Carbon Trust, 2011). Refer also to Chapter 3.3.

This framework will normally have to be integrated with other carbon-saving measures, however. Retrofitting of renewable technologies to a badly insulated building is bad practice, which is why funding for renewable energy retrofit in the UK is conditional on the buildings meeting specified energy performance or insulation requirements (see Chapter 2.3). Similarly the 'Mayor's energy hierarchy', set out in Policy 5.2 of the London Plan, should be applied equally to refurbishment projects anywhere in the world as to new build projects in London. The recommendations are:

Table 2.4.1 *Key stages and tasks in retrofitting renewable technologies*

Assessing feasibility	Buying a system	Installing a system	Operating
Set clear objectives for what you want the project to achieve.	Decide how you wish to manage the contract	Recognize the importance of good commissioning	Liaise closely with the installer during the first 12 months of operation
Use existing information to identify which technologies are best for you, your staff and your site	Prepare your brief and specification, including any possible maintenance and monitoring requirements	Manage the installation contract	Carry out regular checks and meter readings to ensure optimum system performance
Consider whether you want independent expert advice	Select and appoint your preferred installer	Make sure you and your staff are provided with good documentation and training at handover	
Fully understand the cost and benefits of a chosen solution, and the ongoing operation and maintenance costs			

Source: Carbon Trust, 2011.

1　Be lean: use less energy.
2　Be clean: supply energy efficiently.
3　Be green: use renewable energy.

The design process should incorporate investigations of a range of options based on life cycle costing and life cycle assessment. These techniques are required in order to produce a result that optimizes cost over the lifetime of the building and its constituent parts against the carbon/GHG emissions over the same periods. The cost modelling techniques referred to in Chapter 2.2 should be applied. A useful technique is to compare all carbon-saving measures in terms of marginal cost per kg or tonne of carbon dioxide saved, taking into account embodied carbon where data is available.

The tender documents and contract specification should incorporate the carbon targets established for the refurbishment as well as the required BREEAM or similar ratings. The computer simulation or Simplified Building Energy Model (SBEM), or similar, that supports these targets should form part of the contract documentation along with the design stage BREEAM assessment.

Construction

Identification and appointment of suitable contractors are essential for the success of a refurbishment project. As the Carbon Trust confirms, it is important to do the following:

Procure contractors with experience and interest in low-carbon refurbishment, as this will make the journey towards a low-carbon building much easier. The skills, experience and aptitude of contractors in low-energy construction will

> have a major influence on project success and on the low-carbon performance
> of the refurbished building.
>
> (Carbon Trust, 2008)

Of course, not every refurbishment project requires the same skill set. For example, a major office refurbishment in the City of London that requires demolition of all but the façade of an existing building, followed by construction of what is virtually a new building behind, requires very different, and specialized, expertise to that required for converting a cellular office building to open plan.

Many refurbishments incorporate a combination of demolition, retrofitting of services, renovation of fabric and refit of interior accommodation. The success of carbon-saving measures may depend to a large extent on integrating new structural and fabric elements, equipment, plant and controls with those that are retained from the existing building.

Working on an existing building poses different quality control and health and safety issues to new build. The work required to improve carbon performance, such as replacing windows and reducing air leakage can be particularly testing. Hence project management and supervision are even more critical than for new build. Also, since contingencies need to be carefully managed to cater for unforeseen problems arising from working in an existing building, the carbon strategy must not be diluted by pressures on budget.

Use

Once the refurbishment is completed, post-occupancy monitoring and evaluation will allow comparison with the original building. This will also provide important engagement with the occupants and go some way to demonstrating the benefits arising from the refurbishment process. This can also provide feedback for the ongoing commissioning and snagging process, for example, through modifications to control regimes via the BEMS or adaptation of solar protection and daylighting strategies.

As with all new building environments, it is important that the occupants understand the operation of their refurbished workplace or home. A responsive commissioning process and adaptive control system will both help occupants understand how the building and services impact on their environment and provide assurance that the management team will respond promptly to their concerns.

Computer simulation

Of course, all building projects that have to meet Building Regulations target CO_2 emissions require some form of carbon modelling, either through simplified models, such as SBEM for non-residential buildings, SAP for dwellings, or the Passivhaus Planning Package (PHPP, see Chapter 3.1); or through computer simulation (see case history on p. 77). The process is very similar to that required for new buildings and the reader is advised to refer to Chapter 3.7 of *Integrated Sustainable Design of Buildings* (Appleby, 2011a) for a detailed analysis of the options, as well as a case history.

However, simulating an existing building may present some difficulties, since building performance may be poorly documented and the key characteristics and efficiency of the plant and thermal parameters for the building required for input to simulation models may be difficult to ascertain. Sub-metering may be limited or non-existent and a breakdown of significant energy users may not be available, either for major plant or tenancies. Attempting to accurately model such a building can be an expensive and often futile exercise. However, the act of modelling can identify many areas within the building's operation where improvements can be made. It may be easier to model the fully refurbished building, particularly where replacement of a significant proportion of fabric and services is planned.

Commercially available computer simulation and modelling systems do not generally incorporate embodied carbon or greenhouse gases other than those associated with operational energy. These will have to be calculated separately as part of a carbon footprint estimation (see Chapter 1.3).

Computer simulation has also been used to predict specific mass and/or heat transfers in renovated fabrics and spaces. For example, Ecological Building Systems Ltd have investigated the combined heat and moisture transport resulting from various methods of roof renovation[1] (see Chapter 3.1).

Case history: zero-carbon dwelling simulation, Scotland[2]

With a view to determining the characteristics of a UK (Scottish) dwelling that could operate as zero carbon (e.g. Code for Sustainable Homes, level 6), a modelling study was carried out by the University of Strathclyde (Turner and Townsend, 2008) using the current UK regulatory calculation methods: SAP2005 (BRE, 2005) and SBEM (DCLG, 2008b). The study investigated a range of options for achieving carbon reductions beyond the 2007 minimum regulatory requirements. One of the buildings studied was a typical detached dwelling with a floor area of 136 m^2. The building was assumed to be occupied by a family of four, with both parents going out to work and children at school age; occupancy was therefore intermittent; the building performance was assessed for a Scottish west coast climate.

The modelling indicated that for the detached house to achieve the 140 per cent reduction target as set out in the Code for Sustainable Homes (CSH) the following measures would be required:

- Passive House building envelope;
- high-efficiency mechanical ventilation heat recovery (MVHR);
- 4 m^2 solar thermal panels;
- 2 kW biomass heating;
- high A+ rating efficiency appliances;
- high-efficiency lighting; and
- 46 m^2 PV electrical generation (approx 6 kWp).

It should be noted that such a large area of PV would require a mono-pitch roof geometry, rather than the duo-pitch geometry seen on current buildings. A mono-pitch roof maximizes the effective solar collection area of a dwelling.

Performance analysis using detailed simulation

To obtain more detail on the energy performance of the building described above, a detailed modelling study was undertaken using the ESP-r dynamic energy-modelling software (ESRU, 2002).

The model was a thermodynamic (rather than architectural) representation of the detached dwelling, with the interior spaces divided into day and night zones; an approach that has been applied successfully in other housing simulation studies (e.g. Beyer and Kelly, 2008). The building model was furnished with data on the building geometry, construction materials and occupancy, along with explicit representations of the heating, ventilation and renewable energy systems. The occupancy characteristics of the dwelling were derived from work by Jardine (2008).

Two simulations were undertaken, featuring the zero-carbon dwelling model as-is and a base-case model, which was modified so that its insulation characteristics were the same as that of a UK dwelling built after 1997 (Utley and Shorrock, 2008). In the base case the heating system was modified to represent a gas boiler feeding a hot water tank and radiators. Key characteristics from each model are shown in Table 2.4.2.

The model was simulated with a Scottish West coast climate data set, with energy transfer, fluid flows and temperatures calculated at 10-minute intervals over a year.

The aggregate energy performance data from each model is shown in Table 2.4.3. Note that the electrical demand data was generated using a validated power demand profile tool (Borg and Kelly 2010), which generates high-resolution electrical demand data based on diary and time-use-survey information and a user-defined population of appliances. The ratings and energy consumptions of the appliances were reduced between the base and zero-carbon case using scaling factors derived from the UK Market Transformation Programme (DEFRA, 2010). Time-series hot water demand flow rates for the base-case dwelling were generated using profiles generated from Knight and Kreutzer (2008), who define hot water demands for average UK dwellings. The zero-carbon dwelling profiles were modified using anticipated hot water demands defined in the UK Code for Sustainable Homes (DCLG, 2008a)

Table 2.4.2 *Characteristics of the dwelling models in the case history*

	Base-case dwelling	Zero-carbon dwelling
External walls (W/m^{2}K)	0.45	0.11
Floor (W/m^{2}K)	0.6	0.10
Ceiling (W/m^{2}K)	0.25	0.13
Glazing (W/m^{2}K)	2.10	0.70
Average uncontrolled infiltration (ach^{-1})	0.5	0.03
Heating	Gas boiler + radiators	Biomass boiler + heating coil in MVHR

Table 2.4.3 *Detached dwelling base case and zero-carbon annual performance*

	Base-case dwelling	Zero-carbon dwelling
Heating demand (kWh)	3083	372
Hot water heating demand (kWh)	2342	1850
Electrical demand (kWh)	5776	3240
Total demand (kWh)	11201	5462
PV output (kWh)		5023
Solar thermal output (kWh)		1709
Biomass boiler output (kWh)		1172
Total production (kWh)		7904

The analysis clearly indicates that the energy system as sized produces significantly more thermal and electrical energy than is consumed. In comparison to the base case, the requirement for space heating in the zero-carbon dwelling is reduced by 88 per cent, while demands for hot water and electricity are reduced by 21 per cent and 44 per cent, respectively. Electricity becomes the major energy demand, accounting for 59 per cent of the total.

The model indicates that there is a huge seasonal variation in the output of the PV system. It produces 2680 kWh between May and August, offsetting 290 per cent of the electrical demand over the same period. Between November and February the PV system produces only 540 kWh, offsetting only 40 per cent of the electrical demand in the zero-carbon dwelling.

The variability in solar hot water production is as pronounced, with 40 kWh produced by the solar collectors in January, offsetting around 18 per cent of the total thermal demand compared to 219 kWh in June, which exceeds the total thermal demand in the zero-carbon dwelling. Note that the heat output from the solar thermal collectors and the biomass boiler exceed the thermal demand; the excess is attributable to energy losses in the system such as boiler conversion losses, storage tank standing losses and control inefficiencies.

2.5
Community energy and infrastructure

Introduction

Buildings cannot be considered in isolation from the infrastructure that provides them with electricity, gas and water, takes away their sewage and rainwater, and enables access by occupants and service providers. This is true for new and existing buildings alike, although the former may require utilities to be reinforced or access to be improved to cater for the additional burden placed upon them. Only refurbishment involving significant extensions or extreme changes of use, such as warehousing to office work, could have major impacts on infrastructure.

As well as reducing the carbon emissions associated with existing buildings and building 'zero-carbon' new buildings, reaching the 2050 carbon reduction targets across Europe requires decarbonization of electricity grids, while also tackling other sources such as transport and industry.[1] In this chapter we will be examining how national and local infrastructures interact with refurbishment and facilities management strategies, including on-site and community energy generation, water conservation, sustainable drainage and measures to reduce impacts on transport infrastructure.

Energy infrastructure

The carbon intensity of electricity, reported in either g or kg of CO_2/kWh, varies considerably, both between countries and with time. In the UK, where a mixture of coal, oil, gas, nuclear and renewable sources is used to generate electricity, the carbon intensity varied between 214 gCO_2/kWh and 596 gCO_2/kWh in 2011.[2] On average, the minimum values occurred at 0300 and the maximum values between 1000 and 1200. Also maximum values tend to occur in winter: November was the worst month in 2011, while the lowest values occurred in May. As can be seen from Figure 2.5.1, maximum carbon intensities tend to coincide with maximum demand. This is primarily due to the fact that coal- and oil-fired power stations normally have their output increased when generating capacity from lower-carbon sources, such as gas, nuclear and renewables, has been exhausted. Coal and oil firing is less cost effective for energy companies in the UK because of the higher carbon price for coal and oil.

Worldwide, the amount of carbon associated with electricity generation varies even more widely between countries, and Table 2.5.1 gives a selection of

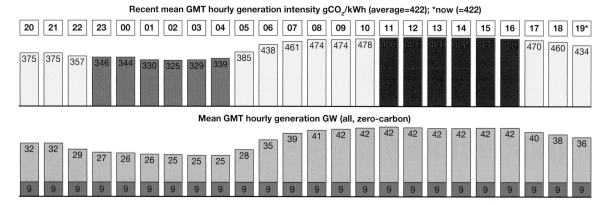

Figure 2.5.1 *Hourly carbon intensity and generation for 28–29 June 2009*

Note: red, yellow and green columns represent periods when carbon content is high, average and low respectively.
Source: Damon Hart-Davis.

Table 2.5.1 *Carbon intensities for electricity generation for selected countries in 2007*

Country	Carbon intensity (gCO$_2$/kWh)
Poland	1002
Australia	891
China	868
India	805
Germany	612
United States	611
United Kingdom	557
Russia	484
Saudi Arabia	385
Japan	365
Canada	213
France	88
Sweden	17
Norway	5

Source: http://lightbucket.wordpress.com/2008/10/22/carbon-emissions-from-electricity-generation-by-country.

the most recent data (2007) from the Carbon Monitoring for Action (CARMA) database as analyzed for the 'lightbucket' website.[3]

The countries that appear at the top of Table 2.5.1 rely heavily on coal- and oil-fired power stations, while at the bottom end generation capacity is dominated by some combination of nuclear power, wind and hydro-electricity. The figures in Table 2.5.1 should not be relied upon for carbon emission calculations for buildings since the generation mix is likely to have altered since 2007; for example, both Germany and Japan have reduced their reliance on nuclear power since the Fukushima disaster of 2011. In the UK, a figure of 0.591 kgCO$_2$/kWh is used in simplified energy models for Building Regulations applications.

Centrally generated electricity tends to be an inefficient method of converting fuel into power. For example, in the UK, on average, only 38.5 per cent of energy in fuel is converted to electricity, while losses in distribution result in only 34 per cent being delivered to the consumer (King and Shaw, 2010).

Carbon intensities can be significantly reduced locally where energy is generated by low- or zero-carbon commercial, community or municipal energy schemes. These could comprise a mix of local wind farms, solar energy farms, combined heat and power plants or energy from waste plants. Across Europe, these are frequently owned and operated by energy service companies (ESCOs), or multi-utility service companies (MUSCOs) (see Chapter 2.3 for more information).

An EU Joint Research Centre (JRC) report provides a useful description of ESCOs, while introducing the concept of energy performance contracting as follows:

Energy service companies (ESCOs) and energy performance contracting (EPC) are common tools to enhance the sustainable use of energy through promoting energy efficiency and renewable energy sources. ESCOs and EPC help to overcome financial constraints to investments and pay off initial costs through the energy cost savings coming from the reduced energy demand. ESCOs provide an opportunity to curb increasing energy demand and control CO_2 emissions while exploiting market benefits for customers by decreasing the energy costs of their clients and making profit for themselves. While ESCOs have been operational on a large scale since the late 1980s/early 1990s, the energy service market in the European Union (and in Europe) is far from utilizing its full potential, even in countries with a particularly developed ESCO sector.

(Bertoldi *et al.*, 2007)

Community partnerships and cooperatives have owned and operated ESCOs across Europe for many years. For example, in Denmark, most wind farms are owned by cooperatives and in Germany the concept of 'citizens' wind farms' has been widely adopted. In the USA, community-owned schemes are less common, although the National Wind organization had 13 projects in development in 2011, having a total capacity of 4 GW and a stated objective of revitalizing local communities.

In the UK, the government is encouraging partnership between local communities and ESCOs[4] in an attempt to provide a catalyst for engagement with local energy bill-payers and voters and reduce resistance to energy projects such as wind farms and energy from waste plants.

The UK action group, Community Pathways, provides information for those wishing to establish community ESCOs. It considers that a community-based or cooperative-run ESCO

can help a community to lower energy bills, reduce fuel poverty and cut CO_2 emissions through spreading uptake (and also the risk) of renewable energy projects between different partners, such as community groups, public authorities and commercial backers. They can operate at a lower rate of return than would be deemed acceptable by a commercial enterprise. An ESCO can offer a range of services tackling climate change from both the energy efficiency and generation angles. By providing an ESCO service the community group takes any risk of investing in these installations from the customer onto themselves until the scheme has proven itself. Provided the ESCO is well organized and sufficiently well trained to undertake these services, the risk to the ESCO is low. An ESCO is a great mechanism to encourage uptake of energy performance measures or use of renewable energy from customers that would otherwise be reluctant to invest up-front in such activities. An additional benefit is that the revenue raised by the ESCO is often then channelled back into other community and energy projects.[5]

In the UK, there are a number of examples of community-owned or supported ESCOs, many of which have been used as vehicles for the installation of renewable technologies such as wind turbines, small-scale hydro-electricity and biomass. Many of these are in rural communities, such as the Westmill windfarm in Oxfordshire, the Settle hydropower scheme in North Yorkshire, and the Kielder biomass combined heat and power (CHP) scheme. See the 'Planning for Climate Change' website for more details.[6] A report published online by

Community Energy Plus also provides useful case histories for community-owned renewable energy schemes in the UK (Hoggett, 2010). The UK Department for Communities & Local Government (CLG) sponsors PlanLoCaL, which 'is a programme of work from the Centre for Sustainable Energy (CSE) which is designed to give communities embarking on a community energy project the confidence, knowledge and ambition to achieve a low-carbon future for their area'.[7] From this website can be downloaded resources and case histories that can be used to assist in the development of a community energy strategy.

Although frequently associated with new construction projects, there are numerous examples of ESCO district energy schemes being connected to a mix of new and existing properties (see case history on p. 88). Where low- or zero-carbon electricity is produced, the connection to existing properties simply requires a modification to metering. For district heating (and cooling) there will need to be modifications to the thermal plant and a new hydraulic interface unit (HIU) provided for each building or tenant, including suitable heat metering devices. Figure 2.5.2 shows a typical HIU for a residential application. The temperatures available from the district mains will need to be compatible with the heating or cooling systems in each building.

Most of the larger district energy schemes combine a mixture of different energy sources serving a wide variety of applications. This maximizes flexibility and enables the scheme to connect to new developments as they are built. An

Figure 2.5.2 *Typical hydraulic interface unit*

Source: © SAV Systems – SAV Flat Station – 5 Series DS.

exemplar for this approach is the district energy scheme in Woking, established in 1999 as a partnership between the Borough Council and a commercial operation called Thameswey. This now comprises a number of gas-fired combined cooling, heat and power (CCHP/trigeneration) plants, a large fuel cell CHP plant and photovoltaic installations, supplying a number of civic and private consumers via a private wire electricity network and district heating and cooling mains.

A number of utility companies offer multi-utility services, covering electricity, gas and water; and the concept of a multi-utility service company (MUSCO) has been developed. Lloyd's Registry maintains a list of companies that hold Multi-Utility Recognition Status (MURS), that is, they are accredited under the UK's National Electricity Registration Scheme (NERS), the Gas Industry Registration Scheme (GIRS) and the Water Industry Registration Scheme (WIRS).[8] MUSCO schemes are also referred to as 'integrated district utility services', one of the best known examples of which serves Hammarby Sjostadt on the edge of Stockholm in Sweden, where the concept has been applied to an entire community, albeit one which has grown from a virtually uninhabited contaminated industrial landscape since the early 1990s. The designers of this remarkable project have been able to incorporate numerous renewable energy sources, including wind power, photovoltaics, hydro-electricity, gas and fertilizer from sewage, and CHP from biomass and waste, as well as evacuated waste conveying systems, waste recycling plant and water treatment for drinking water. See Figure 2.5.3 for a schematic representation of

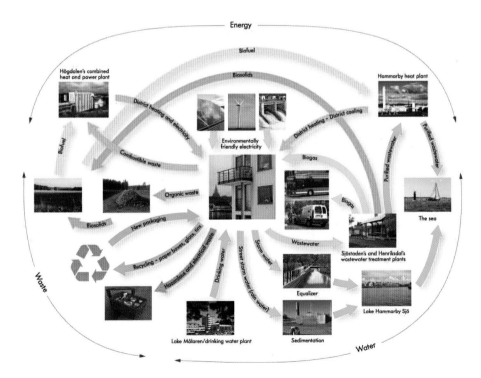

Figure 2.5.3 *The Hammarby Model*
Source: Lena Wettren, Bumlings AB.

the 'Hammarby Model'. See Chapter 3.6 for more information on retrofitting evacuated waste conveying systems.

Water and drainage

The aim of a sustainable water and drainage strategy is to reduce the burden that consumers place on water and drainage infrastructure and resources. For a detailed analysis of water conservation issues and the technical solutions to reducing water consumption for new build projects, many of which can be retrofitted to existing buildings, refer to Chapter 3.9 of *Integrated Sustainable Design of Buildings* (Appleby, 2011a). Refer also to Chapter 3.5 and Chapter 4.3 of this book.

As with electricity generation and supply, there is much lost between the water sources and the supply to the consumer. Take, for example, London, below which there are hundreds of miles of Victorian water mains that, in Thames Water's returns to OFWAT for 2008/09, were leaking at the rate of 700 millions of litres *per day* (Ml/day), corresponding to approximately 280 litres per property.[9] This is despite an aggressive pipework replacement programme by Thames Water that has resulted in a reduction in leakage of 26 per cent since 2003/04. Add the returns from other water companies and the total leakage from Greater London water mains for 2008/09 comes to 892 Ml/day. This compares to a total consumption for the same period and catchment area of 1,709 Ml/day, or a leakage rate of more than 34 per cent. Other cities, such as Paris, with an equally ancient infrastructure, have managed to control leakage rates to around 10 per cent.

Capacity is also an issue for drainage infrastructure. For example, when rainfall in London exceeds a certain rate, the combined sewer system overflows into the River Thames and its tributaries, with up to 39 million tonnes of sewage being discharged into the rivers every year via 57 sewer overflows. It has been estimated that if nothing is done, this rate will nearly double by 2022. At the time of writing, a major project is under way to construct a 25km-long, 7.2 m in diameter tunnel deep beneath the Thames to both attenuate the overflowing sewage and convey it for treatment to an enlarged Beckton sewage treatment works.

Apart from the fact that London's sewers are mostly old, under-sized and carry both sewage and surface water, much of the rain that falls on London runs off hard surfaces and into the underground drains. One of the options considered to reduce the volume of rain water running into these drains was to increase the area of porous surface across London through a combination of 'sustainable urban drainage systems' (SUDSs), attenuation and planted or 'green' roofs (see Chapter 3.14 of *Integrated Sustainable Design of Buildings*, which deals with landscaping, ecology and flood risk (Appleby, 2011a)). Along with installing a new network of drains that separates surface water and sewage, this option has not been pursued because of the difficulty of retrofitting such measures to an overburdened city such as London, being already riddled with underground infrastructure and overground congestion.

Transport

Access to a building and its relationship to transport nodes and community facilities are largely beyond the control of the building owner and occupiers. For example, an office building that caters for cyclists through the provision of cycle sheds, showers and changing facilities loses its credibility if the only access is from a busy dual carriageway that has no provision for cyclists. There may be opportunities to improve access through alterations to the way in which it is configured, particularly if local cycle routes are being reviewed. In the UK, Sustrans provides information on local cycle routes and initiatives[10] and most Local Authorities are involved in improving provision for cyclists and pedestrians in their Local Transport Plans.

Closely affiliated to Sustrans, the CTC is an influential UK cyclists organization that has developed guidance to Local Authorities for use in the development of their Local Transport Plans (LTPs) (CTC, 2010). This includes recommendations that LTPs should do the following:

- Give full recognition to cycling's environmental, health and other benefits.
- Link cycling plans with strategies on road safety, planning and health policies.
- Aim for more, as well as safer, cycling – road safety policies should recognize that cyclists gain from safety in numbers.
- Tackle the fears that deter people from cycling, such as speeding, irresponsible driving, hostile road conditions, danger and intimidation from lorries and complex junctions.
- Ensure developments are, or can be made, easily accessible by cycle, with cycle-friendly infrastructure provided as appropriate.
- Promote cycle-friendly street and highway design in accordance with the 'hierarchy of provision' (see below), including measures to tackle motor traffic volume and speed with, where possible, 20 mph speed limits for most urban streets.
- Include good cycle parking and signage.
- Ensure that highway and path maintenance practices and procedures reflect cyclists' needs.

The 'hierarchy of provision' considers first traffic reduction, followed by speed reduction, junction treatment, designated lanes, separate cycle tracks and shared footways.[11]

When employees or householders do not feel safe when walking to or from local transport nodes and amenities, they will tend to use their cars for even the shortest of journeys. This can also force parents to deliver children to nearby schools by car or result in those without cars becoming virtual prisoners in their own homes. 'Living Streets' is a lobby group for pedestrians that orchestrates campaigns to promote safe walking to school and reduce pavement parking.[12] Simply put, Living Streets' philosophy is that 'Putting walking at the heart of any community can enhance the local economy, increase community cohesion, benefit the health of residents and have a positive environmental impact.'

Case history: Southampton District Energy Scheme

The Southampton District Energy Scheme (SDES) is operated by COFELY District Energy working in partnership with Southampton City Council (SCC), under the name of Southampton Geothermal Heating Company Ltd (SGHC).

Since its launch in 1986 the Southampton District Energy Scheme has grown into a multi-source heating and cooling system, reportedly saving over 10,000 tonnes of carbon dioxide emissions per annum.

Initially, the scheme served a core of consumers from a geothermal well which is now supplemented by large-scale combined heat and power plant with absorption cooling (tri-generation), using conventional gas-fired boilers for 'top up' and standby. The heat from the central plant is distributed through a 14 km district heating network.

At first, the scheme served SCC buildings at a discounted rate but the first commercial customer was Asda in 1987 and more recent commercial participants include IKEA and Carnival (UK) Ltd. The scheme now serves TV studios, a hospital, a university, a shopping centre, a civic centre and several hotels, as well as public and private sector residential developments.

Chilled water supplies were added in 1994 and in 2009 a cable was laid to the Port of Southampton, where electricity from the main CHP engine is now supplied under a 10-year Power Purchase Agreement. This enables the Port to consume all of the electricity generated by the 5.7 MWe and 1.0 MWe CHP engines at the 'Harbour Parade Heat Station' (see Figure 2.5.4). Before this, the electricity was sold back to the grid.

The scheme's main energy centre houses the core energy generation plant that provides heating, power and cooling. The energy centre was built in 1986 to house the geothermal well heat exchanger, district heating pumps and small-scale CHP plant. Since then, the buildings have been expanded to include the 5.7 MW CHP engine in 1998 as well as the district cooling plant, and in 2008 a further 1 MW of CHP was installed.

The district heating was designed to operate at low temperatures and pressures to reduce heat losses and maximize the life of the network. The network is operated using a flow temperature of approximately 80°C and a return of 50°C, with distribution pressures of approximately 5 bar. This enables direct connections into most buildings, removing the need for heat exchangers, further reducing capital costs and energy losses.

The scheme delivers more than 40,000 MWh of heat per annum, 7,000 MWh of chilled water and 24,000 MWh of electricity from the CHP plant. It serves buildings within a 2 km radius of the energy centre with a 1 K temperature loss per km of pipe.

Figure 2.5.4 *Southampton District Energy Scheme: main energy centre*
Source: COFELY.

2.6
Sustainable facilities management strategy

Introduction

In this chapter, the term 'facilities management' (FM) covers management of all kinds of property: commercial, public sector or residential, whether directly managed or through a third party or agent. The aim is to provide a strategic framework for the issues covered in Part 4, 'Sustainable Facilities Management', discussing the various tools available, the principles involved and the structures required to cover the wide range of resources that have to be managed sustainably, such as energy, greenhouse gases, water, materials and waste. An integrated strategy will be outlined that also takes account of management of air quality, indoor environment, hygiene and health and safety of occupants, as well as sustainable procurement and managing biodiversity.

The framework will take account of monitoring and reporting requirements, including corporate social responsibility (CSR) and environmental management systems (EMSs) through collaboration between building owners, occupiers and building managers.

Sustainable facilities management tools

In Chapter 1.3, a number of tools were reviewed that enable assessment and benchmarking of buildings in use. Most of the tools that are designed for assessing existing buildings can also be used as a management tool or framework for sustainable facility management. Assessment tools such as BREEAM In-Use and LEED Existing Buildings are designed for periodic use so that the effectiveness of measures that are drawn out by the assessment process can be tested on a regular basis.

Computer-aided facilities management (CAFM) or total integrated facilities management (TIFM) software packages are available for facilities management and building maintenance departments and organizations to maintain control over repair costs, preventative maintenance of physical assets and space planning (see Chapter 4.7).

The shape of the framework used for sustainable facilities management will be moulded to some extent by the size and nature of the operation. These may vary from an individual company occupying its own office building through an industrial complex, a university campus, a property management company responsible for a mix of commercial and multi-residential buildings, to a Local

Authority managing a mix of its own premises, civic buildings, leisure complexes and social housing.

Private companies may decide to produce annual CSR statements. These are currently voluntary, although there are pressures on larger companies from a number of quarters to produce them. Both the United Nations and the European Commission have produced policy documents setting out the desirability of incorporating CSR into company management processes.

In 2000, the UN published a 'Global Compact'[1] that set out ten high-level principles for companies to follow by defining their moral position in their dealings with others and the environment (see Box 2.6.1). These have been

---

Box 2.6.1 The ten principles of the United Nations Global Compact

The Global Compact asks companies to embrace, support and enact, within their sphere of influence, a set of core values in the areas of human rights, labour standards, the environment and anti-corruption.

Human rights

- Principle 1: Businesses should support and respect the protection of internationally proclaimed human rights.
- Principle 2: Businesses should make sure that they are not complicit in human rights abuses.

Labour

- Principle 3: Businesses should uphold the freedom of association and the effective recognition of the right to collective bargaining.
- Principle 4: The elimination of all forms of forced and compulsory labour.
- Principle 5: The effective abolition of child labour.
- Principle 6: The elimination of discrimination in respect of employment and occupation.

Environment

- Principle 7: Businesses should support a precautionary approach to environmental challenges.
- Principle 8: Businesses should undertake initiatives to promote greater environmental responsibility.
- Principle 9: Businesses should encourage the development and diffusion of environmentally friendly technologies.

Anti-corruption

- Principle 10: Businesses should work against corruption in all its forms, including extortion and bribery.

further refined into a 'Blueprint for corporate sustainability leadership' set out in terms of a Corporate Action Plan in Annex B of the 2010 Review.

The Global Reporting Initiative (GRI) Sustainable Reporting Guidelines summarized in Chapter 1.3 provide a scheme by which the Global Compact can be implemented and measured.

In 2011, the EC produced a 'renewed strategy' that included a definition for CSR as 'the responsibility of enterprises for their impacts on society' (EC, 2011c). It elaborates on this by emphasizing that:

> Respect for applicable legislation, and for collective agreements between social partners, is a prerequisite for meeting that responsibility. To fully meet their corporate social responsibility, enterprises should have in place a process to integrate social, environmental, ethical, human rights and consumer concerns into their business operations and core strategy in close collaboration with their stakeholders, with the aim of:
> - maximizing the creation of shared value for their owners/shareholders and for their other stakeholders and society at large;
> - identifying, preventing and mitigating their possible adverse impacts.

Both Denmark and France have introduced legislation that requires large companies to produce CSR reports. Denmark brought in a law in 2009 that requires each of the 1100 largest companies in Denmark to include a CSR statement in their annual financial report. In France, companies having more than 500 employees and a turnover greater than 43 million euros are encouraged to produce CSR reports under Article 116 of the *Nouvelle Réglementation Economique,* although there are no penalties for failing to comply.

CSR should not be considered as an annual box-ticking exercise and, alongside environmental management systems, CSR should be embedded into the management systems for an organization. Monitoring regimes should provide continuous feedback on performance against established benchmarks, demonstrating progress with time and used as a way of making adjustments where appropriate.

Environmental management

Organizations that are responsible for processes that have considerable environmental impact will mostly introduce management, monitoring and reporting procedures that comply with ISO 14001 or EMAS standards (see Chapter 1.3).

For small and medium-sized enterprises (SMEs), the British Environment Agency has produce a series of toolkits[2] covering general business operations as well as the following sectors:

- food and drink;
- waste businesses;
- end-of-life vehicle treatment facilities;
- metals recycling;

- businesses with sewage discharges to surface or ground water;
- businesses discharging waste agricultural chemicals to land.

These provide a series of checklists and pro-formas for recording and reporting discharges and consumption data. The toolkit for general businesses is designed primarily for use by SMEs that manage industrial processes, with an emphasis on managing and recording emissions and pollution incidents. This covers emissions to air and water, waste management and disposal, energy consumption, land contamination, nuisance from noise and odours and resource consumption, including water and chemical use. The pro-formas allow recording of the following:

- lists of procedures;
- accident and pollution incident management plans;
- maintenance checklists and records;
- training checklists and records;
- complaints records;
- accident and incident records.

Of course, many or all of these should be in the building log book, and operating and maintenance instructions should be handed over following completion of the commissioning of a new or refurbished building.

Building sustainability management

Those who manage or occupy accommodation such as offices or dwellings that have a comparatively low impact may wish to use a method of environmental and sustainability management tailored to the impacts involved. For example, the Better Buildings Partnership has developed a suite of toolkits for use in developing 'green leases' (BBP, 2009), for 'green building management' (BBP, 2010b) and for managing agents (BBP, 2011).

The emphasis in the BBP toolkits is on cooperation and data sharing between landlord, agent and tenant, along with the management, auditing and recording of energy, water, wastewater and waste. For individual buildings, BBP recommend the formation of a Green Building Management Group (GBMG) which would be:

- established to review and improve the environmental and operational performance of the building;
- focused primarily on minimising the consumption of resources, such as electricity, gas (or other heating fuels) and water, and reducing the generation of waste in a building.

The Group should also consider other environmental and sustainability issues such as sustainable procurement, biodiversity, travel, air quality and emissions (as per the Environment Agency toolkits referred to above).

A GBMG would be particularly 'useful in multi-occupied commercial office buildings where shared services are provided to demised areas'. It would also provide 'a forum to share ideas and best practice examples'.

At the heart of the BBP's GBMG is 'a shared commitment to meet regularly, collect resource consumption data, to set and agree common environmental objectives, to develop an Environmental Action Plan (EAP) for a building, to undertake improvement actions and to produce an annual statement of results'. A template for the EAP is provided in an Appendix to the Green Building Management Toolkit (BBP, 2010).

The British Institute of Facilities Management (BIFM) provides a good practice guide (GPG), available to its members, on the implementation of sustainability policy.[3] In summary, the guide 'is based on the principle that the development and effective implementation of a sustainability policy, tailored to the needs and culture of an organization, [are] essential in supporting . . . its strategic sustainability goals'.

This GPG includes sections on:

- the definition and agreement of a suitable organizational strategy – the main roles and responsibilities required for the sustained success of the policy;
- the benefits of a sustainability policy – the construction of a sound business case is particularly addressed;
- the planning, development and implementation stages of a sustainability policy.

The guide sets out the key elements of this policy including:

- defining an appropriate policy statement;
- selecting relevant sustainability topics;
- outlining the policy's boundaries;
- setting appropriate targets and monitoring systems;
- engaging stakeholders;
- effectively reporting on (the) policy's performance;
- providing feedback and adjusting the policy.

Sustainable management framework

Non-residential buildings

Table 1.3.1 in Chapter 1.3 summarizes the issues covered by BREEAM In-Use. As well as an assessment tool, this provides a very useful framework for managing buildings sustainably, drawing together most of the issues covered by the toolkits discussed above where applicable to most applications with relatively low emissions to air, water or land, such as office buildings, retail premises and schools. Similarly, Table 1.3.3 provides a summary for LEED Existing Buildings that has very similar scope to BREEAM, but with some additional features. Box 2.6.2 pulls together all of the strategic issues from BREEAM In-Use and LEED Existing Buildings into a framework for building and facility managers.

Box 2.6.2 Framework sustainable management strategy for non-residential buildings

Policies

- Management of energy and CO_2 emissions, water, waste, emissions to air, ground and water, ground contamination, flood risk, hazardous chemicals, light pollution, refrigerant leakage, environmental management (EMS) and staff responsibility, corporate social responsibility (CSR), stakeholder engagement, occupant satisfaction feedback, staff development, car sharing, deliveries, landscape and biodiversity, fire protection, health and safety and business continuity; security and disabled access.
- Procurement of energy, water, materials and services.
- Refurbishment strategy.

Processes

- Audit, measurement, monitoring and recording of: energy consumption and carbon footprint, water quality and consumption, health and safety management, fire prevention, legionellosis control and cooling tower management, pest control, materials use, waste management, emissions to air, water and land, comfort conditions.
- Exterior fabric and landscape maintenance, erosion control.
- Training of techniques in energy and water saving, waste management, health, safety and fire safety.
- Post-occupancy evaluation (POE)/Building Health Check and condition surveys, building user liaison.
- Planned maintenance and retrofit.

Documentation

- Building user guide,[4] building log book (see text), operating and maintenance manuals, cleaning procedures, Energy Performance Certificate (EPC) and/or Display Energy Certificate (DEC), audit reports, monitoring records, maintenance records, health and safety records, legionellosis and fire risk assessments, security survey report, emergency plan, accident, incident and injury records,[5] POE reports, CSR statements.

The provision of building log books for 'buildings other than dwellings' is a requirement of Part L2 of the Building Regulations. A way of showing compliance with this requirement is to follow the guidance and templates provided in the Chartered Institution of Building Services Engineers (CIBSE) *Technical Memorandum TM31: Building Log Book Toolkit* (CIBSE, 2006b). Templates for log books are available in Word format on a CD-ROM accompanying TM31. The log book provides:

- a summary of all the key information about the building including the original design, commissioning and handover details, and information on its management and performance;

- a concise summary of the principal energy-consuming services in the building;
- key references to the detail held in less accessible O&M manuals, BMS (building management system) manuals and commissioning records;
- a place to log changes to the building and its operation, as well as building performance and actions taken to improve that performance ('fine-tuning');
- information about the metering strategy implemented in the building, and on the scope for monitoring and benchmarking energy consumption data.

The Building Services Research and Information Association (BSRIA) has also produced guidance on the preparation of log books in their 2007 publication *Handover, O&M Manuals and Project Feedback* (BSRIA, 2007). As the title implies, it also provides handover information for building services and a model specification for operating and maintenance instructions, as well as a pro-forma for a condition survey report and occupant satisfaction survey (see Chapter 2.2). Although intended primarily for handing over information to the developer prior to occupancy, the tools in this publication can easily be adapted for use in existing buildings at any stage during their life.

Multiple residential buildings

BREEAM EcoHomes XB is designed as a way of managing and monitoring the sustainability performance of a portfolio of dwellings (see Chapter 1.3). Hence

---

Box 2.6.3 Framework sustainable management strategy for a portfolio of residential buildings

Policies

- Management of energy and CO_2 emissions, water, waste, ground con-tamination, flood risk, deliveries, landscape and biodiversity, fire protection, health and safety, security, disabled access.
- Procurement of energy, water, materials, white goods and services.
- Refurbishment strategy.

Processes

- Audit, measurement, monitoring and recording of energy consumption and carbon footprint, water consumption, materials use and waste.
- Provision of information on techniques in energy and water saving, waste management, public transport, health, safety and fire safety.[6]
- Planned maintenance and retrofit.

Documentation

- Home User Guide,[7] operating and maintenance manuals, cleaning proce-dures, Energy Performance Certificate (EPC), audit reports, monitoring records, maintenance records, health and safety reports, legionellosis and fire risk assessments, security survey report.

it incorporates a series of credits that is designed to rate the performance of a managing agent or registered social landlord (RSL) and provides a useful sustainability framework for managing a portfolio of residential buildings (see Box 2.6.3).

Where a residential portfolio or complex incorporates an energy centre and/or other centralized services such as waste transfer stations, water recycling and treatment plant and the like, some of the elements in Box 2.6.3 will need to be adopted.

Case histories

British Land head office, York House

In 2008, British Land formed a green building management group (GBMG) with the occupiers and managing agent at its head office, York House. In 2010, total

Figure 2.6.1 *British Land head office, York House, London*

Source: © British Land.

building energy use reduced by 1.1 million kWh compared to the previous year, cutting CO_2 emissions by 416 tonnes and saving an estimated £63,000. British Land-controlled energy use reduced by 32 per cent and occupier-controlled energy use by 9 per cent (BBP, 2010b). The proportion of waste recycled also increased to 70 per cent, from 40 per cent, with 98 per cent diverted from landfill. For a more detailed case history, see Chapter 4.10.

Brent Cross Shopping Centre

Hammerson has found that 'Green Working Parties' at its shopping centres have created an environment for proactive owner–occupier relations. At Brent Cross Shopping Centre, the Green Working Party is currently chaired by the Starbucks' manager and meets on a monthly basis.

Figure 2.6.2 *Brent Cross Shopping Centre*
Source: © Martin Addison.

Through these meetings, the Green Working Party has been able to assist in setting and achieving both centre and corporate targets, with reductions in electricity and gas amounting to an energy reduction of over 20 per cent from 2006 baseline levels (BBP, 2010b). Recycling rates have also improved from 48 per cent to 54 per cent for the whole centre in 2009 and 2010. Importantly, the Green Working Party has helped facilitate behavioural change in retailers to improve their own environmental performance as well as facilitate better working relations between all parties.

Cushman & Wakefield and BREEAM In-Use

Cushman & Wakefield implemented BREEAM In-Use in late 2010,[8] as an environmental and sustainability standard to provide meaningful insight into the environmental performance of the buildings it manages throughout the operational life of the building. The aim has been to use the standard to provide owners and occupiers with a robust and independent methodology to benchmark and certify the sustainable performance of its buildings.

By the end of September 2010, Cushman & Wakefield had trained over 50 per cent of its Asset Management staff (across a range of disciplines and specialities) to foundation level Environmental Awareness. Training programmes continued through 2011 with its 'Green Immersion' training programme including additional Environmental Awareness training and LEED Green Associate (GA) training for its specialist teams.

By late 2010 it had registered approximately 200 properties of varying size, location, services and across a number of client portfolios for the BREEAM In-Use scheme. The initial registration process provided Cushman & Wakefield with an opportunity to verify training standards, centralize policies, collate information on every building and review the whole Asset Management portfolio using a uniform measurement standard.

Cushman & Wakefield's teams have since reviewed how BREEAM In-Use can be used as an effective management and operational tool with clear targets for each building across a broad range of property types encompassing retail, offices and other commercial properties. It is also transferring relevant property information from draft ratings off-line to the on-line BREEAM In-Use system.

Cushman & Wakefield has already seen an improvement in ratings for a number of buildings. It envisaged that individual property audits would be completed at selected properties during 2011 to assess and recommend improvements in the key areas of Asset, Building Management and Organizational Performance and Effectiveness. It is committed to continue working in partnership with BRE to ensure BREEAM In-Use is maintained as a valued and integral part of its sustainability platform. Cushman & Wakefield will review the system on a continual basis to identify how sustainability can be increased within its property portfolio.

Figure 2.6.3 *Cushman & Wakefield offices, Portman Square, London*

2.7
Retrofit as part of sustainable facilities management

Introduction

The question we will be addressing in this chapter is: 'When is the right time to retrofit, refurbish or refit an existing building?' The answer to this question will depend on a wide range of factors, such as the condition of the building, provisions in leases, the availability of funds, pressure of running costs, the accommodation needs of occupants, and sustainability drivers, to name but a few.

Although in the interests of economy the term 'retrofit' has been used in both the title of this chapter and indeed the book as a whole, it is important to distinguish retrofit from refurbishment and refit, when examining the question posed above. The term retrofit is frequently used interchangeably with refurbishment, but it is probably more accurate to apply it to adding or replacing building services, including renewable technologies. Replacing or improving the fabric may be called renovation, while refurbishment usually applies to a combination of retrofit and renovation. Refitting, which may also be referred to as restacking, applies to the reconfiguration of office or retail space, usually through stripping out and replacing existing internal fixtures, such as workstations, partitions, shelving and displays. This may also be part of a more general refurbishment process. We will therefore look at the triggers that are likely to generate the need for refurbishment as a whole, along with retrofitting of building services or renewable technologies and refitting of internal spaces, as part of a sustainable facilities management strategy.

Refurbishment

In Chapter 2.1 we looked at the decision-making process that governs the choice between refurbishment and new build. A range of refurbishment options were defined running from major refurbishment through retention of main structural elements or retention of façade only, to demolition and redevelopment. However, there may be less dramatic options available to the facility manager or building owner wishing to upgrade their accommodation. These can be graded in various ways depending on the type and scale of the building or buildings under management. For example, for non-residential buildings, consideration might be given to level of disruption, capital, running and life cycle costs, impact on carbon footprint, environmental benefits (as assessed by one of the protocols in Chapter 1.3) and projected productivity impacts. For those managing residential portfolios, a similar range of issues might be considered, although the pressures and funding issues may be different for those managing social housing compared with private landlords. For example, an article on the Refurbish website from January 2012 states that:

> The need to refurbish the nation's social housing blocks has become more pressing in recent years considering the increased costs in buying land and developing, forcing Local Authorities and Housing Associations to come up with innovative and high-quality schemes to renovate their housing stock.[1]

We saw in Chapters 1.1 and 1.2 that governments in both the UK and the USA are keen to see an increase in green refurbishment in order to improve the energy efficiency of the existing building stock to assist in meeting long-term carbon reduction targets and reduce fuel poverty. This is being driven by devices such as the Green Deal in the UK and the Recovery through Retrofit programme in the USA, with similar schemes offering loans, grants or tax breaks, being offered elsewhere.

However, in many countries, the drivers for refurbishment of dwellings run deeper than the need to improve energy efficiency. For example, in the UK, at

---

Box 2.7.1 Triggers for refurbishment

Managed homes

- Do not meet decency standards.
- Structural defects, such as concrete decay.
- Legislation, e.g. UK Energy Act requirement for landlords to ensure all properties they lease achieve an EPC rating of at least E (from April 2018) (see Box 1.2.1, Chapter 1.2).
- Funding available, e.g. through Local Authority managed scheme, Green Deal, etc.
- Demand from tenants.

Non-residential buildings

- Multi-tenanted buildings – lease renewal provides window for works.
- Dilapidations or defects becoming critical.
- Accommodation no longer meets modern standards.
- Pressure on accommodation predicted to become critical.
- Legislation, e.g. UK Energy Act requirement for landlords to ensure all properties they lease achieve an EPC rating of at least E (from April 2018) (see Box 1.2.1, Chapter 1.2).
- Funds available through commercial loan, Green Deal, tax break, sinking fund or cash flow.
- Demand from tenants/employees.
- Corporate social responsibility (CSR) or environmental policy includes targets for carbon reduction and/or accommodation quality.

the time of writing, more than 30 per cent of homes fall below government decency standards, meaning that they do not meet basic health and safety or hygiene standards (see checklist in Box 1.2.3, Chapter 1.2). Although a proportion of these homes are being renovated through Local Authority programmes, the majority are privately owned and more difficult to reach.

Box 2.7.1 summarizes the main triggers for refurbishment for managed homes and non-residential buildings, where a managed home may be maintained by a private landlord, Local Authority or housing association. It is important to realize that as well as triggers there are opposing forces that may inhibit the uptake of refurbishment and retrofit initiatives. For home owners and office tenants at least, the fear or anticipation of disruption is one of the key barriers to retrofit, more important even than cost.

Retrofitting

Retrofit of building services can be triggered as either a scheduled replacement action under a planned maintenance programme, replacement as indicated by condition-based maintenance or in response to other drivers, such as the Green Deal (see Box 2.7.2).

In the consultation for the roll-out of the Green Deal from a survey of British householders carried out for the Department of Energy and Climate Change in early 2011, it was reported that:

> Discussions with participants identified a number of trigger points for when they would consider taking up energy efficiency measures. These included the purchase of a new property – particularly a long-term investment or final move, a major renovation or refurbishment of a property and the replacement of a boiler or heating system. The survey showed a higher than average likelihood of taking up a Green Deal package among those who had undertaken recent changes and who were planning to move or refurbish their homes soon.
>
> (DECC, 2011c)

In a study reported in the Better Buildings Partnership's *Low-Carbon Retrofit Toolkit*, focusing on non-residential buildings it was found that:

> one most frequently cited [barrier to retrofit] was the perception of disruption. This concern is consistent with the focus of owners and their managing agents being on simply operating their buildings whilst minimizing the impacts on occupiers and reducing complaints, rather than on proactively decreasing carbon emissions and energy use.
>
> (BBP, 2010a)

However, retrofit of building services is potentially far less disruptive than renovation of the fabric or refitting of internal layout, since frequently work can be carried out in plant rooms or externally.

Box 2.7.2 Triggers for retrofit

Managed homes

- Do not meet modern energy standards.
- Households fall within the definition of fuel poverty.[2]
- Scheduled replacement action, or triggered by condition monitoring.
- Legislation, e.g. UK Energy Act requirement for landlords to ensure all properties they lease out achieve an EPC rating of at least 'E' (from April 2018) (see Box 1.2.1, Chapter 1.2).
- Funding available, e.g. through Local Authority managed scheme, Green Deal, etc.
- Demand from tenants.

Non-residential buildings

- Multi-tenanted buildings – lease renewal provides window for works.
- Legislation, e.g. UK Energy Act requirement for landlords to ensure all properties they lease out achieve an EPC rating of at least 'E' (from April 2018) (see Box 1.2.1, Chapter 1.2).
- Scheduled replacement action, or triggered by condition monitoring.
- Funds available through commercial loan, Green Deal, tax break, sinking fund or cash flow.
- Demand from tenants/employees.
- Corporate Social Responsibility (CSR) or environmental policy includes targets for carbon reduction.

Refitting

The terms refitting and restacking are commonly applied to offices, although similar processes apply to other types of accommodation, such as retail outlets and warehouses. There are many reasons why an organization might decide to reconfigure its accommodation, but as proffered in a recent online article from the *Nashville Business Journal*, the need to downsize may be a key trigger in difficult economic times:

> In most cases, a business is facing a lease event and thus has an opportunity to consolidate into less space. A company also may consider a restack to reorganize or reposition teams or departments to address a particular business issue. In either case, businesses are looking at the escalating costs of their real estate and asking the question, 'How can our real estate work better for us?'[3]

Refits are normally triggered by the occupier, whether they own, occupy and manage the building or are a tenant, whereas refurbishment and retrofit of multi-tenanted buildings are frequently initiated and driven by a landlord or agent.

Box 2.7.3 provides a summary of the triggers that drive the decision to refit.

Box 2.7.3 Triggers for refit

- Multi-tenanted buildings – lease renewal provides window for works.
- Accommodation no longer meets modern standards or method of working.
- Business needs to consolidate space.
- Funds available through commercial loan, Green Deal, tax break, sinking fund or cash flow.
- Demand from tenants/employees.

Decision-making process

In Chapter 1.3 we reviewed the various tools available for assessing the environmental impact of refurbishment and refit. The Ska Rating scheme is most suited to minor refurbishment and refitting of non-residential buildings in the UK. For the US market it is likely that Green Globes® Fit-Up would be the most suitable scheme for these types of project. In the residential sector the recently developed BREEAM Domestic Refurbishment scheme should be considered. All of these schemes could be used by the facility or building manager in deciding on a refurbishment or refit strategy by examining the impact of various options on the score/rating achieved under the appropriate scheme.

Part 3

Sustainable retrofit

3.1
Renovation of building fabric

Introduction

In this chapter we are going to examine the standards for improving the performance of existing building fabric and discuss the most cost effective and technically proficient methods of achieving them. We will focus specifically on the European Passivhaus and EnerPHit standards, the British Association of Energy-Conscious Builders' (AECB) CarbonLite standards and the US FSA PowerSaver Home Improvement Standards referred to in Chapter 2.4 for dwellings, as well as good practice for non-residential refurbishment.

Fabric refurbishment standards and strategies

EnerPHit, Passivhaus and AECB standards

'Whilst it is possible to achieve the new build Passivhaus Standard in the refurbishment of an existing building and be fully certified as a "Quality-Approved Passivhaus", it is often difficult to achieve without undertaking major works which involve greater costs.'[1] Hence the EnerPHit Standard has been developed as a good practice refurbishment guide for Passivhaus renovations, with a reduced energy standard in recognition of the difficulty in meeting the new build requirements. EnerPHit is intended for residential refurbishment so, in the absence at the time of writing of a Passivhaus standard for non-residential refurbishment, the standard for new build will be referred to below.[2] The AECB CarbonLite standard incorporates three levels of performance, one of which corresponds to Passivhaus while the others, Silver and Gold, set CO_2 emission targets that are slightly higher and lower than Passivhaus respectively.[3]

Certification to the EnerPHit Standard (Table 3.1.1) can be achieved through two alternative methods. For Method 1 the energy performance of the refurbished building must be verified using the latest version of the *Passivhaus Projektierungs Paket* (Passive House Planning Package, PHPP), which is the design tool produced by the Passivhaus Institut to model the performance of a proposed Passivhaus building.

Where the EnerPHit Specific Heating Demand of 25 kWh/m²annum or lower cannot be met, the use of 'Passivhaus-suitable components' (Method 2) can still result in improvements in comfort, cost-effectiveness and operational energy savings. Buildings that have been modernized using 'Passivhaus-suitable components' but do not meet the Passivhaus or EnerPHit heating demand values, can still receive certification, provided the refurbishment has demonstrated that all

Table 3.1.1 *EnerPHit design criteria for home refurbishment (Method 1)*

Criteria	Passivhaus (new build)	EnerPHit (refurb)
Specific heat demand	$\leq$ 15 kWh/m²annum	$\leq$ 25 kWh/m²annum
Primary energy demand	$\leq$ 120 kWh/m²annum	$\leq$ 120 kWh/m²annum
Limiting air leakage rate	$n_{50} \leq 0.6$ h^{-1}	$n_{50} \leq 1.0$ h^{-1}
Target air leakage rate		$n_{50} \leq 0.6$ h^{-1}

Note: n_{50} is the air change rate at 50 Pa room air pressure.

energy-related building components for certification as 'Passivhaus-suitable components' have been used.

Method 1: Certification via Energy Demand

The whole of the building thermal envelope, e.g. the entire apartment block (or multi-storey office building for Passivhaus non-residential), not individual flats (or tenanted floors), should be considered when calculating the specific heat demand. Combining thermally separated buildings together is not permissible. Buildings that adjoin other buildings must have at least one external wall, one roof surface and a floor slab or basement ceiling in order to certify them individually.

The primary energy demand refers to the total annual kWh for heating, hot water, cooling, auxiliary and household electricity.

Suitable evidence that summertime comfort can be maintained must be provided.

All fabric components must be designed so that there is no excessive surface or interstitial moisture. The 'water activity'[4] of the interior surfaces must be kept at $a_w \leq 80$ per cent (i.e. 80 per cent saturation humidity level at the surface). In case of doubt, evidence for moisture protection based on established techniques must be provided.

The airtightness of the building must be verified using a pressurization test in accordance with CIBSE TM23 (CIBSE, 2000) or DIN EN 13829. If the target n_{50} value of 0.6 h^{-1} is exceeded, a systematic search for leakages must be carried out during the pressurization test and each relevant leak should be rectified.

Windows certified as 'Passivhaus-suitable components', and triple low-emissivity glazing (or equivalent) should be used, adopting the installation principles recommended by the Passive House Institute (PHI).

Method 2 Certification based on Criteria for Individual Components

If the specific heat demand of 25 kWh/m²annum given in Method 1 (above) is exceeded, certification based on the criteria for the individual components may also be possible. Note that all the other general requirements of Method 1 must still be fulfilled.

The PHI has certified the most critical energy-related building components as 'Passivhaus-suitable components'.[5] For products that have not been certified by the PHI as Passivhaus-suitable components, the applicant is obliged to provide 'admissible proof of compliance with the stated criteria'.

The requirements for Passivhaus-suitable components specify maximum thermal transmittance coefficients (U-values), thermal bridging coefficients (Ψ) and minimum internal surface temperatures (t_{si}) for windows and glass (framed and in curtain walling), opaque elements of wall and construction systems and entrance doors.

Windows (including frames) should have an installed U-value of no more than 0.85 W/m²K with the triple-glazed element no more than 0.7 W/m²K based on a standard window size of 1.23 m by 1.48 m. Windows in a 'mullion-transom façade' should achieve the same installed U-value, taking into account the thermal bridging from the transom and mullions, the glass carrier profiles and screws.

Opaque wall and construction systems should achieve a U-value of no more than 0.15 W/m²K and thermal bridging coefficient of 0.1 W/mK for connection details. Internal surface temperatures should be no lower than 17°C when outdoor temperature is –10°C and it is 20°C indoors. In addition, evidence must be provided that connection details will not compromise EnerPHit air tightness requirements. Also details are required of the thermal conductivity of insulation, the fire behaviour of the resultant fabric and details of all junctions between elements or changes of direction.

If there are no suitable products available that comply with the criteria for 'Passivhaus-suitable components', then one should be selected which fulfils the criteria as far as possible. In all cases the required boundary values must be observed at least as an average value. Not meeting this value is only admissible for partial areas if it can be fully compensated for by better values elsewhere.

The Passivhaus standards for non-residential buildings are very similar to those for dwellings.[6] The maximum requirement for heating is an annual energy demand of 15 kWh/m² or 10 W/m² and for cooling is 15 kWh/m² with a maximum primary energy consumption of 120 kWh/m² per annum. Target air leakage (n_{50}) is 0.6 h⁻¹.

Examples of achieving Passivhaus U-values through renovation

Renovation techniques for improving the thermal performance of an existing fabric depend not simply on whether the building is residential or non-residential but on the composition of each of the fabric elements. For example, the fabric of a Victorian building used for offices or retail purposes may be similar or identical to that of a dwelling of the same age. The nature of the internal use and accommodation will be different, however, with office and retail occupation typically presenting higher internal heat gains and different hours of use. Hence an office building renovated to Passivhaus air leakage standards will present greater risk of summer overheating.

In this section we will examine options for insulating existing walls, roofs and floors, replacing windows and doors, whilst meeting Passivhaus U-values and air leakage rates. The environmental impacts of insulation materials will be covered in Chapter 3.8.

Walls

Existing walls may be constructed from some combination of concrete block, brick, stone or *in situ* concrete, with or without air gaps, render or cladding; timber or steel framed with curtain walling. Many older buildings have non-insulated walls or a cavity between internal and external elements. Retrofitting insulation therefore may either involve applying insulation to internal or external surfaces or filling a cavity.

Typically a 225 mm-thick solid brick wall with dense plaster on its internal surface would have a U-value of 2.1 W/m^2K, while a 50 mm cavity would reduce this to 1.44 W/m^2K. A solid 200 mm dense concrete block wall, internally plastered, would have a U-value of around 3 W/m^2K, while a brick/cavity/lightweight block sandwich would have a U-value nearer 1.06 W/m^2K (refer to CIBSE Guide, Section A3, for more details on thermal properties of building structures).

Cavity wall insulation

In the UK, most homes built since the 1920s have been constructed with cavity walls externally. Filling the cavity of an existing brick wall with blown fibre would typically reduce the U-value to around 0.63 W/m^2K, or around 0.52 W/m^2K if the inner layer is lightweight block.[7] This is three to four times greater than that required to meet Passivhaus standards. The most common materials used for blowing into a cavity are mineral fibres, polystyrene beads or granules, and foam (Figure 3.1.1). The wall is drilled from the outside with typically 22 mm holes at 1 m intervals. This is a specialist activity and in the UK standards are regulated by the National Insulation Association (NIA), while most installers offer 25-year guarantees under the Cavity Insulation Guarantee Agency (CIGA) scheme.

Cavities must be surveyed prior to being filled in order to ensure that they have not already been filled and that there are no major blockages. Exposed walls that experience penetration of driving rain through the external layer of brick into the cavity may not be suitable for cavity wall insulation. Similarly, rising damp must be eliminated before filling a cavity with insulation.

Insulation of solid walls (or cavity walls with blocked cavities)

The choice here is between external and internal insulation, the pros and cons of which are outlined by the Energy-Saving Trust[8] as follows:

> External wall insulation:
> - can be applied with minimum disruption to the occupants;
> - does not reduce the floor area of the building;
> - renews the appearance of outer walls;
> - improves weatherproofing and sound resistance;
> - fills cracks and gaps in the fabric, potentially improving air tightness;
> - increases the life of the walls by protecting the outer surface;
> - reduces the risk of condensation on internal walls and can help prevent interstitial condensation (but will not solve rising damp);

Figure 3.1.1 *Insulation being blown into a cavity*
Source: ROCKWOOL©.

- is best installed at the same time as external refurbishment work, such as window replacement;
- is likely to require modifications to roof and guttering to reinstate overhangs;
- may present challenging details around balconies, bay windows, conservatories, etc.;
- may need planning permission if there will be significant alteration in appearance;
- requires good access to the outer walls;
- is not recommended if the outer walls are structurally unsound and cannot be repaired.

Internal wall insulation:

- is generally cheaper to install than external wall insulation;
- will reduce the floor area of any rooms in which it is applied: for example, a 6 m by 4 m room with 150 mm of internal insulation applied to two external walls would be reduced in floor area by around 6 per cent;
- is disruptive, but can be done room by room;
- requires skirting boards, door frames, heating appliances and fittings on external walls to be removed and reattached;
- can make it hard to fix heavy items to the inside surface of external walls – although special fixings are available;
- requires penetrating or rising damp issues to be eliminated prior to installation.

External insulation of walls

Typical insulation thicknesses to achieve a U-value of 0.15 W/m²K are 150 mm of phenolic or polyurethane foam or 250 mm of polystyrene or mineral wool slab, assuming substrate is 215 mm of solid brick and there is minimal cold bridging.

Insulated render systems[9] sometimes include a series of mechanical fixings which are normally made of metal or plastic (Figure 3.1.2). When used to fix the insulation, they form a series of point repeating thermal bridges analogous to the effect of metal cavity wall ties.

Thermal bridging can be largely avoided by:

- Using an adhesive to bond insulation to the substrate. To ensure that there is no air movement behind the insulation, the adhesive should fully cover the insulation, rather than the more usual 'ribbon' of adhesive. This method is not suitable where there are doubts over adhesion quality, such as might occur on a painted or rendered substrate.

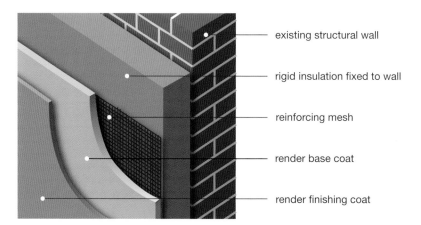

existing structural wall

rigid insulation fixed to wall

reinforcing mesh

render base coat

render finishing coat

Figure 3.1.2 *Typical insulated render system*
Source: GreenSpec.

- Using a mechanical fixing 'track & rail system' where the insulation is supported by metal or plastic tracks attached to the wall. Although this system has the advantage of placing the fixing behind the insulation, a small space is created resulting in an air gap between the insulation and the wall surface.

Brick slips (Figure 3.1.3) are one method of replicating the impression of a traditional brick wall. However, there is a variety of proprietary systems available that alleviate the demanding task of aligning and adhering individual slips onto a simple backing. Modern mounting systems come in a variety of formats including profiled polystyrene and wire mesh backings.

Rainscreen systems provide a greater range of external finishes (Figure 3.1.4), with materials such as wood, laminates, fibre cement, ceramics, terracotta (Figure

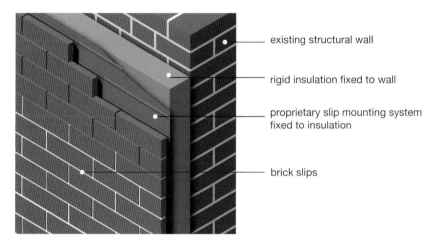

existing structural wall

rigid insulation fixed to wall

proprietary slip mounting system fixed to insulation

brick slips

Figure 3.1.3 *External insulation with brick slips finish*
Source: GreenSpec.

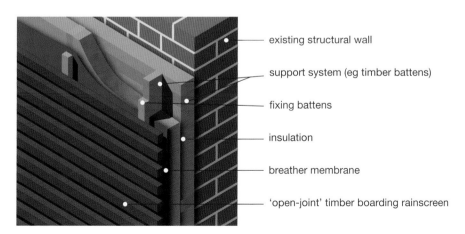

existing structural wall

support system (eg timber battens)

fixing battens

insulation

breather membrane

'open-joint' timber boarding rainscreen

Figure 3.1.4 *Open timber rainscreen on timber battens*
Source: GreenSpec.

3.1.5), metals, stone and glass being among the options in common use. These provide a degree of protection to the material behind, but with some penetration of air and water being allowed into the air gap. For exposed walls this allows pressure equalization across the outer skin and a lower risk of wind damage.

External cladding hung on battens provides a number of options to create a traditional external appearance, enabling tiles, slates, timber panels and shingles to provide a weather-proof external finish (Figure 3.1.6).

Internal wall insulation

Insulation can be applied either directly to existing plaster, to or between studs, or with an air gap created between the insulation and internal wall surface.

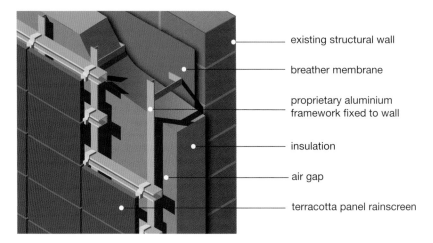

existing structural wall

breather membrane

proprietary aluminium framework fixed to wall

insulation

air gap

terracotta panel rainscreen

Figure 3.1.5 *Terracotta tile rainscreen on metal frame*
Source: GreenSpec.

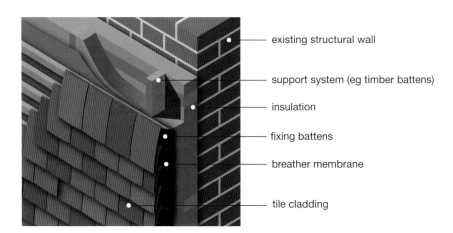

existing structural wall

support system (eg timber battens)

insulation

fixing battens

breather membrane

tile cladding

Figure 3.1.6 *External wall insulation with batten hung cladding*
Source: GreenSpec.

Applying the insulation directly to the surface is the most economical with space, eliminating cold bridges (see Figure 3.1.7) but requires a flat and even surface. Stud fixing may be desirable where the internal wall surface is bowed and in poor condition.

Where there is evidence of rain penetration, an air gap can be created between the insulation and the internal wall surface and a vapour membrane installed to prevent migration of moisture into the plasterboard (see Figure 3.1.8). This might provide unacceptable encroachment into the occupied space, however, and would only be used when external insulation is not feasible.

It is likely that a penetration into the occupied space of more than 150 mm will be unacceptable. Hence, a phenolic or polyurethane foam insulation is likely to be required, having a thermal conductivity of between 0.02 and 0.025 W/mK, compared with 0.035 to 0.042 W/mK for polystyrene or mineral wool.

Curtain walling

Many non-residential buildings have used non-structural mullion and transom-based curtain walling systems that integrate glazing and opaque wall panels into a system supported on the concrete slabs and external columns. Since these systems are independent from the structure, they provide the opportunity for total replacement with a modern high-specification system that incorporates both window and wall elements that comply with Passivhaus insulation standards. There are many modular glazing systems available that meet the Passivhaus U-value requirement of 0.85 W/m²K installed, an example of which is shown in Figure 3.1.9. To achieve the required 0.15 W/m²K wall U-value opaque elements can be formed with impermeable external panels backed by

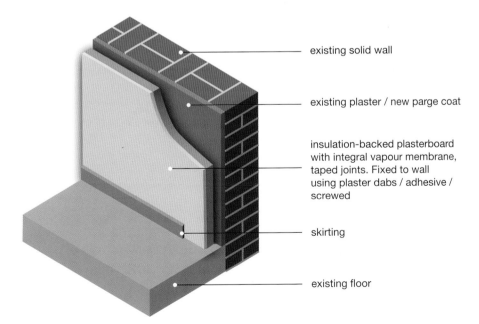

existing solid wall

existing plaster / new parge coat

insulation-backed plasterboard with integral vapour membrane, taped joints. Fixed to wall using plaster dabs / adhesive / screwed

skirting

existing floor

Figure 3.1.7 *Internal wall insulation applied directly to plaster/parge coat*
Source: GreenSpec.

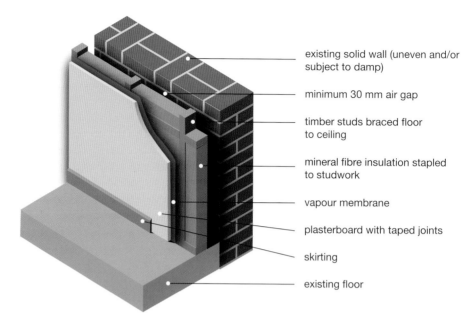

existing solid wall (uneven and/or subject to damp)

minimum 30 mm air gap

timber studs braced floor to ceiling

mineral fibre insulation stapled to studwork

vapour membrane

plasterboard with taped joints

skirting

existing floor

Figure 3.1.8 *Internal wall insulation with air gap*
Source: GreenSpec.

Figure 3.1.9 *Typical Passivhaus certified curtain wall glazing detail*
Source: Schüco International KG.

200 mm of phenolic or polyurethane foam and an internal panel. The entire façade is normally fixed to the leading edge of floor slabs and columns in order to avoid cold bridging.

Windows and doors

When it comes to renovation to achieve Passivhaus performance requirements, windows and doors will normally have to be replaced in conjunction with adding insulation to walls. Windows are always a weak link in the façade of an older building, since not only do they offer low resistance to conductive heat flow, but they also tend to allow significant air leakage and provide a major source of draught in winter. The air leakage itself can create a draught, as well as the adjacent air being cooled, creating downward air movement. Also nearby occupants lose heat to the cool surface by radiation directly from their skin. During summer months windows provide a route for solar heat gain and glare. On the other hand, they provide a source of daylight and access to a view of the outside world.

It is possible to improve the performance of existing windows through renovation (see Empire State Building case history on p. 140) or by installing secondary glazing. However, it will usually be simpler and more cost effective to replace existing windows, especially if it is desired to meet the Passivhaus standard of 0.85 W/m²K installed.

The performance of a window as a whole is dependent on a combination of factors. The glass assembly will usually require a U-value of 0.7 W/m²K to achieve the overall installed rating of 0.85 W/m²K that includes the frame. The U-value depends on a combination of the number of layers of glass, its emissivity and the gas used to fill the cavities between the glass panels.

There are several materials that can be used to create a 'low-E' coating. The best performing are soft and have an emissivity of between 0.05 and 0.1. Harder materials are less prone to damage and have an emissivity of 0.15 or higher.

Inert gases are generally used to fill cavities, rather than air since they have a lower thermal conductivity. Argon is the most common, although krypton and xenon, while being more expensive per unit volume, have lower conductivities than argon and smaller air gaps are possible, reducing the amount of gas required and the thickness of the unit. Historically there have been concerns about gas leakage, but BS EN 1279 Part 3 requires that the leakage rate be lower than 1 per cent per annum (BSI, 2002).

Multiple glazing units are edged and sealed by spacer bars between the panes and around the perimeter of the unit. The traditional material for a spacer bar is aluminium. But as window standards have become more stringent, the heat lost from thermal bridging through the metal has become more significant and hence non-metallic materials such as steel reinforced polymer, glass fibre or structural foam with, typically, a polysulphide seal, have been used. This technology is often referred to as 'warm edge' and results in a more uniform U-value across the full area of the glass.

Of course, the window frame offers a potential cold bridge, while, for openable windows, the seal between the openable and fixed elements is a potential route for infiltration air. Figure 3.1.10 shows a typical cross-section through a triple-pane openable window, showing the sealing arrangement.

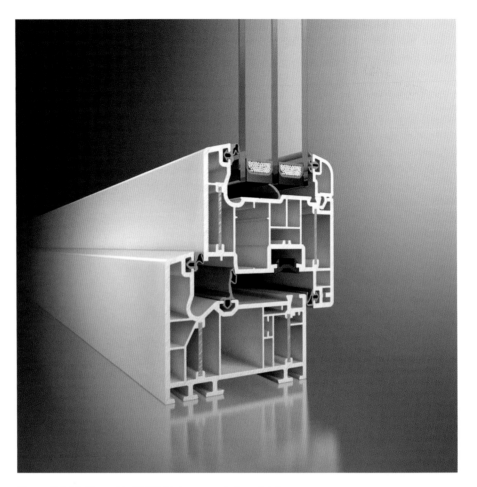

Figure 3.1.10 *Openable UPVC triple-pane window detail*
Source: Schüco International KG.

It is clear that the U-value does not tell the whole story when it comes to the thermal performance of windows. The British Fenestration Rating Council (BFRC) was established to address this[10] and has developed a labelling scheme that has been adopted in Part L of the Building Regulations. This combines overall U-value, solar factor (G) and effective air leakage (W/m^{2}K) into a single Window Energy Rating (WER) (see Figure 3.1.11). This uses an A–G rating scheme, similar to white goods and Energy Performance Certificates (EPCs).

Windows can also provide a useful frame in which trickle ventilators can be mounted, although Passivhaus-compliant buildings would normally require mechanical ventilation with heat recovery (see Chapter 3.2) to avoid the uncontrolled heat loss to ventilation air associated with trickle vents. Windows (and trickle vents in particular) also provide an entry point for noise. Triple glazing performs better in this respect than double (see also Chapter 3.9 of Appleby, 2011a).

The U-value for doors should be the same as for windows and the methods used to achieve the necessary air tightness are very similar. Opaque elements are usually an insulated sandwich, typically around 40mm thick, comprising inner and outer layers of UPVC, timber or aluminium, and foam or cork filling (see Figures 3.1.12 and 3.1.13).

Shading and façade design

Major renovation of a façade provides the opportunity not only to review the impact of windows on heat loss but also daylighting and consequent lighting operation, glare, and potential summer overheating or cooling requirements. There may be opportunities to change the dimensions and position of the windows in the façade, as well as change the solar shading strategy. Depending

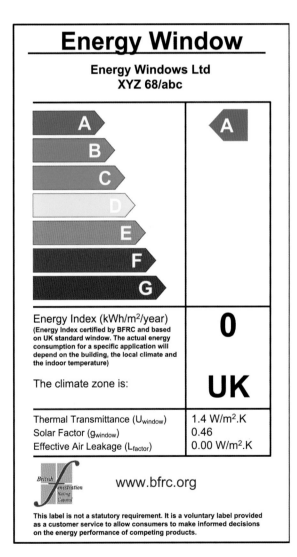

Figure 3.1.11 *Typical BFRC Window Energy Rating sheet*
Source: © BFRC.

Figure 3.1.12 *Cross-section through typical door meeting Passivhaus standards*
Source: Kneer-Südfenster.

Figure 3.1.13 *Example of windows and door meeting Passivhaus standards*
Source: GreenSteps Ltd.

on the condition of the existing façade, economics and aesthetic implications, it may be appropriate to approach the façade design with a clean sheet. In these circumstances the building can be treated as a new build and the passive design measures described in Chapter 3.2 of *Integrated Sustainable Design of Buildings* can be considered (Appleby, 2011a).

It is interesting to note that there has been an ever-increasing polarity between the window-to-wall ratio in houses and high-rise buildings, whether they be apartments or office buildings. Windows (along with room sizes) have tended to shrink as target carbon emissions have come down in the UK Building Regulations/Standards. Individual apartments, on the other hand, may only have one exposed wall. When this is the only source of view and daylight, it is common for this wall to be nearly 100 per cent glazed. The story with office buildings is more complex: view is associated with status of course, but also there has been an on-and-off love affair between architects and fully glazed office buildings since curtain walling was first developed in the late nineteenth century, as exemplified by the Bauhaus-Dessau office building from 1926 shown in Figure 3.1.14.

This photograph beautifully illustrates the dilemma presented by the older generation of fully glazed buildings. Clearly this architecturally important building could have neither double nor triple glazing fitted within the thin glazing bars, nor opaque insulated panels installed, nor external shading fitted, without interfering with the architect's intent and most likely destroying much of the aesthetic value of the building.

Figure 3.1.14 *Bauhaus-Dessau office building with fully glazed curtain walling façade*
Source: Cathegus.

In fact, large areas of high-performance glazing, having U-values of perhaps one-eighth of the windows in Figure 3.1.14, and with controllable external solar protection or solar control glass, may offer optimum carbon efficiency for modern office buildings in temperate climates. This is because, with relatively mild winters, internal heat gains may offset heat losses for much of the winter, while good daylighting, combined with photosensitive lighting, controls will reduce the operating period of the lamps. This should be checked through computer simulation, of course (see Chapter 3.7 of Appleby, 2011a).

The strategy for reducing solar gain through retrofit needs to be integrated with the insulation strategy, and should be based on an analysis of sun paths and shadows from neighbouring buildings and topographic features. A terraced building for which the only exposed elevation is orientated north (in the northern hemisphere), or any orientation that overlooks canyon streets and taller neighbours, is unlikely to suffer excessive solar gain or glare.

Assuming one is required, a solar protection strategy should focus on obstructing or diffusing direct solar gain into the building without reducing daylight to such an extent that the additional carbon emissions from lighting exceed any benefit from the reduction in solar gain. In general, solar protection that diffuses rather than blocks solar gain has a lower impact on daylight. For example, light-coloured perforated roller shutter or venetian blinds allow more daylight than opaque ones. However, for naturally ventilated buildings any shading device that sits adjacent to the internal surface of a window may interfere with internally opening windows and/or move around in the wind, while allowing most of the solar gain to enter the space.

Although between-pane blinds within the opening element will overcome the above problems, they do not allow gas filling of the air gap in which they sit, nor the use of a soft high-emissivity coating, so U-values will be significantly higher than the sealed version. One manufacturer has overcome this problem by incorporating a blind between the sealed triple-pane element and a secondary glass panel (see Figure 3.1.15).

External fins and brises-soleil have the twin benefits of not obstructing views out of the building and having significantly lower impact on daylight within the building. However, they cannot be positioned to prevent low-angle sun from entering the building and are vulnerable to wind damage. When combined with curtain walling, fixings may create a cold bridge, unless they are mounted within a self-supporting structure.

Roofs

Roofs on an existing building may be pitched, with or without a loft space, or flat concrete or timber. The strategy for retrofitting insulation will depend on the type and condition of the existing roof as well as the presence of existing insulation, its location and condition. For pitched roofs, the choice is between a ventilated or unventilated assembly located between and under rafters or loft insulation with a ventilated or unventilated 'breathing' roof space. For flat roofs, the choice is between a warm or inverted warm roof, with insulation on the outside, or a cold roof, with insulation installed internally.

Pitched roofs: insulation at rafters

It is not usually possible for an existing roof to be brought up to the Passivhaus standard by the installation of insulation between the rafters alone. Rafter dimensions vary considerably, with some Victorian buildings having rafters of as little as 75 mm deep and, taking account of the requirement for a continuous 50 mm air gap beneath the sarking, little space will remain for insulation

Figure 3.1.15 *Triple glazing with blind protected by secondary glazing*

Source: Internorm (www.internorm.co.uk). Also see www.ecoglaze.ie/windows/view/timber-aluclad/varion4/.

between the rafters. However, more recently rafters supporting roofs over dwellings have been 150 mm or 200 mm deep, and may be deeper in some commercial properties having larger spans.

The only way to upgrade the thermal performance of a pitched roof and maintain the existing covering and structure, therefore, is to add insulation to the underside of the rafters as well as between. Sometimes this can be achieved by effectively extending the rafters, but this simply extends the thermal bridging effect, so the most common method is to fix rigid insulation with an integral vapour control layer to the underside of the rafters (see Figure 3.1.16).

In order to achieve a U-value for the roof of 0.15 W/m²K, a combined thickness of approximately 250 mm of a rigid lightweight insulation such as polystyrene would be required, if there is no other insulation present between the joists, for example, if the loft is to be used for accommodation. Alternatively a total thickness of between 150 mm and 170 mm of phenolic foam between and below the rafters could achieve the same result, which would have less of an impact on the headroom in the loft.

If the roof tiles or slates require replacing and planning permission can be obtained for a slight increase in ridge height, then it will be possible to improve headroom in the loft by removing the need for a 50 mm air space through installing breathable sarking above the rafters, thus creating an unventilated

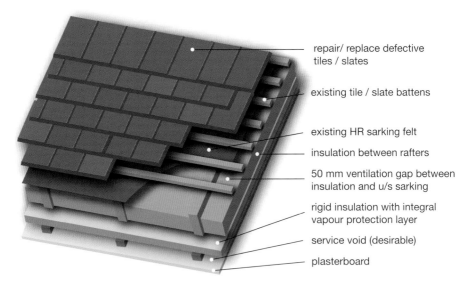

Figure 3.1.16 *Pitched roof with ventilated insulation assembly between and under rafters*
Source: GreenSpec.

insulation assembly (Figure 3.1.17). This enables insulation to be installed for the full depth of the rafters and, depending on the depth of the rafters, may obviate the need for further insulation beneath. For example, with 170 mm phenolic foam, a U-value of 0.15 W/m²K should be achievable.

The concept of an 'unventilated' pitched roof is relatively new and requires the installation of a low vapour resistance (LR) 'breathable' sarking membrane, allowing internally produced water vapour to pass through the membrane,

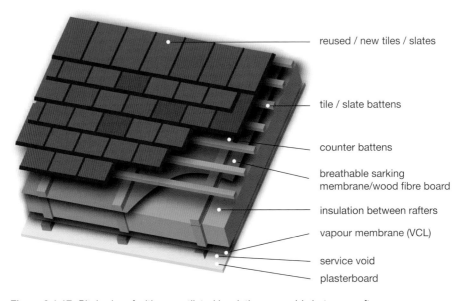

Figure 3.1.17 *Pitched roof with unventilated insulation assembly between rafters*
Source: GreenSpec.

whilst preventing the ingress of water in its liquid state or infiltration air. Moisture passing through the breather membrane is dispersed through the ventilated cavity formed by counter battens over the rafters. The water vapour resistance for breather membranes suitable for pitched roofing is specified by BS 5250:2002 at less than 0.25 MNs/g.

Loft insulation

Adding layers of loft insulation over or between the joists may be the simplest and cheapest way of enhancing the insulation of an existing roof.

The traditional 'cold roof' or 'loft' found in most existing pitch-roofed buildings allows moist air from inside the building to diffuse through the ceiling into the loft space from where it is removed by cross-ventilation (see Figure 3.1.18). When laying additional insulation over the existing loft, note the following:

- A ventilation path of at least 25 mm in width is required between the insulation and the underside of the sarking at the eaves.
- Holes and gaps in the ceiling should be sealed to restrict the amount of moist air entering the roof space.
- Moisture within the loft space is prevented from penetrating the roof finish by a high-moisture-resistance sarking.
- For roofs over 35° pitch, or over 10 m span, ridge ventilation is required, equivalent to a continuous 5 mm gap along the full length of the ridge.

Ventilated or cold lofts tend to become dirtier over time than unventilated roofs and the risk of condensation is higher should the vents become blocked. On the other hand, damaged vents may allow infestation from wasps or bees, and even allow nesting birds or bats to make their homes in the loft space. More seriously, if squirrels can gain entry, then there is the potential for damage to electrical wiring which could result in a roof fire.

An unventilated pitched roof with insulation above and between the joists incorporates a breathable sarking beneath the roof finish and a moisture

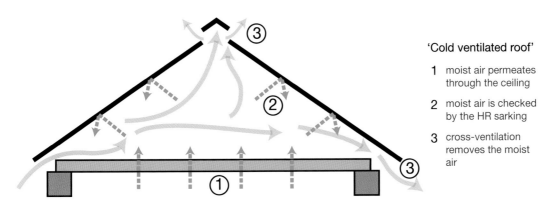

'Cold ventilated roof'

1 moist air permeates through the ceiling

2 moist air is checked by the HR sarking

3 cross-ventilation removes the moist air

Figure 3.1.18 *Principles of insulating a ventilated roof*
Source: GreenSpec.

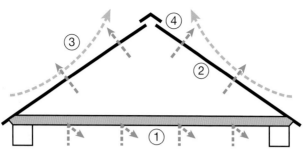

'Cold un-ventilated roof'

1 moist air is checked
   by well-wealed ceiling

2 moist air is diffused
   through LR sarking

3 external ventilation
   removes the moist air

4 5 mm ventilation gap
   if required by BS 5250

Figure 3.1.19 *Principles of an unventilated roof*
Source: GreenSpec.

resistant layer beneath the ceiling insulation (see Figure 3.1.19). This will normally require major refurbishment of the roof but the result is likely to provide significantly lower air leakage through the ceiling than the ventilated option.

A U-value of 0.15 W/m²K or less can be achieved relatively easily by laying a combined thickness of 300 mm of mineral wool or loose-fill cellulose (recycled paper) insulation, for example, over and between the joists (see Figure 3.1.20). If a solid loft floor is required for access or storage, then it might be necessary to fix battens above the joists to the full depth of the insulation on which to fix flooring. Alternatively, rigid laminated chipboard insulation panels can be used to form a floor by fixing above the joists.

Flat roofs

Though a very common and cheap form of construction, flat roofing is prone to significant defects such as leakage, component decay, condensation and, in the more extreme cases, structural failure. Millions of pounds a year are spent on the refurbishment of flat roofing. This might involve simply patching, re-coating or re-covering through to the more comprehensive stripping off and replacement of the entire roof. Figure 3.1.21 shows a typical re-covering of a flat roof using a synthetic rubber material (EPDM, ethylene propolene diene monomer).

As with pitched roofs, insulation can be located either above or below the main fabric element – usually timber or concrete. Many of the older roofs that experience problems with condensation have internal insulation. Known as a 'cold roof', similar conditions prevail to the ventilated pitched roof referred to above. However, with a flat roof construction there is little space for the moist air that permeates through the insulation from the space below to be carried away, hence condensation has been a common problem within this air gap.

Figures 3.1.22 and 3.1.23 show typical arrangements for externally insulating a flat roof. Similar principles apply to both concrete and timber roofs. In most cases existing roofs will require external finishes to be removed and a foam insulation applied with an external membrane, such as the EPDM shown in Figure 3.1.21. When this layer forms the upper layer of the roof as in Figure 3.1.22, the material must not only be resistant to moisture penetration but, as is the case for EPDM, to ultraviolet light, mechanical damage and thermal stress. Other materials that are used to provide an external waterproof layer are:

Figure 3.1.20 *Typical loose-fill cellulose retrofit*
Source: Excel Fibre Technology – Warmcel Insulation.

- TPO (thermoplastic olefin), a cold-formed synthetic rubber membrane, similar to EPDM;
- bitumen membrane reinforced with APP (atactic polypropylene) which has to be hot formed;
- bitumen membrane reinforced with SBS (styrene butadiene styrene) which can be hot or cold formed.

In an inverted warm roof the insulation is placed above a combined vapour control layer and waterproofing membrane. The insulation effectively protects this membrane from thermal stress, ultraviolet light and mechanical damage. The insulation is prevented from lifting by adding ballast or paving slabs.

Thermal mass and phase change materials

Older buildings that have not undergone extensive internal renovation are frequently thermally massive, with large areas of dense plastered masonry walls, for example. Before there was a need to conceal services above false ceilings or

Figure 3.1.21 *Example of flat roof refurbishment*

Source: www.permaroofing.co.uk.

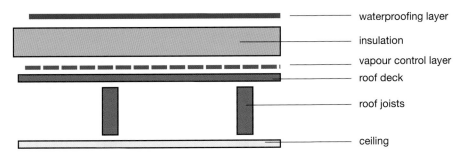

Figure 3.1.22 *'Warm' flat timber roof*
Source: GreenSpec.

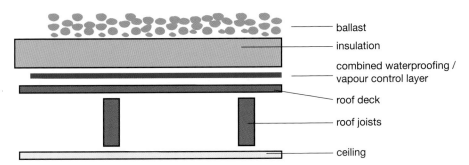

Figure 3.1.23 *Inverted warm flat concrete roof*
Source: GreenSpec.

beneath access floors, many office buildings had exposed concrete ceilings and floors, increasing the exposed thermal mass still further. These types of building respond slowly to changes in thermal stimuli and, for example, if allowed to cool at night, daytime temperatures are suppressed, thus reducing the need for artificial cooling or air conditioning. In modern buildings located in temperate climate zones this 'night cooling' has been used successfully in naturally ventilated buildings by eliminating false ceilings, leaving soffits exposed and opening windows at night during the cooling season (see Chapter 3.4 of Appleby, 2011a). Summer overheating of an existing building could be reduced to some extent by removing false ceilings during refurbishment and tidying up the services and general clutter that are normally concealed by the false ceiling. The repercussions from doing this are considerable; for example:

• Luminaires will have to be replaced with suspended fittings.
• Reverberation time of space will increase.
• Fire protection will need reviewing, with sprinklers replaced as necessary.
• Services previously located above ceiling will need concealing or rerouting.
• Underside of concrete slab may need renovating and/or resurfacing.

One alternative to exposed thermal mass is to install phase change materials (PCMs). PCMs use the characteristics of certain substances, known as eutectics, to change from solid to liquid form at normal ambient temperatures. Products are available that use micro-encapsulated PCMs in board form which can be used in place of mass. The most common materials used are inorganic salt hydrates and organic materials such as paraffin wax. Salt hydrates generally have a high heat of fusion compared with organic materials, but can suffer from supercooling which can affect the heat transfer during the cooling phase and also tend to degrade with time. Organic materials are more stable but do not perform so well thermally. Although most organic PCMs are inherently flammable, this can be corrected using suitable additives. As the material cools, it solidifies, and when heated, it liquefies and releases the energy absorbed as 'coolth'. The reverse occurs when used for solar heat absorption. For example, a typical PCM panel containing microencapsulated pure paraffin wax melts at 22°C and solidifies at 18°C. A 15 mm-thick PCM panel has a similar thermal storage performance to 90 mm of exposed concrete. A number of commercially available products are available using paraffin wax with additives such as a copolymer for use in place of plasterboard, for example.

According to a paper reporting on studies carried out at the Oak Ridge National Laboratory in the USA:

> PCM's have been tested as a thermal mass component in buildings for at least 40 years, and most studies have found that PCM's enhance building energy performance. However, problems such as high initial cost, loss of phase-change capability, corrosion, and PCM leaking have hampered widespread adoption. Paraffinic hydrocarbon PCM's generally performed well, but they increased the flammability of the building envelope. Traditionally, PCM's were used to stabilize interior building temperature. Thus the best locations for PCM were interior building surfaces – walls, ceilings, or floors.
>
> (Kosny *et al.*, 2007)

This US study demonstrated that PCMs do not have to be directly exposed to the air in the occupied space and demonstrated impressive performance under summer conditions. Hence incorporating PCMs into an existing thermally lightweight building can closely simulate performance with exposed thermal mass.

Floors

Section A3 of the CIBSE Guide provides a method for calculating U-values for floors (CIBSE, 2006c). For solid uninsulated concrete or suspended floors, the U-value depends on the exposed perimeter length divided by the floor area and the type of ground on which it sits. Generally speaking, the resistance to heat flow of concrete and a typical floor covering would be negligible and hence the U-value for a 6 m by 4 m room having a 4 m exposed wall, say, would be approximately 0.35 W/m²K if sat on clay, 0.42 W/m²K if sat on gravel or sand and 0.82 W/m²K if sat on homogeneous rock. A suspended ground floor must be ventilated to prevent condensation and the U-value will depend to some extent on the area of ventilation opening over the length of perimeter wall (α). Generally α will be no greater than 0.003 m²/m.

Insulation can be located either above or beneath the floor, or at the edge of exposed perimeters.

Figures 3.1.24 and 3.1.25 show the main options for concrete and suspended timber floors. The latter also includes access floors that may be adopted to contain services under an office floor.

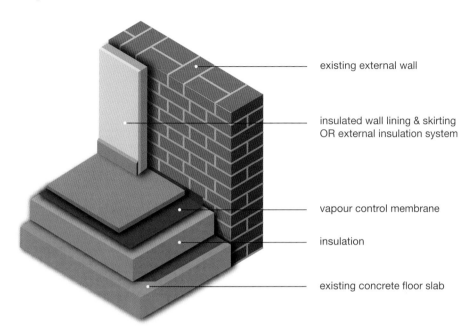

existing external wall

insulated wall lining & skirting OR external insulation system

vapour control membrane

insulation

existing concrete floor slab

Figure 3.1.24 *Insulation over concrete floor*
Source: GreenSpec.

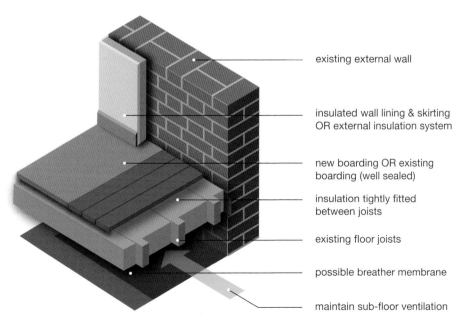

existing external wall

insulated wall lining & skirting OR external insulation system

new boarding OR existing boarding (well sealed)

insulation tightly fitted between joists

existing floor joists

possible breather membrane

maintain sub-floor ventilation

Figure 3.1.25 *Insulation under suspended timber floor*
Source: GreenSpec.

The options for retrofitting will depend on the type of floor existing and the level of disruption and replacement of existing fabric that is acceptable. For example, it is unlikely that a refurbishment would require the breaking up and removal of an existing uninsulated concrete ground floor, followed by further excavation to facilitate the installation of underfloor insulation, and the casting of a new concrete floor. On the other hand, the major refurbishment of an existing office building that has sufficient headroom or in which new floor slabs are to be laid may incorporate new access flooring which can incorporate insulation within the ground-floor void.

Problems and factors to take into account are:

- Insulation laid on top of an existing floor must be able to take the impact and point loads associated with the activities expected. Though seemingly a simple option, raising the floor level through adding insulation will usually require doors to be modified, as well as skirting boards, power sockets, fitted kitchens, WCs, radiators and other fixtures to be removed and re-fixed. Other problems might include unequal step heights at staircases and the raising of step heights at external doors.
- Suspended timber ground floors, on the other hand, can be easily upgraded. Foam insulation slabs can be friction-fitted between joists from above against timber bearings nailed to the sides of the joists. Mineral wool quilts can be installed upon mesh or netting suspended between and/or below the joists. Blown insulation, on the other hand, can be contained by mesh or boarding beneath the joists.
- Timber floors tend to suffer from air leakage. Where old floorboards are relaid, or new ones installed, careful attention is needed to ensure that all joints between individual boards and between the skirting board and floor are adequately sealed.
- Insulation should be taken right up to the edge of the floor and any space close to the outside wall filled with insulation to avoid any gaps. Also gaps between the insulation and the underside of the floor should be sealed.
- The insulation must not interfere with the sub-floor ventilation by blocking the air bricks in the outside wall, nor bridge the damp-proof course.
- A fire-resistant board should be fixed to the underside of the joists if the floor is above a garage or basement.
- The thickness of insulation required to meet Passivhaus standards will depend on the ground type and exposed perimeter-to-area ratio, but typically, for a suspended timber or access floor, around 200 mm of mineral wool or polystyrene or 150 mm of polyurethane or phenolic foam should achieve a U-value of 0.15 W/m^2K for a 6 m by 4 m room with 4 m exposed perimeter.

Air tightness

In the UK, air leakage rate is expressed as a flow of outdoor air into a building in m^3/h per unit gross internal floor area at a pressure of 50 Pa. For a floor-to-ceiling height of 2.5 m one air change per hour is equivalent to an air leakage rate of 2.5 $m^3/h/m^2$. Part L of the Building Regulations requires a maximum air leakage rate of 10 $m^3/h/m^2$, or four air changes per hour (h^{-1}) for a room of the same height. The 50 Pa refers to the pressure at which a building has to be maintained when subject to an air tightness test with all ventilation openings closed or taped up (CIBSE, 2000). In reality, a building will rarely be subject to such high pressures or experience the air change rates that occur during its air tightness test. For example, Ridley estimated from his modelling of a typical house that with a 3 $m^3/h/m^2$ air tightness (1.2 h^{-1} for 2.5 m ceiling height) measured at 50 Pa, the infiltration rate, which varies with wind force and occupant behaviour, is likely to be 0.4 h^{-1} or below for 48% of the time (Ridley, 2009).

Infiltration is a major source of energy loss in existing buildings. Because older buildings are frequently better built than those developed during the boom years following the Second World War, they tend to suffer from less infiltration. Since the introduction of insulation standards in the UK, there has been a marked reduction in heat loss through the fabric. However, until air testing became mandatory for non-residential buildings in 2006, there was no commensurate improvement in infiltration losses. Hence it is not unusual for the infiltration heat loss from post-war buildings to be 35–40 per cent of the total.

When refurbishing an existing building it is only possible to address air leakage properly and get anywhere near the Passivhaus standard if the entire envelope is being insulated and refurbished. The key to achieving a high standard of insulation and air tightness is to ensure continuity of insulation and airtight seal around the entire building envelope, while avoiding condensation and air quality problems. This is much easier to achieve for a new build project, but a refurbishment requires a similar attention to detail and quality control during construction. Wherever there is a penetration through the envelope between a heated and unheated space, a seal needs to be formed that maintains continuity with the impermeable layer formed by the fabric. Every joint that will be subject to movement must incorporate inherent flexibility and not open up when exposed to changing temperatures, moisture, sunlight, traffic or wind pressure, where applicable.

US retrofit insulation standards

The Federal Housing Agency PowerSaver Home Energy Improvement Standards refer to the US Energy Star Recommended Levels of Insulation.[11] Because of the large range of climates experienced in the USA, these recommend different levels of insulation for different climate zones, which run from Zone 1 covering the likes of Hawaii and the southern tip of Florida, to Zone 8 in the coldest parts of Alaska. Recommendations are given for those planning on retrofitting insulation to the roof, walls and floors of wood-framed buildings. For example, for a building in Zones 5 through to 8, which span most of the middle and northern States of the US, the recommendations are for insulation levels of R49 to R60 in an uninsulated loft. The R-value refers to the resistance of the insulation in hft^2degF/Btu. For example, R49 is equivalent to a conductance of 0.116 W/m^2K and would require 350 mm of mineral wool or 160 mm of phenolic foam at k values of 0.04 and 0.018 W/mK respectively. R60, on the other hand, is equivalent to 0.095 W/m^2K and would require 420 mm of mineral wool or 190 mm phenolic foam.

The Energy Star recommendation for timber framed walls for the same Zones is to blow insulation into the cavity and apply R5 to R6 insulation to inside or out, which works out at approximately 40 mm of mineral wool or equivalent.

Where floors are accessible for adding insulation, Energy Star recommend insulation levels of R25 to R30, or 180 mm to 210 mm of mineral wool respectively.

Courtyards and atria

One method of improving the performance of a complex multi-faceted building is to reduce the area of external surfaces by converting courtyards or niches into atria. This works provided that the resultant daylight levels in spaces bordering the atrium do not fall to a level that results in carbon emissions associated with increased artificial lighting usage offsetting the savings in heating-associated carbon emissions. Adding an atrium may also render natural ventilation inadequate for controlling summertime temperatures, necessitating mechanical ventilation or air conditioning.

On the other hand, atria can be designed to both provide a stack for solar-assisted natural ventilation and provide solar protection to the spaces bordering it. They can also create a sheltered meeting space or entrance and enliven a neglected courtyard (see case history for Indiana State University on p. 141).

Case histories

Mayville Community Centre, Islington, London

The award-winning Mayville Community Centre (Figure 3.1.26) was the first certified Passivhaus non-domestic retrofit in the UK. The building achieved full Passivhaus Certification in December 2011:

> The Mayville Community Centre was able to surpass the Passivhaus standard because of rigorous detailing by Bere architects, a high level of support and on-site training and continual monitoring of construction detailing throughout the build process, which were particularly important in meeting the Passivhaus air tightness requirements.
>
> Built circa 1890, the centre is located within the Mayville estate in Islington, London, ranked in the top 10% most deprived areas in London. The centre provides a focal point for the local residents as a valuable community resource.[12]

One key objective of the refurbishment was to maximize the efficiency of investment by providing more usable space of a higher quality than previously within the original building footprint. The building fabric has been improved considerably in order to reduce the building's energy consumption and meet the onerous Passivhaus standard. 'The finished building is predicted to consume 90%–94% less energy than before the refurbishment' (ibid.).

Reduced energy consumption and associated CO_2 emissions have been achieved through excellent levels of insulation, ensuring draught-free construction, triple-glazed windows and integrated renewables. All junction details were designed to prevent or minimize thermal bridges, ensure continuity of insulation and reduce air leakage. Figure 3.1.27 shows the results of energy

Figure 3.1.26 *Mayville Community Centre Passivhaus refurbishment*
Source: Mark Martines.

monitoring between November 2011 and February 2012 compared with the same months prior to refurbishment.

On-site energy generation has been made possible through the retrofitting of 126 m^2 of photovoltaic panels generating 18 kWp of electricity, 3 m^2 of solar thermal panels providing domestic hot water and a ground-source heat pump that is employed for space heating. Other sustainability features include rainwater harvesting, two 'green' roofs planted with native meadow flowers and ecologically sensitive gardens for community food growing projects.

Grove Cottage, Hereford

Grove Cottage was the first refurbishment in the UK to be formally certified under the Passivhaus Institute's EnerPHit refurbishment standard.[13] Designed by Simmonds Mills Architects, Grove Cottage is a solid-walled Victorian townhouse dating from 1869 that was extended and refurbished using the Association of Energy-Conscious Builders' (AECB) CarbonLite principles and aiming for Passivhaus levels of energy performance.

The whole house's CO$_2$ emissions for cooking, space and water heating energy have been reduced by 80 per cent compared to the average measured

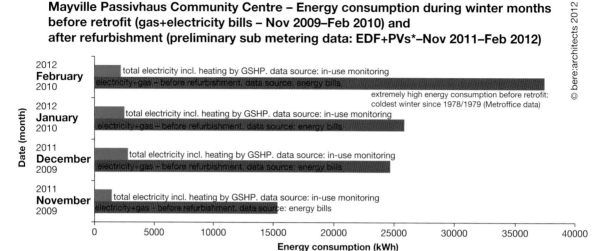

Mayville Passivhaus Community Centre – Energy consumption during winter months before retrofit (gas+electricity bills – Nov 2009–Feb 2010) and after refurbishment (preliminary sub metering data: EDF+PVs*–Nov 2011–Feb 2012)

© bere:architects 2012

* data collected before PV export sub-meter installed; assumes all electricty generated by PVs was used in the billing, nothing exported back to grid

Figure 3.1.27 *Mayville Community Centre: energy consumption monitoring results*

Source: bere:architects.

performance of a typical UK house of the same size. Energy performance and comfort monitored between 2009 and 2011 found that around 80 per cent less gas was used and 45 per cent less electricity than an equivalent-sized home, while internal temperatures remained at around 21°C when required during the heating season.

This was achieved by upgrading insulation levels to 400 mm in the roof, 250 mm on the walls and retrofitting triple-glazed windows, while an airtight-ness level (n_{50}) of 0.79 h^{-1} was achieved through attention to detailing junctions and penetrations through the external fabric.

The Empire State Building

The iconic Empire State Building (Figure 3.1.28) has been subject to a major refurbishment programme of energy-saving measures (Pearson, 2011). This has included retrofitting chillers, rationalization of variable air volume air conditioning, optimizing ventilation controls, improving energy management and enhancing existing windows. Total costs are likely to reach around $13.2 million with a resultant reduction in annual energy bills of $4.4 million, corresponding to an energy saving of 38 per cent.[14]

The 6,500 existing windows in its façade were upgraded by removing the sashes from their frames and replacing them with temporary windows. The windows were taken to a workshop established on the fifth floor, where they were dismantled and cleaned. A new super-insulating glass unit was created by taking one of the original panes of clear uncoated glass, laying a warm edge spacer on it and then a suspended low-emissivity film to help reduce solar gain and heat flow.

Another edge spacer was added so that the outer glass could be laid on top, creating a triple-glazed unit from the reused components, to the same dimensions

Figure 3.1.28 *The Empire State Building*
Source: Thinkstock.

as the original. The assembly was then baked in an oven for about 90 minutes to shrink the film, turning it taut and translucent. The process improves the window's thermal performance from a U-value of 5 W/m^2 K to 1.25 W/m^2 K, while halving solar gain.

See also the case histories at the end of Chapter 3.2.

Indiana State University College of Education: University Hall refurbishment

The refurbishment of University Hall at Indiana State University was completed in the summer of 2009. This project involved the renovation of a 70-year-old rectangular building with a large interior courtyard into a state-of-the-art facility with the intention of attracting incoming students, alumni and community leaders. The existing building made considerable use of natural light and ventilation in occupied spaces. The renovations were designed to retain these features as well as incorporating other sustainable design features.

One of the most visible improvements to the facility is the conversion of the central courtyard into an enclosed atrium space. This allows the 6,900-square feet, three-and-a-half-storey space to be used throughout the year for events and daily interaction. Large skylights have been incorporated into the new atrium roof to maintain the natural daylighting and allow plants to be located in the space.

To maximize natural light and energy performance in the atrium, a focused study was conducted during design. The goals for the atrium daylighting were to do the following:

- Provide sufficient quantity and quality of light into the space to promote healthy plant growth.
- Provide the majority of light required for plant growth from daylight instead of electric lights.
- Control the entry of the direct sunlight particularly during spring, summer and fall months.
- Maximize winter solar heat gains.
- Minimize daylight glare in offices bordering the atrium, suitable for laptop usage.
- Provide a uniform distribution of daylight.

The result was a series of triangular-shaped skylights designed to specifically meet the goals described using the angles of the skylights and ceramic frits on the glass.

Crossbank and Summervail Houses in Oldham[15]

Typical of many blocks of flats built in the 1960s and 1970s, thermal performance of the walls and windows was very poor. Wall U-values were around 1.5 W/m²K and windows were single glazed with very high air leakage. The flats were refurbished in the early noughties, using Dryvit polystyrene 'Outsulation' and UPVC double glazing. This external cladding system reduced wall U-values to 0.28 W/m²K and when combined with a halving of window U-values and major improvements in air tightness, carbon emissions and running costs were reduced significantly.

FACING PAGE AND ABOVE

Figure 3.1.29 *Crossbank and Summervail Houses, Oldham: before and after refurbishment*
Source: Dryvit Ltd.

3.2

Retrofit of building services and controls

Introduction

A building that has been renovated to minimize heat loss and infiltration, while avoiding the risk of overheating in summer, will require very little in the way of environmental services. For example, a building located in the south of England and renovated to Passivhaus or EnerPHit standards is likely to be heated by its internal heat sources for most of the winter. In fact, the main problem will be to avoid these same sources causing overheating, even during the winter months. Many existing buildings obtain enough air from outside through leakage to meet the hygiene and comfort requirements of their occupants, even when windows are fully closed. Once this source of fortuitous ventilation air is cut off, through Passivhaus or similar air tightness measures, ventilation will have to enter via alternative routes. Trickle vents would allow an uncontrolled variable rate of ventilation depending primarily on wind pressure and direction. If these vents are closed through the intervention of occupants, then no outside air would enter the building, apart from that entering through opening and closing of doors to outside. When this leads to discomfort, occupants are likely to open windows, allowing significantly more outdoor air to enter the building than if trickle vents had been provided. See also the CarbonLite report comparing natural ventilation with mechanical ventilation with heat recovery (MVHR) in a Passivhaus house.[1]

Existing buildings may be heated from radiators, natural convectors or some form of mechanical ventilation, in some cases via an air-conditioning system that also provides cooling and humidity control. Traditionally, where there is a significant winter heat loss through windows, along with draught from leakage and cold surfaces, radiators have been placed at the perimeter to deal with the heat loss, offset the downdraught and counter some of the radiant loss from occupants' skin to cold window surfaces. Once heat loss and internal surface temperatures no longer present these challenges, then perimeter radiators will be surplus to requirement. Indeed, the challenge becomes one of maintaining good air quality and preventing overheating. Heating will be required primarily for bringing the room temperature up to a comfortable level after a cold weekend or Christmas break, for example. Hence the dominant need will be for ventilation and mitigating against overheating, but ideally without creating major carbon emissions associated with refrigeration-based comfort cooling.

This chapter will examine the options for the sustainable retrofit of building services, either as part of a refurbishment strategy or by upgrading existing plant or services, for residential or non-residential buildings, and applying the principles of Passivhaus, EnerPHit or similar. Here we will focus on heating, ventilation and air conditioning (HVAC) and their control, as well as lighting, white goods, refrigeration and other services. Retrofitting of water services will be covered in Chapter 3.5. Although renewable technologies, such as biomass boilers and solar hot water panels can be considered as building services, we will examine them, together with photovoltaic panels, wind turbines, etc., in Chapter 3.3.

Residential heating and ventilation

In the on-line guidance on 'housing refurbishment/retrofit' provided by GreenSpec, it states:

> In older houses around 20% of the energy lost from space heating is through ventilation. Within more modern, well-insulated houses where less heat is lost through other means, the [proportion] increases to above 35%. This loss of heat occurs through the opening of windows and doors, but also through the more chronic uncontrolled ventilation provided by gaps around windows, doors and services penetrations, airbricks and chimney flues, etc. If this rate of heat loss is to be significantly reduced, other mechanisms of ventilation have to be introduced.[2]

In Chapter 2.1 we have already seen how the fabric can be renovated to reduce this air leakage. However, in order to maintain a satisfactory indoor air quality and comply with Building Regulations Part F requirements in England and Wales, in the absence of trickle vents, some form of mechanical ventilation is required (HMG, 2010). Approved Document F sets out minimum ventilation rates for new buildings that are applicable to refurbishment involving upgrading fabric performance of existing buildings. It sets out minimum rates for individual rooms, such as kitchens, bathrooms and sanitary accommodation, for intermittent or continuous operation, as well as whole-house minima, based on number of bedrooms or internal floor area. The minimum whole-dwelling rate is 0.3 litres/s per m^2 internal floor area, which is equivalent to 0.43 air changes per hour (ach^{-1}) for a ceiling height of 2.5 m. This compares to the minimum rate required by the Passivhaus standard of 0.3 ach^{-1}. On the other hand, Approved Document F also specifies minimum rates for a kitchen of 13 litres/s when extracted continuously via a canopy located between 650 mm and 750 mm above the hob, as well as 8 litres/s from a bathroom and 6 litres/s from sanitary accommodation. So a dwelling with one of each of these would have 27 litres/s extracted from these rooms, or 0.6 ach^{-1} for a floor area of 80 m^2 and ceiling height of 2.5 m. Approved Document F also requires that each room can be purged at a rate of 4 ach^{-1}, when required, to remove excessive heat, moisture or pollution. Where possible, this can be achieved through opening windows, otherwise the ventilation system should ideally be sized to purge at its highest setting. For example, extracting 8 litres/s from an internal bathroom measuring 4 m by 3 m by 2.5 m will move around one air change per hour, so the extractor fan will have to be able to operate at 32 litres/s during the purge cycle. Approved Document F is vague on this issue, however, and achieving such a boost with standard equipment may not be realistic. It is interesting to note that some

Figure 3.2.1 *MVHR unit in roof space*
Source: Glow-worm.

mechanical ventilation heat recovery (MVHR) units are provided with a multi-speed fan enabling a boost function to be switched on manually. However, heat recovery will not function efficiently during purge mode, and noise levels will be significantly higher than normal running mode.

One unit manufactured for the UK market quotes its maximum rate as the purge setting of 100 per cent, with normal rate at 30 per cent, 50 per cent as boost and 20 per cent low. If there are habitable rooms that do not have openable windows, then the designer will have to decide whether to select a unit to achieve the desired purge rate, or to base the unit selection on the normal rate, meeting the sum total of the minimum extract rates required for kitchen, bathroom, sanitary accommodation and utility rooms. Rather than installing an oversized MVHR unit, it may be more cost effective to install a separate extract fan for each internal room concerned. On the other hand, the purge setting may be useful for increasing ventilation rates when occupancy increases temporarily, such as during a social gathering.

The MVHR unit incorporates a heat exchanger to allow heat in the extract air to be transferred to incoming air. Efficiencies of heat exchange are quoted typically at between 90 and 95 per cent, which compares with a best practice standard set by the Energy-Saving Trust of 85 per cent (EST, 2006a). The air is supplied at the same temperature throughout the house, regardless of differences in heat load in individual rooms or different requirements for thermal comfort. For example, CIBSE recommend winter 'operative' temperatures[3] of between 20°C and 22°C for a bathroom, 17°C and 19°C for bedrooms and kitchens, and between 22°C and 23°C for living rooms (CIBSE, 2006c). These are based on a predicted mean vote (PMV) of +/−0.25 at typical clothing (clo) and activity (met) levels for each room using the methodology set out in ISO 7730 (BSI, 2005). It is interesting to note that the Passivhaus Planning Package (PHPP) assumes a constant indoor temperature in winter of 20°C, but this cannot be guaranteed without individual thermostatically controlled heaters in each room. As can be seen from Figure 3.2.1, normal practice for a dwelling served from an MVHR unit is to extract air from the rooms containing sources of moisture, heat and odour, such as the bathroom and kitchen, and to supply air into living rooms and bedrooms. Hence air will transfer from the latter to the former via undercut doors or air transfer grilles. This should result in the supply air cooling if there is a net heat loss in the rooms served. So by the time it is drawn into the kitchen, bathroom, etc., the air could be at close to 20°C. If there is cooking taking place in the kitchen, for example, room temperatures are likely to rise above CIBSE comfort levels, although occupants can of course adjust their clothing to compensate.

If overheating is to be avoided, it is very important that the MVHR unit incorporates a damper that allows for extract air to bypass the heat exchanger when the supply air exceeds a temperature that is useful. This should be achieved automatically, normally through an outside sensor, mounted in the shade, that switches the unit to bypass when the outside air temperature is the same as indoors, say, 20°C.

Of course, there is an energy penalty for using MVHR since the dual fans required for extract and supply have electrical demand at all times during occupancy. The magnitude of this demand will depend on the volume flow rates and pressure drops through the two systems. The former depends on the size of the dwelling and the number of rooms requiring extract, while the latter depends on the length and roughness of the ductwork and pressure drop through grease and supply air filters. According to guidance from the Energy-Saving Trust:

> [MVHR] systems can provide the ideal ventilation system, delivering the required ventilation rate almost independently of the weather conditions. However, the energy-saving benefits are only realized for airtight properties (<5 m³/h/m² at 50 Pa) when almost all ventilation air passes through the heat exchanger.
>
> (EST, 2006a)

The Passivhaus standard specifies a target maximum air leakage rate of 0.6 h⁻¹, which corresponds to 1.5 m³/h/m², at 50 Pa, for a floor-to-ceiling height of 2.5 m, which means that MVHR is suited to Passivhaus-compliant dwellings.

The EST gives a recommended specific fan power for best practice of 1 W per litre/s 'when running at each of its settings'. This is half the default figure used in SAP (Standard Assessment Procedure) calculations for UK Building

Regulations and compares with a maximum of 1.62 W/litre/s (0.45 Wh/m^3) specified in the Passivhaus standard. In order to achieve these low values, the system must be designed and installed without sharp bends in the ductwork, sized to operate at 2 to 2.5 m/s under normal air flows, and with filters and heat exchangers that are selected with optimum efficiency against pressure drop. Pressure drops increase as filters become soiled, hence they need replacing or cleaning two or three times a year. This imposes a maintenance burden on the householder that is outside the control of the designer. Historically, for ease of installation, flexible ducting has been used to connect between the MVHR unit and outlets or risers. If not fully stretched, the pressure drop through flexible ducting increases dramatically and, if badly kinked or compressed, by up to ten times. This can badly impact on both the balance of the system and the performance of the fans. For this reason the installation guidance for MVHR in Appendix Q to SAP states that 'flexible ducting should be avoided',[4] but then goes on to say that, if installed, it should be stretched taut, not be allowed to sag, and that all bends should have a minimum radius the same as that of the duct cross-section, or greater. All ductwork should be insulated and intake ducts carrying cold air protected against condensation.

It is important that supply air filters be installed upstream of heat exchangers in order that heat transfer surfaces be kept clean, which means that these filters may be exposed to external air temperatures. When these are well below zero, there is a risk that the filters will freeze and reduce air flows sufficiently to trip out the supply fan motor. This risk is reduced provided the MVHR is installed in a 'warm' loft space or basement and the intake duct is of sufficient length to allow some pre-heating of incoming air. Some manufacturers supply electric frost coils to temper incoming air, although this will impact on the carbon efficiency of the unit.

Once an existing loft is insulated, very often there may be limited space available for installing an MVHR unit, hence it is essential to ensure that there is sufficient space available to allow regular access to the unit for replacing or cleaning filters and dismantling the unit to clean internal surfaces from time to time.

Outdoor air intakes and exhaust outlets should be designed so that strong winds do not interfere with the operation of the ventilation system. If a suitable sheltered location is not available, then omnidirectional cowls should be used or a split ductwork connected to openings facing in opposite directions. Intakes and outlets must also be positioned so that discharge air does not get drawn back into the dwelling. Intakes and outlets must be designed to prevent the ingress of rain, birds and insects, and must not be located so that they allow entry of polluted air. The unit should incorporate good quality dampers that shut when the fans are switched off so that air cannot enter the house through the system. Gravity-operated non-return flaps are not up to the task since they tend to leak when shut.

With air being supplied into bedrooms and living rooms directly from the MVHR unit, it is important that noise transmitted from the supply fan does not exceed acceptable levels, which are NR 25 and NR 30 respectively (CIBSE, 2006c). Units should be selected with this in mind, but it may be necessary to use acoustically lined ductwork for supplying air to bedrooms and living rooms (see Chapter 3.4 for more details).

Each room is connected separately to the MVHR unit. With fans running continuously, this means that odours generated in kitchens or sanitary accommodation are unlikely to permeate through the rest of the house.

Where it is decided that individual control of room temperature is required and/or sub-Passivhaus levels of insulation are to be achieved, resulting in periods when recovered heat from the MVHR cannot deal with heat loss, then thermostatically controlled radiators in each room may be installed. These may be served with low-pressure hot water from a boiler or heat pump that also provides domestic hot water. Alternatively electric panel heaters can be installed.

With such a low heat loss the size of radiator required will be tiny, typically between 300 W and 400 W for a large living room. With heat emissions from televisions, hi-fi equipment, lighting and people, this heat loss will be offset for much of the time in most households. Bedrooms will have lower casual gains, although lower operative temperatures are acceptable.

At the time of writing, the smallest gas-fired combination boilers available for the residential market are capable of generating around 20 kW. If installed in a Passivhaus dwelling, they will primarily be used for domestic hot water, with heating mode mostly being used for start-up in mid-winter.

Rather than radiators, another option might be to install underfloor heating. This requires much lower water temperatures than radiators, with a maximum floor surface temperature of 28°C (CIBSE, 2006c) and hence can be served from ground-coupled or air-to-air heat pumps and solar 'combisystems' (see Chapter 3.3). This is an expensive option, but could be integrated with the works required to retrofit ground-floor insulation. Underfloor heating usually comprises polyethylene pipework embedded in a screed that may either be laid on a concrete floor (Figure 3.2.2) or between floor joists (Figure 3.2.3). Because of the slow response of this type of heating, it is not suitable for dwellings where occupancy is unpredictable or heat loads vary rapidly.

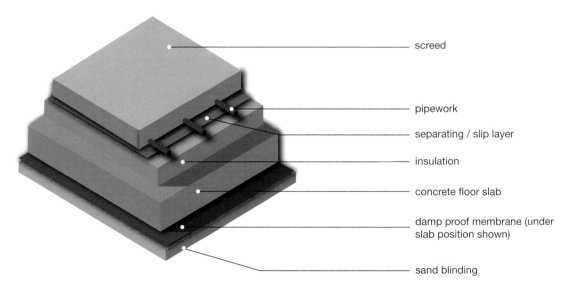

— screed
— pipework
— separating / slip layer
— insulation
— concrete floor slab
— damp proof membrane (under slab position shown)
— sand blinding

Figure 3.2.2 *Underfloor heating: arrangement with concrete substrate*
Source: GreenSpec.

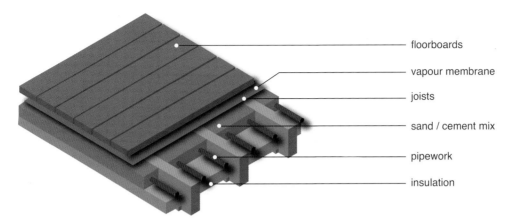

floorboards

vapour membrane

joists

sand / cement mix

pipework

insulation

Figure 3.2.3 *Underfloor heating: arrangement with suspended timber floor*
Source: GreenSpec.

If it is viable to retain existing radiators, then it may be possible to achieve the desired output by supplying them with water at between 35°C and 40°C from a heat pump, which will reduce output to approximately one third of that achieved from operating a boiler at maximum flow and return temperatures.

However, the decision on primary heating source must address the domestic hot water (DHW) demand, which is likely to be much higher than heating energy, both instantaneously and over the whole year. Crucially, DHW must be heated to at least 60°C to avoid legionellosis risk and hence it must be possible to take low-grade heat from sources, such as heat pumps and solar hot water panels (see Chapter 3.3), and store and deliver it at this temperature. This will require a vertical DHW storage cylinder having dual heat exchangers: the lower fed with water from the low temperature source, the upper being either an electric immersion heater or a coil fed from a conventional boiler (see Figure 3.2.4). The demand for domestic hot water should also be addressed by the refurbishment process and this will be examined further in Chapter 3.5.

MVHR and refurbishing multi-residential buildings

When retrofitting apartment buildings, finding space for MVHR may be more problematic than for individual houses. However, every case is different, so providing general guidance is difficult. As can be seen from Figure 3.2.5, units can be installed within individual apartments, provided there is a suitable cupboard or void that can be linked to the distribution ductwork. Alternative locations include lofts and basements, provided there are vertical routes available for ductwork.

As with all ventilation systems serving individual apartments, whether new or existing, the biggest challenge is likely to be finding suitable locations for intake and discharge. This would normally involve running ducts to external walls, avoiding short circuiting between intake openings, discharge openings, and boiler flues where applicable. Terminals also need to be designed to prevent

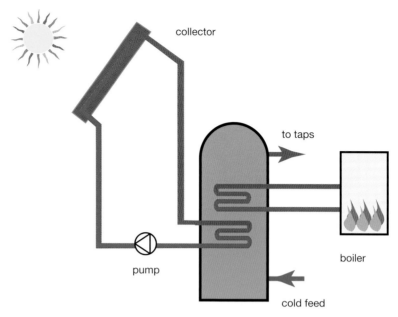

Figure 3.2.4 *Simplified schematic for solar hot water systems*
Source: GreenSpec.

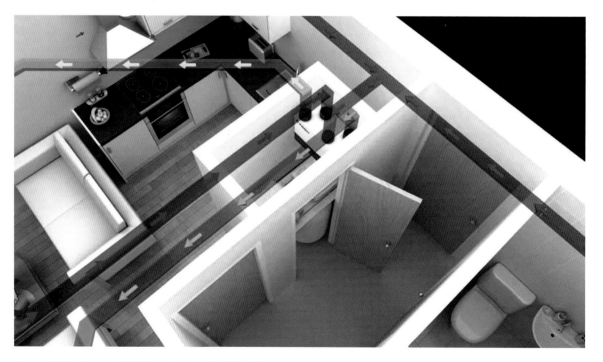

Figure 3.2.5 *Compact MVHR unit serving individual flat*
Source: Titon HRV1 Q Plus.

wind pressure interference and to avoid spoiling the external appearance of the building. One solution is to integrate intakes into the underside of existing balconies, where present.

Where there is an existing loft space, MVHR units could be located immediately above the apartments they serve. Although it may be tempting to serve multiple apartments from a single MVHR, this creates a route for both the spread of fire and the transfer of noise between apartments. These risks can be mitigated using fire dampers and sound attenuators respectively, but they would add to the complexity of the retrofit. Furthermore this option would remove the capability of controlling the fans from an individual apartment since any change in ventilation rate would impact on other apartments served.

MVHR, EnerPHit and retrofitting renewables

For those targeting zero- or near-zero-carbon refurbishment, it will be necessary to go beyond meeting the insulation and air tightness requirements of the Passivhaus EnerPHit standard. This means developing strategies for heating domestic water and catering for a portion of electrical demand from renewable sources of energy. We will be reviewing these technologies in Chapter 3.3; however, here we will look at the specific issues around retrofitting them to super-insulated dwellings and apartment buildings ventilated via MVHR systems.

For most existing dwellings the feasibility of solar hot water panels and photovoltaic cells will depend in part on the type and orientation of roof. Flat roofs offer the greatest flexibility, allowing panels to be installed at optimum inclination and orientation to the sun. As can be seen in Figures 3.3.1 and 3.3.8, in both cases, optimum orientation is south and optimum angle of inclination to the horizontal is between 30° and 40°. These apply in the south of England, but will vary with latitude.

The amount of energy that can be obtained from solar hot water panels will depend in part on the area installed and in part on the efficiency of the collector and storage apparatus, but it is limited in most locations by the availability of sunlight, which is dependent on solar geometry and cloud cover. This means that in the south of England, for example, the maximum energy that can be derived from solar hot water panels is typically between 50 and 70 per cent of the total hot water demand.

With photovoltaics (PVs), on the other hand, it is generally not feasible (or necessary) to store the electricity generated from the sun. This is because electricity generated can either be used on site or fed back to the grid. The primary economic driver for this is the rate that energy companies can pay as a feed-in tariff (see Chapter 1.2). If the return on investment is good enough, then the only limit on the economic area of panels will be the space available.

Unfortunately because of the vagaries of solar radiation and the demand for electricity and hot water during hours of darkness and cloud cover, it is not possible to exactly match demand with generation for either solar panels or PV. There are a number of definitions coined for zero-carbon and zero-energy homes and buildings. The requirement for Level 6 in the Code for Sustainable Homes (CSH) incorporates 'unregulated' carbon emissions, including plug-in appliances that are not within the target emissions calculated for Building Regulations compliance. However, these will not be counted in the zero-carbon model used in the UK 2016 SAP calculations. The requirement for CSH Level 6 allows for the carbon emissions to be assessed over a 12-month period, so that, provided the net energy generated on site exceeds that consumed over that period, then zero carbon is achieved.

Bearing in mind the difficulty in finding enough space on an existing roof for both solar hot water and PV panels and that solar energy is so variable in many parts of the world, there may be a strong argument for considering wind turbines. In Chapter 2.6 of *Integrated Sustainable Design of Buildings* (Appleby, 2011a), it was concluded that most urban and suburban areas would be too sheltered for wind turbines, bearing in mind the likelihood that embodied carbon would be greater than that saved during the life of the turbine. Exceptions to this might include locating wind turbines atop exposed multi-storey buildings, hills or coastal stretches.

Where space heating demand is close to zero and at least 50 per cent of domestic hot water demand is offset by solar hot water panels, the feasibility of retrofitting biomass boilers for individual dwellings requires close scrutiny. If there is no space for solar hot water panels or the building is overshadowed, biomass may be worth considering, primarily for heating domestic hot water. However, biomass boilers require large storage bunkers and conventional chimneys to be taken above roof level, so the availability of suitable space is critical.

The following guidance is taken from the Scottish Passive House Centre website:[5]

The equipment must be sized appropriately to the heat load of the house. This will be defined by the 'Verification' page in the PHPP (Passivhaus Planning Package) software. In a 110 m² house with 3.6 occupants, a stove of 3 kW output would be sufficient for all space heating and DHW needs. For a small Passive House, most models will be too large, i.e. the output will be too high. Therefore suitable models have to be chosen carefully.

- A combustion air supply must be provided to any stove or boiler in a Passive House bearing in mind the level of airtightness that has to be achieved. The provision of an air supply and flue for stoves or boilers will generally not adversely impact on the airtightness or balancing of ventilation flows due to the 'closed' nature of their construction. Air required for combustion is drawn in through a relatively small diameter duct and expelled through the flue.
- A stove or boiler that directs most of the heat output to the DHW tank is essential if the hot water is to be used to heat the ventilation air. A model that simply radiates all the heat into the space in which it is located cannot generally be used for whole-house heating. Most Passive House models with a back boiler deliver 20–30% of the heat produced into the room and 70–80% to the water.
- Wood (whether logs, chipped or in pellets) is bulky and a considerable volume is required for storage, especially if it is purchased in bulk to keep costs to a minimum.
- Most wood stoves are highly efficient (up to 90%), and when burning pellets there is very little ash remaining following combustion. A flue and

a fresh-air supply (independent of the room air if placed inside the thermal envelope) will be required.

- Biomass boilers have a slow response time (i.e. they need a while to fire up and even longer to cool down). Therefore, the DHW tank or thermal store has to be certified for use with biomass boilers (these might, for example, be a vented system type). To catch the sluggish response time, and in order to make the boilers efficient, you will often find accumulator tanks, even up to 3000 litres or more! This is not a must, of course, and will have to be decided in each individual case.

See the case history for the Barbrook Passivhaus Retrofit on p. 170.

The viability of solar hot water and PVs for retrofitting multi-residential buildings will depend on the space available on the roof or elsewhere. The smaller the footprint-to-total-floor-area ratio, the less viable these options become. With PVs there is the possibility of incorporating panels into façade treatments, either as rainscreens or brises-soleil, although this tends to be more costly than roof mounting, while, when mounted vertically, output will drop by some 30 per cent from optimum, even for a southerly orientation.

Tower blocks with exposed roofs represent one of the few instances where wind turbines may be feasible in an urban location.

It is important that the renewable technology is not impacted on by existing or future neighbouring buildings. Crystalline photovoltaic panels are connected in series and if any part of the array is in shade, output drops to near zero. Output from solar hot water panels will also drop considerably if shaded. Wind turbine performance, on the other hand, will be severely impacted by obstructions upwind that reduce velocities and create eddies.

Control and metering

Controls for use by the householder must be simple, robust and easy to understand. Most householders will not be familiar with dwellings that are designed for maximum energy efficiency and windows that should be left shut during cold weather, relying on MVHR for ventilation air.

A report from the Zero-Carbon Hub (ZCH), published in 2012 in response to concerns about the quality of some MVHR installation, recommends that:

> All MVHR systems should be fitted with indicators that show they are working, and whether they are in normal or boost and/or bypass mode. There should be a clear indication, preferably both visual and audible to show when the unit is not working and when maintenance is needed.
>
> Appropriate, simple user controls should be provided in sensible, accessible locations (e.g. not tucked away awkwardly inside a cupboard). They should be easy to use, and clear and intuitive for occupants. The controls should encourage the selection of the correct operation for different external weather conditions; for example, summer bypass and frost protection.

The touch screen panel in Figure 3.2.6 shows the typical functionality available, with three fan speeds for 'normal' operation, and a further three for unoccupied, boost and purge operation. In addition, there is facility for adjusting summer

Figure 3.2.6 *Thin-film transistor (TFT) touch screen control panel for MVHR unit serving individual dwelling*

Source: Paul Heat Recovery.

bypass temperature settings and running supply fan only or extract fan only. Display panels should include warning lights indicating that the filter should be replaced or cleaned, that summer bypass is operating and frost protection is functioning, if provided.

Smart meters combine two-way communication of gas and electricity data between the consumer and the Data and Communications Company (in the UK) and provide feedback on consumption to the customer via an in-home display. As well as allowing consumers to understand how their behaviour impacts on energy consumption and providing automated billing, these also allow the energy company some degree of control over consumers' connected load, including demand management and remote disablement of supply (see also Chapter 1.2).

Lighting, white goods and other energy-saving measures

When a dwelling has been renovated to Passivhaus EnerPHit or near-zero-energy/carbon standards and DHW consumption and emissions have been minimized, the energy consumption and carbon emissions associated with lighting, white goods and other appliances become dominant. For example, the modelling exercise described in the case history in Chapter 2.4 on p. 77 indicates that around 60 per cent of post-refurbishment energy demand is associated with the supply of electricity. Refurbishment provides the opportunity to retrofit light fittings and lamps with energy-efficient products, while it may also be desirable to replace white goods and other appliances.

Tungsten lamps are steadily being replaced with compact fluorescent (CFL) as the main artificial light source. It has been speculated by some (mostly manufacturers) that lamps that use light-emitting diodes (LED) will eventually replace fluorescent lamps as the most energy-efficient and cost-effective means of lighting.[6] At the time of writing, LED 'bulbs' and spotlights are available as 'like for like' replacements for tungsten or CFL and halogen lamps respectively, but at a considerable premium. At up to 90 lumens/W the amount of light emitted by cool white LED lamps per unit of electrical power required (luminous efficacy) can be as much as 50 per cent higher than for CFL,[7] while at up to 50,000 hours, life expectancy can be five times longer. Warm white LED lamps, on the other hand, although having the same life expectancy, can have a luminous efficacy nearer to or below that for CFL. Historically LED lamps have been used primarily for spotlights or decorative lighting; however, some of the modern globe types have an upward light component similar to a tungsten light bulb.

The LED globe and spotlight lamps shown in Figure 3.2.7 are designed so that they can fit into standard light fittings. Hence their take-up is likely to depend on consumer choice and their availability in the marketplace at an attractive price.

Figure 3.2.7
Typical LED globe and spotlight lamps
Source: Philips Consumer Care.

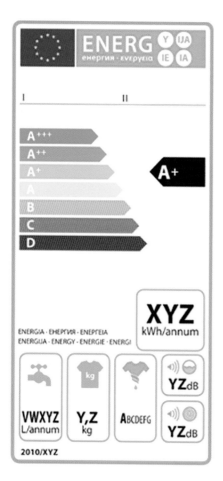

Figure 3.2.8 *Typical EU Energy Label for a washing machine*

Source: www.newenergylabel.com/uk/labelcontent/washers.

A similar situation exists for white goods, with manufacturers competing with each other to produce more efficient products that can sport an attractive EU Energy Label (see Figure 3.2.8). From 2011, the EU labelling scheme became compulsory for new televisions, as well as washing machines, dishwashers, fridges, freezers, fridge-freezers, tumble dryers, washer-dryers, electric ovens and light bulbs[8] (EC, 2010b).

Most modern white goods can claim at least an A rating. Indeed in recognition of the improvements in performance achieved by the products covered, the EU Energy Rating scheme had to be extended to A+++ while omitting E, F and G ratings. One exception is the labelling of televisions which was introduced in December 2011 as a mandatory A to G scheme, although higher ratings will be phased in from 2014. The Energy-Saving Trust has also introduced a labelling scheme, for the UK only, which essentially covers the top 20 per cent of products in each category.

Each product rating scheme is based on a specified testing regime. For example, washing machines are rated on annual energy consumption based on 60°C and 40°C cotton washes at part and full load, with a specified number of washes per week and set periods on standby and switched off. Annual water consumption is rated using the same sequence. Also rated are energy efficiency during spin cycle and peak noise levels when full and half-loaded.

The energy rating is established from the energy efficiency index (EEI) which in turn is calculated from a different formula for each appliance type. For example, the EEI for a washing machine is calculated from the ratio of actual annual energy consumption to a reference annual energy consumption, expressed as a percentage.

At the time of writing, the best performing washing machines in Europe have an EEI of 41.9 per cent (A+++) corresponding with an annual energy consumption of 160 kWh, and water consumption of approximately 10,800 litres/annum.[9]

An EU Energy Label is also required for electric ovens, but not gas ovens or hobs of any kind. Table 3.2.1 compares energy consumption and carbon emissions for typical gas and electric hobs and ovens, as well as small, medium and large A-rated electric ovens.

Clearly the gas appliances, although using more energy than the electrical equivalents, are responsible for lower carbon emissions, and are likely to be cheaper to run.

Non-residential HVAC

We have seen already that non-residential refurbishment opportunities cover a large range of building types and characteristics. At one end of the spectrum, a Victorian house converted for use as an office may present near identical refurbishment challenges to those faced when retrofitting building services in a

Table 3.2.1 *Ovens and hobs: typical energy consumption and carbon emissions*

	kWh	kg CO_2 per 'use'
Ovens		
Typical gas	1.52	0.28
Typical electric	1.09	0.59
Small A rated (12–35 litres)	0.6	0.32
Medium A rated (36–65 litres)	0.8	0.43
Large A rated (>65 litres)	1.0	0.54
Hobs		
Typical gas	0.9	0.17
Typical electric	0.72	0.39
Induction	0.5	0.27

Source: www.confusedaboutenergy.co.uk/index.php/buying-household-appliances/cookers.

large house of similar age and size. At the other sit a 50-storey office building in Dubai, a teaching hospital in Glasgow, the Sydney opera house or the Royal Festival Hall.

There is not the space here to cover all of the technical options available for every conceivable refurbishment project. In fact, most of the methodologies involved and the technologies available are used for new build, and many of these are covered in the section headed 'Energy-efficient building services' in Chapter 3.2 of *Integrated Sustainable Design of Buildings* (Appleby, 2011a). In this section therefore we will restrict ourselves to the specific issues associated with non-residential retrofits and the technologies best suited for retrofitting where these are different from those used in new build projects. Energy management issues will be covered in Chapter 4.1.

There are two very different scenarios within which we must consider retrofitting of building services: first, as part of a major refurbishment that might incorporate improving the performance to Passivhaus, low or zero carbon (LZC), or similar standards; second, upgrading equipment and plant that require replacing as part of an ongoing condition monitoring or planned maintenance programme.

The concept of Passivhaus evolved in Germany from a desire to develop low-energy dwellings in a climate that regularly drops below –10°C in winter. As we saw in Chapter 3.1, translating this to non-residential buildings in countries that experience warmer winters changes the emphasis. Where the average UK dwelling in 2008 had some 57 per cent of energy use from heating and 25 per cent from DHW, with 18 per cent from appliances, lighting and cooking, the average for an office building was closer to 25 per cent for heating and hot water combined, 18 per cent from lighting, 21 per cent from office equipment and catering, and 36 per cent from cooling, humidification, fans and pumps (see Figures 2.7 and 2.8 in Appleby, 2011a).

By the same token, many non-residential buildings have significantly higher heat gains during summer per unit floor area, with associated potential for overheating, driving the need for air conditioning in some cases. In offices, for example, this is due to more people, lighting and office equipment per unit floor area than in a typical dwelling. As well as improving energy performance, one of the aims of refurbishment may be to improve comfort conditions. A lot of the draught and temperature problems inherent in poorly constructed and insulated buildings are mitigated through the Passivhaus insulation and air tightness measure, hence the main challenges will be to ensure good indoor air quality and prevent overheating.

As with refurbishing dwellings to Passivhaus standards, an existing non-residential building that is naturally ventilated and relies on trickle ventilation in winter will require a form of MVHR to ensure winter comfort and control of ventilation-related energy demand. For summer operation, computer modelling should be used to assess whether temperatures exceed criteria for longer than is acceptable with a viable window opening regime (see case history in Chapter 3.7 in Appleby, 2011a). If not, then the MVHR system should be designed for comfort cooling.

Any building which has not been designed to be mechanically ventilated is likely to present a challenge when retrofitting air-handling plant, ductwork and air terminal devices. Although older buildings tend to have high enough floor to ceiling heights to cater for the installation of false ceilings, the challenge may be how to install these, along with riser ducts and plant rooms, while retaining some of the historical character of the building.

The following issues need to be addressed to minimize overheating risk or reduce cooling load:

- Develop a rational lighting strategy that optimizes daylight use and solar protection, while incorporating efficient lamps and intelligent lighting controls.
- Set a limit on occupant density, if negotiable. This also impacts on the number of computers and other office equipment. It is interesting to note that the default value for Passivhaus non-residential buildings is 35 m² per person. This compares with the British Council for Offices' (BCO) 2009 recommendation of between 8 m² and 13 m² per person.[10] A typical commercial office building in the UK is likely to have a density nearer to 10 m² per person, depending on the balance between open-plan and cellular offices.
- Specify 'Energy Star'-rated office equipment (see p. 163).
- Optimize shading, solar protective glazing and exposed thermal mass, or phase change material (PCM) board (see Chapter 3.1).

Lighting

For lighting of the workplace the amount of light reaching the working plane is normally important for visual acuity. This is dependent not only on the luminous efficacy of the lamp but on the type and cleanliness of the luminaire and the internal reflectance of room surfaces. Where most occupants are working at display screens the absence of distracting glare in their line of sight and on the screens is also important.

The actual amount of light reaching the working plane per W of electrical input power is referred to by Baker as the 'global lighting efficacy' (Baker, 2009). It is the product of luminous efficacy, light loss factor (LLF) and utilization factor (UF). For a poorly maintained luminaire having degraded diffusers, LLF can be as low as 0.4. UF, on the other hand, depends on the distance of the lamp from the reference plane and the reflectance values for the room surfaces. For an open-plan office with high ceiling and wall reflectances (0.7 and 0.5 respectively), UF would be around 0.83. However, with low-reflectance surfaces on the walls and ceiling (0.3, say), UF drops to 0.62.

Many offices are designed to achieve a maintained illuminance of 400 to 500 lux at desk level. Indeed, in the 1970s, some office lighting was designed to achieve 1000 lux on the working plane. An example from Section 7.6 of Nick Baker's *Handbook of Sustainable Refurbishment* describes an office having a uniform illuminance of 500 lux achieved with T5 fluorescent tubes requiring 10 W/m^2 floor area of electrical energy. By providing background illumination of 150 lux and a 12W task light to each workstation, achieving 600 lux over a 1 m^2 area, the total load can be reduced to 4.1 W/m^2, a reduction in both electrical energy and heat emitted from the lighting of 59 per cent (Baker, 2009). Also with task lighting the reflectance of ceiling and wall surfaces is less important, but, on the other hand, daylight controls are less effective (see next section).

Generally, where office activities are dominated by computer use, maintained illuminance levels can be dropped to 300 lux, as recommended in the BS EN 12464-1: 2011 (BSI, 2011b).

The most common type of lamp used in non-residential applications is the fluorescent tube, particularly in offices, hospitals, schools, warehouses, shops and supermarkets. The type of lamp and ballast installed in the existing building and opportunities for renovating the ceiling will drive the strategy for reducing lighting energy and carbon emissions. If the existing suspended ceiling is to be replaced, then the lighting can be designed as if for new accommodation. If the ceiling is to be retained, then a decision will have to be made on whether to replace lamps only, lamps and ballasts or the entire luminaire.

The three most common types of fluorescent lamp are T12, T8 and T5, where the T stands for 'tubular' and the number refers to the diameter in multiples of one-eighth of an inch; T12 is 1.5 inches, T8 is 1 inch and T5 is 5/8 inch diameter. T12 lamps were designed to operate with a magnetic ballast and typically have a luminous efficacy of 55 lm/W (compared with 14 lm/W for a tungsten lamp). T8 and T5 lamps typically have the more recently developed high-frequency (HF) electronic ballast and have average luminous efficacies of 90 and 105 lm/W respectively. The main reason for the difference in efficacy between T12, T8 and T5 lamps is the ballast. HF ballasts can be retrofitted to T12 lamps, resulting in an increase in efficacy from around 55 to between 75 and 85 lm/W. At the time of writing, T5 products are manufactured in different lengths to T8 and T12 tubes, but adaptors are available that incorporate high-frequency electronic ballasts and fit into the longer T8 or T12 fittings.

At the time of writing, an ever-increasing number of light-emitting diode (LED) tubular lamps are being offered as a retrofit to T8 lamps, but at a factor of between 50 and 100 times the unit cost of T5 or T8 tubes. However, if the labour cost of replacement is taken into account, with a life expectancy of perhaps twice that of a T5 lamp, the LED lamp can provide a return on investment within 5 to 10 years.[11] However, the luminance from a lamp of the same length currently is perhaps 35 per cent lower, so clearly a prediction of the reduction in maintained illuminance will be required. Although lower lighting levels may fall within RLL guidelines, they may not be acceptable to all occupants. Furthermore, current designs for LED lamps have low or zero upward light emissions, so will not be suitable where a design requires some

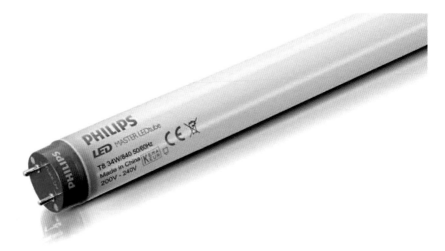

Figure 3.2.9 *Typical LED tube lamp*
Source: Philips Consumer Care.

illumination of the ceiling to avoid gloom. Also, because of their temperature sensitivity, LED lamps must not be fully enclosed (see Figure 3.2.9). With significantly lower mercury content the T5 lamp presents a lower environmental risk than either the T8 or the T12 lamps, while the LED lamp presents no disposal impacts, and is also less fragile.

Retrofitting lighting controls

Because lighting represents such a significant component of carbon emissions associated with most non-residential buildings, retrofitting 'intelligent' lighting controls is often considered an 'easy win'. For a building that can utilize daylight through well-designed solar protection, energy savings of approaching 70 per cent of the total from lights have been reported (Chapter 3.6 of Appleby, 2011a).

Some types of lighting control can be retrofitted with little disruption and hence represent a good option where a major refurbishment is not planned. In its *Lighting Handbook*, the Society of Light and Lighting (SLL, 2009) provides a useful overview:

> There are a number of factors that need to be considered in any control system; these are the inputs to system, how the system controls the lighting equipment and what is the control process that decides how a particular set of inputs will impact on the lighting. Thus, for a control system to work it must have:
> - input devices: such as switches, presence detectors, timers and photocells;
> - control processes: these may consist of a simple wiring network through to a computer-based control system;
> - controlled luminaires: the system may control luminaires in a number of ways, from simply switching them on and off to dimming the lamp and in more complex systems causing movement and colour changes.

We will focus here on occupancy and daylight detection. In the Carbon Trust's leaflet on *How to Implement Lighting Controls*, it recommends that:

Lighting controls are best deployed as a reliable means of turning off the lighting. People will turn lights on when they need them; sometimes they forget to turn them off. So the most effective control strategy is:

- Request on.
- Auto off.

This is also known as absence detection and is particularly suited to an office application. Presence detection, where lights are switched on when movement is detected, is best suited to intermittent occupancy, such as a corridor or cupboard.

All types of movement sensors

rely on movement, or the absence of it, to inform the lighting controls. Three different ways to detect occupancy are generally available, and the choice is often determined by the application:

1   Passive infra-red (PIR).
2   Ultrasonic.
3   Microwave.

Generally speaking, PIR sensors are more economical than the other two and more suited to close range, small area, applications.

(Carbon Trust, 2010)

Daylight sensors, also referred to as photocells and photoelectric switches, measure light levels to determine whether artificial lighting should be on or off. Daylight sensors are often included with movement sensors as a combined unit, sometimes referred to as an intelligent lighting control system.

Although combined units can reduce costs and installation times, there is no point in installing daylight sensors in locations that do not benefit from daylight, usually where the daylight factor falls below 2 per cent (see Chapter 3.6 of Appleby, 2011a). Luminaires are available that have integrated controls, with sensors located within the luminaire.

Sensors need to be carefully calibrated so that they provide a proxy to the lighting level and occupant activity at the nearest workstations. To simplify the work required above a suspended ceiling or where luminaires are fixed to an exposed soffit, wireless lighting control systems have been developed, as well as systems that use existing power wiring for transmission of control signals.

Office equipment

According to the Carbon Trust, 'Office equipment is the fastest growing energy user in the business world, consuming 15% of the total electricity used in offices. This is expected to rise to 30% by 2020' (Carbon Trust, 2006). Replacement of office equipment may form part of a major refurbishment, an energy management strategy or a procurement programme (see Chapter 4.1 and Chapter 4.8). Ideally it should form part of the overall carbon reduction strategy for a business, and its procurement given the priority it deserves.

The EU has adopted the US Energy Star rating system for office equipment, providing a unique database of approved equipment including computers, printers, copiers, scanners, fax machines and multi-function devices.[12] Large photocopiers tend to have the greatest energy consumption per item, while the sheer number of computers in most offices will tend to put them top of the list of energy consumers overall.

Johnson *et al.* (2011) have set out a number of scenarios for future office use, examining a range of trends in computer and internet technology and the impact that 'Generation Y' computer-savvy people will have on the electronic workplace. One trend is for a more mobile workforce with greater use of 'hot-desking' and with storage to be largely removed from the desk and transferred to the 'cloud' (i.e. secure warehouses containing massive amounts of data storage) and printing made largely redundant through the implementation of a paperless office policy. Another scenario envisages the advent of 'surface computing', with touch-screen interactive working via 'media walls'.

It has been estimated that cloud computing can reduce energy consumption from computers by between 75 and 80 per cent. Johnson *et al.* have estimated that an office based on cloud computing, one monitor per person and no printing, would result in an overall energy saving of 56 per cent compared with the base case for a typical office. An office in which each person works at multiple touch screens and has access to large media walls would have a 40 per cent larger energy consumption than typical.

The future is likely to be a combination of the two of course. While cloud storage is gaining in popularity, the paperless office has been the future of office working for many years, and is likely to remain so. Multiple touch screens are also likely to gain in popularity, particularly for those involved in design, simulation and visualization.

Air conditioning, ventilation and heat recovery

Moving air around a building with fans has historically produced greater carbon emissions than that required to heat the building and provide domestic hot water. If this air is also cooled and dehumidified, then the resultant overall carbon emissions can be more than twice that for the same building with natural ventilation.

One of the reasons why fan energy is so high for air-conditioned buildings is because of the large quantities of air and momentum required to distribute the air through the building to ensure it is thoroughly mixed with room air, offsetting heat gains and creating a comfortable working environment. This can require perhaps eight or ten air changes per hour. Blowing the air through a labyrinthine network of ductwork itself requires much of the total fan power to overcome system resistances. Many systems use high velocities to reduce duct sizes so that they can fit into suspended ceilings, while generating enough back pressure at control devices to enable balancing and stable damper operation.

If heat gains can be reduced, through renovation and retrofit of lighting and office equipment, such that peak internal summer temperatures fall within acceptable limits (see Chapter 3.4 of Appleby, 2011a), then the building can be considered for natural ventilation. Its suitability will also depend on being able to open windows without allowing the ingress of unacceptable quantities of noise and air pollution (see Chapter 3.4).

When seeking to meet Passivhaus standards for non-residential buildings, or similar low- or zero-carbon (LZC) requirements, there is a strong argument for providing an equivalent to the MVHR approach used for dwellings. The system will have to provide sufficient outdoor air to meet occupant requirements during the winter months. For the UK, CIBSE recommend 10 litres/s of outdoor air per person (CIBSE, 2006c). For office accommodation with one person per 10 m^2 and a floor-to-ceiling height of 2.5 m, this is equivalent to 1.44 air changes per hour (ach^{-1}). This compares with a default value in the Passivhaus standard of 0.3 ach^{-1}, which assumes 35 m^2 per person occupant density.

The challenges are to ensure that the outdoor air finds its way into the breathing zones of occupants and that other sources of contamination do not pollute the incoming air. Methods of minimizing air quality problems will be tackled in Chapter 3.4. The extract air system should remove air from locations where there are specific fixed sources of heat and pollution, such as large printers and food preparation areas. Toilets would normally have their own supply and extract system, with heat recovery (MVHR) to prevent cross-contamination with the work area ventilation.

During much of the heating season, air will be supplied at or above room temperature. Hence if air is supplied close to the ceiling, for example, using existing air distribution outlets, and extract air is also removed at high level, for example, via air-handling luminaires, then there is a good chance that very little of the outdoor air will find its way into the occupied zone. This is because the air distribution system would have been designed to handle six to eight times more air than is required to meet the outdoor air requirements of the occupants, and supplied at a temperature below that in the room when there is a cooling demand. Thus the momentum in the supply air would have created mixing with the room air, ensuring heat and air exchange with the air in the occupied zone.

To avoid this risk of short circuiting, the air distribution system will need to be modified so that air is introduced directly into the occupied zone, but without creating draught, and removed from locations away from the supply air terminal devices. For a narrow plan building, the ideal location for supplying air might be under the windows, behind or under perimeter heating, if required. This may be compatible with some existing air-conditioning systems that utilize perimeter units fed with outdoor air from central plant sized to meet the outdoor air requirements of occupants. Extract air could then continue to be drawn from above the luminaires, provided those closest to the perimeter are blanked off to avoid short circuiting, as well as above the fixed office equipment.

Where necessary, extract air will need to be re-routed to a heat recovery device in the central plant. The two most common heat recovery devices available utilize plate cross-flow heat recovery devices (also known as recuperators) or thermal wheels (Figure 3.2.10).

Efficiencies depend on size, internal configuration and the method of heat transfer. Modern versions of both types have quoted efficiencies of between 80 and 90 per cent. Thermal wheels are available in either impermeable or hygroscopic materials, the latter enabling transfer of moisture in either direction, depending on the vapour pressure gradient. Recuperators are usually manufactured from either impermeable aluminium, plastic composite or polystyrene, with latent heat transfer through condensation on the heat exchangers which has to be drained off.

For workplaces that have a variable occupancy, there is an argument for retrofitting variable volume inverter drive fans controlled from a sensor that responds to occupancy levels, such as a carbon dioxide sensor located in the

Figure 3.2.10 *Air-handling unit with thermal wheel*
Source: Nuaire.

extract air. However this is only feasible when the ventilation system serves a single open-plan space that is not likely to suffer from clusters of high occupant density.

Refrigeration and heat rejection plant

It is not always possible to eliminate the need for cooling, but if a major refurbishment is being planned, then existing chillers and heat rejection plant are likely to be too large. Depending on when they were installed, they also may be extremely inefficient. The following issues should be considered:

- Type of chiller: refrigeration plant can be driven by reciprocating, centrifugal or rotary screw compressors, or through absorption. Large centrifugal chillers tend to have the highest efficiencies, with maximum coefficient of performance (CoP = condenser heat divided by power input) of between 6.0 and 7.0. A typical rotary screw chiller has a CoP of 5.5, while CoPs for reciprocating chillers might fall between 3.5 and 4.5. Absorption chillers might have a CoP of 0.7 to 1.0.
- Older chillers have significantly lower CoPs than their modern equivalent. For example, a centrifugal chiller made between 1985 and 1990 might have had a CoP of 4.7 when new, falling to around 3.5 over 20 years of operation or so; while the equivalent chiller manufactured today is likely to have a CoP of 6.0 or more.
- Modern centrifugal chillers have variable speed drives, enabling high efficiencies at low load. Retrofit, however, is usually too difficult to contemplate.
- In general, chillers work more efficiently with higher chilled water temperatures entering. For example, an increase from 7.2°C to 10°C typically results in a 6 per cent energy reduction for chillers operating with refrigerant R134a and 12 per cent for chillers operating with R123.[13]
- Older chillers tend to suffer from refrigerant loss, which not only adds high global warming potential (GWP) gases to the atmosphere but also reduces chiller efficiency through contamination.
- Although larger chillers may be nominally more efficient, their efficiency drops at part load, so it may be more efficient to install multiple smaller chillers, which also adds resilience in case of chiller breakdown.
- Some chillers allow lower than normal condenser entering water temperatures (CEWTs). For example, energy consumption can fall by between 20 and 40 per cent if the CEWT is allowed to drop from 30°C to 18°C.
- Although absorption chillers seemingly offer a prohibitively low CoP, their main advantage is that they can use low-grade heat to provide an energy source to drive the refrigeration cycle. Hence they can use heat rejected from a combined heat and power plant (see below) or solar panels, as well as direct gas-firing.
- Depending on external conditions, there may be long periods when cooling water can be diverted from condensers and used in chilled water coils. This is particularly relevant if there are evaporative cooling towers or water available from ground coupling.
- Although cooling towers offer the most efficient means of heat rejection, running costs tend to be high because of measures required for legionellosis prevention (see Chapter 4.5).

Boilers and combined heat and power

Boiler technology has also moved on, with seasonal efficiencies higher than 90 per cent and condensing boilers as standard, compared with boilers from the early 1990s achieving perhaps 50 to 60 per cent. For a 10,000 m² office building refurbished to Passivhaus standards or similar, it is likely that a compact boiler capable of generating around 100kW might satisfy heating demand, particularly if domestic hot water (DHW) is primed from solar panels.

Unless there is a kitchen for hot meal preparation, showers for sports changing or laundry with washing machines that have a hot water connection, DHW demand can be extremely low. Hand washing in sanitary accommodation alone can draw off very little hot water, and it would be useful to have monitored consumption prior to refurbishment before sizing solar panels and boiler plant.

Combined heat and power (CHP or cogeneration) machines generate electricity and use the 'waste' heat produced for heating and DHW. Combined cooling heat and power (CCHP or trigeneration) uses this heat via absorption chillers to provide cooling. For a more detailed discussion on the types of equipment available, see Chapter 2.6 of Appleby (2011a), while Chapter 3.2 of Appleby (2011a) includes a section that examines some of the economic aspects of their application.

Typically a medium-sized gas engine CHP will generate 1.5 times as much heat as electricity. Hence unless there is a major heat demand, such as might be the case for a sports centre with a swimming pool, whirlpool spa, showers, etc., CHP is unlikely to be feasible for most LZC or Passivhaus non-residential buildings.

Lifts and electrical services

On average, lifts or elevators contribute between 3 and 5 per cent to a building's energy consumption, although this can be significantly higher for very tall buildings. The two main categories of lift are hydraulic and traction, with hydraulic generally restricted to buildings that have five or six floors. Hydraulic lifts operate at around 1.0 m/s and are very inefficient, using typically three to five times as much energy per unit of travel distance when compared to a traction lift. Traction lifts can operate at speeds of between 2.5 m/s and 10 m/s. Older lifts tend to use DC motors that are quite inefficient, particularly at low loads, and generate a lot of heat. Modern lifts use induction AC motors with sophisticated control systems, such as the pulse width modulation (PWM) inverter which uses variable voltage, variable frequency (VVVF) gearless technology, most commonly with a permanent magnet motor. This has the effect of increasing efficiencies across the normal operating range of loads and speeds for a typical lift, for example, by a power factor correction to close to unity at all times. When combined with regenerative braking, this reduces energy consumption by some 80 per cent compared with a 'conventional pole changing drive' (Intelligent Energy Europe, 2010).

Regenerative braking uses the energy generated through braking to generate electricity through reversing the motor, i.e.:

> When the lift is going down, and the load weight (people inside) is larger than the counterweight, then the motor torque is in opposite direction to the speed, i.e., the motor is braking. In the same way, when the lift is going up unloaded, energy savings can be reached if the motor is controlled with a regenerative VVVF drive.

Regenerative braking can be retrofitted to existing lifts and some manufacturers offer a regenerative braking retrofit package.

Standby energy consumption can be 20 per cent or more of the total, hence automatic isolation of lights and fans when lift cars are not in use can produce a significant energy saving.

Power factor (PF) is the ratio of the useful power to the apparent power, where the useful power is that which is doing the work and the apparent power is that measured at the meter. The primary reasons why they are different are due to:

- phase differences between supply and demand caused by an inductive load, such as is caused by AC induction motors and fluorescent lamp ballasts;
- distorted waveforms caused by inverters and variable speed drives.

Without PF correction, losses of between 0.5 and 1 per cent of the power supplied to the inductive loads can result. PF correction is easily retrofitted through a combination of suitably sized capacitors, installed close to the loads to compensate for lagging current, and harmonic correction to correct for distorted waveforms.

Building energy management systems and controls

The strategy for modifying control of indoor environmental conditions and energy consumption monitoring will depend on the extent of refurbishment planned. However, modifying or retrofitting automatic control and building energy management systems (BEMSs) can be one of the least intrusive and most cost-effective tools for improving energy efficiency.

Almost all buildings have a degree of automatic control, whether it be through timed operation of boilers and other plant, or the thermostatic control of radiators or air-conditioning units. Ultimately the aim is to achieve a balance between satisfying as many occupants as possible and minimizing energy consumption.

A BEMS provides a framework for linking sensors with controllers and actuators, enabling adjustment of control parameters, monitoring and recording temperatures, and incorporating, for example, intelligence to learn the building's thermal characteristics and reduce hysteresis (see also Chapter 4.1).

Advanced control techniques that incorporate predictive control algorithms based on computer simulation models have been investigated, with the potential for incorporating into an existing BEMS through a software update, for example.

Many building heating and ventilation systems operate for longer than necessary; for example, when heating systems are switched on and off at the same time every day, rather than adapting to external conditions and the thermal response of the building (optimum start).

We do not have space here to cover all aspects of the design of control and BEMS and the reader is referred to the CIBSE Guide H for further reading and guidance (CIBSE, 2009).

Case histories

Barbrook Passivhaus, Devon

Barbrook Passivhaus Retrofit[14] is a demonstration project within Exmoor National Park. The overarching aim of the project has been to develop techniques to reduce carbon dioxide emissions from existing social housing by 80 per cent through refurbishment.

The project was initiated by Energy Action Devon (EAD) who brought the team together, including North Devon Homes, who own the two properties at Barbrook. In 2009, Phase 1 of the National Retrofit for the Future competition was launched to carry out feasibility modelling.[15] In January 2010 EAD were awarded £150,000 to carry out the build in Phase 2 of the competition.

The refurbishment included the following measures:

- continuous insulation all around walls and roof with 350 mm Warmcel insulation blown into the purpose-built timber frame built around existing concrete walls, resulting in U-value of 0.1 W/m²K for walls and roof;
- ground-floor slab replaced with a new slab, including 250 mm insulation beneath it;
- insulation fitted around the edge of the slab and to sides of foundations;
- existing concrete walls retained within the thermal envelope to act as thermal mass and regulate the temperature;
- new triple-glazed, argon-filled windows with overall U-value of 0.75 W/m²K;
- new 'Ecopassiv' glazed doors fitted with a U-value of 0.92 W/m²K;
- air leakage rate of 1.1 h⁻¹ at 50 Pa achieved;
- mechanical ventilation with heat recovery (MVHR) installed in loft spaces above each dwelling;
- wood pellet boiler installed to provide low-carbon heating to both properties;
- carbon emissions from the heating system predicted to be 150 kgCO₂/annum.

Each property has an MVHR unit installed in its loft space. Extract air is drawn from the bathrooms and kitchens, and outdoor air is blown into the bedrooms and living rooms, warmed from heat recovered from the extract air in the MVHR unit. The ducting was integrated into the refurbishment from the outset to avoid unnecessary drilling through air barriers after installation.

In the summer, the MVHR system may be switched off and open windows used for ventilation. The intention is that in the winter the ventilation air provided via the MVHR system will make the house feel 'fresh' enough so that the occupants do not feel driven to open the windows.

It was considered that the ducting design was crucial to the success of the retrofit. To ensure the most efficient delivery of air it was installed using straight, rigid and well-insulated sections, and kept as short as possible.

The MVHR units are Paul Focus 200, supplied by the Green Building Store, with a heat recovery rate of 91 per cent and electrical efficiency of 0.31 Wh/m³. These units have been certified by the Passivhaus Institut which means that the efficiency has been independently tested. Both units are individually controllable using a touch screen programmer. The filters in the units will need to be changed approximately every six months. This will be done by a maintenance person from North Devon Homes.

The two properties are heated using a single wood pellet boiler, providing space and domestic hot water via a 500-litre cylinder.

Typically a Passivhaus should not require additional space heating, but due to the lack of solar gain on this site, it was decided to install a heating system. The Austrian Okofen pellet boiler was chosen because of its reported high efficiency, controllability and reliability. The pellets are stored in an adjacent store and fed automatically into the boiler as required. Due to the limited space available on site, there was room only for a small store, so pellets have to be delivered bagged rather than blown from a delivery vehicle.

Each property has a heat meter monitoring space and water heating as part of the Retrofit for the Future requirements. This provides feedback to each occupant and it is hoped that this will encourage them to use the system efficiently.

The tenants are able to fully control the heating pattern in their own home. An easy-to-use programmer allows time and temperature settings for three on-periods for each individual day of the week.

The boiler is a modulating 2.8 kW Okofen Pellematic, with a quoted seasonal efficiency of 90.5 per cent. It has been estimated that it should use around 800 kg pellets per year fed from a fuel store that can hold 450 kg of pellets. The pellets were initially imported from Austria, because their performance had been proven in the Okofen boiler. Once the boiler was well established, the aim was to source pellets more locally.

The Empire State Building

This famous landmark on the New York skyline measures 443 m from base to the tip of its antenna, with 102 floors between and a total floor area of approximately 257,000 m².

It has been estimated that the overall reduction in energy consumption will be 38 per cent, saving some 105,000 tonnes of CO_2 over 15 years.[16] As well as the renovation to its windows, described in the case history in Chapter 3.1 on p. 140, a number of modifications were made to the buildings services (Pearson, 2011), as follows:

- *Lighting and power*: The lighting power density and associated energy use were reduced in tenant spaces by making better use of daylight and task lighting. Photosensors and dimmable ballasts were installed to control lighting in perimeter zones. Tenant areas were also provided with a plug load occupancy sensor to turn desk-top devices on and off depending on whether occupants are at their desk. The owners have also constructed a model LEED platinum office space in the building to demonstrate to tenants what a low-energy office should look like.
- *Chiller retrofit*: The cooling load reduction projects referred to above and in Chapter 3.1 made it possible to reduce chiller capacity, allowing refurbishment of the existing chillers, including installing variable speed drives and upgrading their controls, rather than installing new units. In

addition, the existing R500 refrigerant has been replaced with ozone-friendly R134.

- *Variable air volume (VAV) air-handling units*: Alteration to the internal layout of the building has meant that the number of constant volume air handling units could be halved. Two VAV units have replaced four constant volume air-handling units. This has resulted in reduced maintenance and energy consumption, and improved comfort through lower noise levels and better control.

- *Controls*: Demand control ventilation has been installed with CO_2 sensors linked to mixing dampers to bring in appropriate quantities of outside air based on occupancy levels. The existing control system has been replaced with a modern direct digital control based on Johnson Control's Metasys building automation and control system. New sub-metering has been installed for each tenanted area and tenants will be provided with access to online energy benchmarking information, allowing them to compare their energy use against other tenants.

3.3
Retrofitting renewable technologies

Introduction

The primary objective of retrofitting renewable technologies is to reduce the operational carbon emissions associated with providing energy to a building; the implication being that there should be no carbon emissions associated with doing so. However, unless the life cycle is genuinely carbon-neutral, all renewable technologies contain embodied carbon: in their materials, processing, assembly, transportation, maintenance and disposal. In the case of biomass boilers, the fuel itself embodies carbon from harvesting, processing and delivery, while heat pumps use mains electricity to drive the refrigeration process and ground coupling requires electric pumps to circulate water through underground pipework.

The selection of renewable technologies requires an approach based on life cycle assessment, as well as life cycle costing, availability of funding, physical constraints, environmental impact, etc. In this chapter we will focus on those issues that impact on the suitability of the various options for retrofit, highlighting where a difference in approach is required for residential and other applications. For a more detailed analysis of the technologies and their integration into new building designs, the reader is directed to Chapters 2.6 and 3.2 of *Integrated Sustainable Design of Buildings* (Appleby, 2011a).

Feasibility

The Carbon Trust provides a useful guide to those wishing to install renewable technologies into existing buildings, including the following advice on feasibility studies:

> Predicting performance during feasibility is important as it provides a benchmark to check whether the system is designed and installed correctly. Our research shows that these predictions are not always fully accurate and sometimes miss key factors. These include:
> - For wind turbines: local wind conditions, including impact of nearby obstacles and terrain.
> - For solar hot water and photovoltaics: overshadowing and system losses.

- For ground-source heat pumps and biomass heating: realistic average efficiencies, ground conditions (GSHP only), how the building will be used, system losses and heat load assessment.
- For small hydro: hydro resource (head of water and flow), estimated system efficiency.

(Carbon Trust, 2011)

To this should be added the availability of a sustainable source of fuel for biomass plant at a predictably economic rate. In the same leaflet, the Carbon Trust also suggests that:

> Typically, a feasibility study should cover the following:
> - compatibility with your site, buildings and infrastructure
> - space requirements
> - estimated capital costs
> - estimated annual energy yield, cost savings, carbon savings and simple payback
> - maintenance costs and time required
> - whether planning permission or any other regulatory permits are required
> - funding or grant opportunities and other incentives, in particular FiTs, RHI and ECAs [feed-in tariffs, the Renewable Heat Incentive and enhanced capital allowances, see Chapter 1.2].

Feasibility studies should also, where possible, compare the embodied carbon of the options being considered and the carbon emissions saved during the life expectancy of the plant. This can be a particular issue for wind turbines in urban locations, which BRE has demonstrated may not save the embodied carbon used in construction during the life of the turbine (Philips *et al.*, 2007). The summary to this paper states that:

> In windy locations, micro-wind turbines can generate enough energy to pay back their carbon emissions within a few months or years but in large urban areas, micro-wind turbines may never pay back their carbon emissions. Life cycle costing suggests that, even in favourable urban locations, financial payback is unlikely for all but the most durable, efficient and low-maintenance turbines.

However, it is important that an assessment be based on trustworthy data for the products being considered since, according to the BRE report, the embodied carbon in the products studied varied from 180 $kgCO_2$ to 1,444 $kgCO_2$ for manufacture; and from 18 to 147 $kgCO_2$ for delivery, installation and maintenance.

The picture is very different for photovoltaics which, as a summary of recent research by the UK's Centre for Alternative Technology reports, typically have a payback time of 2.5 years for the energy invested in manufacture.[1]

Renewable electricity technologies

As we have already seen in Chapter 3.2, a building that is refurbished to Passivhaus or similar standards will normally have a demand profile dominated by electricity. Bearing in mind retrofitting renewables should not be carried out unless passive measures have been addressed, thermal energy for heating should always be minimized. Thermal loads will always be higher where DHW demand is prevalent, such as residential buildings, sports centres, hospitals, restaurants, schools and hotels, or any application that requires hot process water, including indoor swimming pools.

Solar photovoltaics

Solar photovoltaic cells (PV) are the most 'tried and tested' of the renewable technologies, and arguably the more suitable at a domestic scale. Initially developed in the middle of the twentieth century for providing power to satellites, PV cells have now become a consumer product in the mass market. Development of more efficient materials and processes, combined with the economies of scale and the aggressive expansion in Chinese involvement in the global marketplace, will ensure increasing growth through a reduction in unit price and greater energy deliverability.

PV modules convert sunlight into a direct current, so for most applications, an inverter will be required to produce alternating current (AC). This will also be necessary to enable grid connection and to sell surplus electricity to an energy company through a feed-in tariff arrangement. Depending on the particular PV technology installed, a typical 1 m^2 module will generate anywhere between 60 and 110 kWh per year.

The most common types of PV panel use monocrystalline or polycrystalline cells manufactured from a purified thin wafer of silicon laminated into a glass or plastic sandwich. Thin-film panels are manufactured by depositing a thin layer of dielectric material in vapour form within a vacuum onto a substrate such as glass, plastic or metal. This is a process that suits a production line and is therefore significantly cheaper than crystalline cell manufacture. It also has allowed the production of a flexible product that can be retrofitted onto an existing smooth surface. However, thin-film products generally have an electrical output of less than half that for the equivalent crystalline product, although at half the cost per unit area.

For optimum output, a panel should be installed on a roof facing between south east and south west (see Figure 3.3.1) and be unobstructed by shade throughout the day.

The GreenSpec website provides the following rule of thumb: 'For optimum output, the tilt from the horizontal should be equal to the latitude of the site minus 20°. For example, 30° is an optimal tilt in Southern England, increasing to almost 40° in Northern Scotland.'[2] A wall-mounted vertical array produces around 70 per cent of maximum output.

PV cells are available as homogeneous panels, roof tiles, in rolls for application to a smooth roof or integrated into glazing systems. When panels are linked together, the installation thus formed is known as an array. An array can either be integrated flush with an existing roof or glazing system, or mounted

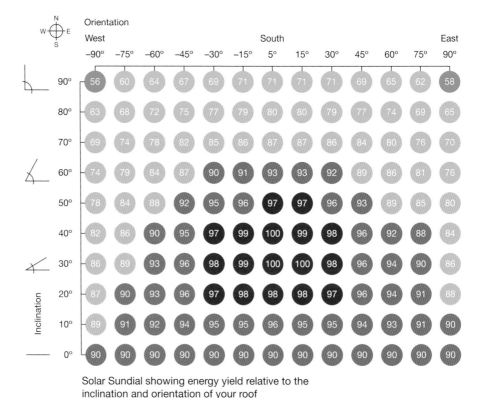

Figure 3.3.1 *Optimum orientation and inclination angles for solar photovoltaic panels located in the South of England*

Source: solarcentury.co.uk.

proud of a roof (Figure 3.3.2), either parallel with a slope or in frames installed at the optimum inclination (Figure 3.3.3).

Roof integrated PV tiles are available which might be considered as part of an overall roof covering replacement (Figure 3.3.4). Tiles are supplied pre-wired with connectors to adjacent tiles.

Flexible thin-film PV laminates are typically made using amorphous silicon technology and can be fitted to flat or profiled standing seam roofs as shown in Figure 3.3.5.

Another option for retrofitting PV is to install them into brises-soleil, or sun shades. Typically, PV cells are installed that allow a certain amount of light through between cells, although this reduces the electricity generated accordingly.

PV panels and arrays are rated in terms of power output in full sunlight, known as kilowatt peak (kWp). For example, a typical residential array based on crystalline PV panels might be rated at 3.6 kWp, occupying around 36 m^2 of roof area and generating between 2,700 and 3,300 kWh of electricity per annum in the South of England. This might represent some 50–60 per cent of the consumption of an average household (assuming an annual consumption of 5,500 kWh per year for a family home), although there will be times when the amount of electricity generated exceeds demand. At these times the surplus electricity would normally be allowed to flow into the electricity grid via a

Figure 3.3.2 *Typical residential retrofit with 3.6 kWp PV array proud of tiled roof*
Source: Shutterstock.

Figure 3.3.3 *PV installation retrofitted to flat roof*
Source: Lucas Braun.

Figure 3.3.4 *Typical PV slate installation*
Source: solarcentury.co.uk.

two-way meter, unless the building is not grid-connected. This method of 'export' effectively uses the grid in place of a battery and overcomes many of the shortcomings of using regular batteries including: high cost, storage space, limited useful lifespan and environmentally damaging components.

For an existing building the design process requires the following actions:

- Ensure there are no planning restrictions on visual impact of PV installations.
- Check angle of inclination, orientation and shaded areas.
- Determine extent of available roof area.
- Estimate demand profile and decide on maximum economic area of PV panel based on economic equation for suitable PV options and feed-in tariff available.
- Determine extra weight on roof structure and compare against predicted load-bearing capacity of existing roof.
- Investigate mains connection and 'export' facilities.
- Find accessible location for power conditioning equipment (inverter and metering).

The size of the PV installation may be dictated by the size of a suitable unshaded area available, the capital funding available, the return on investment provided

Figure 3.3.5 *Thin-film PV on a curved standing seam roof*
Source: Architectsea.

by the feed-in tariff, or some combination of the three. Where there are large areas of exposed roof available, such as those on supermarkets and warehouses for example, there may be an economic argument for investing in covering the entire roof, even if the power generated exceeds demand for much of the time, on the basis of an attractive long-term feed-in tariff.

Wind turbines

Although wind provides a potential valuable resource for the generation of renewable electricity, its force varies with time, proximity to ground and obstructions. Wind turbines use the energy in the wind to rotate blades that drive a turbine which generates alternating current at a variable frequency which has to be first converted to direct current then back to AC at the same frequency as the grid. Because of the friction and losses in the system, most horizontal axis wind turbines will not start rotating until wind speeds reach 2.5 m/s and require an average wind speed of 5 or 6 m/s to operate economically. The helical type shown in Figure 3.3.6 has a 'cut-in' speed of 5 m/s.[3]

The roofscape of urban and suburban locations offers mostly a sheltered and turbulent wind environment. Apart from above the tallest of buildings, the wind speed will struggle to exceed 2.5 m/s in most locations close to buildings, particularly where upstream obstructions create eddies and turbulence. Where there is some confidence that wind resources will be adequate, then it is wise to have a 12-month wind speed assessment carried out, during which a directional anemometer will be mounted in the proposed location, connected to a data logger that continually records the wind speed and direction.

Figure 3.3.6 *Vertical axis helical wind turbine*

Source: quietrevolution.

The two main categories of wind turbine are horizontal axis (HAWT) and vertical axis (VAWT). The former has the turbine in a housing at the top of a stem, connected in-line with the blade shaft, while a VAWT has the turbine at its base and may be inherently more stable and easier to work on.

Micro hydropower

Like wind turbines, turbines that use the energy in flowing water to generate electricity have been around for many years. Where there has been a valley to flood and resources available for the major civil engineering works required, the principle has been employed on a large scale in hydroelectric dams since the end of the nineteenth century.

Micro hydropower generally use a 'run of the river' arrangement that is commonly associated with a weir, but avoids construction of a dam (see Figure 3.3.7).

Most micro hydropower projects are community-based, with a particular focus on the developing world. Clearly building owners or managers that want to tap into this source of electrical energy must have access to a suitable source of running water.

Figure 3.3.7 *Torrs hydropower scheme in the Peak District, UK, with Archimedes screw turbine and weir*
Source: Clem Rutter.

There are a number of different types of turbine used in micro hydropower schemes (see Chapter 2.6 in Appleby, 2011a) but the most common for 'run of the river' applications is the Archimedes screw type shown in Figure 3.3.7.

In England, the Environment Agency is responsible for permitting work on rivers and in its guidance for people considering the installation of a hydropower scheme they set out the key areas of environmental impact that need to be addressed:

- *Abstraction*: You need the Environment Agency's agreement for the amount of water your scheme can take from the river to flow through a hydropower turbine.
- *Impoundment*: Any new or raised weir will change the water levels and flows in the river by impounding more water above it. The Environment Agency will need to agree these changes with you.
- *Flood risk*: You need the Environment Agency's agreement for any works in or near rivers that have the potential to increase flood risk. This will include both the construction works and the finished scheme.
- *Fish passage*: For many schemes, the Environment Agency will require a fish pass to allow fish to pass safely up and down the river.

(Environment Agency, 2010)

Provided the river used as the source of energy does not dry up during periods of drought, then hydropower provides the only source of renewable energy that is continuous, 24 hours per day, 365 days a year. The amount of electrical power generated depends on the head and the flow that can be diverted from the river. One rule of thumb states that the power (kW) is five times the flow (m^3/s) times the head (m). For example, from a reasonably sized river it may be possible to draw an average of 4 m^3/s, and if the drop between the turbine inlet and downstream river (i.e. the head) is 2 m, then the average power generated will be 40 kW, or 350,400 kWh per annum (assuming no downtime). The turbine needs to be sized on peak flow, for example, the Torrs hydro turbine shown in Figure 3.3.7 is rated at 63 kW but is predicted to generate 240,000 kWh per annum.

The lower the flow, the greater the head required to make a system viable. For example a stream flowing at an average of 0.05 m^3/s requires a head greater than 10m,[4] which is likely to require construction of a small dam and reservoir and will rarely be feasible.

Because of the continuous generation capability, it is essential that the turbine can export surplus power to the grid, while benefitting from feed-in tariff, and that the local connection is capable of taking the maximum current generated.

Renewable heat technologies

Unlike renewable electricity, there are only limited opportunities for exporting renewable heat generated on site. Export is possible with large-scale biomass and geothermal plants where surplus heat can be distributed locally via a district heating scheme (see Chapter 2.5).

The most suitable technologies for retrofitting are solar hot water, biomass and ground-coupled heat pumps.

Solar hot water

Like photovoltaics, solar hot water panels should be mounted on an unshaded surface, such as a sloping roof. Figure 3.3.8 shows the optimum orientation and inclination for an installation in Southern England. Unlike PVs, however, the optimum area of panel is limited by the predicted hot water demand and the tendency to lose heat from the panels when sunlight is not available.

There are two types of solar collector in common use: flat plate and evacuated tube (see Figures 3.3.9 and 3.3.10 respectively). Similar to PV, these can be mounted parallel with and proud from a roof slope, integrated into a roof covering or in a suitably inclined framework on a flat roof.

Key issues relating to the design of a solar hot water installation include the following:

- Where there is a risk of freezing, the fluid circulated through the panels must contain anti-freeze.
- The temperature of the water leaving the panels will fall well below the level at which *legionella* bacteria can proliferate, hence it must be pumped to a storage system so that the temperature delivered to taps can be raised to 60°C at the top of the cylinder when necessary (see Figure 3.3.11).
- Ideally a new bespoke cylinder should be installed which will have to be tall enough to cater for heat exchangers arranged vertically as shown in Figure 3.3.11 and ensure stratification in the cylinder. Alternatively, the existing cylinder could be retained with a new cylinder arranged to preheat the supply to the existing one.
- Panel area and storage volume must be optimized for each application, which will normally require a suitable computer model.
- Evacuated tube collectors are fragile and must not be located where there is a risk of damage: for example, where tree branches could be blown onto them, stones can be dropped by birds or vandalism is likely.

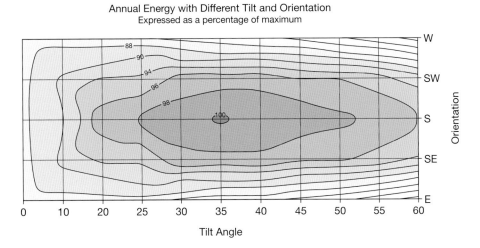

Figure 3.3.8 *Optimum orientation and inclination angles for solar hot water panels*

Source: Viridian Solar.

Figure 3.3.9 *Typical flat plate solar collectors integrated into roof slates*
Source: GDC Group ©.

- A control system is required that monitors the collector and cylinder temperatures and starts the pump when there is useful solar energy to be gained. When there is no more useful solar energy, the controller stops the circulating pump so that the water in the cylinder cannot be cooled.

For detailed design guidance, refer to publications from the Energy-Saving Trust and CIBSE (EST, 2006; CIBSE, 2007).

It is possible to use solar energy to supplement the heat from a boiler to provide hot water for heating as well as DHW. Figure 3.3.12 shows a typical arrangement based on the 'combisystem', which has been widely installed across mainland Europe and Canada although, at the time of writing, this arrangement is yet to make an impact on the UK market. However, with the minimal heating demand associated with Passivhaus and similar standards, this may change. Key factors that might influence its choice include the following:

- Typically a combisystem can contribute more than 30 per cent of the combined DHW and space heating requirement. For buildings built to Passivhaus standards, this can be significantly higher.
- Because heating water is drawn off at a position below the DHW heat exchanger, the flow temperature will be below 60°C, making it potentially suitable for either underfloor heating or existing radiators that require down-rating.

Figure 3.3.10 *Evacuated tube solar collectors mounted on a tiled roof*
Source: Norbert Nagel.

- The design of the storage tank and the water stratification therein is critical to the effectiveness of the system. A typical height-to-diameter ratio should be 2.5:1 or 3:1.
- The solar collector area supplying a combisystem will be typically three times the area supplying a DHW system alone.[5]

Combisystems have been the subject of a major European project, under the Altener programme, that reported in 2003.[6]

Biomass

We have already discussed biomass in the context of community energy systems (Chapter 2.5) and retrofitting building services for dwellings, including the case

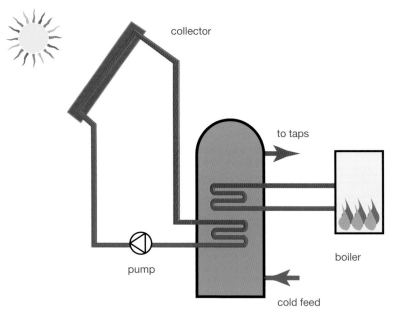

Figure 3.3.11 *Simplified schematic for solar hot water systems*
Source: GreenSpec.

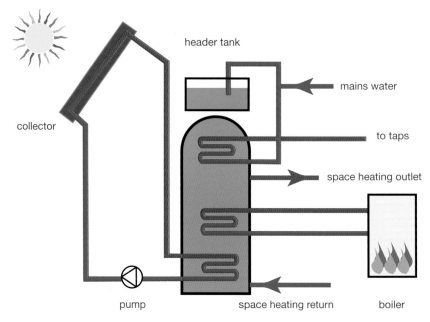

Figure 3.3.12 *Schematic of 'combisystem' solar-assisted heating and hot water system*
Source: GreenSpec.

history for the Barbrook Passivhaus scheme (Chapter 3.2), while there is a detailed analysis of the technologies for biomass and bioliquid combustion in Chapter 2.6 and their integration into building designs in Chapter 3.2 of Appleby (2011a).

The decision whether to retrofit biomass boilers into individual non-residential buildings will depend on a number of factors, including:

- The availability of space for both boilers and storage, in a location where there is access for deliveries without major disruption to either occupants or neighbours. The space required for delivery vehicles must be assessed, along with whether they can use hose connections or require head room for a tip-up truck.
- The long-term sustainability of biomass fuel supply, and the potential impact on cost, carbon emissions and sustainability of having to import from overseas if local sources disappear.
- The availability of a route for a chimney to be taken above roof level.
- The cumulative impact of NO_x and particulate emissions. Although in rural areas the emissions from road traffic is likely to be quite low away from busy roads, so the contribution from biomass boilers should not be significant. However, the cumulative effect of numerous new biomass installations and traffic in urban locations is likely to have an impact on the ability of UK Local Authorities to meet their Air Quality Objectives under the Air Quality Standards Regulations.[7]

Note that the UK Renewable Heat Incentive (RHI) stipulates a maximum NO_x emission of 150 mg/MJ (540 mg/kWh). This compares with 216 mg/kWh for the most efficient Austrian wood pellet boilers and typically between 18 mg/kWh and 70 mg/kWh for gas-fired boilers. Also the European Commission has brought in a requirement under the recast Ecodesign Directive that oil-fired boilers should not exceed 105 mg/kWh, with a maximum of 50 mg/kWh for gas-fired boilers (EC, 2009d).

The following paraphrases the conclusions from a 2008 report on *Biomass for London* (BioRegional, 2008):

- Wood fuel boilers can be as much as five times as expensive as fossil fuel equivalents once auxiliary equipment is included.
- Other costs include any civil works necessary to prepare a suitable fuel store and plant room.
- Wood fuel systems normally have long life expectancy reducing lifecycle costs.
- Electricity from biomass CHP units qualifies for Renewables Obligation Certificates (in the UK).
- The Renewable Heat Incentive applies, with four different tariffs available, depending on the rated heat output of the plant.
- Installations inside Smoke Control Areas must only be of 'exempt appliances'.
- Wood fuel boilers whose burn rate exceeds 45.4 kg/hr must apply to the local authority for chimney height approval.

Geothermal energy and heat pumps

Geothermal energy can be used as a source of heating or cooling a building with or without the assistance of a heat pump. There are locations where heat from volcanic activity or radioactive decay is accessible and can be economically conveyed to surface buildings. Indeed, whole cities, such as Reykjavik in Iceland, have benefitted from this phenomenon for many years. Wherever porous rocks are found, such as the chalk layer below the clay on which London sits, bore-holes can be drilled to access water. Throughout history, wells have been drilled to obtain drinking water from these aquifers. Provided there is no deleterious environmental impact, water from aquifers, typically at a temperature of between 10°C and 12°C, can be drawn from the aquifer and used via a heat exchanger to provide cooling for buildings.

The economics of utilizing this geothermal energy depend largely on how far beneath the ground the source lies. Typically in London, for example, it is necessary to drill between 150 m and 250 m to reach suitably productive rock. Not only does this involve expensive drilling, but the amount of pipework required, the size of pumps and the electrical power required to circulate the water can all mitigate against the feasibility of these schemes.

Where there is no aquifer nor 'hot rocks' accessible, then coupling a heat pump to the ground through burying a coil between one and two metres below the surface may be a more cost-effective option. A ground-coupled heat pump (GCHP) comprises a refrigeration circuit with the evaporator connected to a buried pipe loop ('slinky' coil) or closed-circuit borehole, and its condenser is used to heat water which in turn can be employed in space heating or pre-heating of DHW. The refrigeration circuit incorporates a compressor that heats a refrigerant (low-boiling-point fluid) that has been turned into a vapour by heating it in the evaporator. The high-pressure hot vapour releases its heat in the condenser where it becomes a liquid, losing its pressure in a restriction before entering the evaporator once more. Reverse-cycle heat pumps are widely available that can convert to cooling devices in summer through changing over the refrigeration circuit so that the condenser becomes the evaporator and vice versa.

For retrofitting a medium to large building, a large curtilage would be required for the shallow coil option, with significant ground works and refurbishment of landscaping (see Figure 3.3.13). This might be acceptable where major reconfiguring of the landscape or a new car park are planned (see case history for Suffolk One below), but otherwise boreholes might be the less disruptive option (see Figure 3.3.14).

All external pipework above ground will need frost protection, either by adding anti-freeze to the heat transfer medium or providing trace heating to the exposed pipework.

When comparing these systems with gas-fired or biomass boilers, clearly, unless they use PV or wind turbines to provide electrical power for the pumps and heat pumps, they cannot be considered a zero-carbon heat source. The carbon efficiency depends on the seasonal coefficient of performance (CoP) of the heat pump. CoP is the ratio of heat out to electrical power in, so the higher the value, the stronger the argument for a GCHP. However, to this must be added pump power, which for complex pipework systems can be significant. The carbon intensity of gas in the UK is on average a factor of 2.2 times lower than

Figure 3.3.13 *Trenches for ground-coupled heat pump coils by Ice Energy Heat Pumps Ltd.*
Source: David C. Hobbs.

electricity although, as we saw in Chapter 2.5, the carbon intensity of electricity varies with time of year, time of day and country, and is likely to fall as the electricity grids are decarbonized in coming years.

The seasonal CoP of a ground-coupled system, taking into account pump power, needs to be greater than 2.2 in order to compete with gas-fired plant in carbon terms. CoP depends in part on the flow temperature demanded, and can be as high as 4.0 if this can be kept to 40°C or lower. The same plant delivering water at 60°C would achieve a CoP of around 2.5. Capital costs are perhaps three or four times greater than for a gas-fired boiler, however, but less than for the equivalent biomass boiler. Hence life cycle costing, with a subsidy from such sources as the Renewable Heat Incentive, has to be factored into the decision-making matrix.

Figure 3.3.14 *Typical apparatus for borehole drilling for a GSHP*
Source: Tetris L.

Case histories

Suffolk One Sixth Form College, Ipswich

Although not a refurbishment project, this case history is incorporated because of its novel use of coils buried below a car park for inter-seasonal heat transfer in conjunction with a heat pump. The text below is extracted from the website of the developer of this system, ICAX.[8]

> Inter-seasonal heat transfer has been chosen as the sustainable heating source for the exciting new centre of learning for 16-to-19-year-olds built on a 12-acre site on the outskirts of Ipswich, known as Suffolk One.
>
> Suffolk One is a landmark development providing modern and flexible teaching since it opened in September 2010. The 20,200 m² building – funded by the Learning and Skills Council – accommodates 2,200 students from Ipswich and South Suffolk.
>
> The ICAX design collects heat from asphalt solar collectors in the bus turning areas in summer, stores the heat in 'thermal banks' in the ground, and releases heat to Suffolk One in winter using ground-source heat pumps [Figures 3.3.15 and 3.3.16].
>
> A thermal bank is a bank of earth used to store heat energy collected in the summer for use in winter to heat buildings. A thermal bank is an integral part of an inter-seasonal heat transfer system, invented, developed and patented by ICAX to answer the need for on-site renewable energy without burning fossil fuels.

Figure 3.3.15 *Solar thermal collector for interseasonal heat transfer employs 14 km of pipework embedded in the bus turning area*

Source: www.icax.co.uk/Suffolk_One_College.html.

Figure 3.3.16 *Tarmac bus turning area acting as solar collector for interseasonal heat transfer*

Source: www.icax.co.uk/Suffolk_One_College.html.

The ICAX skid-mounted equipment also captures surplus heat from the roof-mounted solar thermal collectors, whose primary function is to provide hot water, so that the heat generated from thermal panels in the long summer holidays is not wasted (and the life of the panels will be prolonged).

A wide range of energy-efficient mechanical and electrical systems has being installed at Suffolk One with the aim of achieving a targeted BREEAM rating of 'very good'. As well as inter-seasonal heat transfer, rainwater harvesting, Windcatcher and Sunpipe systems are being employed to provide natural ventilation and light. Suffolk One also includes the first installation of Sanyo's co-generation VRF air-conditioning system in the UK. These systems will enable Suffolk One to make long-term savings and reduce its carbon emissions.

Black roads tend to absorb the heat of the sun up to the point when they radiate heat as quickly as they are absorbing it. The surface temperature of roads in direct sunshine can often reach 15°C higher than the ambient air temperature. ICAX collects heat using fluid circulating through an array of pipes embedded in the surface of the road and deposits it in thermal banks constructed beneath the insulated foundation of buildings. The temperature across a large thermal bank can be increased from its natural temperature of 10°C to over 25°C in the course of the summer months.

Solar photovoltaic retrofit to care home at Hanwell in London

This residential care home is located on a busy road in a prominent position in Hanwell, West London. As can be seen in Figure 3.3.17 the building has an L-shaped plan with roofs sloping at 35°, facing South East and South West. Maintaining the original roof line, two large solar PV arrays were installed in place of the roof tiles, having a total rating of 34 kWp.

The care home in Hanwell, London, operates its own kitchens, laundries and lifts, in addition to needing power for the staff and residents' TVs, computers, radios, lights, etc.[9]

Energy demand has been minimized by incorporating a number of energy efficiency improvements into the building prior to installing the PV panels. The installation meets most of the electrical demand for the building, apart from after dark and on overcast days, while exporting power to the grid when there is a surplus generated by the PV panels.

On average, over the course of a whole year, the care home will be close to generating as much power from the roof as is used inside the building.

Figure 3.3.17 *Photovoltaic panels retrofitted to SE- and SW-facing roofs of a care home in Hanwell, London*

Source: In Balance Energy Ltd.

3.4

Indoor environment and hygiene issues

Introduction

As we have already seen, there are many reasons to consider refurbishment or refitting of an existing building, but more often than not the indoor environment of the original will have deteriorated to an extent where complaints are frequent. This may be a particular issue for buildings for which the primary function is office work, with long-term sedentary occupation. The modern densely occupied office presents a potentially stressful environment that, in some instances, results in high levels of dissatisfaction and discomfort, resulting sometimes in illness, absenteeism and low productivity. At the same time, millions of homes throughout the world fall below decency standards, not meeting even the most basic requirements for health, safety and hygiene.

In this chapter we will look at how refurbishment can address these issues and, in particular, prevent recurrence of problems such as sick building syndrome, indoor pollution, thermal, visual and aural discomfort, building-related allergies and Legionnaires' disease.

Of course, it is also important that undertaking refurbishment does not result in any of these problems arising. For example, sealing a building to meet strict airtightness standards, such as those required to create a Passivhaus, results in a reliance on mechanical ventilation during winter months, while extending the period during which overheating can occur. We will examine how these issues should be addressed by the designer of a refurbishment project.

For detailed guidance for designers of new buildings on a 'strategy for avoiding sick buildings', refer to Chapter 3.1 of *Integrated Sustainable Design of Buildings* (Appleby, 2011a, pp. 199–200). This same book also has chapters on thermal comfort (Chapter 3.3), air quality, hygiene and ventilation (Chapter 3.5), light and lighting (Chapter 3.6) and noise and vibration (Chapter 3.8). Much of the guidance in these chapters applies also to refurbishment projects.

In Chapter 2.2, we looked at how questionnaires and physical surveys can be used to identify the extent of discomfort and symptoms being experienced by occupants of an existing building. Below, we will look at how the analysis of these surveys can be used to identify measures for incorporation into refurbishment and refit projects. In Chapter 4.4, we will examine how building and facility managers should follow this up to prevent further problems occurring.

Sick building syndrome and indoor environmental problems

Sick building syndrome (SBS) by definition has no readily identifiable cause, but can be described only by a group of symptoms including the following which have been reported by numerous researchers:

- irritated, itching, dry or watering eyes;
- irritated, itching, runny, dry or blocked nose;
- sore or constricted throat;
- dry mouth;
- headache, lethargy, irritability, difficulty in concentrating;
- dry, itching or irritated skin and rashes.

Box 3.4.1 Risk factors for sick building syndrome

Characteristics of work and building:

- sedentary occupation, clerical work;
- more than half of occupants using display screen equipment for more than 5 hours a day;
- maintenance problems identified;
- low ceilings – typically lower than 2.4 m (between floor finish and underside of ceiling);
- many changes or movements of furniture and equipment (high churn rate);
- public sector tenant or occupants;
- large areas of open shelving and exposed paper;
- sealed building and city centre location;
- large size – typically an occupied floor area greater than 2000 m²;
- building more than 15 years old;
- scruffy appearance;
- large areas of soft furnishings, carpets and fabrics.

Environmental factors include:

- low room humidities;
- low supply rate of outdoor air;
- smoking permitted in work areas;
- damp areas and mould growth;
- dust, solvents and ozone emissions from printers and photocopiers;
- low-frequency fluorescent lamps creating subliminal flicker;
- high room temperatures;
- dusty atmosphere;
- gaseous emissions (volatile organic compounds) from building materials and cleaning materials;
- low-frequency noise.

SBS may be diagnosed when a significant proportion of a building's occupants report a large number of these symptoms during the time they spend in the building, but note that they disappear or steadily reduce when people are away from the building. SBS has generally been associated with office buildings, although the risk factors listed in Box 3.4.1, which is extracted from Chapter 3.1 of Appleby (2011a), may be found wherever there is long-term occupancy. Clearly individual risk factors may be present in many workplaces, and may be easily identifiable and remedied. SBS, however, usually results from a combination of factors that can work together to create a cumulative response for which a single cause cannot be identified. For example, a combination of low humidity with moderately high dust concentrations and irritants such as ozone (an irritant frequently associated with electrical machinery such as photocopiers) and certain volatile organic compounds (VOCs) can cause irritation of eyes, nose and throat. Normally airborne pollutants are absorbed into the mucosa and irrigated away. However, when humidity falls below 30 per cent saturation (%sat) (= 30 per cent relative humidity) for long periods, mucosal irritation is common. The humidity level indoors depends on a number of factors. If a building is naturally or mechanically ventilated, with no artificial humidification, the % saturation will depend on the moisture content of the outdoor air, the air change rate and the amount of moisture emitted from sources indoors, such as human perspiration and expiration, as well as steam from cooking and boiling water. For an unoccupied room having no water present, the moisture content will be the same as outdoors, so when the temperature outdoors falls below about 3°C, the room humidity will fall below 30%sat at an air temperature of 20°C indoors. If outdoor air is supplied at the CIBSE recommended rate of 10 litres/s for every person in an occupied space, then the room humidity will not drop below 30%sat until the outdoor temperature falls below freezing, assuming a typical latent heat gain for each occupant of 55 W and no other source of moisture. At minus 10°C outside, the air is very dry and room humidity will be at about 12%sat. At these levels the air quality must be very good if complaints of mucosal irritation are to be avoided. Also at such low humidities, conditions associated with dry skin tend to appear with some individuals.

Use of computers and display screen equipment is a fact of life for most office workers. Clearly eye irritation is most unwelcome for those spending most of their day staring at a screen. This can be exacerbated if the visual environment for working at a screen is not good, for example, if the screen suffers from reflections, the images are poorly defined or visual acuity is poor on other media being scrutinized, such as books or drawings.

In the UK, the Display Screen Equipment Regulations require, among other things, 'an appropriate contrast between the screen and the background environment' and that 'possible disturbing glare and reflections on the screen . . . be prevented by coordinating workplace and workstation layout with the positioning and technical characteristics of the artificial light sources' (HSE, 1992). It also requires that 'sources of natural light . . . cause no direct glare and no distracting reflections on the screen' and consequently that windows 'be fitted with a suitable system of adjustable covering to attenuate the daylight that falls on the workstation'.

Flicker from fluorescent lamps can contribute to eye strain and headache. But this phenomenon has only been reported for lamps that have ballasts that operate at the mains frequency of 50 or 60 Hz. Modern fluorescent lamps fitted with high-frequency lamps operating at a frequency of 30 kHz have overcome this problem.

Low temperatures and draught are not normally associated with SBS, but they are very often a cause for complaint, and in some instances may result in illness, and even hypothermia and death in vulnerable populations.

According to Section 1 of CIBSE Guide A, for a level of dissatisfaction amongt office workers below 6 per cent, 'operative temperature' (θ_c) should fall between 21°C and 23°C in winter months, assuming typical insulation properties of clothing and chairs, and metabolic rates associated with sedentary activity (CIBSE, 2006d). These recommendations are derived from the international comfort standard, BS EN ISO 7730, that formulates the relationship between these parameters using predicted percentage dissatisfied (PPD) and predicted mean vote (PMV) as statistical representations of the likely response by a typical mix of people (BSI, 2005).

Operative temperature is the internationally recognized comfort temperature that is determined from air and mean radiant temperatures (MRT) and air speed. At air speeds below 0.1 m/s, θ_c approximates to the average between the two temperatures, while MRT is entirely dependent on the surface temperatures surrounding a point and the solid angles subtended to them. MRT approximately replicates the thermal sensations on the skin exposed to these temperatures, and also the temperature measured by a 25 mm globe thermometer and most types of wall thermostat.

In theory, the further outside the CIBSE comfort range operative temperature is, the more people will express dissatisfaction with their thermal environment, although other factors may also create dissatisfaction such as draught, vertical temperature gradient and radiant temperature asymmetry.

As the speed of air relative to exposed skin increases, the temperature feels lower: a phenomenon known as the 'wind chill factor' when associated with cold windy weather. An air speed of 1.0 m/s corresponds with a perceived reduction in temperature of 2.7 K, while if the air speed is 0.25 m/s, an elevation of 1 K in operative temperature is required for the same PPD as at 0.1 m/s or lower. In general, draught risk is greater if velocities exceed 0.15 m/s across occupants' exposed necks or ankles. Draught is frequently combined with temperature gradients, since if the temperature is lower across an occupant's ankles and their ankles are significantly cooler than their heads, while also experiencing a draught across their ankles, then dual discomfort stimuli are at play. For example, if the temperature gradient is 3 K, with, say, 23°C at the head and 20°C at the feet, then around 6 per cent of people would be dissatisfied, but if there is an air speed of 0.15 m/s across those same ankles, then at least 15 per cent of people would express dissatisfaction. If a nearby window is responsible for a radiant temperature asymmetry of 10 K or more, then 5 per cent of people may report dissatisfaction. Of course, some of these dissatisfactions may overlap, but there is no method for estimating a cumulative dissatisfaction with all of these factors. Radiant temperature asymmetry is determined from the difference in radiant temperatures on either side of a body (see CIBSE, 2006d, for more information). These phenomena are not uncommon in older buildings having single-glazed leaky windows that tend to generate draught when it is cold outdoors due to dense cool air being driven downwards and across the adjacent floor.

Prolonged exposure to low temperatures can result in the reduction in core body temperature to below 35°C and the onset of hypothermia, which can be fatal. The risk is dependent primarily on the health and activity level of the person. Those most at risk include the elderly, alcoholics and drug addicts, but medical conditions and medication that interfere with the body's thermo-regulatory system can increase risk. There have been cases where vulnerable individuals have succumbed to hypothermia at temperatures of around 18°C. Clearly, design temperatures should be higher where the majority occupancy is inactive, which is why care homes and nursing homes frequently are kept at between 23°C and 24°C for winter heating.

The above illustrates the intimate relationship in winter between air quality and the thermal and visual environments. At the other end of the scale, excessive temperatures and, to a lesser extent, high humidities can also interact with air quality. Clearly there is a level of dissatisfaction associated with increasing operative temperature, but when associated with high humidity, the body is more likely to overheat because evaporation rates decrease as percentage saturation rises. Also high humidity tends to be associated with condensation onto surfaces at a lower temperature than room air, resulting in a greater risk of fungal and algal growth and associated odours and health risk (see section dealing with allergies on p. 201). For example, if air at 21°C and 70%sat comes into contact with a surface at 15.5°C (i.e. its 'dew point'), then condensation would occur. As well as occurring fortuitously on poorly insulated walls in bathrooms and kitchens, and within ducts carrying warm air through cold environments, condensation occurs deliberately in cooling coils to provide dehumidification. Wherever condensation occurs, if it is allowed to linger and combine with dirt and microorganisms, a substrate can form that supports the growth of mould or algae. Unfortunately, providing humidification can also be associated with trapped moisture within air-handling systems, especially when water has been sprayed into the air and poor maintenance has allowed liquid water that has not been absorbed into the air to pool in the air-handling system, providing a sink for sludge and microorganisms. This can be overcome through the use of steam humidification, although with a significantly greater energy burden.

Noise can be the source of everything from minor discomfort, through annoyance, interference with speech intelligibility to hearing damage. Although individual susceptibility varies, the statistically derived thresholds for these phenomena are understood and guidelines are available from CIBSE and others to help building and services designers prevent complaints from occupants. There are sources of noise both inside and out, some of which are constant and predictable and others which are variable and more difficult to predict.

Noise and vibration are inextricably linked since some of the energy involved in producing noise can also generate vibrations in the solid components of a building which can be felt by occupants in contact therewith.

It has been suggested that exposure to sound frequencies below 20 Hz (infrasound) results in many of the symptoms associated with SBS, but in particular fatigue, headaches, nausea, disorientation and vision problems.

However, a thorough review of the literature carried out by the US National Toxicology Program in 2001 reports that the link between infrasound and symptoms is inconclusive.[1]

Environmental control strategy for workplaces

Anyone contemplating refurbishing a building that contains workplaces should examine Box 3.4.1 and reflect on how many of the risk factors listed are present in their existing building, and what can be done to prevent those that cannot be eliminated from impacting on the refurbished building.

Clearly there are some, such as sedentary occupation, clerical work, display screen use, public sector occupant, building age, large size, low floor-to-ceiling height, city-centre location and high churn rate, that may be beyond the control of those responsible for refurbishment. However, if some or all of these are present, then it highlights the need to identify what measures are required to mitigate the negative impacts of these risk factors and the environmental factors associated with them.

It should be clear from the previous section that one of the key causative factors of SBS symptoms is air quality, particularly when combined with low humidity. Hence taking steps to avoid the release of irritant and malodorous substances into the workplace atmosphere should be a priority.

Air quality and ventilation

For an approach to 'design for good indoor air quality (IAQ)', the reader is referred to Chapter 3.5 of Appleby (2011a) which sets out the following decision-making hierarchy to eliminate or reduce exposure to airborne contaminants:

1   Eliminate contaminants at source.
2   Substitute with substances that produce non-toxic or less malodorous emissions.
3   Reduce emission rate of substances.
4   Segregate occupants from potential sources.
5   Improve ventilation, e.g. by local exhaust, displacement or dilution.
6   Provide personal protection.

This has been adapted from a strategy for minimizing exposure to airborne contamination in an industrial setting; however, apart from providing personal protection perhaps, it is directly applicable to most workplaces.

Substantial improvements in IAQ are possible if low-emission materials are used in the building fabric, finishes, furnishings, ventilation plant and for cleaning. In the USA the Carpet and Rug Institute (CRI) has developed a green label for carpets and adhesives,[2] which involves testing products for 24-hour and 14-day emission rates and test chamber concentrations for 'target contaminants'.

A voluntary American standard is also available for testing office furniture which also uses a 14-day emissions test for a menu of volatile organic compounds (VOCs) (ANSI/BIFMA, 2007).

The use of VOCs and hazardous materials in the manufacture of wood-based furniture is addressed in a decision by the European Commission amending the 1980 Eco-label regulations (EC, 2009e), and individual countries have already introduced proposals for their own mandatory labelling schemes, such as the French 'Emissions dans l'air intérieur' label, which came into force for new products on 1 January 2012 and for existing products at the beginning of 2013, and covers VOC emissions from construction, decoration and furnishing products.

Both the BREEAM and LEED assessment schemes (see Chapter 1.3) give credit for selecting 'low-emitting materials'. For example, BREEAM rewards the procurement of timber panels, structures and flooring, floor coverings and adhesives, ceiling tiles, wall coverings, paints and adhesives that have met relevant standards covering emissions of VOCs, including formaldehyde. LEED sets out a series of VOC content requirements covering adhesives and solvents, paints and coatings, carpet systems, and composite and 'agrifiber' products.

Ozone is an irritant to which the respiratory tract is particularly sensitive, with the eyes affected at higher concentrations. It can also bring on asthma attacks in sensitized individuals. It is formed by the bombardment of oxygen with ultraviolet radiation and through high-voltage electrical discharge through air. It is found in the lower atmosphere through the action of sunlight on oxygen in the air and in the workplace from a number of sources, such as imaging equipment (photocopiers, printers, etc.) electrostatic precipitators and X-ray machines. In the UK, the 15-minute occupational exposure limit (OEL) is 0.2 ppm (HSE, 1996). Although it is rare that concentrations in the office atmosphere ever approach this level, emission limits are being placed on imaging equipment as part of a new European Ecolabel, being drafted at the time of writing (Kougoulis et al., 2011). Based on the German Blue Angel labelling scheme,[3] this sets an emission limit for colour printing of 3 mg/h for ozone, as well as limits for total volatile organic compounds (TVOCs) of 18 mg/h, benzene of <0.05 mg/h, styrene of 1.8 mg/h and dust of 4 mg/h. The standards set for monochrome printers for ozone, TVOCs and styrene are 1.5 mg/h, 10 mg/h and 1.0 mg/h respectively, with other limits staying the same. The US-based EcoLogo scheme refers to the monochrome limits only and omits benzene and styrene from its standard.[4] Refer also to Chapter 1.3 for more information on these labelling schemes and Chapter 4.8 for how they fit into a sustainable procurement strategy.

Clearly, as we saw in Chapter 3.2, office equipment can be a heat source and hence should be a focal point for mechanical extract. The same principle applies to emissions of ozone, TVOCs, etc., and for larger equipment there may be an argument for locating it within a dedicated enclosure, provided with a mechanical exhaust that creates a slight negative pressure, preventing heat and pollutants from migrating to neighbouring areas.

Overheating

Overheating of the workplace can be prevented through a combination of measures. When considering strategies for minimizing SBS risk, there is a dichotomy, however, since SBS is more prevalent in sealed buildings that require air conditioning, but also in buildings that suffer from overheating. As we saw in the previous section, symptoms are more likely when humidity is low, but air quality problems can also be associated with humidification, which is a common function of air conditioning in winter.

Furthermore, a building located adjacent to busy roads, or other sources of noise and pollution, simply may not be able to benefit from natural ventilation because of the unacceptable air pollutant and noise levels that would result.

For an existing building to be suited for refurbishment as a naturally ventilated building, there are a number of factors that should be addressed:

- If the building is already naturally ventilated, is it effective? Results from long-term monitoring of indoor temperatures, noise levels and air quality, as well as occupant satisfaction would be very useful.
- How polluted and noisy is the environment immediately adjacent to the perimeter walls? If there are concerns, then data on noise and air pollutant levels should be obtained, either through monitoring, or from Local Authority data. An example is given in Chapter 3.9 of Appleby (2011a, p. 286) for a building with a window opening 20 m from the edge of a motorway (or similar busy road), where the 18 h average noise level at the façade would typically be around 77 dB, corresponding to between 62 dB and 67 dB for someone sitting close to the window. This compares with the BREEAM credit standard for a cellular office of 40 dB. Similar modelling can be carried out for pollution concentrations outdoors and indoors.
- Are there opportunities to channel air through office spaces from openings that will not allow unacceptably high levels of noise and air pollution into the building? For example, if there are façades that open onto quiet areas outdoors, the problem façades could be protected by creating a double skin that also forms a stack used to draw ventilation air across the entire floor area (see Figure 3.4.1).
- How deep is the floor plan and can the refurbished space be open plan? If workstations have to be located more than 6m from an openable window, natural ventilation is difficult to achieve without connection to a central atrium.
- If the existing building is sealed and mechanically ventilated or air conditioned, can the façade be re-engineered to incorporate openable windows? Could the air conditioning be retained for low-volume winter ventilation with heat recovery (MVHR), with the option to boost for summer cooling should internal temperatures exceed comfort levels (mixed mode operation)?
- Summertime temperatures can be reduced through night cooling. Can the refurbishment strategy allow for exposing the underside of existing concrete slabs or could phase change materials be incorporated into a new suspended ceiling? (See Chapter 3.1.)
- Any natural ventilation strategy will need to be developed and justified using computer simulation predicting summer temperature limits, noise levels and air pollutant levels. Refer to Chapters 3.4 and 3.7 of Appleby (2011a).

Figure 3.4.1 *Berlaymont building, Brussels, with retrofitted glass structure creating double-skin façade*

Source: J. Logan.

Allergies and allergens

Most airborne allergens (aeroallergens) are organic particles with a mean mass aerodynamic diameter of less than 10 microns (μm), while some are in aerosol or vapour form, hence they are respirable.

The concentration of most allergens tends to be highest in the home, particularly in older houses with gardens and pets. Here the most common airborne allergens are house dust mite excreta, animal dander, pollens and moulds.

Because of the smaller volume of soft furnishings, offices tend not to have the same levels of infestation with house dust mites. Where moulds in homes may form in bathrooms, kitchens, on poorly insulated internal surfaces and interstitially (see Figure 3.4.2), offices may have them hidden in air-handling systems. Prevention and remediation strategies for existing buildings will be addressed in Chapter 4.4 and Chapter 4.5. However, a building that has suffered from mould growth presents a continuing risk of proliferation following refurbishment unless all signs of fungal growth are removed, including the substrate on which the spores have lodged, and the conditions that have supported mould growth are eradicated.

The insulation and air tightness measures set out in Chapter 3.1 should prevent surface temperatures dropping below the dew point at which condensation forms. Extract ventilation from 'wet rooms' in dwellings, such as bathrooms and kitchens should prevent room humidities reaching levels at which moisture can form. The greatest risk of condensation in both homes and non-residential buildings is within the air-handling systems (see Chapter 3.2), particularly if warm moist extract air is allowed to pass through a cold space. For this reason it is best to avoid installing MVHR and air-handling units in cold lofts and plant rooms and to keep intake ducts carrying cold air in winter well insulated and as short as possible. Rain should not be allowed to penetrate ductwork or filters. Where humidification is required, this should be via a steam humidifier located in a straight duct run that does not allow unmixed steam to

Figure 3.4.2 *Mould on roof timbers due to interstitial condensation in a poorly ventilated void*

come into contact with duct walls. Cooling coils that also provide dehumidification must be provided with sloping drain trays that can be easily accessed for inspection and cleaning.

Legionellosis cause and prevention

Legionellosis, of which the most common form is Legionnaires' disease, is probably the best known building-related illness, although outbreaks are relatively rare, with between 350 and 400 cases per annum in the UK in recent years.[5] However, it is thought to be under-reported by a factor of ten, because the symptoms are easily confused with other types of pneumonia.

Most infections occur through inhalation of aerosols generated from contaminated water systems associated with buildings. Most serious outbreaks have been associated with contaminated cooling towers, although there has been a steady trickle of cases involving people exposed to aerosols from hot and cold water systems. There are also occasional cases arising from exposure to aerosols generated by spa pools, humidifiers, misting devices, indoor fountains, safety showers, sprinkler testing and vehicle washes. Essentially contamination and exposure to an aerosol are possible for any equipment or system that features some or all of the risk factors set out in Box 3.4.2 (Appleby, 2011a).

For detailed design guidance, refer to CIBSE Technical Memorandum 13 (CIBSE, 2002). We will also be setting out the measures required for minimizing legionellosis risk associated with existing water systems in Chapter 4.5.

When planning a refurbishment, however, there are a number of issues that need to be considered:

* Should the existing air conditioning or processes rely on an evaporative cooling tower or condenser for heat rejection, the opportunity should be

---

Box 3.4.2 Risk factors in outbreaks of legionellosis

* Water temperatures between 20°C and 50°C.
* Nutrients available for growth, such as proteins and rust.
* Niches which protect *Legionella* from the penetration of heat and biocides, such as limescale, sludge and algae.
* Generation of a fine, invisible aerosol such as that produced from taps, shower heads, cooling towers and spray humidifiers.
* Low water turnover which may create conditions during which temperatures drift into the risk zone, biocides decay and sediment precipitates to form a sludge.
* Water system open to ingress of animals, insects, dirt and sun: direct sunlight encourages algal growth which provides an ideal niche for *Legionella*.
* Susceptible people exposed to aerosol, such as those with impaired lung capacity or immune system.

taken to review the risks and maintenance burden they present against the economics of replacing them with a dry method of heat rejection. Clearly, if the refurbishment involves removing the need for cooling entirely, then the problem is solved. If the cooling load has been reduced considerably, but it is decided to retain what will become an oversized evaporative cooling tower, then it must be recognized that legionellosis risk will increase significantly because an under-used tower provides an ideal location for the multiplication of *legionella* bacteria.

- Modifications to water systems must be designed to ensure that no 'dead legs' remain once the alterations have been made. For example, if the domestic water pipework has been re-routed, then all redundant existing pipework must be removed and the opportunity should be taken to extend the primary circulation loop so that dead leg connections to taps are kept as short as possible. This also minimizes the amount of water wasted as people wait for hot water to reach the taps, reducing both water and energy consumption. It also means that people are more likely to wash their hands properly, although care has to be taken where a vulnerable population has access to the taps, such as in a care home, through the installation of mixer taps, typically set to a maximum of 43°C (see Chapter 10 in Brundrett, 1992).

- Cold water storage tanks that are located in warm environments present a risk of legionella multiplication where water throughputs are low and temperatures can rise above 20°C. Retrofitting low-water-consumption appliances may result in a significant reduction in water consumption (see Chapter 3.5), resulting in much greater dwell times in storage tanks. Where multiple tanks have been installed, it is not unusual for one tank to be favoured over others, resulting in stagnation and sedimentation in the others. The need for water storage should be reviewed, based on the risk of mains failure, and new tanks installed based on predicted 12- or 24-hour consumption, as appropriate.

Decency standards for housing

In Chapter 1.2, we saw that there are millions of homes in the UK that do not meet the government's own standards for decent homes. The criteria covered in the Housing Health & Safety Rating System (HHSRS) definition for a decent home are listed in Box 1.2.3 on p. 24.

Local Authorities can take action under the Housing Act 2004 and the HHSRS Regulations 2005 to force landlords to make necessary improvements to dwellings where an inspector finds that the rating under the HHSRS can be described as 'Category 1'. This requires an assessment of the likelihood of harm arising from all of the hazards listed in Box 1.2.3, based on a complex procedure set out in the Regulations. Box 3.4.3 is extracted from the CLG guidance (CLG, 2006).

Box 3.4.3 Definition of a decent home

A decent home meets the following four criteria:

(a) It meets the current statutory minimum standard for housing.
- Dwellings which fail to meet this criterion are those containing one or more hazards assessed as serious ('Category 1') under the HHSRS.

(b) It is in a reasonable state of repair.
- Dwellings which fail to meet this criterion are those where either:
    - one or more of the key building components are old and, because of their condition, need replacing or major repair; or:
    - two or more of the other building components are old and, because of their condition, need replacing or major repair.

(c) It has reasonably modern facilities and services.
- Dwellings which fail to meet this criterion are those which lack three or more of the following:
    - a reasonably modern kitchen (20 years old or less);
    - a kitchen with adequate space and layout;
    - a reasonably modern bathroom (30 years old or less);
    - an appropriately located bathroom and WC;
    - adequate insulation against external noise (where external noise is a problem); and:
    - adequate size and layout of common areas for blocks of flats.

A home lacking two or fewer of the above is still classed as decent, therefore it is not necessary to modernize kitchens and bathrooms if a home meets the remaining criteria.

(d) It provides a reasonable degree of thermal comfort

It should be noted that, while dwellings meeting criteria (b), (c) and (d) are likely also to meet criterion (a), some Category 1 hazards may remain to be addressed. For example, a dwelling meeting criterion (d) may still contain a Category 1 damp or cold hazard.

Any dwelling that falls below the decent homes standards will clearly need a major refurbishment just to make it habitable. If the building is structurally unsound, then it may have to be demolished. However, in many cases the amount of work required will provide an opportunity for the owner, landlord or property manager to bring thermal performance up to a high standard, while tapping into funding streams, such as the Energy Company Obligation (ECO).

3.5
Water-saving measures

Introduction

Water is a valuable resource and although there are some regions that have more than they need, long periods of drought impact on a large proportion of the world population. The developed world in particular is profligate with the resources it has, with nations such as the USA and Australia having daily per capita abstraction rates of 4740 and 3562 litres per person respectively, compared with 630 litres for the UK.[1] Estimates for developing countries vary from 50 to 100 litres/person/day. These data cover water supplying agriculture, industry, households and commercial demand. The corresponding rates drawn off by households are 575 litres/person/day in the USA, 493 in Australia and 150 in the UK. This compares with household use of 20 litres/person/day in countries such as Ethiopia, Rwanda and Uganda.[2]

In the UK, most authorities agree that office water consumption averages at between 30 and 50 litres/worker/day, depending on whether there is a canteen, showers, humidifiers and evaporative cooling towers.[3] However, it is hospitals, sports centres, hotels, garden centres, residential care homes, car wash facilities and certain industrial processes that tend to have the greatest intensity of water consumption, particularly where there are swimming pools or spa pools, and water is used for washing, air cleaning, manufacture, therapy or treatment.

Abstraction, chemical treatment and distribution of water and its discharge as sewage have a range of environmental impacts, including carbon emissions associated with energy use and pollution, which we will be discussing in the next section.

Elsewhere we will be focusing on what measures can be taken during refurbishment to reduce water consumption, including retrofitting water-efficient fittings and appliances and the installation of rainwater harvesting or grey water recycling systems. For water management strategies and measures applicable to existing buildings please refer to Chapter 4.2. The reader might also like to read Chapter 3.9 of *Integrated Sustainable Design of Buildings* (Appleby, 2011a) for more detailed guidance on the design of water-conserving systems for new buildings.

Environmental impact of water use

Figure 3.5.1 illustrates one impact of over-consumption when combined with below average rainfall for a number of years. The process of abstracting and storing water, adding chemicals, distributing it to consumers, then handling,

Figure 3.5.1 *North Platte River, Wyoming USA, May 2002*
Source: Kirk Miller.

processing and discharging or recycling the sewage uses primary energy, resulting in associated carbon emissions, whilst having a number of environmental impacts associated with sewage management and chemical water treatment.

Around 90 per cent of greenhouse gas emissions associated with water use come from heating of domestic hot water (EST, 2011), while the emissions associated with treatment and pumping have been estimated by Anglian Water as 0.452 $kgCO_{2eq}$ per m^3 for water and 0.781 $kgCO_{2eq}$ per m^3 for sewage.[4] In 2004/05, an average of 15,807 million litres of water were delivered to the 'public distribution system' in England and Wales per day. Assuming this was all pumped and treated, the total annual greenhouse gas emissions associated with this supply was around 2.608 million tonnes CO_{2eq} per year. With an estimated 10 billion litres of sewage being treated daily in England and Wales,[5] the associated annual greenhouse gas emissions are approximately 285,000 tonnes CO_{2eq}. These figures should be compared with a total for England and Wales from all sources of 560 million tonnes for 2005.

The Energy-Saving Trust determined that the total CO_2 emissions associated with water use for a typical existing household is 959 kg per annum (EST, 2009). The balance of predicted carbon emissions from this study is shown in Figure 3.5.2. The model used for these figures allows not only for the energy used by the utility companies but also the contribution that hot water use makes to space heating and the heat loss to cold water sitting in pipes and cisterns.

The water consumption data on which the CO_2 predictions are based is shown in Figure 3.5.3. Note that the EST model assumes a proportion of washing machine supply was from a gas-fired boiler, while all dishwasher water was heated electrically.

There are a number of other environmental impacts associated with water supply, mostly from treatment of waste water and sewage. Although chemicals

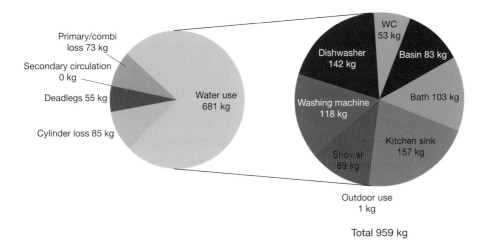

Figure 3.5.2 *CO$_2$ emissions breakdown for existing housing stock based on average household of 2.4 persons*

Source: Clarke, Grant and Thornton (EST, 2009).

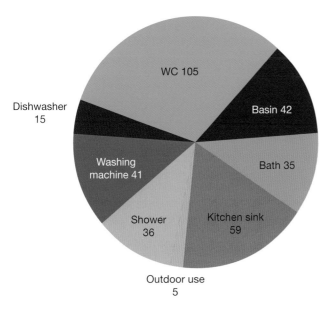

Figure 3.5.3 *Water use data in litres/day for an average household, used for CO$_2$ predictions in Figure 3.5.2*

Source: Clarke, Grant and Thornton (EST, 2009).

that have significant impact in high enough concentrations, such as chlorine, are used in water treatment, the most significant impacts come from sewage settlement and treatment, with associated handling of liquid, slurry, sludge and solid residuals. Odour comes from the occasional overflow of untreated sewage as well as the formation of acetic acid and methyl acetate during settlement.

Retrofitting water-saving appliances

Many of the same types of appliance and fitting are used in both residential and non-residential applications, and when it comes to retrofitting, the same issues need to be considered. However, the behaviour of occupants in using water services differs significantly with the nature of occupancy. For example, the length of time an individual spends washing hands after using sanitary accommodation and their tendency to leave a tap running are typically different when they are in their own home compared with their workplace or a motorway service station.

WCs

As can be seen from Figure 3.5.3, water use in flushing toilets tends to be the single greatest contributor to household water consumption. Most WCs installed before 2001 had 9-litre cisterns or larger, with a siphon-operating mechanism. It is interesting to note that the lever-operated siphon mechanism was developed to avoid the risk of cisterns leaking directly into the pan. Since 2001 the Water Fittings Regulations have allowed approved button-operated drop and flap valves, which, when they fail, allow a continuous trickle of water to flow into the pan. The same Regulations required that maximum cistern capacity be reduced to 6 litres and allowed for the introduction of dual-flush cisterns.

In a recent publication, the Environment Agency reported a study that showed a massive increase in water bills from water leakage via sticking drop valves in 6 per cent of homes in a sample of 500 (EA, 2007). The door was opened for valve-operated flushing to bring the UK into line with the rest of the European Union, but the problem also exists elsewhere, such as the USA, for example:

> It is estimated that in the US about 20% of WCs leak at a rate of about 20,000 US gallons per year per WC (76 m³/year). A standard allowance for WC leakage in US textbooks is 15–30 litres per person per day i.e. the water use of a 6-litre WC could be doubled due to leakage. If we assume 4 people sharing a single WC this equates to about 60–120 litres per WC per day. 60 litres per day is a lot of water but only equals 2.5 litres per hour, which is below the starting flow of domestic water meters (hence would be difficult to detect). When this 0.04 litres/minute leak is simulated, the resulting flow down the pan is not noticeable to the untrained eye.[6]

Waste also can occur through inlet valves allowing water to enter a cistern while the water is leaving, which typically increases water use by around 17 per cent. This can be prevented through the installation of a delayed action inlet valve.

Although dual-flush WCs have become the norm, their performance can be disappointing. In theory, it is likely they would be used on low flush three times for every single full-flush operation, resulting in an average water use of 4 litres per flush for a 6:3 full:reduced flush ratio (a 33 per cent reduction). However, studies in a residential context have found that water consumption only dropped by 18 per cent of full-flush volume compared with a 6-litre cistern. On the other hand, studies involving retrofitting dual-flush insert devices (see Figure 3.5.4)

Figure 3.5.4 *Typical dual-flush insert device*
Source: www.multikwik.com.

Figure 3.5.5 *Variable flow siphon flush*
Source: Opella.

into cisterns of various sizes resulted in a reduction in flush volume of 27 per cent and an average reduction in water consumption per household of 8.5 per cent.[7] The reasons for this departure from the theory may be in part due to a lack of understanding of the push button controls and multiple flushing for stubborn deposits.

Variable volume siphon flushing devices are also available, such as the one shown in Figure 3.5.5, which allows manual control over the flushing process, so that the flow can be interrupted when the bowl is clean.

For non-residential applications wherever there are urinals, there is no point in installing dual-flush cisterns because the WCs will tend only to be used for solids.

Bearing in mind the risk of leakage through standard valve cisterns, the designer should consider retrofitting dual-flush or controllable siphon devices along with delayed action inlet valves. Table 3.5.1 is extracted from the Environment Agency guidance and summarizes the options available, indicating water volume saved and cost rating.

Table 3.5.1 *Siphon devices suitable for retrofit*

Device	Saving per flush	Advantages	Disadvantages	Cost
Cistern displacement devices	0.5 to 2.5 litres	• Low cost or DIY labour only	• Only beneficial if the existing full flush is excessive	£
Interruptible flush – user releases lever or pushes a button when the pan is clear	30%	• Low-flush default forces regular user to learn the operation • Accurate control of flush volume possible	• First-time users may assume the flush is ineffective unless instructions are provided	££
Variable flush – knob rotated for high, medium and low flush	30%	• Obvious operation without instructions	• Might not appeal visually to all users • Requires two operations, adjust and flush • Potential for double flushing	££
Dual-flush retrofit or replacement siphon – default to part flush	30%	• Low-flush default forces regular user to learn the operation	• First-time users may assume the flush is ineffective unless instructions are provided • Potential for double flushing	£££
Dual-flush retrofit or replacement siphon – default to full flush	30%	• Pan should always be cleared	• Without instructions, users might never discover the part-flush function	£££

Source: EA, 2007.

Urinals

Older urinal installations might typically have a continuous flow of water, consuming perhaps 500 m³ of water a year to flush four or five stalls, regardless of use. In fact, the Water Supply Regulations stipulate that each stall should be flushed with no more than 7.5 litres per hour per stall. However, rather than using a manually adjusted valve to allow a continual flow at this rate, a variety of low-cost automatic systems is available, including solenoid valves operated from timers, door switches, infra-red presence detector or water pressure fluctuation when a hot tap is operated. For maximum economy, flushing for individual stalls can be provided using IR devices or a sprung-loaded push button or lever-operated valve.

Alternatively, where a major refurbishment of sanitary accommodation is planned, existing stalls can be replaced with waterless urinals. These incorporate a deodorizing chemical seal that is lighter than urine and caps the outlet, thus masking the odour from the drain (see Figure 3.5.6).

Taps

The type of tap that offers the greatest water saving will depend on how it is to be used. A tap over a kitchen sink or bath will usually be used for filling things and hence the flow rate is probably not very important. Taps used primarily for washing hands, however, can perform well with low flow rates, provided their wetting capability is maximized. Hence aerated or spray taps are ideally suited

Cross-Section of the Patented Vertical EcoTrap®

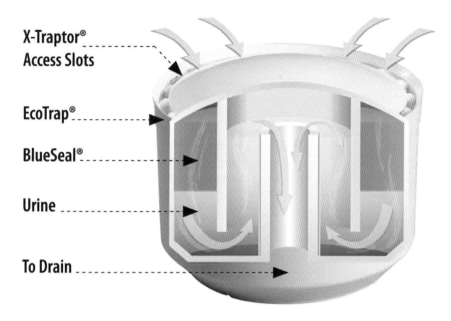

X-Traptor®
Access Slots

EcoTrap®

BlueSeal®

Urine

To Drain

Figure 3.5.6 *Waterless urinal: typical outlet showing the operating principle*
Source: Waterless Co.

to hand washing and can save up to 80 per cent of water consumption compared with a conventional bib tap. However, in a residential application and with a flow rate of typically around 1.7 to 2 litres/min., a single spray tap will not generate sufficient flow through a combination boiler for it to operate.

Products are available that operate as a spray tap when the handle is partially turned then open to full bore for basin filling when operation is continued. Where there is a risk of taps being left running, which applies to most taps used for hand washing, particularly outside the home, then a degree of automation is worth considering. This can be achieved with infra-red operation or self-closing push button taps, although the reliability of the latter is varied, with large variations in delay before closing possible. Infra-red has the advantage of hygienic operation, although batteries or electricity supply will be required.

Baths and showers

Many homes have both a bath and a shower, either with the shower over the bath or in a separate cubicle. Multiple showers in a single household are not unusual. The maximum bath size allowed by the Water Supply Regulations is 230 litres, corresponding to a water capacity of approximately 160 litres when occupied. A modern water-efficient bath will contain around 70 litres of water when in use.

According to a report from the Energy-Saving Trust, water consumption associated with both bath and shower use is on the rise, and reductions in water use due to more efficient white goods and dual-flush WCs are being offset by these increases (EST, 2011). A detailed report by Waterwise published in 2009 reported that around 80 per cent of households contained showers in 2006 compared with 5 per cent in 1970. Another survey reported in the same publication that approximately 40 per cent of respondents stated that they always shower rather than take a bath (Waterwise, 2009). This same report also identifies the significant increase in the retrofitting of power showers: one survey indicating that some 28 per cent of households have them. These devices boost the flow of water to anything up to 20 litres/min., compared with less than 5 litres/min. for electric showers and between 5 and 7 litres/min. for those with aerating shower heads, resulting in an increase in energy demand and associated carbon emissions. Although there is evidence that power showers are operated at below full flow, with a median operating time of 5 minutes, this represents perhaps 75 litres for a typical shower per use.

User satisfaction is an important factor in retrofitting showers. The main reason why many people purchase power showers is to 'enjoy the shower experience', although others may see them as a luxury good and status symbol. Some people find the needle jets from power showers uncomfortable and that the sheer volume of water washes away soap suds too quickly.

Although electric showers are the most popular choice for retrofitting, the quality of the shower experience is variable and the duration of showers may need to be longer because of the time required to rinse soap away, particularly from long hair. Aerated shower heads achieve better wetting at similar flow rates because the spray is mixed with air. Some aerated shower heads are advertised as being suitable for use with electric showers.

According to the UK Water Technology List: 'An efficient aerated shower-head is defined as a showerhead that mixes air and water and delivers a fully formed spray pattern, with a flow rate of no more than 9 litres/minute when operated at dynamic pressures up to 5 bar (for all spray settings).'[8]

Another source of wastage associated with showering is the water run-off while adjusting temperatures with a mixer tap. This can be avoided by retro-fitting a mixer having a separate thermostatic adjustment that can be left at the desired setting while the water valve is opened (see Figure 3.5.7).

Showers installed in non-residential buildings tend to be used by those who have undertaken athletic activities such as cycling, swimming or running. Generally time spent in the shower will be shorter, but there is a greater risk of showers being left operating once the person has left. This can be avoided by installing timed push-button valves or infra-red presence detection, with a fixed temperature setting.

White goods and commercial washing equipment

With the developments there have been in washing powders and liquids in recent years, many washing machines are operated for much of the time at a wash temperature of 40°C or lower. Partly because of this, but also to reduce manufacturing costs, manufacturers have taken the opportunity to drop hot fill options from their product ranges. This means that most washing machines use electricity to heat water, even for higher temperature washes. A consequence of this is that machines need to be cleaned more frequently, at temperatures as high

Figure 3.5.7 *Typical thermostatic shower mixer*
Source: Ideal Standard International.

as 90°C, to clear soap residue that previously would have been dissolved at the higher temperatures. At the same time water consumption per load has fallen drastically: from around 150 litres in 1990 to 50 litres and less in 2010. The most efficient washing machines have a water consumption of below 7.5 litres per wash.[9]

To be listed in the UK's Water Technology List and qualify for enhanced capital allowances (ECAs), commercial washing machines must be of the 'horizontal axis (type) with an energy and wash performance equivalent to the European Energy Label rating of AA for energy consumption and wash performance respectively. The machine must also not exceed a maximum water consumption of 12 l/kg wash load'[10] (see also Chapter 3.2). The list also covers industrial washing machines such as batch washers, washer tunnels and washer extractors.

Dishwashers use between 12 and 14 litres to wash 12 place settings when fully loaded, compared with some 40 litres that would be required to wash the same amount by hand. This assumes that there is no hand rinsing prior to loading the dishwasher, however. Unlike washing machines, dishwashers generally operate at 60°C or higher and it should be possible to connect them up to a hot water supply. Most have only one connection and are designed to heat water supplied from the mains, so the manufacturer's literature should be consulted prior to operating the machine for the first time.

Typically, large restaurants and food service operations utilize commercial dishwashers. Prior to loading the dishwasher, plates and dishes are manually sprayed (pre-rinsed) to remove loose or 'sticky' food. The washing of dishes typically consumes two-thirds of all water use from the restaurant. The water used in this pre-rinsing operation is often twice the volume of water used by the dishwashing equipment. The most cost-effective water conservation measure in a commercial food service operation is improving the efficiency of the pre-rinse spray valve.[11]

The Water Technology List does not cover dishwashers but the UK 'Government Buying Standards' site refers to the EU Energy Label scheme[12] for domestic-scale appliances and the US Energy Star specification[13] for larger commercial dishwashers. For the former, the mandatory standard is for a minimum A rating covering energy, cleaning and drying with water consumption of 12 litres for 14 place settings, dropping to 10 litres for a best practice standard.

Swimming pools

Water consumption associated with a swimming pool depends on a number of factors including:

- whether located indoors or out and the climate conditions to which it is exposed;
- the surface area of water;
- the type and frequency of use;
- the presence of a cover and how frequently it can be deployed;
- the filter type and the amount of back-washing required;
- the water recycling strategy;
- the chemical dosing and maintenance regime;
- the leak prevention strategy;
- the contribution from rain water.

Any retrofit strategy to reduce water consumption will depend partly on whether the use is residential or commercial, whether the pool is located outdoors or indoors and the constraints imposed by the site or building. The following might be considered, if not already in place:

- Fit a cover: particularly important for outdoor pools and/or ones that have long periods out of use.
- Fit a water meter as a leak detector.
- Install automatic top-up.
- Recycle filter back-wash water.
- Install a cyclone device to take out larger solids upstream of the filter.
- Install rainwater harvesting to supplement water supply for top-up and back-wash,[14] see below.

Evaporative cooling towers and condensers

As we saw in Chapter 3.4, there are compelling reasons why evaporative cooling towers or condensers should be removed as part of a refurbishment strategy. The amount of water used in an open cooling tower depends on how much is lost through drift, evaporation, leakage and windage/splashing from the water that cascades through the pack or heat exchanger into the open pond at its base, along with the amount of 'blowdown' or bleed required to control the concentration of salts, such as chlorides, and other dissolved impurities (total dissolved solids, TDSs), in the circulating water. Evaporative loss depends on the amount of heat rejected, while other losses depend on the spray generated and the amount captured in the drift eliminators located normally at the tower discharge and the splash guards located at the air inlets. Modern towers are designed with very effective drift eliminators to reduce the risk of *legionella* bacteria being carried out of the tower in very fine water droplets. Typically between 2.8 and 3 litres/h of make-up water will be required per kW of heat rejection capacity. Evaporation losses depend on the water circulation rate and the difference between the water temperature and the dew point temperature of the air. Hence, as the amount of heat rejected reduces, the evaporation rate should fall, assuming water is diverted from circulating through the tower as demand reduces. A cooling tower serving an office building having a significant cooling load might use around 800 litres/m^2/annum. For a 10,000 m^2 office block, this equates to 8,000 m^3 of water per annum.

Humidifiers

The amount of water required for humidification depends on the amount of air to be humidified, the percentage saturation to which the building is controlled, the amount of fortuitous moisture gain to the treated space and the moisture content of the outside air. The latter value varies with time, while moisture emissions will vary with occupancy and other sources, such as cooking and kettle boiling.

Steam humidification requires a source of steam, either from a central boiler or from an electric or gas-fired steam generator, piped into a supply air duct via a header containing an array of nozzles. Not all of the water supplied ends up increasing room humidity: some is 'blown down' for the same reasons described above for evaporative cooling towers; while some is lost through condensation on surfaces within the ductwork. These factors can result in 50–100 per cent more water being drawn from the mains than is used for humidification.

When retrofitting humidification equipment, it is worth considering devices that incorporate condensate recovery.

Car wash systems

Pollution prevention guidelines PPG 13 published for the UK by the Environment Agency and Scottish Environmental Protection Agency (SEPA) states that:

> Recycling effluent and reusing the water (from a commercial car wash) is the best environmental option for dealing with vehicle washing and cleaning effluent. Use washing equipment that has a collection and re-use or recirculation process. These systems usually require regular, off-site removal of some water, silt or sludge so waste management licensing legislation will apply.[15]

Figure 3.5.8 shows a typical arrangement for a car wash recycling system with sludge pit and associated water filtration and treatment system.

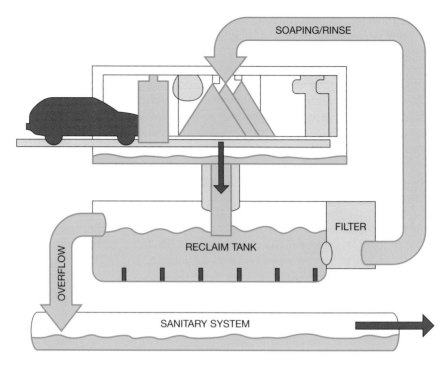

Figure 3.5.8 *Typical car wash recycling system*

Source: www.dontdrivedirty.com

Piped distribution and metering

When a refurbishment enables replacement of distribution pipework, the opportunity should be taken to reduce the length of hot water 'dead legs' in order to minimize the amount of water that has to be run off in order to attain the desired temperatures. This is also a requirement to reduce the risk of legionella bacteria multiplication (see Chapter 3.4).

According to a report from the Environment Agency (EA) published in 2009, only 32 per cent of households in England and Wales paid metered charges for their water at the time when the research was done for the report (EA, 2009). Research has indicated that water use should fall by between 10 and 15 per cent once water meters are installed, while bills will be lower for around 75 per cent of households fitted with meters compared with those paying standard water charges. The EA has therefore recommended a roll-out of water meters, so that at least 80 per cent of households in England and Wales are metered by 2020.

For retrofitting non-residential or multi-residential buildings, it is a good idea to install meters having a pulsed output for linking with a building energy management system (BEMS), along with other utilities, and via a phone line to the energy company for billing purposes. Similarly for individual dwellings, meters should be either located so as to be easily read by the occupier or form part of 'smart metering' systems that provide readily accessible feedback on consumption and include output from electricity and heat or gas meters.

Major leaks can be sensed through the pulsed output from a meter linked to the BEMS which includes trend analysis software that is able to tell when flows exceed the norm and hence raise the alarm. For small buildings with no BEMS, bespoke leak detectors are available that can be installed in the main water supply.

Small leaks in toilet areas or blocks that might go undetected overnight or at the weekend can have their impact minimized through the installation of proximity detectors; these are positioned to sense occupation that operate solenoid valves in the water supply to the area/block.

Pulsed metering, leak detection and sanitary supply shut-off all gain credits under the BREEAM scheme.

Retrofitting rainwater harvesting and grey water recycling

Rainwater harvesting systems vary in complexity from a simple rainwater butt at one end of the spectrum to a large-scale bespoke system comprising catchpits, filters, underground storage, water treatment and pump. The former may store rainwater from the roof of a house for irrigation purposes, while the latter might use roof and surface water for toilet flushing, swimming pool or cooling tower feed, as well as irrigation.

The storage tank is normally sized from the amount of rainwater likely to be available, which depends on the surface area of the roof and the slope and type of roof surface. For example, typically only 50 per cent of rain that falls on a flat roof is available for harvesting (i.e. a drainage factor of 0.5). This proportion falls to even lower levels for green or landscaped roofs, which do not make an ideal catchment area for rainwater harvesting. Smooth sloping roofs can have a drainage factor as high as 0.9. The amount of water stored is usually calculated from 5 per cent of the total annual rainfall adjusted for the drainage factor of the roof and the filter efficiency of the installation (available from the manufacturer, but typically 0.9). Coarse filters are required to remove leaves and other large solids. Beyond this, the level of filtration and water treatment provided depends on the appliances being supplied. It may be considered that coarse filtration is sufficient for irrigation and even supplying WC cisterns, although there have been some problems with staining of WC basins from residues in the harvested water. Some installations have incorporated additional filtration and ultraviolet biocidal control, although the cost, energy consumption and additional maintenance from these must be factored into the feasibility study for the installation.

Water that has been used for washing purposes can also be collected, cleaned to some extent and re-used for flushing toilets and to supply washing machines, if the quality is good enough. Generally speaking, water is collected from showers, baths and wash hand basins, and possibly from washing machines and dishwashers, although the cleaning system would have to be sufficiently robust to handle the additional detergent and grease loads from these appliances. Stored water is held for a time to allow sludge to collect and surface scum to be removed automatically and both flushed away. The whole system is drained and flushed through if there is no demand for a pre-determined period.

For larger installations a water treatment plant can be installed on similar lines to a municipal plant, but the additional carbon emissions associated with water treatment will have to be justified by the water savings achieved.

Both of these types of system require complete re-plumbing and space for storage, hence they would only be suitable for major refurbishments.

For detailed design guidance, refer to the *Reclaimed Water* publication from CIBSE (CIBSE, 2005) and advice and guidance from Anglian Water and downloadable from the UK Rainwater Harvesting Association website.[16] Rainwater harvesting equipment appears in the Water Technology List[17] and hence qualifies for tax relief in the UK through enhanced capital allowances (ECAs).

3.6
Measures to reduce and recycle waste

Introduction

According to the Department for the Environment, Food and Rural Affairs (DEFRA), 'The UK consumes natural resources at an unsustainable rate and contributes unnecessarily to climate change. Each year we generate approximately 290 million tonnes of waste, which causes environmental damage and costs businesses and consumers money.'[1]

Processing and landfill of waste have considerable environmental impacts, including greenhouse gas emissions associated with methane production at landfills and wastewater treatment plants. The US Environmental Protection Agency (EPA) reports that 161 million tonnes of CO_{2eq} were emitted from these sources in 2006 (EPA, 2008). Elsewhere the EPA claims that the recycling rate across the USA in 2005 was 32 per cent, saving some 49.9 $MtCO_{2eq}$.[2] DEFRA report that 'over 40% of household waste was recycled in England in 2010/11, compared to 11% in 2000/01', while figures calculated by RecycleNow indicate that 'UK recycling saves more than 18 million tonnes of carbon dioxide a year.'[3]

In 2008, the EC Waste Directive introduced the principles of the 'waste hierarchy' and that the 'polluter pays'. It defined the waste hierarchy, in order of preference, as:

1   prevention;
2   preparing for re-use;
3   recycling;
4   other recovery, such as energy from waste;
5   disposal.

This has been transposed into law in England and Wales through the 2011 Waste (England and Wales) Regulations (see Chapter 1.2). We will be examining strategies that can be introduced by businesses and households to meet the requirements of these Regulations in Chapter 4.3. Chapter 3.8 will examine the impact of recycling and re-use on the sustainability of materials used in refurbishment. Chapters 3.11 and 4.3 of *Integrated Sustainable Design of Buildings* cover design and construction issues around waste management respectively (Appleby, 2011a).

Retrofit strategy to encourage recycling and composting

When planning for refurbishment, a review of the existing waste strategy should reveal whether there is sufficient provision for recycling of waste generated from the activities carried out within the building. Most councils and local authorities will have a collection strategy for recyclable waste, although these are reviewed from time to time when there are changes in legislation and budgetary constraints. Space needs to be allocated for suitably sized bins close to locations where waste is generated and where it is to be collected by the refuse collection vehicles.

The types of waste to be separated and the volumes generated will depend on the activities for which the building is intended and the policy of the local authority on grouping of recyclable wastes, which in turn depends on the design of the facilities to which the waste is sent. For example, household waste may be grouped into three separate streams, i.e. glass; food waste; and plastic bottles with cans, paper and card. This can be confusing for the householder since some types of plastic are not deemed recyclable, such as packaging, tubs and bags. The reason for this is given on the UK's 'recycle-more' website as follows:

> Plastic bottles are specified as they are made from one of only three polymer types and are very easily identified, both by members of the public and those sorting the collected bottles. The three polymer types used are PET (polyethylene terephthalate) (e.g. fizzy drink bottles and squash bottles), HDPE (high-density polyethylene) (e.g. milk bottles and detergent bottles) and PVC (polyvinyl chloride) (e.g. large squash bottles), although the use of PVC in such applications is in decline.
>
> Items such as margarine tubs and rigid food containers are often made from a very wide range of polymer, many of which are blends. These are much more difficult to identify and separate efficiently.
>
> It is also more difficult to secure an outlet for the material as mixed plastics are not in high demand.[4]

Plastic bags are difficult to separate from other plastics, although there is some recycling in supermarkets, while shoppers are being encouraged to use alternative, more sustainable bags.

Space planning for waste receptacles for recyclables is covered by environmental assessment schemes such as BREEAM and LEED (see detailed discussion in Chapter 3.11 of Appleby, 2011a).

Retrofitting evacuated waste conveying systems

The principle of piped waste conveying using a vacuum was developed as a retrofit solution for a hospital in Sweden in the late 1950s as a logical extension of the central vacuum cleaning systems already in use at that time for large buildings. The concept was simple, but developing a system that was reliable, hygienic and did not suffer from periodic blockage was quite a challenge.

Vacuum waste conveying systems have now been installed globally, many of them serving entire communities or large mixed-use developments. Users deposit their solid waste into colour-coded waste collection points which may be located indoors or out, and the waste is held temporarily above a closed storage valve. Once the inlet is full the valve opens under the dictates of a central control system that only allows waste of the same type into the underground pipes at any one time.

When the control system senses it is time to empty the inlets, central fans are started creating a vacuum in the pipework and a supply air valve is opened in order to allow transport air to enter the system (Figure 3.6.1). The storage valves beneath the inlets are opened one at a time, allowing the waste to fall into the underground pipework (Figure 3.6.2) and be evacuated away to the collection station where it is drawn through a cyclone and separated from the transport air. The waste then falls into a compactor where it is compressed and transferred into a sealed container designated for the specific waste type. The transport air is discharged to the atmosphere after having passed through filters and silencers.

Although expensive to install, these systems offer significant advantages over the normal approach to waste collection. For example, refuse vehicles are kept away from most of the site, reducing nuisance from noise, odour and spilt waste as well as reducing the fuel consumption, carbon emissions, pollution and risk of accidents associated with the operation of these vehicles. The carbon emissions associated with the fans operating four or five times a day for an average of 30 minutes is usually significantly lower than from the fuel consumption of refuse vehicles handling the same volume of waste. There is also far less manual lifting of waste bags, especially if inlet points are provided on every floor of apartment buildings. Furthermore the risk of vandalism and arson are significantly reduced because of the reduced storage time.

Not everything can be handled by these systems. The size of waste handled is limited by the size of the inlet openings and underground pipework, which are typically 300–400 mm in diameter. Clearly it is possible that there could be some abuse of the system, in particular those designed for access by the public. Blockages could be caused if large highly absorbent articles are disposed of and exposed to moisture, while a separate system would be required to handle large volumes of slurry from kitchens. Problems could also arise from depositing

Figure 3.6.1 *Underground vacuum waste conveying system*
Source: Envac Group.

Figure 3.6.2 *Typical waste collection points for underground conveying system*
Source: Envac Group.

heavy items such as builder's rubble or scrap metal into the system. The system is not intended for the disposal of dead animals, faeces, highly acidic or alkaline solutions, paints and adhesives. Appropriate signage and community information are therefore very important.

There is a small but real risk that someone could deposit an explosive device into one of the inlets. However, this is true of any waste bin, and the underground system is more likely to contain the explosion and limit the damage than a street-level bomb would. When installed as part of a private community, it is possible to introduce a measure of security by installing lockable inlets accessed with a swipe card.

These systems tend to be most economically retrofitted to high-density districts and developments, with most buildings being four storeys or more. However, they will free up space, usually at ground-floor level, which was previously used for waste storage.

Large-scale retrofit systems have been installed in 15 city centres across Spain and covering 10 per cent of Macau city centre in China, for example.

In Vollsmose, a suburb of Odense in Denmark, waste points often became a target for gangs of troublemakers who set them on fire, and collecting refuse became a personal risk to the collectors. In early 2000, renovation began on the estate and a waste vacuum system installed. Following the installation of this system, along with other measures, such as educating environmental ambassadors, the cleanliness of the estate was transformed.[5]

3.7
Catering for sustainable transport strategies

Introduction

The environmental impact of transport is considerable, particularly in the developed world. For example, in 2006, according to the US EPA greenhouse gas (GHG) inventory, 1,975 million tonnes of CO_{2eq} emitted into the atmosphere were associated with transportation, corresponding to 28 per cent of total emissions in the US (EPA, 2008). Of this total, 84 per cent was from road vehicles, with rail only contributing 3 per cent. Data for 2010 from the UK GHG inventory indicates an emission rate associated with transportation of 139.3 $MtCO_{2eq}$, or approximately 23.7 per cent of total emissions.[1] Road vehicles contribute some 88 per cent of this total, with rail at 1.8 per cent. It is interesting to note that the US transportation emissions corresponded to 6.5 tonnes CO_{2eq} per person in 2006, while the UK figure for 2010 was equivalent to 1.9 tCO_{2eq}/person.

These figures indicate the reliance placed on road transport in these two countries. The USA, in particular, suffers from greater distances travelled and inefficient vehicles. A report from the FIA (*Fédération Internationale de l'Automobile*) Foundation reveals that 86 per cent of trips undertaken in the USA in 2003 were by road, compared with 62 per cent for EU countries, with the average American making 50 per cent more trips per day and each car travelling 19,100 km per annum,[2] compared with 14,000 km for the average European car.[3]

In this chapter we are going to discuss what measures should be considered to reduce vehicle use and impacts when refurbishing buildings, while in Chapter 4.6 we will be looking at the management strategies required to achieve the same aim. For a detailed account of the measures required to integrate sustainable transportation planning into new developments and reduce vehicle impacts, refer to Chapters 2.7 and 3.10 of *Integrated Sustainable Design of Buildings* (Appleby, 2011a).

Sustainable transport strategy

The operator of the building to be refurbished may already have a green travel plan. Since in the UK this has been a planning requirement since 2001, it may have been handed over by the original developer, or been mandated by the corporate social reporting (CSR) policy of the building owner. The Planning Policy Guidance PPG13, although now superseded by the National Planning Policy Framework, provides a useful set of objectives for this plan:

1   reductions in car usage (particularly single-occupancy journeys) and increased use of public transport, walking and cycling;
2   reduced traffic speeds and improved road safety and personal security particularly for pedestrians and cyclists; and
3   more environmentally friendly delivery and freight movements, including home delivery services.

(CLG, 2001)

Below we cover the key measures required to achieve these objectives for a refurbishment project.

Improving facilities for cyclists and pedestrians

The key to creating an environment in which people want to cycle or walk to work is a combination of safety and comfort through the following measures:

- providing secure, dedicated, sheltered and convenient cycle storage and changing facilities, including suitable lockers and showers;
- pedestrian-, wheelchair- and cycle-friendly design for all types of user regardless of the level of mobility or visual impairment, through the provision of cycle lanes, safe crossing points, direct routes and with appropriate tactile surfaces;
- ensuring all access routes are well lit and signposted to other amenities, public transport nodes and adjoining off-site pedestrian and cycle routes.

For new developments, many local authorities in the UK have developed cycle storage standards, which may be relevant for major refurbishments that require planning permissions. In the absence of these it may be appropriate to refer to the BREEAM protocol (see Chapter 1.3), particularly if it is desired to achieve a specific rating under this assessment scheme. The 2011 BREEAM scheme covers a wide variety of non-residential and multi-residential buildings and thus incorporates complex guidelines for achieving the credits allocated under the 'Cyclist facilities' heading. The number of 'compliant cycle spaces' to be provided is typically based on 10 per cent of those who might make use of them occupying buildings catering for up to 500 occupants, although there are a number of exceptions depending on types of use, likelihood of visitors using the facilities and the like. For any occupancy greater than this, 6.67 per cent of the number between 501 and 1,000 should be allocated spaces, while for 1,001 and above, the percentage drops to 5 per cent.

BREEAM also recognizes that fewer people will want to make use of cycle storage if public transport is good or where the average commuting distance is likely to be 10 miles or greater, and hence reduces the requirement by 50 per cent.

'Compliant storage' should be no more than 100 m from the main entrance, be overlooked, well lit, secure and sheltered, with a covering overhead as a minimum. It should be possible to secure both a wheel and the frame of a cycle. For example, the 'Sheffield' design is both compliant, robust and simple, comprising a sturdy tubular frame set into the ground. However, there are a number of bike storage products available that can be used where space is restricted (see Figures 3.7.1 and 3.7.2).

Finding space for showers, changing facilities and lockers may be more difficult than bike storage. The BREEAM requirement is for one shower per ten cycles, hence for an office building in the centre of London with 1,000 occupants requiring 42 cycle stands, space would have to be found for four showers, with associated changing facilities, accessible by both male and female cyclists. Where lockers are to be provided, there should be one per stand and they must be large enough to contain a helmet, backpack, clothing, etc.

Promoting public transport

The travel plan needs to consider how occupants are both to be discouraged from using their cars and encouraged to use either cycles or public transport. Where the building is located within walking distance of a public transport node, typically considered as less than one kilometre, occupants need to be aware of the location of the node and that the route is both safe and well lit. If services are infrequent, or if there are multiple services and routes, then consideration should be given to installing a display screen in a suitable central location that provides live information on times and destinations for the various services. This information can also be streamed to all workstations via an office intranet service for example, along with a system for car sharing (see p. 228).

Figure 3.7.1 *Automated bicycle parking system over an underground storage chamber for 46 bikes in Zaragoza, Spain*

Source: Jezhotwells.

Figure 3.7.2 *Double-storey racking system*
Source: Cycle-Works Ltd.

If there is sufficient critical mass from a site, then it may be possible to negotiate with a local bus company to re-route one of their services to a new stop adjacent to the site.

Improving parking facilities

The provision of parking spaces will be linked to the success of strategies to persuade people to use cycles or public transport. Clearly the better the public transport, the less parking should be provided, not only because of the convenience but also because the cost of providing parking spaces in city centres is extremely high.

Where public transport access is not very good, then car-sharing schemes should be promoted. The car park should be reorganized to incorporate dedicated spaces for the use of cars that can have multiple users, either as part of a community or commercial car club or a car-sharing scheme for the commuters. Incentives can be provided in the form of allocating reserved spaces close to entrances and/or offering discounted or free parking. Charging can also provide a disincentive to solo car users.

Similar incentives can be provided for those who use electric or hybrid cars for commuting, with spaces set aside for electric vehicles having suitable charging points (see Figures 3.7.3 and 3.7.4). One option is to establish a car club fleet which uses primarily electric vehicles, with hybrid cars available for longer journeys if necessary.

BREEAM does not include any credits that cover low-emission vehicles, while LEED includes three options for encouraging use of low-emitting and

Figure 3.7.3 *Electric vehicle charging point*

Source: Myles Barker.

Figure 3.7.4 *Dedicated parking bays for electric cars at Belgrade Plaza car park, Coventry*
Source: Myles Barker.

fuel-efficient vehicles. Option 1 involves providing these vehicles to 3 per cent of the FTE (full-time equivalent) workforce, along with preferred parking. Option 2 requires preferred parking for occupants using low-emission vehicles for at least 5 per cent of the car parking spaces. Option 3 rewards the provision of refueling facilities to cater for at least 3 per cent of the car parking capacity. The last option refers to alternative fuels such as hydrogen for fuel cells.

Safety and security

Those planning refurbishment projects that include car parking may wish to review the safety and security measures provided, particularly if the facility is used by the public. The UK has an award scheme, owned by the Association of Chief Police Officers (ACPO) and managed by the British Parking Association (BPA) called the Park Mark® Safer Parking Scheme.[4] Even if it is not anticipated that an application will be made for an award under this scheme, the associated design guidance provides a very useful framework within which a refurbishment can be designed. Box 3.7.1 summarizes the main points covered by the guidance.

Box 3.7.1 Summary of main points covered by Park Mark® Safer Parking Scheme

Boundaries

- These should deter potential offenders through restricting access to an appropriate extent; for example, private car parks may need to be completely enclosed with secure walls, gates and doors, designed to be impenetrable.
- Open-access car parks should have boundaries that deter the unauthorized removal of vehicles, through bollards, walls, etc.
- Access control should be via shutters or barriers, depending on the level of security required, and designed to Loss Prevention Standard 1175 (LPCB, 2010).
- Automated shutters and gates will need to be operated so that they deter tail-gating.
- Top levels of multi-storey car parks should be designed with suicide risk in mind, having perimeter walls designed to be un-climbable where risk is high.

Lighting

- Lighting should be designed to meet or exceed BS5489-1:2003, BS EN 12464-1: 2011 and BS EN 12464-2: 2007 which include the horizontal maintained illuminance levels in Table 3.7.1.
- External lighting and, where possible, lighting for perimeter areas should be provided with daylight controls from photocells.
- External lighting should be designed to avoid light pollution and switched off when the car park is closed.
- Emergency lighting should be designed to BS 5266-1 (BSI, 2011b).

Table 3.7.1 *Level of lighting for car parks*

Location	Average lux	Minimum lux
Outdoor car parks	30	10
Indoor car parks		
Parking bays	75	50
Ramps, corners, intersections	150	75
Vehicular access points	Night: 75 Day: 300	50
Pedestrian routes	100	50

Source: BSi, 2003b, 2007, 2011b.

Pedestrian access

- Access should be kept to a small number of controlled points, monitored by CCTV, with people not using the facility discouraged from entry, where possible.

- Access points should be clearly signposted, with pedestrians kept separate from vehicles and providing no hiding places out of sight of pedestrians or CCTV.
- Stairways should have see-through banisters with vandal-proof mirrors at stair turns and be overlooked from trafficked areas outdoors and CCTV.
- Lifts should be provided with vision panels in doors, fully mirrored internal walls, vandal resistant buttons and hands-free emergency communication.

Signage

Signage should be clearly visible and used to control, warn or instruct visitors. Signs should be sited so that information is visible from all parts of the parking facility, but they should not be so restrictive as to obscure views, CCTV or natural surveillance.

Surveillance

Landscaping next to and on a parking facility should not restrict surveillance opportunities or provide areas of concealment. Dense prickly shrubs and thorn hedges may be used to physically reinforce boundaries, but all landscaping, including that on pedestrian access routes, should be maintained to ensure that there is no dense foliage between 1 m and 2.5 m in height. For example, hedges and bushes should be planted that do not grow in excess of 1.0 m and trees should be used that do not have branches below 2.5 m.

The following is an extract from the Park Mark® guidance:[5]

- CCTV cameras should be located to cover the vehicle and pedestrian entrances/exits as well as any help points.
- When installing cameras on vehicle entrance/exits they should be positioned on each full-time or part-time lane so that the front of the vehicle is viewed where possible. The following criteria should be complied with:
  - The registration plate is easily readable when the vehicle is stationary at the barrier and, if possible, a view of the front seat occupants is provided.
  - The recorded image of the vehicle registration number is not obscured by date, time and/or recording mode.
  - Images of the vehicle registration number recorded from the rear on exit shall not be obscured by the flow of traffic.

When installing cameras on pedestrian entrance/exits, the following criteria should be complied with:

- Record individuals entering, not a mixture of persons entering and exiting.
- Provide clear facial recognition for evidential purposes.

Where the number of pedestrian entrances or other areas of access is too great to cover without large installations, consideration should be given to the following measures:

- Installing cameras at ground-floor lift lobbies, stairwells and ramps, thereby offering better protection to the upper levels;
- Fitting grilles or fences so that pedestrians can be channelled past a particular camera.

Vehicular access

- The number of access and exit routes should be minimized, incorporating a degree of control that will depend upon factors such as location, type of parking facility and management practices.
- Control can be provided by some combination of barrier access, flow plates or staffed control points.
- Features such as narrowed entrances or height restrictors may be required to control the type of vehicles permitted within a parking facility. Height or width restrictors must be able to be easily opened or removed to enable access for emergency or maintenance vehicles.

3.8

Material impacts in refurbishment

Introduction

As we saw in Chapter 2.1, one of the key advantages of refurbishment over new build is the opportunity to re-use existing building materials. This may be in-situ: for example the building shell; or through removing and re-conditioning existing materials or components, such as roof slates or windows (see the Empire State Building case history in Chapter 3.1).

According to the introduction to the Building Research Establishment's Envest environmental assessment tool website:

> From material extraction, processing, component assembly, transport and construction, to maintenance and disposal, construction products have an environmental impact over their entire life cycle [such that]:
> - 10% of the UK CO_2 emissions arise from the production and use of building materials.
> - Each year the UK construction industry uses 6 tonnes of building materials per head of population.
> - Materials production and construction accounts for an estimated 122 million tonnes of waste, or 30% of the total arising in the UK.[1]

Of course, every component that is used in the refurbishment of a building has an embedded environmental impact. Each component will have gone through a process prior to construction, which may vary from adaptation or re-conditioning of a re-used component through to a complex industrial process involving extraction of numerous raw materials, processing, assembly and delivery. Once installed, some components will need periodic maintenance or replacement using additional materials and processes. Eventually, as with new buildings, the whole assembly may need to be demolished and disposed of, refurbished again, or adapted for another use.

A detailed account of the sustainable sourcing and procurement of materials for new buildings is given in Chapter 3.12 of *Integrated Sustainable Design of Buildings* (Appleby, 2011a), which deals with materials specification, including a review of the schemes available for assessing and rating the life cycle environmental impacts of construction materials. Chapter 4.2 sets out the principles of sustainable procurement, including modern methods of construction (ibid.).

Environmental impact of construction products

As we saw in Chapter 1.3, many activities and processes can be compared using an environmental rating system and in Chapter 2.1 we examined the BRE's Office Scorer, which uses the Ecopoints system to compare the environmental impacts associated with new build and refurbishment projects. The Ecopoints system, along with the similar US-based BEES Life Cycle Assessment Model,[2] are used to pull together an array of impacts into a single rating.

The environmental impacts of importance include:

- climate change: embodied carbon in $kgCO_{2eq}$, i.e. the greenhouse gas (GHG) emissions giving global warming potential (GWP) over 100 years;
- water extraction: mains, surface and ground water extraction;
- mineral resource extraction: virgin irreplaceable materials such as ores and aggregates;
- stratospheric ozone depletion: chlorinated and brominated gases that destroy the ozone layer;
- human toxicity potential (HTP): based on the full life cycle of the material;
- ecotoxicity to freshwater: maximum tolerable concentrations in water for ecosystems;
- ecotoxicity to land: maximum tolerable emissions to land;
- high-level nuclear waste: volume of high-level waste requiring long-term storage before it may be safe;
- waste disposal: tonnes of solid waste going to landfill or incineration in terms of loss of resource;
- fossil fuel depletion;
- eutrophication: over-enrichment of water courses causing algal growth and oxygen depletion;
- photochemical ozone creation: emissions of oxides of nitrogen (NO_x) and volatile organic compounds (VOCs) that convert to ozone in presence of sunlight;
- acidification: emissions of sulphur dioxide (SO_2) and NO_x that lead to acid deposition (acid rain).

The Ecopoint system is used as the basis for a database of ratings developed by the BRE and published online in the Green Guide library.[3] Green Guide ratings provide an indication of the environmental performance of the average composite element available in the UK marketplace installed anywhere in the UK. It does not reward the designer for specifying materials that are entirely native to the development location, for example, unless an environmental profile is available from a company who is responsible for manufacture of the whole building element. However, BRE has developed a 'Green Guide Calculator' that enables BREEAM and CSH assessors to generate Green Guide ratings for a significant proportion of specifications not listed in the Green Guide Online.[4]

Re-using building elements has five separate benefits for a refurbishment project, as recognized in the assessment protocols associated with BREEAM:

1   Because the environmental impact associated with re-using materials is minimal, the Ecopoints are likely to be close to zero and hence the Green Guide rating is awarded at the maximum A+ level by default.

2   Credit is given for making use of existing façades that constitute more than
    50 per cent of the external envelope of the building by area and 80 per cent
    by mass.
3   Similarly if more than 80 per cent of the volume of the primary structure is
    re-used without significant reinforcement or alteration, an additional credit
    can be won.
4   Because no procurement is required, re-used elements achieve a Tier 1 rating
    under the Responsible Sourcing credit (see below).
5   Lastly, the credit dealing with construction waste management benefits from
    the re-use of existing building materials because of the lower volume of
    waste generated.

Responsible sourcing and sustainable procurement

Sourcing of construction products occurs in at least two stages. Products and
materials will be specified to meet the cost and sustainability criteria to varying
levels of detail depending on how critical they are to the refurbishment. This will
be followed during the refurbishment works by value engineering and procurement based on exact specifications and measured quantities.

Apart from achieving the specified BRE Green Guide rating and Tier level
for responsible sourcing, materials and products should where possible be
purchased from local suppliers and manufacturers. This will also help in achieving targets for minimizing CO_2 emissions associated with deliveries established
from the Construction Site Impacts credits in BREEAM. 'Local' can be defined
as within 30 km; however, a realistic aim should be to procure from as close as
possible to the site and avoid products that are manufactured overseas as far as
possible. Of course, for specialist products this may be impossible, while some
products that are manufactured locally may have a greater life cycle environmental impact or carbon footprint because of the materials imported or
processes used.

BREEAM rewards the responsible sourcing of materials for a list of eight
main building elements that covers the structural frame, ground and upper
floors, roof, external and internal floors, foundations, substructure and
staircases, not all of which are relevant to refurbishment projects of course.

Fit-outs are assessed separately for materials used in stairs, windows, doors,
skirting, paneling, furniture and fascias. There are no credits associated with
responsible sourcing of building services.

The BREEAM protocol is based on measurable standards of environmental
management in the manufacture of materials from 'cradle to gate'. The protocol
refers to four 'tiers' of quality, with Tier 1 meeting all of BRE's criteria. These
require certification that certain standards of organizational and supply chain
management and environmental and social responsibility have been met. There
are a number of well-established national and international certification systems
that do this, including the Forest Stewardship Council (FSC) and the Programme
for the Endorsement of Forest Certification (PEFC) schemes for timber. BRE has
developed a framework standard that assesses all of these issues for specific
materials or products, administered by the British Standards Institute (BRE,
2009). BSI awards certificates on a scale from Pass to Excellent, with Very Good

and Excellent ratings qualifying for Tier 1 and Pass and Good for Tier 2. A register of certified products can be found at the Green Book Live website.[5]

Where a product has not been certified under the BRE scheme, it is necessary to obtain evidence of a certified environmental management system (EMS) being in place for the whole of the supply chain (Tier 3) or if this only applies to the 'key process', such as product manufacture but not abstraction of raw materials, for example, then only a Tier 4 can be allocated. BRE has developed a calculator that enables credits to be awarded based on an area weighted scoring of the Tiers allocated to the applicable materials for the various building elements.

For information on specific products, including building services plant and equipment, there are numerous on-line product directories, some of which provide useful technical information and background, links to suppliers' and manufacturers' websites and key sustainability information, such as recycled content.[6, 7, 8]

In the USA, the National Institute of Building Science has produced the on-line Whole Building Design Guide which includes the Federal Green Construction Guide for Specifiers.[9]

As we saw in Chapters 3.2 and 3.5, labelling schemes are also available for a range of building services, consumer and office equipment under the EU Energy Labelling and Ecolabel schemes, the EU/US Energy Star scheme and the UK ECA (Enhanced Capital Allowance) Directories. However, these are primarily concerned with resource (and particularly energy) use during operation.

Insulation

The dominant material required for many refurbishment projects will be insulation. Hence when deciding on the types of insulation to be installed, it is important to factor in the environmental impact of each type of insulation as well as its thermal performance. BRE provides an approach that is embedded into their assessment protocol that provides a useful tool for option studies. The Insulation Index takes into account the volume of each type of insulation, its conductivity and its Green Guide rating converted into a number (e.g. 0.25 for D rating, 3 for A+ rating). So the rating used to assess the whole building is weighted by volume and thermal performance.

The insulating materials that perform best under the Green Guide rating system are loose products blown in-situ, including cellulosic materials (recycled newspaper), blown either wet or dry, and blown glass or stone wool. Low-density sheep's wool, glass and stone (mineral) wools also do well. Factory gas blown products, such as expanded and extruded polystyrenes or rigid urethane, do well if blown with pentane or CO_2, but any foam insulation blown with a hydrogenated fluorocarbon performs poorly. For example, commonly used blowing agents HFC 134a and HFC 152a have a global warming potential (GWP) 1,300 and 140 times that of CO_2 respectively.

Innovative insulation products

It is clear from Chapter 3.1 that the thickness of insulation is important in retrofit. Hence it is not surprising that innovative high-performance materials and products, known collectively as super-insulation, are being investigated as an alternative to the current range of fibrous and foam materials. Two such products which are starting to gain a foothold in the retrofit marketplace are vacuum insulation panels (VIPs) and aerogel. VIPs use micro-porous fumed silica in powder form, vacuum-packed into a metalized plastic membrane and heat-sealed to form a panel (Figure 3.8.1). The resultant conductivity is extremely low, typically between 0.006 and 0.008 W/mK, compared with typical values for foam and fibre insulation of 0.024 and 0.04 respectively. Hence a U-value of 0.15 W/m²K might be achieved with a panel thickness of 40 mm or less. The resultant panel has the stability of vacuum packed coffee and if unprotected could easily be damaged. For obvious reasons on-site trimming to size is not possible. The technology has so far been applied mainly to fridges and freezers in which it is protected by metal panels. According to an International Energy Agency (IEA) report from around 2005, the high cost of the product was inhibiting its adoption in the construction sector, but 'in renovations by the use of VIPs, additional expenses can be avoided, as for instance the lengthening of the roof when insulating the façade. Often VIPs are used as a problem solver,

Figure 3.8.1 *Vacuum insulation panel*

Source: Ian Abley; www.audacity.com.

e.g. for terrace insulation, VIPs are here the only possibility to prevent a step between the heated room and the terrace.'[10]

The same report compares the environmental impact of VIPs with that for 'glass wool' and expanded polystyrene (EPS) using European protocols similar to the BRE Ecopoints scheme referred to above. It concluded that some 90 per cent of the impacts were due to the high energy use in the manufacture of microporous fumed silica; however, overall impacts, according to the Eco-indicator 99 scheme, were better than EPS. Although there have been a number of retrofits using VIPs in Germany, at the time of writing, the market in the UK is very small, although it may be significant that new products have recently appeared on the market.[11]

Another material that has transferred from other applications is aerogel, which consists of 2–5 nm diameter particles which form a highly porous cluster having pores in the 1–100 nm range. When based on silica, the aerogel produced is effectively transparent, although some light scattering occurs. Because the average pore size of 1–100 nm is less than the mean free path of air molecules, (typically 70 nm), the silica matrix thermal conductivity is very low. Silica-based aerogels can achieve thermal conductivities of less than that of still air, reportedly as low as 0.005 W/mK. However, the incorporation of reinforcing fibres into commercially available flexible insulation blankets to make them suitable for building applications increases the conductivity to around 0.012 W/mK. A number of products have been developed that incorporate reinforced aerogel, including a cladding system that protects the aerogel with a magnesium silicate outer layer[12] and a blanket that can be used as loft insulation, see Figure 3.8.2.[13]

A US standard has been developed for flexible aerogel insulation (ASTM, 2012). Although no environmental impact data could be found at the time of writing, the consensus appears to be that the manufacturing process is relatively benign.

Aerogel has also been used as a basis of glazing systems, the most common being translucent, although products are being developed that are transparent. One product, that is available in a variety of thicknesses, achieves a U-value of 0.64 W/m²K with a single 25-mm sheet of aerogel, allowing 55 per cent of daylight to be transmitted.[14]

Robustness

Life cycle assessment of the environmental impact of building materials is based on an assumed life expectancy for each material. Mechanical and electrical plant and equipment may be subject to reduction in efficiency through use or breakdown due to mechanical failure. Materials, on the other hand, may be subject to weathering or wear and damage through attrition, abuse or moisture. Life expectancy for materials will therefore depend on the selection of suitably robust materials for the level of abuse expected.

Clearly, the whole of the external envelope must be designed to exclude penetration of moisture into the building from precipitation, while prevention of surface and interstitial condensation requires suitable positioning of insulation and damp-proofing. Also robust construction depends on the use of materials that will withstand wear and tear. This is rewarded in BREEAM by incorporating a credit: 'to recognize and encourage adequate protection of

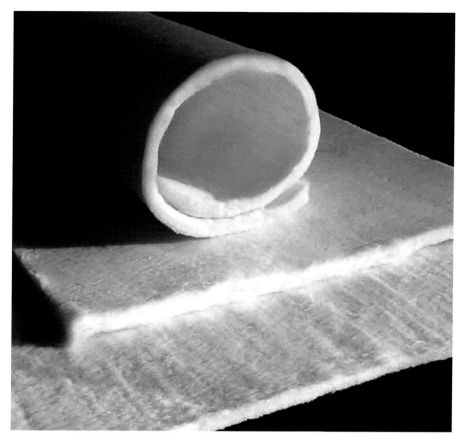

Figure 3.8.2 *Aerogel-based blanket insulation*
Source: Aerogels Australia.

exposed elements of the building and landscape, therefore minimizing the frequency of replacement and maximizing materials optimization'.[15]

During the planning of refurbishment it is useful to review the movements of people and vehicles around the building and carry out an 'impact' assessment on the routes they take around the building. This should identify the following:

- external locations where vehicle manoeuvres are required close to walls or soft landscaping that might need protection, such as loading bays and lawns;
- internal areas in which fork lift trucks (or similar) will be manoeuvred;
- internal areas through which trolleys will be wheeled;
- internal areas with high pedestrian traffic loads;
- areas that are likely to experience above average soiling and hence high cleaning intensities.

The following mitigation measures might be expected to increase the life expectancy of surfaces exposed to the above risks:

- bollards, barriers and/or raised kerbs protecting external walls in delivery and vehicle drop-off areas;

- robust external wall construction up to 2 m from the ground – this could mean avoiding fragile rainscreens, such as hung slates, at this level;
- corridor walls to be suitable for 'Severe Duty' (SD) as specified in BS 5234-2 (BSI, 1992) (Figure 3.8.3);
- protection rails fitted at an appropriate height along corridor walls;
- protection to doors from impact by trolleys, etc;
- hard-wearing and easily washable floor finishes in heavily used areas, such as main entrances, corridors, public areas, etc.

Figure 3.8.3 *Hospital corridor showing rubber protective wall and corner profiles and kick plates on doors*
Source: Lindsay Fowke.

3.9
Enhancing ecology by refurbishment

Introduction

While the construction of a new building frequently involves destroying habitats or disturbing ecosystems, refurbishment of an existing building may be possible without having a negative impact on the ecological value of soft landscaped areas surrounding the building. This will depend on the amount of work required externally: building an extension, for example, may be as challenging as new build, while applying external insulation may disturb or destroy vegetation close to the walls.

On the other hand, refurbishment may provide an opportunity to enhance the ecological value of a previously barren landscape. Similarly there may be opportunities to reduce flood risk by increasing the permeability of the site and introducing sustainable drainage systems. Also it might be worth exploring the potential to create green roofs, brown roofs, or green walls on the building envelope.

Many of the same principles and strategies required for refurbishment also apply to new build and the reader is directed to Chapter 3.14 of *Integrated Sustainable Design of Buildings* for a more detailed account of landscaping, ecology and flood risk associated with new developments (Appleby, 2011a).

Ecological enhancement

Most buildings have relatively small curtilages, particularly those in urban locations, where land values are high and buildings have historically taken up most of the available land. For these buildings all is not lost, however, and we will be looking at the potential for ecological enhancement through retrofitting green roofs, brown roofs and green walls, later in this chapter. However, if we consider the example of a university campus or mixed-use development on the edge of a town, there are numerous opportunities for enhancing ecological value and creating bridges and corridors that provide links to biodiverse neighbouring landscapes.

Refurbishing landscape is not a short-term project. If much of the existing landscape has been degraded to such an extent that there are very few native species remaining, then it will be necessary to obtain advice from a suitably qualified ecologist on a programme of introducing native species that are compatible with both the substrates available and the activities proposed for the site.

Reference should be made to the local Biodiversity Action Plan (BAP), which should identify priority habitats for the local neighbourhood. For example, the London Biodiversity Partnership (LBP) publishes 'habitat suitability maps' for the whole of Greater London. 'These maps identify areas which if used to create one or more of the nine selected BAP priority habitats would give the best benefit to biodiversity in London.'[1] The nine priority habitats are given as: acid grassland, calcareous grassland, floodplain grazing marsh, heathland, lowland meadow, reedbed, rivers and streams, standing water (ponds) and woodland.

We have already seen that the golden rule for maximizing ecological enhancement is to incorporate as far as possible species that are native to the area. With this in mind, the Natural History Museum has developed a database that gives a list of native plant species for a given postcode.[2] This lists plants under the headings of annual, biennial, perennial, shrub, tree, etc., and provides information on family, provenance, protected status and whether suitable for garden use, as well as an image for most of those listed.

A major concern that must be addressed prior to restoring a degraded landscape is the identification and eradication of invasive species. Invasive alien species, such as the notoriously destructive Japanese knotweed and the phototoxic giant hogweed (see Figures 3.9.1 and 3.9.2), have become a major focus of international conservation concern and the subject of cooperative international efforts, such as the Global Invasive Species Programme (GISP).[3] In the Introduction to its landmark strategy document, GISP states that 'Invasive alien species are now recognized as one of the greatest biological threats to our planet's environmental and economic well-being.'

Figure 3.9.1 *Japanese knotweed*
Source: Gav.

Figure 3.9.2 *Giant hogweed*
Source: Appaloosa.

If invasive species are identified, an eradication method should be developed and implemented, using a specialist contractor. Various eradication techniques are used with varying degrees of success. Critical to the complete eradication of Japanese knotweed, for example, is killing the rhizomes and the complete removal and disposal of all plant material, either by deep burial on site or removal and disposal in a licensed site. In the UK, Japanese knotweed is defined as a controlled waste. The method employed will depend primarily on the length of time available for treatment. The Environment Agency has published *The Knotweed Code of Practice* which sets out the treatment options and the techniques available for management and eradication of the weed (EA, 2006).

Sustainable drainage

The efficient and rapid removal of storm water without overflow or back-up is important in mitigating the risk of flood, land pollution and soil erosion, with the related risks from undermining of foundations, damage to property and destruction of flora. The extent of impermeable surfaces in landscaped areas around a building directly impacts on the volume of storm water that has to be handled by the drains and hence the flood risk. Where combined sewers are prevalent, such as across most of London, this can lead to discharge of untreated sewage into watercourses, or even backing up of sewage. Reducing the volume of water that is discharged into a combined sewer can also result in significant savings in sewer charges (see Holywell Primary School case history on p. 252).

The above points are reinforced by the Environment Agency in their 2007 report on SUDS retrofit in urban areas in which they stated that:

> Retrofitted SUDSs may prove useful in any situation where inadequate stormwater management leads to poor performance of the urban drainage system. This includes problems associated with excessive Combined Sewer Overflow (CSO) discharges, separate storm sewer outfalls and flooding of urban watercourses. Retrofitting also has a potentially important role to play in tackling sewer flooding risk; expanding the capacity of sewers and drainage systems to take on more 'load' deals with just one side of the supply-demand balance.
>
> (EA, 2007b)

Sustainable urban drainage systems (SUDSs) typically make use of a combination of permeable surfaces for source control; permeable conveying through swales and infiltration trenches; and shallow ponds with emergent vegetation, such as reed beds, for passive treatment over long retention times. A swale is a shallow ditch lined with vegetation, while an infiltration trench incorporates a layer of gravel. Ponds can also be incorporated to attenuate storm water, referred to as balancing ponds or detention basins.

According to the Environment Agency:

> There are many SUDS design options to choose from and they can be tailored to fit all types of development, from hard surfaced areas to soft landscaped features. They can also be designed to improve amenity and biodiversity in developed areas. For instance, ponds can be designed as a local feature for recreational purposes and to provide valuable local wildlife habitat nodes and corridors.
>
> (EA, 2008)

In other words, retrofitting SUDSs can provide significant enhancement to ecological value. Even for a building such as a supermarket that has landscaping entirely devoted to car parking, permeable paving and other sustainable drainage features can be introduced. Porous surfaces and swales can be retrofitted to car parking areas, along with native plant species and trees that both increase ecological value and provide shading for parked cars (see Figures 3.9.3 and 3.9.4).

Figure 3.9.3 *Swale under construction with complete one behind*
Source: Duk.

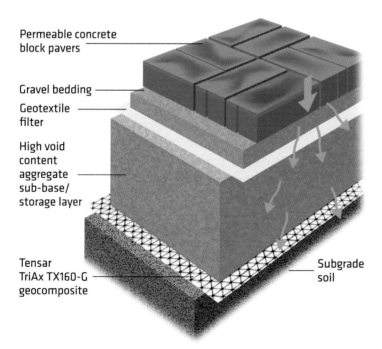

Permeable concrete
block pavers

Gravel bedding

Geotextile
filter

High void
content
aggregate
sub-base/
storage layer

Tensar
TriAx TX160-G
geocomposite

Subgrade
soil

Figure 3.9.4 *Example of permeable block paving suitable for car park SUDSs*
Source: Tensar International Ltd.

With regard to the marginal life cycle cost of SUDSs, CIRIA states:

In general a SUDS scheme should not cost more than a traditional drainage system. There is strong evidence suggesting that the construction and operational costs of SUDSs, particularly multifunctional landscaped components, are less expensive than traditional drainage. This is because SUDSs do not involve deep excavation or expensive materials.[4]

The Environment Agency report from 2007 referred to above confirms the cost benefits of permeable paving, based on their cost model, that demonstrates that:

Permeable paving costs less on a lifecycle basis than traditional surfaces, with reduced maintenance costs outweighing increased capital costs. While extra excavations are required to lay permeable paving, replacing worn out paving blocks is less costly than the digging required to renew worn out tarmac. For those areas where water companies only charge for surface drainage on hard surfaces, there will be further financial savings [from] no charges for permeable surfaces.

Retrofitting green and brown roofs

Green roofs are sometimes, perhaps more accurately, known as vegetated roofs. The principle is very simple, and has been around for centuries, i.e. turning a frequently neglected area of the building into a landscape. This can either be used as an amenity space, such as a roof garden, also known as an intensive green roof; or as a relatively lightweight covering providing a substrate for native plant species, or an extensive green roof.

Extensive roofs sit on top of a waterproof membrane and comprise further layers to protect the roof from roots that penetrate a drainage layer, over which sits a filter mat that prevents the growing medium from washing into the growing layer. The most common plant species grown on extensive green roofs are those within the sedum genus, or stonecrop. These flowering plants are low maintenance, self-propagating and are available in varieties that are native to most of the UK and Europe (see Figure 3.9.5).

Whereas intensive green roofs are invariably flat, extensive roofs can be sloping, with typically a maximum incline of 30° to avoid slippage of the growing medium. Box 3.9.1 sets out the key characteristics of green roofs and their associated benefits and challenges.

Generally speaking, if the primary aim of retrofitting a green roof is to enhance ecological value, then an extensive roof is the best option, located so as to avoid disturbance and encourage visiting insects and birds (see Figure 3.9.6).

Similarly, brown roofs are created primarily to enhance biodiversity, but generally do not incorporate bought-in plants. The substrate usually comprises local earth and materials, including stones and logs, while flora are allowed to colonize the roof opportunistically.

Walls can also be used as a substrate for plant life, although historically this has usually entailed the fortuitous growth of climbers, such as ivy, that in some cases have damaged walls and penetrated interiors. Modern green walls, however, are normally better trained and require a vertical growing medium to

Figure 3.9.5 *Sedum spectabile*

Source: Jurgen Howaldt.

Box 3.9.1 Key characteristics of green roofs

Benefits

- Potential for enhancing ecological value by the incorporation of native species.
- The amount of stormwater retention depends on the depth of growing medium, with an intensive roof having the greater retention capacity.
- Absorption of solar radiation in summer and evaporation of retained water can significantly reduce heat gain to floor below.
- Provides thermal insulation, although this may be compromised if growing medium freezes.
- Has potential to reduce heat island effect.
- Plants absorb CO_2 and other gaseous pollutants, as well as trapping particulates.
- Adds to sound insulation properties of roof.

- Protects roof membranes from damaging effects of solar radiation, increasing replacement intervals and reducing life cycle cost potentially to that of a conventional roof.
- Aesthetic value – enhances view for those overlooking the roof.
- Intensive roofs have amenity value, providing secure and pleasant space for building occupants.

Challenges

- Long-term maintenance required, especially intensive type (see Chapter 4.9).
- Potential for leakage, particularly if root systems are allowed to break through membrane.
- Potential for spread of fire across roof, although breakthrough from or into building less likely than conventional roof because of density of growing medium and retained moisture.
- Structure may need strengthening, particularly for intensive variety.
- May not be compatible with rainwater harvesting because of water retention characteristics.

Figure 3.9.6 *Green roof using native species of sedum in Lanxmeer, the Netherlands*

Source: Lamiot.

be fixed to the wall surface, planted with small, creeping herbaceous perennials, ferns, grasses and small shrubs. This can be used to create attractive patterns and textures (see Figure 3.9.7). However, this system requires an integrated irrigation system to be built into its structure, normally employing hydroponics, which adds to the installation and maintenance cost of the installation.

The 'living wall' in Figure 3.9.7, although very striking, demonstrates one of the problems with growing plants on a façade containing windows. There is clearly a risk that plants obstruct views and will limit daylight if allowed to grow unhindered.

Case histories

Green Mountain College, Poultney, Vermont, USA

In 2010, the Sierra Club's *Sierra Magazine* rated Vermont's Green Mountain College the nation's most eco-friendly college.[5] The college emphasizes environmental sustainability as an essential element of its course studies. It is the first college in the USA to achieve climate neutrality. The college has its own

Figure 3.9.7 *Retrofitted 'living wall' at the European Environment Agency, Copenhagen*
Source: Loozrboy.

biomass facility, uses electricity produced by extracting methane gas from manure on Vermont dairy farms, and grows its own organic produce.

The following is an abstract taken from one of a series of case studies downloadable from the American Green Infrastructure website:[6]

> Green Mountain College is a private liberal arts college with approximately 750 undergraduates, and master's programs in Environmental Studies and Business Administration, located in Poultney, in the northern Taconics region of Vermont. As part of its mission, the college challenges each student to bring knowledge and creativity to issues of sustainable environmental, economic, and social systems.
>
> Among its sustainability initiatives, Green Mountain College is developing land management policies and campus gardens and landscapes that support regional and global plant conservation goals, as well as academic programs in biology, environmental studies, and natural resource management. As guides to meeting conservation goals, (they have) used the North American Botanic Garden Strategy for Plant Conservation and similar initiatives, and researched land management and landscaping policies and practices at other colleges. The college adopted its Invasive Species Policy and Natural Areas Policy in 2006 to promote sustainable land management of college natural areas. In landscaped areas of campus, native species gardens have been established, beginning in 2000, by students and faculty, including class projects in Botany and Local Flora courses. Native species landscaping educates students and the public about a rich regional flora that many people are not aware of, and maintains a unique sense of place associated with an ancient legacy of plant life. After extensive input and review by students, faculty, and staff in spring 2010, the college administration approved a proposal to replace invasive ornamentals on the landscaped campus, and in September 2010 approved the new campus-wide Native Species Landscaping Policy.

Walsley Hills High School and Holywell Primary School, Worcestershire

A retrofit SUDS scheme has been installed at the sites of Holywell Primary School and Walsley Hills High School in Worcestershire.[7] This system has involved intercepting overland flow from adjacent land in collector swales, storage of unpredictable water volumes in landscaped features, replacement of conventional drainage infrastructure that is undersized for severe storms and reduction of silt blockages, using silt interceptors, and re-routing of drainage to natural features.

Cascade and feature wetland have been developed which provide amenity benefit. The SUDS saves on sewerage disposal charges, which amounted to an annual cost of £3,879 combined.

Part 4

Sustainable facilities management

4.1
Energy management

Introduction

Energy management is a core activity for most organizations that occupy or manage buildings. It is a term that has been around for many years, and which has seen the evolution of an entire discipline, with associated qualifications and professional associations. In its 2011 guidance the Carbon Trust defines energy management as

> [t]he systematic use of management and technology to improve an organization's energy performance. It needs to be integrated, proactive, and incorporate energy procurement, energy efficiency and renewable energy to be fully effective.
>   Energy management is essential if you want to control costs, be fully compliant with legislation and enhance the organization's reputation.
> (Carbon Trust, 2011b)

More recently, and overlapping with this, the concept of carbon management has been developed (CPSL, 2009). Usually this refers to the total equivalent carbon dioxide emissions of the six greenhouse gases listed in the Kyoto Protocol, that is:

*   carbon dioxide (CO_2)
*   methane (CH_4)
*   nitrous oxide (N_2O)
*   sulphur hexafluoride (SF_6)
*   hydrofluorocarbons (HFCs)
*   perfluorocarbons (PFCs).

In practice, many organizations will only need to measure and manage carbon dioxide emissions, since most sectors do not produce significant amounts of the other five greenhouse gases. However, there are important exceptions, including industrial processes that use HFC-based solvents, as well as the agricultural and sewage treatment industries, which produce significant methane and N_2O emissions.

Historically, energy management has focused on operational energy and rarely taken account of the embodied energy or CO_2 emissions associated with the materials, transport and disposal of consumables. However, for a thorough calculation of carbon footprint, total life cycle GHG emissions should be determined (see Chapter 1.3).

One of the objectives of this chapter is to encourage managers to integrate energy, carbon and greenhouse gas (GHG) management since an organization's GHG inventory is the same as its carbon footprint and requires consumption data from energy metering to establish operational CO_2 emissions.

The policy commitments required by management and the relationship with the operation of the business are frequently grouped with other environmental and sustainability issues, along with water use, waste strategy and emissions; and sometimes also with fire, health and safety. These may come under the umbrella of an environmental management system (EMS) and input to corporate social reporting (CSR) (see Chapter 2.6).

This chapter will focus on operational energy efficiency and the management of the building services to optimize energy consumption and associated CO_2 emissions. It should be read in conjunction with Chapter 2.4 which sets out a strategy for refurbishing existing buildings to reduce CO_2 emissions; this is developed further in Chapters 3.1, 3.2 and 3.3 which run through the options for improving carbon performance by renovating the building fabric and retrofitting building services and renewables.

Energy policy and management framework

An energy policy would normally be developed by an organization, which may be the occupier of one or more buildings, the landlord of multi-tenanted buildings or an agent acting for various landlords across a variety of building types. For an individual building, it is possible that multiple policies may apply; developed by landlord, managing agent and tenants, for example. It is important that these policies are compatible, while leases should require sharing of relevant information (BBP, 2009).

The energy policy should require management to sign up to best practice and take ownership of the implementation of the 'action plan'. The Carbon Trust guidance (Carbon Trust, 2011b) proposes the following checklist of good practice:

- Energy is reviewed as a strategic issue and there is a mandate to manage energy that is endorsed and actively supported at the highest levels in the organization.
- Adequate resources (financial and human) are allocated to energy management.
- There is a reliable and effective system for monitoring and reporting energy performance.
- Energy procurement is an integrated, proactive process.
- There is planning to meet upcoming regulation.
- There is a maintained level of energy awareness throughout the organization.
- There is active engagement of the workforce around energy issues.
- There is full integration of energy management with other management systems.
- Energy management is seen as an opportunity.

Box 4.1.1 Summary of BS EN 16001 Energy Management Systems

BS EN 16001 is based on a methodology known as 'plan-do-check-act':

1   *Plan*: Identify energy aspects and legal obligations; establish energy objectives and targets.
2   *Do*: Assign resources and responsibilities; raise organizational awareness and provide training; communicate internally and externally; establish documentation; implement operational controls.
3   *Check*: Establish the monitoring of energy management programmes; evaluate compliance with legal obligations; identify and manage non-conformance; control records; carry out internal audits of the energy management system.
4   *Act*: Review energy management systems by management, resulting in potential changes.

The management system format of plan-do-check-act is designed to ensure that BS EN 16001 can be used by any organization. The requirements of the standard can also be aligned with those of other management systems such as quality (ISO9001) and environment (ISO 14001).

An energy policy should include reference to its context within a corporate vision, EMS, CSR, etc., relating it to environmental management and quality assurance systems. It should incorporate high-level commitments to the energy strategy and provide adequate resources to implement it, including employment of competent energy management personnel, provision of energy awareness training, regular formal reviews and accreditation against a suitable energy management standard such as BS EN 16001 (BSI, 2009) (see Box 4.1.1).[1]

Energy survey and data analysis

Before an energy management system can be fully implemented an energy survey is required to establish current energy usage, identify energy-saving opportunities and define practical next steps (Carbon Trust, 2011c). This will normally have to be carried out by someone with energy management or building services expertise and repeated every three to five years:

*   *Review energy usage (energy audit)*: By analyzing bills or readouts from the building energy management system (BEMS), consumption figures for each energy supply can be determined. This should be broken down into each fuel type or energy source and to as small a time frame as available. The more information can be gleaned on seasonal differences, even down to diurnal variations, the more sophisticated the analysis.
*   *Identify energy-saving opportunities* : This can be based on a combination of a walk-through survey, analysis of energy consumption data and a design review. An analysis of operating and maintenance records should also highlight plant and equipment that is coming to the end of its efficient

working life,[2] or where there are problems with reliability, that can also be associated with a reduced operating efficiency.

- *Define practical next steps*: The survey should identify energy-saving measures in terms of potential energy and CO_2 emission reductions and payback period, identifying 'low-hanging fruit' with a payback period of one year or less, 'nice to haves' with a payback period of one to two years and then longer-term objectives, depending on funding availability and company 'return on investment' (RoI) policy. This should be turned into an 'action plan' that can be integrated into the maintenance or small works programme, depending on the scale and cost of the measure. Some measures may result in a change in procurement policy and may require signing-off at the appropriate level.

Box 4.1.2 sets out the scope of an energy survey as envisaged in Section 18.3.1 of CIBSE Guide F. Section 18 of the Guide provides a detailed procedure for an energy survey (CIBSE, 2012).

The following sections provide some pointers to what should be investigated during an energy survey and some of the opportunities that may be uncovered.

Box 4.1.2 Scope of a typical energy survey

- *Building*: levels of insulation, ventilation, air infiltration, etc.
- *Pattern of use*: periods of occupancy, the types of control, the temperatures and humidities maintained, the use of electric lighting, the activities and processes being undertaken, including their operating temperatures, insulation, etc.
- *Energy supply*: examination of energy supply and distribution arrangements.
- *Main building services*: primary heating, cooling and air-handling plant.
- *Electric lighting*: quality, illuminance, luminance efficiency, extent to which daylight could reduce energy use, flexibility of control, etc.
- *Transport of energy within the building*: fans and pumps, insulation of hot water and steam pipes and air ducts, evidence of leakage, etc.
- *Plant room*: state and condition, insulation of boilers, chillers, tanks, pipe work, recovery of condensate, plant efficiency checks, etc.
- *Small power*: both on occupied floors and in common areas.
- *Energy management*: determining who is responsible for energy management in each department, how energy consumption is reviewed, recorded and analyzed, monitoring and target setting, investment, planning and maintenance.
- *Building performance*: compared to standard benchmarks.
- *Identification of opportunities*: for energy and cost savings with recommendations for action.

Metering

The number of meters and their connectivity dictate the quality of information available as a snapshot. At one end of the spectrum will be manually read single meters for each fuel, with quarterly billing, for example. At the other will be a network of pulsed-output meters connected to a BEMS that incorporates software for real-time energy analysis, also referred to as 'advanced metering', with sub-metering for each main energy demand and tenant. Automatic meter reading (AMR) provides the billing organization with real-time energy consumption data from electricity, gas, energy and water meters (Carbon Trust, 2007a). A 'smart' meter allows two-way communication between the consumer and the billing organization.

Where electrical loads are greater than 100 kW, a 'Code 5'[3] primary half-hour meter should have been provided by the electricity supplier. This connects directly to the billing organization (AMR) and can be linked to a BEMS via a pulsed output. Most gas meters installed since 1992 have had a pulsed output capability, allowing connection to a battery-operated data logger with GSM (Global System for Mobile communications) connection to the billing organization (AMR), which can also be linked to a BEMS. Similarly, pulsed output energy meters are used with district heating and cooling to meter energy consumption by measuring variations in water temperature differential between the flow and return connections to each consumer. Figure 4.1.1 shows a typical snapshot of the daily energy consumption for a large office building based on real-time data taken from sub-meters for each main energy use.

For complex sites having multiple tenants and numerous meters operating at various tariffs, meter types and reference numbers should be recorded on drawings.

The quality of analysis can be enhanced if data are also available on the operating times of plant and equipment, indoor and outdoor temperature variations and operating and maintenance records.

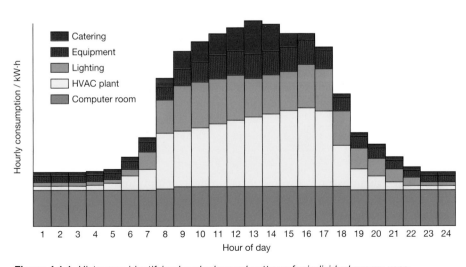

Figure 4.1.1 *Histogram identifying hourly demand patterns for individual energy uses*
Source: CIBSE, 2012.

Controls and BEMSs

In its simplest form, automatic control is primarily concerned with maintaining thermal comfort and starting and stopping plant and equipment at suitable times. If the control system is not set up correctly, then dissatisfaction will result and energy may be wasted. In many buildings, control functions are not fully integrated into a central control panel or BEMS, but have some equipment independently controlled, such as thermostatic radiator valves (TRVs) controlling the output from individual radiators for winter heating in an air-conditioned building that has separate controls for cooling. This opens up the potential for some areas to be simultaneously heated and cooled, for example: clearly a waste of energy. Most control systems incorporate interfaces with building occupants, not only through adjustable TRVs, but also wall thermostats, desktop handsets and adjustable vents. There may also be sensors located externally and within ducts and voids. These all need to be identified, their functions understood, their design set points and band widths determined and compared with the actual settings. Any difference between the design and actual values needs to be explained. For example:

• Is there a reason why occupants have set a room thermostat at 24°C, when it should be 21°C?
• Has the set point of a thermostat drifted over time?

The first question may require further investigation on user satisfaction (see Chapter 2.2) or the accuracy of the thermostat. The second may need a simple recalibration of the sensor, although if this recurs, then a better quality sensor may be required.

Assuming the building is not operated 24 hours per day, the control system will also switch plant on and off. The energy survey should check whether this is carried out at the same time every day, using a simple time clock, or whether optimum start and stop have been provided, bringing in the plant and switching it off at times that are dependent upon the outside conditions and the thermal response of the building. According to Section 10.3.3 of CIBSE Guide F:

> The greatest energy savings from optimum start control are likely to be gained in buildings of lightweight construction and with heating systems of low thermal capacity. Heavyweight buildings are less influenced by external fluctuations and are likely to require smaller variations in required start-up times. Similarly, heating systems with a slow response require a longer preheat time and are, therefore, likely to realize reduced savings with optimum start control.
>
> (CIBSE, 2012)

Figure 4.1.2 demonstrates the potential impact of optimum start, offering a saving of up to 10 per cent of total annual heating energy use. Hence this is well worth considering as a modification to the existing control regime.

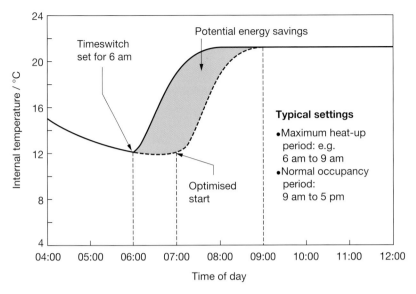

Figure 4.1.2 *Example of operation of optimum start control*
Source: CIBSE, 2012.

Building fabric

A non-intrusive survey of the building fabric may identify some critical defects that impact on the operation of the building services and the energy efficiency of the building.

At first glance, it may not be easy to determine the level of insulation present within the built fabric, or the routes of air leakage; however, the following methods may help build a better picture:

- If there are any as-built drawings and specifications they should indicate the type and thickness of insulation.
- Evidence of Building Regulations Part L approval should indicate predicted thermal performance and results of air tightness test (for non-residential buildings built to versions of Part L2 that came into force since 2002).
- Compare annual energy bills or total energy consumption (kWh) against typical or best practices figures (e.g. for offices built prior to 2002 refer to *Energy Consumption Guide 19* (BRE, 2000b)).
- A thermal imaging survey should pin-point weaknesses in thermal performance of envelope, including thermal bridging and gaps in cavity wall insulation (see Figure 4.1.3).
- A visual survey should identify major routes for air leakage into the building, while more subtle leaks can be traced using a simple smoke generating tube, or through an air leakage test. Note that thermal imaging can also indicate routes of air leakage.
- Mould growth on internal surfaces could indicate rain water penetration from outside, a leaking pipe or condensation. The latter indicates a poorly insulated element or a defective damp proof course, depending on its location.

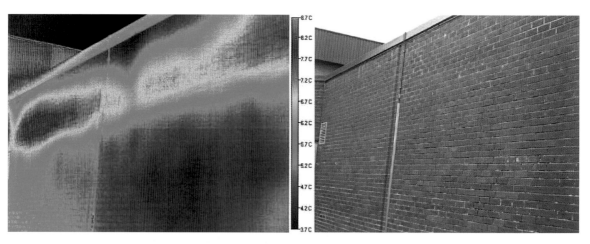

Figure 4.1.3 *Thermal image of wall: red areas indicate where there is no thermal insulation*
Source: www.thermalimageuk.com.

- Check that external doors close properly and the amount of time busy access doors remain open, whether automatic doors operate properly and how loading bay and vehicular access doors impact on outdoor air flows into adjacent spaces.

If overheating and glare from windows in summer are a problem, then the effectiveness of solar shading should be reviewed. See Chapter 3.1 for retrofitting options to improve the thermal performance of the fabric.

Lighting

It is rare to find lighting separately metered from other loads; however, it is important to determine what contribution it makes to the overall demand and what measures can be introduced to reduce load without impacting on its effectiveness. If half-hourly meter readings are available, it should be possible to determine the impact on load of switching lights on and off which, for safety reasons, should be done when the building is unoccupied.

The energy survey should check whether:

- lighting levels meet design or good practice illuminance levels, by measuring lux values on the working plane;
- efficient lamps are installed (see section on retrofitting lighting in Chapter 3.2);
- lighting is operating when it is not required (both internal and external) – either because there is enough illumination from daylight or there are no occupants present (see section on lighting controls in Chapter 3.2);
- switching systems allow isolation of unoccupied or daylit areas;
- there are redundant lights operating, above cupboards or false ceilings, for example;
- luminaire diffusers, windows and upper surfaces of rooms are dirty.

Heating, ventilation and air conditioning

Some buildings will have separate systems, plant and equipment providing heating, ventilation, air conditioning and heat recovery. Others may have heating only, while still others may combine all functions into package equipment. Hence the first task of an energy survey is to identify the main items of plant and how they deliver their energy output to provide space heating, cooling or humidification, and heat domestic hot water.

Heating

Heating may be from electricity (direct or night storage), boiler plant, a heat pump, combined heat and power (CHP) or from district heating that is not within the control of the building owner or occupier. The primary objectives of the energy survey are to check whether the plant is converting fuel to heating energy efficiently, whether that energy is being distributed through the building efficiently and whether heat emitters are releasing heat to the room air efficiently. The following issues need to be considered:

- Boiler efficiencies have increased significantly over the years, with modern gas-fired condensing boilers achieving seasonal efficiencies greater than 90 per cent when new (see Chapter 3.2). However, seasonal efficiency for a condensing boiler depends on return temperatures being low enough for condensation to occur, hence maximum efficiency will only be possible when the boiler is serving underfloor heating alone, for example. When connected to a radiator system that allows flow and return temperatures to drop when external temperatures are lower, seasonal efficiency might drop to around 87 per cent, whereas if fixed flow and return temperatures are required efficiency drops typically to 85 per cent (see Section 10.1.2 of CIBSE, 2012). Efficiency will also drop off if a boiler is operating all the time at low loads, hence it is important to determine whether a boiler is oversized. For example, a large non-condensing boiler may achieve 80 per cent when operating at full load but only 30 per cent at one sixth of full load. This can be a particular problem if a single boiler is operated out of the heating season in order to heat domestic hot water. If the boiler is old and measures have been introduced to reduce heat loss then it may be time to replace it. Consider installing a separate boiler for domestic hot water, or instantaneous water heaters for remote outlets (see below).
- If regular boiler efficiency tests have been carried out, then the trend should be checked to determine whether there has been a recent steep decrease in efficiency and whether boiler maintenance has made any difference. If the plant is old and there has been an increasing rate of efficiency decay, then consideration should be given to replacement. Life expectancies vary from 15 years for a typical condensing boiler to 25 years for a well-maintained sectional or shell and tube boiler.[4]
- If there are multiple boilers connected in parallel, check that control valves are installed that prevent water flowing through inoperative boilers and heat being lost up the chimney. Satisfactory operation can be checked by measuring temperature difference across each boiler when only one is operating.

- Ensure that boilers can only run when there is a heat demand. Unnecessary firing is known as 'dry cycling' and may be due to a fault with the boiler thermostat. In multiple boiler installations, dry cycling can be prevented by increasing the band width over which boilers are cycled.
- Check maintenance logs against operating and maintenance instructions and note any gaps in records.
- Check that all hot surfaces, apart from heat emitters, are adequately insulated.
- Check frequency of alarms relating to operation of heating from BEMS records.
- Check whether heat emitters are located so that heat is lost directly to cold surfaces such as windows without benefitting occupants, for example, radiators located in front of windows; check whether emissions from radiators directly to external walls have been reduced through the installation of a reflective (high-emissivity) layer between the radiator and the wall.
- Some older air-conditioning systems circulate air at a constant temperature, perhaps as low as 10°C or 12°C throughout the building to cater for cooling requirements in internal areas, while heating to higher temperatures where room loads are not at design values. This can lead to refrigeration and boiler plant operating simultaneously for much of the year. Obviously this is wasteful and consideration should be given to a major retrofit of the air conditioning (see Chapter 3.2).
- For perimeter areas that have separate systems or heat exchangers for heating and cooling, check that there is a dead zone between the operating bands for the two systems, so that they cannot operate simultaneously.
- Check that the domestic hot water system is suitable for meeting current demand. Many hot water storage vessels are oversized, with heat lost through both hot water standing in the cylinder and circulating through the building. Check flow and return temperatures at cylinder (should be no less than 60°C and 50°C respectively), locate furthest outlet and measure the time it takes to reach maximum temperature: it should take no longer than one minute to reach its maximum temperature (typically around 55°C). Make sure the outlet has not been recently flushed by doing this test before first occupants arrive in morning. If this test indicates a problem, then consideration might be given to removing hot water storage and replacing with local instantaneous water heaters. If the storage is required to capture heat from solar panels, then it may be necessary to upgrade thermal insulation and reduce lengths of 'dead legs'. Low hot water temperatures in the cylinder also represent a legionellosis risk (see Chapter 4.5).
- The efficient use of CHP depends on being able to make use of the 'waste' heat from electricity generation. If the system has been designed to 'dump' heat that is not required via an external heat exchanger, there should be a means for monitoring this. If the amount of heat being dumped seems excessive, this could indicate that either the CHP plant has been oversized, the thermal buffer storage has been under-sized or the controls have not been set up correctly.
- Check that controls for heat pumps are set so that there are adequate dead zones between the operation of the heat pump, auxiliary heating and reverse

cycle cooling mode, so that auxiliary heating is not operated unless the room temperature continues to fall and the heat pump has reached maximum capacity. This will also ensure that the cooling cycle cannot operate at the same time as the auxiliary heating.

- Check room humidity at which the humidifier is brought in and ensure that this matches the humidity being achieved in the treated space. Humidistats are frequently located in extract air systems that may experience temperatures of 2 K or 3 K higher than the space. This means that the space humidity could be up to 10 per cent higher than the set point of the humidistat.
- Historically, the design criterion for winter humidity has been 50 per cent sat, which is unnecessarily high for comfort conditions. Approximately six times as much energy is required to control minimum humidity to 45 per cent compared with 35 per cent sat (see Section 7.2.3 of CIBSE Guide F). Consideration should be given to resetting controls to achieve a minimum room humidity of 35 to 40 per cent sat.

Ventilation, cooling and refrigeration

Air conditioning and mechanical ventilation can either be centralized, with air-handling plant connected to a ductwork distribution system, or designed with local air-conditioning or ventilation units.

Where a mechanical ventilation system might contain only fans, heating coil and filter, an air-conditioning system incorporates either: a direct expansion cooling coil that takes heat out of the air by evaporating refrigerant within the coil and rejects it via an air-cooled condenser; or a chilled water coil that rejects heat through a refrigeration plant incorporating a condenser that transfers heat to outside via a cooling tower. This latter arrangement tends to be used for larger installations, while the former may be used either for packaged units or distributed refrigerant systems, such as the 'variable refrigerant flow' (VRF) system.

For retail or food storage applications and drink or food manufacture,[5] separate refrigeration plant may be dedicated to cold stores and display cabinets.

Life expectancy of cooling towers depends on materials used in construction and varies from 10 years for timber and 12 years for galvanized steel, up to 30 years for stainless steel. For chillers, however, the principal factor influencing life expectancy is the type of compressor, with most lasting for around 20 years, apart from centrifugal compressors that might be expected to last 15 years. Similarly most good quality fans should last for some 20 years.[6]

- Where there are evaporative cooling towers, check whether there is a circuit that allows filtered cooling water flowing from the pond to the condenser to be diverted to supply the chilled water circuit when its temperature is below the required chilled water temperature. This is particularly useful when there is a high cooling load at moderate outdoor air temperatures, and can supplement the 'free cooling' from outdoor air referred to above.
- Check that cooling towers have been well maintained: dirty towers will not operate efficiently but, more importantly, represent a significant legionellosis risk (see Chapter 4.5).

- Large chillers represent a significant maintenance burden and great care is required to avoid release of refrigerants having very high global warming potential (see Chapter 3.2). Check maintenance records for signs of excessive top-up of refrigerant.
- According to CIBSE Guide F: 'Compressor refrigeration duty and system energy efficiency can be increased by using electronic expansion valves (EEVs). These provide a robust and more efficient alternative to the thermostatic expansion valve, the valve opening being controlled electronically. The valve can control superheat far more effectively. Also, it does not have the restricted pressure operating range of the thermostatic valve' (CIBSE, 2012). EEVs can be fitted cost-effectively to most existing chillers.
- As with boilers, chiller efficiency drops off at part load. This varies with the type of compressor and control, but where records indicate poor efficiency at part load, it may be worth considering installing chilled water storage (buffer). The most effective method of achieving this is with a store containing eutectic (phase change) material. This allows the chiller to operate at full load for short periods of time, until the eutectic requires recharging. If a low off-peak tariff is available, this means chillers can be run during these periods at lower cost and greater coefficient of performance (CoP).
- There is a direct relationship between the evaporating and condensing temperature difference (lift) and efficiency, such that either a drop in condensing temperature or rise in evaporating temperature of 1 K results in a 3 per cent increase in chiller efficiency. Hence it is worth checking that condensing water temperature is at its lowest and chilled water is at its highest realistic value.
- Ensure that the filters within the air-handling system are not dirty and that the pressure drop across them is not excessive.
- If the air-handling unit incorporates means for mixing return and outdoor air, check to see whether there are motorized dampers and how these are controlled. These should allow for 'free cooling' when the enthalpy (energy content) of the outdoor air is lower than in the treated space. If there are significant variations in occupancy, then check whether the outdoor air supply rate is controlled from a CO_2 sensor in the extract air.
- Local packaged air-conditioning units, such as 'through the wall' units, are far less efficient than central systems, and typically associated with 50 per cent higher carbon emissions (CIBSE, 2012). However, because of their energy-efficient features, variable refrigerant flow (VRF) and reversible heat pumps tend to have carbon emissions close to those associated with central systems. Life expectancy of a package unit can be as short as 10 years,[7] and, depending on condition, consideration might be given to replacing any found during the survey.

Motors and drives

During the energy survey, an inventory should be made of all electric motors, noting details from their labels, what they are driving, their drive type, their age and condition. Motors might typically have a life expectancy of 15 years, while variable speed drives might last for as little as 10 years.[8] The following issues should be highlighted:

- All induction motors, especially those with variable speed drives, should be fitted with power factor correction (see Chapter 3.2).
- V belt pulley drives are prone to slippage and should be replaced with modern flat, synchronous or ribbed belt drives where possible.
- Where there is a variable load, significant energy savings can be made if variable speed drives are retrofitted, for example, to the following items:
  - fans that have to deal with varying pressure drops across filters;
  - cooling towers fans, linked to control system;
  - pumps connected to a circuit incorporating two port control valves, such as TRVs;
  - lift motors (see Chapter 3.2).

Office, washroom and kitchen equipment

Office equipment generally falls into three categories: fixed, portable and 'unofficial'. The latter category is normally portable, brought in by employees and includes any electrical apparatus that has not been safety checked by the company's portable appliance testing (PAT) regime. This might include laptop computers, electric fires, hair dryers, etc. An inventory of all office equipment should be prepared, indicating rated power requirement (nameplate rating), fixed or portable, and usual location where used. See Chapter 3.2 for ideas on retrofitting office equipment.

This inventory should also identify kitchen, washroom and laundry equipment, including any gas and electric cooking appliances, commercial washing machines, dishwashers, refrigerators, freezers, kettles, hand dryers, etc.

The above list probably applies to most large office buildings; however, other types of building will have specialist equipment associated with their end use which we do not have space to cover here. This includes, for example, sports centres, with their swimming pools, spa baths, saunas, steam rooms, gym equipment, etc.; hospitals, hotels, factories and a wide range of other applications. The Carbon Trust provides downloadable sector-specific publications at their website. [9] Similarly the US EPA Energy Star programme provides energy management guidance across a wide range of applications.[10]

Monitoring and targeting (M&T)

> Monitoring and targeting (M&T) provides mechanisms for the long-term management of energy use and for highlighting potential improvements in the efficiency of energy use.
>
> (CIBSE, 2012)

The role of M&T is to do the following:

- establish current consumption;
- compare current consumption with historical data and benchmarks;

- set future targets;
- compare current consumption with the targets;
- identify trends in consumption;
- produce exception reports when targets are exceeded.

M&T is at the heart of good energy management, while the tools required are likely to gain in sophistication with the complexity of the buildings and services being monitored.

There are a number of techniques available for analyzing the data obtained from metering and bills. Although manual analysis is possible with simple energy profiles, there are long-established software tools that incorporate sophisticated analysis techniques and standard reports, as well as database and exception management capabilities.

Targets should be set 'that will stimulate management to make improvements. These targets must be realistic and achievable, taking into account the likely savings from improvements in housekeeping, maintenance and other efficiency measures' (CIBSE, 2012). Targets can be based on established benchmarks, depending on the level of ambition to which senior management have committed in the energy strategy. For example, energy benchmarks are published in Section 20 of CIBSE Guide F for good and typical practice for a wide range of applications located in the UK. These may not be considered ambitious enough for those wishing to make significant inroads into energy, carbon and cost performance. In which case, a programme of steadily improving targets may be set, for example, a reduction in energy use of 10 per cent per annum, or meeting Passivhaus standards within ten years (see Chapters 3.1–3.3).

The tools available for energy analysis are designed to help the energy manager understand trends in order to detect avoidable waste, identify potentially fruitful lines of investigation, quantify the effect of energy efficiency measures, provide feedback for staff awareness and improve budget setting. As well as testing performance against targets, these tools can also be used to determine the relationship between heating fuel consumption and outside temperature and, through regression analysis, establish the baseline fuel consumption, such as that associated with domestic hot water heating for example. Traditionally in the UK this analysis has used the relatively crude degree day techniques (Carbon Trust, 2007b), but in recent years some computer simulation software has been integrated into energy management packages that more accurately models the energy performance of existing buildings. Some software packages incorporate a 'tracker' feature that learns the shape of the energy/fuel use profile and provides a warning when it differs: similar to leak detection from pulsed water metering. Figure 4.1.4 shows a typical readout indicating a problem, resulting in an exception report.

Energy strategy, action plan and priorities

Once a policy has been developed and the survey has been used to establish what measures can be introduced to improve energy performance, then a strategy needs to be developed to implement an action plan. This is effectively a management framework which, according to the Carbon Trust *Energy Management* guide (2011b), should include:

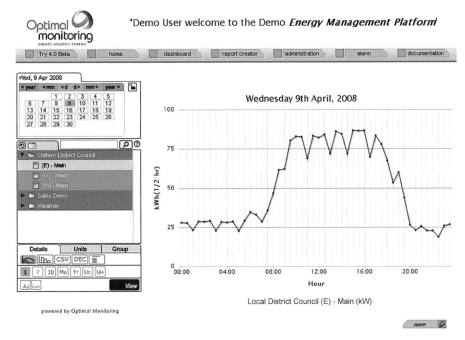

Figure 4.1.4 *Typical screen dump from M&T software*

Source: Optimal Monitoring.

- Assignment of energy roles and responsibilities across the organization with sufficient resources allocated to ensure that these responsibilities can be properly delivered. This includes staff time, staff grades and budgets.
- Development and maintenance of organizational structures so they support energy management and related processes.
- Compliance with energy and carbon regulation.
- Development and maintenance of procedures for operational and capital financing of energy efficiency activities and projects, which are consistent with the policy aims.
- Development and maintenance of procedures for the procurement of energy-consuming equipment, energy-related services and energy itself.
- Energy information management including metering, monitoring, analysis and reporting of energy performance and related issues.
- Methods and processes for identifying energy reduction opportunities.
- Training and development of staff across the organization, which supports the energy policy objectives.
- Communicating the energy policy, targets and particular initiatives both internally and externally where appropriate.

The shape of the action plan and implementation programme will depend on factors such as the size of the organization, the funds available for energy efficiency and the targets set. Priorities will need to be set based on cost and importance. Clearly the 'low-hanging fruit' can be addressed at low to zero cost, but if additional monitoring equipment is required to understand better the impact of energy efficiency measures, then there is a strong argument for installing this first.

The action plan should allocate budgets, delivery dates and potential energy-saving and payback targets for each item.

Housekeeping and engagement

Most of the 'low-hanging fruit' referred to above will involve housekeeping measures and require engagement with all staff:

> A good housekeeping campaign will recognize the importance of cleaning and security staff, particularly as they are often the first and last people in the building. Implementing a good housekeeping policy can also promote staff awareness of their responsibility to the environment as a whole.
>
> (Section 15.4 of CIBSE, 2012)

Also:

> Like health and safety, everyone in the organization should be responsible for their own actions with respect to energy efficiency. While health and safety regulations impose legal obligations on all employees, energy-efficient behaviour is more appropriately driven by developing an energy-efficient culture . . . This means making employees aware of the importance of saving energy, both for the organization and for their own working conditions. People are more likely to change their own habits if they understand how their actions affect consumption. Staff should feel confident about making suggestions and be informed enough to take action.
>
> (Carbon Trust, 2011b)

All building users need to understand how to interact with their building in an energy-efficient manner. Much of the appropriate behaviour, such as switching off lights, is common sense. However, where the occupant/building interface gets more complicated, such as openable windows and adjustable thermostats, there may be significant scope for user error and conflict. Although in many cases an operating manual may be sufficient to address these issues, training will help reinforce the message, which in many instances can be combined with courses in health and safety, fire and environment, for example.

Energy procurement

Another important component of energy management is cost management, including procuring energy at the best tariff. In the UK the choice of tariffs is currently excessive, which makes obtaining the best tariff complicated, even for domestic users. The Government Procurement Service offers assistance to the public sector in obtaining the most beneficial rates for all utilities.[11]

Where district energy schemes are operated by an energy services company (ESCO) there may be the opportunity to enter into an energy performance contract (see Chapter 2.5) with the potential to incorporate contract energy management (CEM) into the services provided by the ESCO. The resultant linking of energy savings with the cost of energy management could be attractive for an organization that does not have the resources to manage its own energy efficiency programme.

4.2
Water management

Introduction

The management of water in non-residential buildings, property portfolios, campuses and industrial processes is very often combined with energy management. Sometimes the same plant, equipment or system is involved, such as cooling towers, humidifiers, domestic hot water, swimming pools and spa pools. In manufacturing, laundries, car washes and industrial cleaning, water is frequently used as part of a process.

This chapter should be read in conjunction with Chapter 3.5, which describes the options for reducing water consumption through retrofitting water systems, fittings and appliances. The water management process follows very much the same principles as energy management and in most instances the energy survey described in the previous chapter will incorporate water use issues, as will the policy, monitoring and targeting (M&T), strategy, action plan and utility procurement process.

This chapter will focus on water management as part of facility or property management of non-residential and multi-residential buildings, portfolios or estates, rather than for individual households.

Benchmarking and analysis

In the UK, most non-residential buildings have had water meters fitted. In most cases these will require reading *in situ*, although pulsed-output meters have occasionally been installed, while many newer meters have pulsed-output capability, allowing for connection to a data logger, laptop, mobile phone or BEMS.

A water use survey should start by checking water consumption from utility bills, or results from data logging or BEMS records. Annual water use figures should be compared with an appropriate benchmark, such as those published by the Environment Agency.[1]

The UK Government's Business Link website[2] suggests that:

> The benchmarking process involves establishing your own performance level and measuring it against peer businesses on a like-for-like basis. To benchmark your water use, you should follow a systematic process:
> *   Planning: decide who is going to carry out the benchmarking and agree on the objectives, criteria and businesses against which you want to benchmark.

- Information gathering: establish your own water use, e.g. by using a water balance, record that of similar businesses using the same measurement criteria and then collate the findings so that you can make comparisons.
- Analysis: review the information you have gathered, find and fill any gaps, ensure that comparisons are realistic and identify opportunities for improvement.
- Implementation: make an action plan consisting of quick wins and longer-term initiatives, assign responsibilities and put the plan into action, making sure that it is properly monitored.
- Evaluation and review: benchmarking is a process of continual improvement so you should review the results of your action plan and repeat the benchmarking exercise regularly to see what further improvements you can make.
- You can find data on other businesses using government sources, trade associations and trade publications. It is also worth approaching comparable businesses directly, as they may also benefit from benchmarking.

Many high-water-use industries have published benchmarks on the internet, which can be accessed using a suitable search engine.

Identifying water-saving measures

Metering

If there is no sub-metering on the premises, then it will be necessary to identify the heaviest users of water by observation and experience. As we saw in Chapter 3.5, this will depend on the building type, the water-consuming equipment found and the behaviour of the users. However, as a general approach the following is proposed:

- Check meter readings or utility bills to determine whether there has been a sudden increase in the flow rate: this may indicate a leak.
- Check for any obvious signs of leakage during a walk round, such as damp patches, mould, cracks in plaster or concrete, warping of timber and, if the leak has been major and long term, undermining of foundations and subsidence.
- Pulsed-output meters can be used via trend analyzing software to give a warning of 'exceptions', using the same techniques discussed in Chapter 4.1 for energy management.

Sanitary accommodation

- Note WC cistern capacity and evidence of overflow and failure of cistern valves. If cisterns hold more than 6 litres, are single flush or are showing signs of continuous flow, consider reducing capacity with displacement devices and/or replace the flushing device with a dual-flush siphon and install a delayed action inlet valve (see Chapter 3.5).
- Check whether urinal flushing is continuous or excessive. Consider retrofitting timed or infra-red (IR) presence detection control of flushing.

- For sanitary accommodation with heavy use, check for evidence that taps are regularly left running and consider replacing with IR-operated aerated taps or installing solenoid valves in hot and cold water supplies operated from an IR detector. Note that this same detector can also operate lighting for the accommodation and, where there is a separate ventilation system, switch the fan(s) on and off.
- If it takes longer than one minute for the hot water to reach its maximum value at taps and showers, not only is water and energy being wasted, but the risk of legionellosis is increased, so check that hot water pipework is adequately insulated, or consider extending the circulation pipe to as close to the taps as possible in order to reduce dead legs (see Chapter 4.5).

Showers

In an office building shower use may form a small portion of the overall water consumption, consisting mainly of cyclists and runners in the morning and at lunch time, and likely to represent no more than 10 per cent of the workforce. However, for a sports centre or club and some 'dirty' industries, shower use may dominate demand. If flow appears to be high, it is a good idea to check the flow rate through a typical shower head by measuring the time taken to fill a container of known size. If the rate is greater than 9 litres/min., then it is worth considering replacing shower heads with an aerated type, ideally rated at 5–6 litres/min. Where there is evidence that showers are left running, then consideration should be given to replacing manual taps with push button or IR-operated types, or install an IR detector-operated solenoid valve in hot and cold water supplies to the shower room.

Kitchen equipment

If there is a kitchen on the premises being surveyed, it is a good idea to observe water use during preparation and washing up. Note whether there is a tendency to leave taps running during food preparation and for rinsing prior to dish-washer loading. Some commercial kitchens have pre-rinse spray valves (PRSVs) that consume perhaps twice as much water per sitting as the dishwasher.[3] If there appears to be heavy reliance on a PRSV, check its water consumption using the method described above for a shower. If this exceeds 9 litres/min., consider replacing it with a high-efficiency model, rated at 5.5 litres/min. or less. Note the manufacturer of the dishwasher and the model reference and check its energy rating from the literature. If it is a commercial model, then it is worth checking compliance with the Energy Star standard.[4] Domestic dishwashers are reported to last between 9 and 12 years, so if the appliance is within this age range and starting to perform badly, it might be time to replace it with an A-rated machine or better.

Laundry equipment

Identify any washing machines on the premises and determine how often they are operated. Ascertain manufacturer and model and determine what the rated water consumption is. If these are commercial washing machines, then check whether they appear in the UK Water Technology List,[5] in which case they will have been subject to enhanced capital allowances (ECAs). Domestic washing machines might typically last for 10 to 13 years. See Chapter 3.5 for more information on performance and labelling.

Swimming pools and spa pools

If the facility has a swimming pool and/or spa pool, then it will be necessary to discuss water management with those responsible for maintenance. Water use through pool and bath top-up is directly related to water treatment chemical use and costs.

Check hours of use and whether the pool is covered when not in use to reduce evaporation: evaporation losses can equal half the pool capacity per year. If water supply is sub-metered, check to see whether water consumption patterns accurately track filter backwash intervals and periods of maximum use. If there are any unexplained increases, this may indicate a leak: if there are no obvious gaps in the lining, leaking pipe joints or signs of seepage around the pool or spa pool, then a specialist survey might be required.

Discuss filter backwashing procedure and interval with maintenance staff. Compare actual backwash interval with that specified in operating and maintenance instructions. Determine whether backwash water is drawn from mains and discharged to sewer. For external pools there may be an opportunity to use backwash water for irrigation purposes.

A great deal of water is lost through splashing, particularly from busy leisure pools and spa pools with a young demographic. This can be significantly reduced if the surface of the water is dropped below rim level.

Check how frequently the pool and spa pools are emptied for maintenance. It is rare that it is necessary to empty a pool more frequently than once every three years, while a busy spa pool will need the water replacing weekly for cleaning and disinfection (see Chapter 4.5).

See Chapter 3.5 for potential retrofit ideas for reducing swimming pool water consumption.

Evaporative cooling towers and condensers

If the make-up water to the tower or towers is separately metered, determine seasonal profile over recent years and check for exceptional usage. Cross-check this against maintenance records and discuss with maintenance personnel to determine whether there have been any problems that might explain high water use.

With the cooling towers turned off, carry out a condition check on the towers to ascertain whether drift eliminators are in place and of a type that is likely to be effective (see Figure 4.2.1). Check pond, casing, pipework and water treatment equipment for any signs of leakage or excessive splashing. This survey might incorporate observations required to assess risk of legionellosis (see Chapter 4.5).

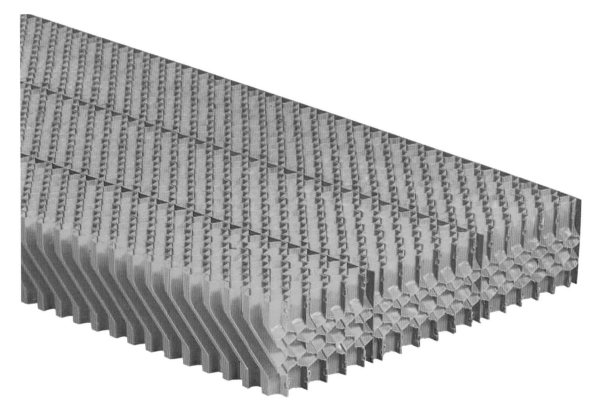

Figure 4.2.1 *Typical high-efficiency drift eliminator*
Source: GEA 2H Water Technologies.

Humidifiers

To ensure that it is not calling for excessive humidification, check the set point of the humidistat and compare with records of room humidity for cold winter days (see Chapter 4.1). If water supply to humidifiers is separately metered, it is possible to check whether water consumption tracks periods when the controls should be calling for humidification (i.e. during cold weather). Make sure there are no signs of leakage around the humidifier and associated make-up water pipework. If possible, check the condition of downstream ductwork internally for signs of condensation or ponding, indicating that not all water vapour is reaching the treated space. A simple duct-mounted steam humidifier will wet downstream obstructions within 2 or 3 m, resulting in pooling or saturation of duct linings for example.

Action plan and implementation

In Chapter 4.1 we discussed setting up a monitoring and targeting (M&T) regime as part of an energy management strategy. This same regime can incorporate targets for water consumption checked by on-going monitoring from pulsed-output metering. Ideally, one of the first actions following the water strategy will be the installation of additional sub-meters to cover, for example, major users of water and supplies to tenanted areas. These can also provide a more sensitive leak detection regime, based on trend analysis and exception identification software.

The survey will have identified 'low-hanging fruit' that have low or zero cost associated with them, and which clearly can be implemented without delay. Since many of the same plant, equipment and systems are impacted the implementation programme should be integrated with the energy action plan and the legionellosis risk prevention measures (see Chapters 4.1 and 4.5).

As with energy management, engagement with occupants is important, for example, the WRAP (Waste & Resources Action Programme) advises businesses to 'make sure staff are fully aware of the importance of water minimization and encourage them to report leaks'.[6] It is logical to incorporate this awareness raising into training and literature designed to engage staff in energy management.

In the UK, WRAP has introduced its 'Rippleffect' support package for businesses which, according to its website [7] 'provides a wealth of free advice and support to help your business to save money by using water more efficiently'. After registering for the Rippleffect, the following features will be available for use:

- online training modules;
- freephone advice line;
- online videos;
- guides and case studies;
- online tools.

4.3
Waste management

Introduction

For any business or household there are two key management functions that impact on waste arising. First, there is the way in which the processes are designed and materials are procured to minimize the generation of non-recyclable waste, and, second, there is the separation and storage of waste for collection from the premises. For this we have to apply the waste hierarchy discussed in Chapter 3.6, that is:

1   prevention;
2   preparing for re-use;
3   recycling;
4   other recovery, such as energy from waste;
5   disposal.

The process of minimizing waste through procurement and process design stretches from deciding on which food to purchase based on the amount and type of packaging in which it is encased, through to the optimization of materials use and waste arising from manufacturing. Decision-making in the first case may be confined within a moral framework, whereas there are clear economic drivers for the latter case.

Of course, waste takes a number of forms, for example, in transforming inputs of raw materials, energy, water, etc., into a finished product, there will not only be waste materials, but wasted energy, waste emissions to air and waste emissions to sewers or water courses.

We will be examining the key issues that define sustainable procurement in Chapter 4.8, including the amount of waste generated in the manufacture and use of the options available.

For a review of the design requirements for recycling and composting, refer to Chapter 3.11 of *Integrated Sustainable Design of Buildings*, which also includes a chapter on construction waste management (Appleby, 2011a).

Minimization of waste arising

A significant proportion of waste arises through a combination of over-purchasing perishable products, inefficient use of materials and over-packaging. The following extract from a US guide on minimizing laboratory waste[1] illustrates the first point well:

Purchasing chemicals in larger containers at an initial lower unit cost, rather than smaller containers, appears to be a good way to save money. However, consideration of the total costs of such purchases makes it clear this may not be the case. When a large container of a chemical is purchased, often a small quantity is taken out for use and the rest is stored. As a result, partially filled containers accumulate in laboratories and storerooms, and the chemicals, many of which have exceeded safe storage time periods or have unreadable labels, are disposed of as wastes. In a laboratory that has not adequately implemented waste minimization programs, unused chemicals typically constitute 40% or more of the hazardous waste stream generated.

Waste streams should be divided into those which are re-usable on site, recyclable, disposable to landfill and hazardous. These must be separated and dealt with accordingly, and we will examine the management of recyclables in the next section.

The electronics sector is particularly important because of its exponential growth in both consumer and business sectors:

As new technologies hit the stores fast, the demand for higher performance and faster processing capabilities make new models of laptop computers obsolete in a relatively short amount of time: the average lifespan of a laptop is typically between 3 and 4 years. When old computers become obsolete or lack the required functional capabilities, they often end up in landfills or get shipped to Third World countries, where the wastes can become a major environmental and health concern.[2]

Electronic goods contain a variety of hazardous substances, many of which end up in landfill, with the potential for contaminating land and water courses. A number of the larger electronics manufacturers now offer a 'take-back' facility. In Europe, a Distributor Take-Back Scheme (DTS) has been introduced through the 2002 Waste Electrical and Electronic Equipment (WEEE) Directive and in England and Wales via the 2006 WEEE Regulations (see Chapter 1.2). Despite this, some 66 per cent of electrical and electronic waste is being disposed of elsewhere, much of which is likely to be ending up as landfill.[3]

The design of a process can have a significant impact on the amount and type of waste generated. This can range from the way in which a dress is cut from cloth, depending on the width of cloth procured and the skill of the dressmaker, for example, through to the accuracy of machinery used for manufacturing engine components and the tolerances acceptable. In both these examples there will be some surplus material and rejects, but the amount of waste going to landfill can be minimized if the material procured is of a type that can be re-used or recycled.

Office waste

Extending this analysis to office processes, there are a number of situations where waste minimization principles can be applied,[4, 5] for example:

- introducing a paperless office system, requiring all communication and filing to be electronic, with strict control of printer and photocopier use;
- where print-outs are essential, these should be double-sided;
- all waste paper and card to be sent for recycling;
- all bought-in paper, card and packaging to be from recycled or Forest Stewardship Council (FSC) certified sources;
- toner cartridges for printers and photocopies to be refillable;
- buying consumables in bulk to reduce packaging, but only if fragile materials can be protected against damage;
- not over-buying products that could become outdated;
- all redundant or irretrievably broken electrical and electronic equipment to be disposed of through WEEE DTS;
- identifying hazardous wastes such as fluorescent lamps, batteries and some cleaning products, and providing suitable labelled containment for collection;
- all redundant furniture to be disposed of for re-use, or for recycling of materials if not suitable for re-use.

Food waste

Another area that generates significant waste is food processing, packaging and catering. According to an item from September 2011 on the EU Europa website:[6]

> It is estimated that in the European Union every person wastes about 179 kg of food a year. In total this is about 89 million tonnes per year. Agricultural food waste and fish discards are not included in these estimates. This means that the total annual food waste is even higher. Food waste is expected to rise to about 126 million tonnes (up by 40 per cent) by 2020 without additional prevention policies or activities.
>
> Food is wasted at all stages of the food chain: from producers, manufacturers, retailers, caterers and consumers.
>
> Food waste occurs for various reasons. For example, in the manufacturing sector it is mainly caused by overproduction, misshapen products (wrong size or shape), and by product & packaging damage. In the retail sector it is caused by marketing standards (aesthetic issues or packaging defects), stock mismanagement and marketing strategies (two-for-one deals).
>
> In households, reasons include a lack of awareness on quantities of food wasted and on the environmental and economical costs of food waste. The lack of knowledge on how to use food efficiently (e.g. making the most of leftovers, cooking with available ingredients) also contributes to food waste from households as does a lack of shopping planning and the misreading of date labels.
>
> Finally, the catering sector contributes to food waste (for example) by offering only one portion size (while individuals have different portion needs), because of a difficulty in anticipating the right number of clients, and because taking leftovers home is not yet an accepted habit in Europe.

The Department for Environment, Food and Rural Affairs (DEFRA) food and catering services standards[7] set out the following requirements for catering contracting in the public sector for England and Wales:

> Packaging waste in delivering food for the catering service (should be) minimized so that:
> - tertiary (bulk) and secondary packaging consists of at least 70 per cent recycled cardboard; and:
> - where other materials are used, the tertiary packaging must either be reusable or all materials contain some recycled content.
>
> Any contractor (should have) a food waste minimization plan in place, including actions and estimated quantifiable reductions, and ensures appropriate training is given to staff to ensure best practice in terms of food waste minimization.
>
> An appropriately-licensed separate food waste collection service should be procured as part of overall site waste management with the food waste collected going either for treatment at an in-vessel composting or anaerobic digestion facility or other suitable facility (as opposed to landfill).

Hazardous waste

The way in which wastes are identified as hazardous and thereafter labelled, controlled and disposed of is governed in England and Wales by the Hazardous Waste (England and Wales) Regulations 2005, amended in 2011 to take account of the revised EU Waste Framework Directive (see Chapter 1.2). At the core of this legislation is the identification of hazardous wastes, which are identified as having one out of a list of 16 'hazardous properties'[8] which range from 'explosive' to the recently introduced 'sensitizing'. The EU has developed a coding system for wastes, enshrined in the European Waste Catalogue (EWC). This has been adapted for use in England and Wales by the Environment Agency in their 'List of Wastes'.[9] In order to identify whether a particular waste is hazardous, it is necessary to ascertain whether it is identified in this list as hazardous, using the method described in the Environment Agency guidance.[10]

In the UK, WRAP offers a service to businesses which it calls the 'Waste hierarchy interactive tool'.[11] This provides tailored advice on waste management based on the type of business and the size of the organization.

Management of re-usable and recyclable waste

In Chapter 3.6, we examined a retrofit strategy to encourage recycling and composting, referring to the provision of storage receptacles to enable separation of different recyclables both close to the place where they are generated and accessible for collection. Where there are opportunities for re-use on site, it may be necessary to provide collection points for these materials, as well as recyclables. For example, some spoilt photocopier paper may be printed on one side only and be re-usable for jotting or drafts, whereas that printed on both sides will have to go for recycling.

Where there are large volumes of recyclable waste generated, such as super-markets and shopping centres, the space required for storing waste can be significant. This space can be dramatically reduced by the use of compactors and balers.

Balers are best suited to cater for an application where either there are large volumes of each recyclable waste stream; in which case a separate baler would be required for each type of waste; or where one type of waste dominates, such as cardboard packaging at a shopping centre, for example. It is important not to compress mixed recyclables in a baler if they need to be separated for processing at the recycling depot. A heavy-duty compactor or baler can reduce the volume of waste by up to a factor of four to one. There are also versions designed to reduce tyres to around one third of their original size.

Staff engagement

As with energy and water management, staff engagement in the process of waste minimization is vital. The California Department of Health Services guidance on pollution prevention states: 'Effective and successful management of the medical waste system within a hospital can best be accomplished when everyone involved is allowed to take responsibility and ownership for the process.'[12] The strategy should

> encourage employees to participate in hazardous materials source reduction as a way to reduce or eliminate hazardous waste generation. Hospitals should consider an incentive program to encourage employees to follow good house-keeping practices that reduce hazardous materials use. An incentive program can easily be instituted through an employee or team recognition or awards program.

The principles expressed in the above apply to any workplace and any type of waste, and should be introduced through training, signage and information dissemination as part of the environmental management system (EMS) and health, safety and environmental awareness programme for the business.

4.4

Air and environmental quality management

Introduction

In this chapter we are going to build on the background provided in Chapter 3.4, where we looked at problems that can be experienced with the indoor environment in an existing building and how this can contribute to the symptoms associated with sick building syndrome (SBS). We will refer to the tools used to establish the extent of any dissatisfaction with the indoor environment and to investigate the causes, described in Chapter 2.2. This chapter will set out the management operations required to mitigate against SBS, indoor air pollution, building-related allergies and discomfort due to thermal, visual and aural factors.

Monitoring of the indoor environment

There are essentially four methods available to the building or facility manager for monitoring the indoor environment:

1   taking snapshots of environmental conditions with portable equipment;
2   using data harvested from a building energy management system (BEMS);
3   making observations while moving around the building;
4   asking the occupants.

Within the fast-growing area of computer-aided facilities management (CAFM) there are a number of intranet-based tools available that provide an occupant feedback capability. In their simplest form they incorporate a screen view such as that shown in Figure 4.4.1, allowing occupants to report dissatisfaction with temperature, air quality and lighting, for example.

In the USA, the Center for the Built Environment (CBE) has developed an integrated facilities management tool that links reports from occupants via a GEMNet intranet protocol to a tenant interface for energy and maintenance system (TIEMS) and maintenance and operations recommender (MORE). GEMNet is the US General Services Administration (GSA) Energy and Maintenance Network, which provides an infrastructure that permits the GSA to support local building managers, provide a framework for management and analysis of maintenance and building performance data, automate certain

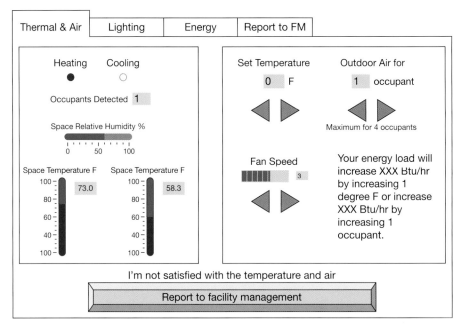

Figure 4.4.1 *Typical occupant interface for automatic control*
Source: Cisco.

computerized maintenance management system (CMMS) functions, provide common interfaces, and monitor and control facilities remotely.

The CBE project 'Using occupant feedback to improve building operations: A system to help facility managers utilize and respond to building occupant complaints' was completed in 2007 (Federspiel and Villafana, 2003).

MORE uses information from CMMSs and energy management and control systems (EMCSs) (or BEMSs) to recommend what maintenance personnel should do in response to a maintenance service request or other event requiring a maintenance or control system action. The recommender integrates text information from a CMMS database and sensor information from an EMCS/BEMS to provide recommendations. It also uses reported maintenance actions to learn to improve its recommendations.

A protocol for automating this process is described in a paper by UK-based Shimmin and Khoo on 'web-based occupant feedback for BEMS' as follows:

> When an occupant feels discomfort with their environment they submit their 'complaint' via the on-line web-based interface to the central intranet server. The details are logged in a database for subsequent processing of the occupants' complaints. At predetermined intervals a fuzzy logic engine running on the server will compile the occupant submissions for each interval and attempt to find the best compromise to satisfy the 'complaints' of discomfort in each zone by a form of democratic voting and averaging. The fuzzy logic engine will then adjust related set points through the BEMS, which controls the HVAC plant. The feedback loop closes when the occupant experiences a change in their immediate environment as set points are updated.
>
> (Shimmin and Koo, 2002)

An automated protocol may pick up relatively simple problems that depend on adjustment of a controllable parameter such as temperature, humidity or lighting level but, as we saw in Chapter 3.4, causation of SBS is more complicated than that. One way to approach this is to adopt one of the questionnaire-based surveys described in Chapter 2.2, such as the Building Health Check or Appraise scheme. Although evolving from 'sick building' investigations, these can be adapted for periodic building appraisals that can be used to both adjust building maintenance strategies and involve occupants in the operation of their workplace. These can be integrated with periodic energy and water use surveys, health and safety and legionellosis assessments and reviews of waste minimization and recycling strategies (see Chapter 2.6).

For example, an intranet-based questionnaire made available to all occupants annually might indicate a large number of reports of eye irritation in winter, while humidity readings recorded by the BEMS indicate that during cold weather, room percentage saturation is below 30 per cent for long periods. Also periodic air quality monitoring indicates that both particle and volatile organic compound (VOC) concentrations are above limit values. Further investigation finds that a filter has collapsed in the main air-handling unit, allowing dust to be circulated through the building from a neighbouring building site, while VOCs are being generated from recently laid carpets. This episode indicates problems with filter maintenance, carpet procurement and air quality management which need to be addressed by the facilities management team. There may also be a dust suppression issue with contractors working on the neighbouring site that needs to be raised with the project manager.

Section 8.8 of the CIBSE Guide M provides guidance on 'repeat testing and commissioning' including recommended actions following complaints from building users (CIBSE, 2008). As well as gleaning information from the occupants, maintenance records and BEMS, a design review is required to ascertain whether the relevant services are performing according to the original design intent and whether there is an inherent design problem that could be leading to the situation being experienced.

Prevention of ongoing indoor environment problems

It should be evident from Chapter 3.4 that there are a wide range of reasons why a building and its occupants might experience indoor environment problems. These can be inherent in the building location, type, use or services design; caused by poor maintenance or neglect; or some combination of these. We discussed potential retrofit opportunities to tackle these problems in Chapter 3.4, so in this section we will look at preventative measures associated with facility and building management, while in Chapter 4.7 we will be setting out planned and condition-based maintenance strategies in general.

Wherever possible, indoor air and environmental quality problems should be prevented before they can be measured or cause complaint, hence potential problems from sources of exceptional heat gain, noise, air pollution, etc., should be mitigated in advance. In other words action should be taken where these sources are likely to impose a load on the environment that goes beyond what the building and its services were designed for. For example, in the case referred to above, where the building site-generated dust was circulating around the building, and VOCs were being emitted from newly laid carpets; these should have been anticipated as sources of discomfort and the necessary action taken before becoming cause for complaints.

Apart from meeting good practice in planned maintenance and inspections of plant and systems, conditions should be monitored, preferably through a BEMS having a comprehensive network of sensors. Alarms should be set in the BEMS software to warn when conditions drift out of design comfort bands, and a protocol developed on what actions should be taken when particular scenarios occur. It is important that all alarm events be recorded, along with the actions taken and the results therefrom. The protocol should remain a live document and be amended from the mitigation history for each alarm event.

4.5
Legionellosis prevention and hygiene

Introduction

As we saw in Chapter 3.4, there is a particular risk of contracting legionellosis if one inhales a contaminated aerosol emanating from poorly maintained evaporative cooling towers or condensers, domestic water systems and spa pools. Other potential sources include humidifiers, misting devices, indoor fountains, safety showers, sprinkler testing and vehicle washes. It is important to note that *Legionella* bacteria are found naturally in water supplies and that a significant proportion of people are likely to have inhaled airborne *Legionella* at some time. For example, a 2008 study of hospital workers from four cities in Italy found that 28.5 per cent had *Legionella* antibodies in their blood.[1] However, it has been reported that 'only between 0.1 and 5% of persons exposed to *Legionella* develop Legionnaires' disease [and that] most *Legionella* infections may be subclinical or result in an influenza-like illness (i.e. Pontiac fever)'.[2] Also it has been estimated that only 10 per cent of Legionnaires' disease cases are reported due to the confusion with pneumonia from other causes.

Apart from *Legionella* bacteria there are a number of respirable micro-organisms that can be released into the atmosphere in aqueous aerosols and as fungal spores. Heavily contaminated humidifiers and misting devices have not only been found to cause legionellosis, but also extrinsic allergic alveolitis, humidifier fever and asthma attacks. Extrinsic allergic alveolitis is a disease of the gas-exchanging parts of the lung (alveoli) which in some cases has led to irreversible lung damage and death. With humidifier fever, however, although exhibiting some of the same symptoms as extrinsic allergic alveolitis, such as fever, sweating, aching limbs, breathlessness and wheezing, most victims fully recover. In some outbreaks involving exposure to a contaminated aerosol from a humidifier, some of those exposed have contracted extrinsic allergic alveolitis, others humidifier fever and still others have suffered asthma attacks. According to Sherwood Burge (1992), 'most outbreaks of building-related extrinsic allergic alveolitis have resulted from exposure to aerosols from a mixed growth of a wide range of organisms, many of which are usually not identified', but typically include a cocktail of fungae, bacteria, actinomycetes and protozoa. Most of the outbreaks have been associated with humidifiers serving paper and textile factories, where there has been a proliferation of nutrients to support microbial growth.

Microbiological contamination and other soiling can also occur within air-handling systems. This can arise because of neglected or absent filtration allowing particulates to coat heat exchangers and internal surfaces of ductwork. This can be exacerbated where there is condensation or ponding in cooling coil trays or downstream of humidifiers, for example. It may be necessary to inspect internal surfaces periodically and commission duct cleaning and, in some cases, disinfection where contamination is found.

General rules for management of risk

Managing the risk of legionellosis, humidifier fever and extrinsic allergic alveolitis requires the same approach in general to that required to maximize the reliable operation and life expectancy of building services and minimize risks from health and safety hazards. There is well-established guidance available from CIBSE and the Health & Safety Executive (HSE) in the UK and ASHRAE and the Centers for Disease Control and Prevention (CDC)[3] in the USA, which includes advice on the operation and maintenance of building services systems to minimize the risk of legionellosis (ASHRAE, 2000; CIBSE, 2002; HSC, 2002).

The facility or building manager must ensure that operating and maintenance systems are in place that reflect the outcome of a current risk assessment, which has taken account of any modifications to the water systems that pose a risk of legionellosis or other water-borne illnesses.

Crucial to a legionellosis control strategy is addressing the risk factors listed in Box 3.4.2. It is important to note that complete elimination of risk would require all of the risk factors to be removed, including the generation of an aerosol. Although this is possible if dry alternatives to cooling towers can be installed or spray humidifiers removed, this is not possible for domestic water systems, spa baths or car washes, for example. Hence in these cases, risk control is dependent upon a rigorous operating and maintenance regime that is proportionate to risk.

The key features of risk management general to all types of equipment and application are as follows:

- Ensure that the risk assessment is up to date and includes as a minimum:
  - description of building and relevant systems, including accurate layout and schematic drawings;
  - name and title of responsible person, usually the 'operations manager';
  - risk evaluation for each relevant system and details of relevant records of microbiological quality, water treatment and maintenance activity;
  - review of 'written scheme' including accuracy of drawings and record keeping;
  - names and responsibilities of maintenance personnel and contractors.
- Condition survey for each risk item, such as cooling towers, water treatment equipment, humidifiers, cold water storage tanks, hot water cylinders, distribution pipework, showers and other outlets, spa baths, fountains, car wash equipment, etc.

For a detailed risk assessment methodology, see the *BSRIA Guide to Legionellosis Risk Assessment* (Brown and Roper, 2000a), which includes a proforma risk assessment form.

It is very important that operation and maintenance and risk assessment documentation do not conflict and that record keeping reflects the requirements set out in the documentation.

Evaporative cooling towers and condensers

In the UK there is a requirement under the 1992 Notification of Cooling Towers and Evaporative Condensers Regulations to provide the local authority with:

- the address of the premises where the plant is located;
- the contact details for the person who has control of the premises;
- the number and location of the cooling towers or evaporative condensers.

The operation and maintenance of evaporative cooling towers and condensers have to address the following issues:

- the cleanliness of surfaces in contact with the water;
- control of water quality through water treatment;
- monitoring of the effectiveness of the water treatment regime;
- record keeping.

Cleaning and disinfection

CIBSE states that 'a simple, itemized schedule of maintenance is essential, and this should include the intervals at which the necessary inspection, checks and cleaning (including disinfection) should be carried out' (CIBSE, 2002). It goes on to recommend that 'cooling towers serving air-conditioning systems and those in continuous use . . . be cleaned and disinfected twice each year, in early spring and early autumn'. This should include descaling and removal and cleaning of the packs and drift eliminators (Figures 4.5.1 and 4.5.2), where possible. In any case a tower should be cleaned and disinfected prior to being brought in after a long down-time, while intervals might have to be reduced in locations where atmospheric pollution is particularly bad. Towers should be inspected on a one- to three-month cycle to check control functions, blow down, uniformity of water distribution and the condition of all accessible surfaces in contact with water. Refer to the CIBSE guidance for a detailed procedure for cleaning and disinfection.

Water treatment

Controlling water quality in an open cooling water circuit is a sensitive operation that would normally be carried out by a water treatment specialist. It requires the correct and often conflicting control of hardness, corrosion, total dissolved solids (TDSs), microbiological content and debris/particles (straining/filtration).

- The degree of hardness control required to prevent scale and sediment formation (Figure 4.5.3) will depend on the hardness of mains water supplied to the tower and usually requires some form of water softening.

Figure 4.5.1 *Internal view of badly soiled pack above cooling tower pond*
Source: www.debaltd.co.uk.

- Corrosion can create niches for *Legionella* colonization and is primarily dependent upon the resistance of surfaces in contact with water and may require the addition of corrosion inhibitors.
- TDS increases as water is lost through evaporation, drift and splashing, increasing the concentration of impurities in the water along with its electrical conductivity, while increasing both scale formation and corrosion potential. This is controlled through blowing down a proportion of the recirculating water and diluting the remainder with incoming mains water. This make-up water will require additional water treatment and add to the overall water consumption of the tower (see Chapter 3.4).
- There should be a screen or strainer fitted to the outlet from the tower which will need clearing of particulate matter from time to time. An accumulation of detritus will undermine the effectiveness of water treatment chemicals, increasing dosage and cost. If the atmosphere is particularly dusty, a bypass backwash filter might be fitted.
- If all of the above are working effectively, then the amount of chemical treatment required for microbiological control can be kept to a minimum. The choice of 'biocides' falls between oxidizing and non-oxidizing methods. Oxidizing chemicals include chlorine (bleach) and bromine, the effectiveness of which are pH-dependent. For example, approximately 20 times as much chlorine is required at a pH of 9.0 (alkaline) compared with a pH of 6.0 (acidic), hence for highly alkaline water, it may be necessary to use an additive to increase acidity. There is a variety of non-oxidizing biocides that are usually dosed intermittently to prevent *Legionella* from acquiring immunity, which they are not able to do with oxidizing biocides.

Figure 4.5.2 *Drift eliminators suffering from severe neglect*
Source: www.debaltd.co.uk.

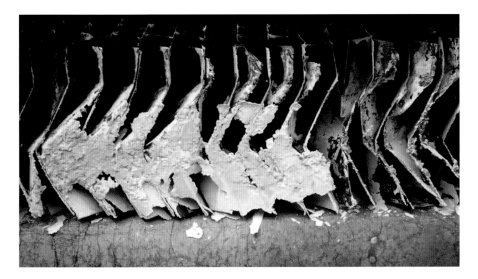

Figure 4.5.3 *Scale can have a major impact on cooling tower performance, here blocking air inlets to a pond*
Source: www.debaltd.co.uk.

Monitoring

According to CIBSE TM13:

> The monitoring programme should . . . include routine sampling and testing for the presence of bacteria, both general (aerobic) bacterial species and *Legionella* bacteria. Since the detection of *Legionella* bacteria requires specialist laboratory techniques, routine monitoring for aerobic bacteria (using dip slides) is used as an indication of whether microbiological control is being achieved.
>
> (CIBSE, 2002)

It recommends that dip slide samples be taken on a weekly basis and samples for the laboratory analysis for *Legionella* be taken quarterly. Samples should normally be taken via a drain point immediately downstream of the condenser (or the pond of an evaporative condenser). If high dip slide readings are obtained, then CIBSE recommends that further samples be taken for analysis by an 'accredited laboratory'. It is highly likely that low concentrations of *Legionella* will be found occasionally (<100 colony forming units/litre – cfu/l). However, if a small number of samples indicate between 100 and 1000 cfu/l, then the system should be re-sampled. 'If a similar count is found again, then a review of the control measures and risk assessment should be carried out to identify any remedial action' (ibid.). If sampling indicates extensive colonization with *Legionella* or more than 1000 cfu/l is found and confirmed following re-sampling, then disinfection of the entire system should be considered.

It will also be necessary to check the effectiveness of the various control regimes described above through a series of measurements from samples of cooling and make-up water as set out in Table 4.5.1.

Table 4.5.1 *Recommended frequencies for cooling tower water monitoring*

Parameter	Units	Make-up water	Cooling water
Calcium hardness	mg/l CaCO$_3$	Monthly	Monthly
Magnesium hardness	mg/l MgCO$_3$	Monthly	Monthly
Total hardness	mg/l CaCO$_3$	Monthly	Monthly
Total alkalinity	mg/l CaCO$_3$	Quarterly	Quarterly
Chloride	mg/l Cl	Monthly	Monthly
Sulphate	mg/l SO$_4$	Quarterly	Quarterly
Conductivity	µS (TDS)	Monthly	Weekly
Suspended solids	mg/l	Quarterly	Quarterly
Corrosion inhibitor	mg/l	–	Monthly
Oxidizing biocide	mg/l	–	Weekly
Temperature	°C	–	Weekly
pH		Quarterly	Weekly
Soluble iron	mg/l Fe	Quarterly	Quarterly
Total iron	mg /l Fe	Quarterly	Quarterly
Concentration factor*		–	Monthly
Microbiological activity	dip slide	Quarterly	Weekly
Legionella	colony forming units/l	–	Quarterly

Note: *The ratio of calcium or magnesium hardness of the cooling water to that in the make-up water.
Source: CIBSE, 2002.

Domestic water services

Because dosing with biocides is not appropriate for domestic hot and cold water services, the primary control methods are the following:

- Minimize the period that water sits in storage equipment or pipework (Figure 4.5.4).
- Minimize the time during which temperatures fall between 20°C and 50°C.
- Ensure that internal surfaces in contact with water are kept free of any sediment or coating that can form a substrate for colonization by *Legionella*.

These should all have been mitigated against through the design process, and any design faults should have been picked up during the legionellosis risk assessment and dealt with.

Box 4.5.1 details the key measures to be taken in monitoring and maintaining domestic water services (see also CIBSE, 2002).

Figure 4.5.4 *Example of poorly maintained cold water storage tank with low throughput*
Source: Thameside Mechanical Services Ltd.

Box 4.5.1 Monitoring and maintaining domestic services

On a weekly basis

Flush through little-used outlets.

On a monthly basis

- Check flow, return and drain water temperatures at hot water cylinder, and note any discoloration of drain water. Take a sample of drain water for dip slide if concerned about its quality: if there are signs of significant microbiological activity, consideration might be given to draining and disinfecting the entire hot and cold domestic water system.
- Check the time that it takes for hot water to reach 50°C at the most remote hot water tap: this should be less than one minute. If this time is exceeded, check that the circulation pump is operating. If this is a persistent problem, then it is worth checking whether the lengths of dead legs are excessive and/or pipework is adequately insulated.
- Check the time that it takes for cold water to drop to 20°C at the most remote cold water outlet: this should be less than two minutes. If this time is exceeded, determine where the heat gain is occurring by measuring temperatures in the storage tank and at other outlets. If the problem is with the tank, see below, otherwise either additional insulation or re-routing of pipework away from the heat source may be necessary.

Summer and winter

- Check water temperature in the cold water storage tank(s) remote from ball valve and compare with the mains water temperature entering tank. If a max/min thermometer has been fitted in the remote spot, note the maximum temperature that has occurred since the last inspection.
- Also note the air temperature in tank room and any sources of heat gain. If the tank regularly exceeds 20°C, check for signs of stagnation within tank and whether heat gain to the tank room can be mitigated.

On a quarterly basis

Dismantle, clean and descale shower heads and hoses.

On an annual basis

- Visually inspect cold water storage tank for evidence of stagnation, sludge and corrosion, note any defects in thermal insulation and take remedial action where appropriate.
- Check the daily water throughput of the cold water storage, and if significantly less than once per day, consider reducing the storage volume by either removing one or more of the tanks from a multiple tank installation or lowering the float valve.

- If the internal surfaces of hot water cylinder are accessible, drain and remove the access hatch for internal inspection to check for scale, sludge and corrosion.
- The hot and cold water systems should be inspected to ensure that the risk assessment, schematics and layouts are accurate.
- Check operation and maintenance records to ensure that actions have been taken as scheduled and recorded properly.
- Check that all thermometers have been calibrated.

Humidifiers

The two main types of humidifier of concern are the recirculating water spray type found in some air-conditioning systems and small portable devices, either using a pump or ultra-sonic waves to generate an aerosol. The former have been associated with outbreaks of humidifier fever and extrinsic allergic alveolitis, the latter with Legionnaires' disease.[4]

In all cases, a scrupulous cleaning regime must be instigated. Water reservoirs should be drained daily and the equipment cleaned and disinfected at least twice during a 12-month period. In most cases one of these will be prior to being operated for the first time at the start of the winter. Some equipment may incorporate non-chemical water treatment, such as ultra-violet (UV) radiation treatment. This will need checking on a weekly basis in accordance with the manufacturer's requirements, but as a minimum include checking that UV lamps are functioning and that the water in the control reservoir is sufficiently clear to allow effective transmission of UV light along its full length.

Spa pools

Typically a spa pool, or whirlpool spa, is maintained at a temperature between 32°C and 40°C, contains significant concentrations of anthropogenic detritus and generates an aerosol within the breathing zone of its occupants: ideal conditions for the multiplication and dissemination of *Legionella*. Other bacteria can proliferate, such as *Pseudomonas aeruginosa* which is associated with skin infections. Hence there is a heavy reliance on water treatment and maintenance to control microbiological contamination.

Management of commercial spa pools is a specialized activity and requires daily actions by trained personnel, including the following (CIBSE, 2002):

- Every two hours check the clarity of water and pH value, ensuring that the dosing rate for the oxidizing biocide is suitable for the pH of the water, which should be between 7.4 and 7.6.
- Clean the water line, overflow channels and pool surround.
- Inspect strainers, remove debris and clean thoroughly.
- Check total dissolved solids (TDSs).
- Check water use – should be equivalent to 50 per cent of volume of pool each day.
- Sand filters will need backwashing daily – other types in accordance with manufacturer's directions.

Typically the whole system should be drained, cleaned and disinfected weekly, and the water balance checked to ensure all branches are operating at design flows.

Microbiological testing should be carried out at least once per month, along with testing that all automatic systems are working properly and the air filter in the air blower system is clean.

See also the Health & Safety Executive (HSE) Information sheet: *Legionnaires' Disease: Controlling the Risks Associated with Using Spa Baths.*[5]

Other equipment and services

As a general rule, the control system for water systems that pose a risk of legionellosis or other airborne disease should be based on eliminating the risk factors that do not interfere with the effective operation of the system. The following hierarchy is suggested:

1   Keep all surfaces in contact with water clean and free of sludge, scale and corrosion.
2   Maintain water temperatures throughout the system at below 20°C and above 50°C.
3   If point (2) is not possible, instigate a water treatment regime including biocidal control that controls microbiological quality to within acceptable parameters.
4   If neither points (2) nor (3) are possible, then the intensity of monitoring, cleaning and disinfection must increase in proportion to the risk of exposure and the susceptibility of the exposed population.

Table 4.5.2 has been adapted from CIBSE (2002) and details the recommended maintenance tasks.

Contamination of air-handling systems

Like the internal surfaces of a hot water cylinder or cooling tower, a ducted ventilation system is generally hidden from view and historically has not been subject to regular inspection or maintenance. However, as we saw in Chapter 3.4, investigations into the causes of complaints and clusters of symptoms in some buildings in the 1980s and since have brought into focus the internal condition of these systems. Studies on odour sources in buildings carried out at the University of Denmark, investigating sources in poorly maintained air-handling systems, discovered that they emit odour and allergens from dirt and mould accumulated in filters, drip trays and other internal surfaces (Pejtersen *et al.*, 1989).

Concern about contamination of the internal surfaces of air-handling systems led to a flurry of activity in the mid-1990s, resulting in the Building Services Research and Information Association (BSRIA) developing a Standard Specification for Ventilation Hygiene, and the Heating and Ventilation Contractors Association (HVCA) publishing a guide on internal cleanliness of new ductwork installations; while, in the USA, the National Air Duct Cleaners Association (NADCA) published a standard for Mechanical Cleaning of Non-

Table 4.5.2 *Maintenance tasks for minimizing controlling legionellosis risk for miscellaneous equipment and services*

Equipment/service	Task	Frequency
Water softener	Clean and disinfect resin and brine tank (check with manufacturer what chemicals can be used to disinfect resin bed)	As recommended by manufacturer
Emergency showers and eye wash sprays	Flush through and purge to drain	6-monthly or more frequently if recommended by manufacturer
	Check thermostat	Annually
Sprinkler and hose reel systems	Witness tests of sprinkler blow-down and hose reels to ensure that maintenance operatives are exposed to minimum risk of legionellosis	6-monthly or to coincide with tests
Lathe and machine tool coolant	Clean and disinfect storage and distribution system	6-monthly
Dental equipment	Drain down and clean	At the end of each working day
Car/bus washes	Check filtration and treatment system, clean and disinfect system	See manufacturer's instructions
Indoor fountains and water features	Clean and disinfect ponds, spray heads and make-up tanks, including all wetted surfaces, descaling as necessary	Interval depending on condition

Porous Air Conveyance System Components (NADCA, 1992; Loyd, 1997; HVCA, 1998). Whereas these standards dealt primarily with the mechanics of duct cleaning, CIBSE turned its attention to the life forms that might be cultivated within the air-handling system and developed a methodology for testing for these in its 2000 Technical Memorandum, the *Hygienic Maintenance of Office Ventilation Ductwork* (CIBSE, 2000b). This includes a decision-making protocol for duct cleaning, based on sampling for microorganisms on the internal surfaces of the air-handling system and in the office air. Microorganisms generally require a substrate on which to adhere and multiply. For example, bacteria are unlikely to betray their presence by clearly recognizable surface growths, but they can be seen as slime or films in areas where standing water occurs. Fungi, on the other hand, can live on any substrate where adequate nutrients are available. They cannot use a smooth duct surface as a source of nutrients, but live on the accumulated dirt or organic detritus that may find its way into air-handling systems. They may also use the metabolites of other organisms or the decaying remains of other colonizers.

The CIBSE methodology requires extensive sampling of surface colonization within the air-handling plant and air distribution system, along with air sampling within the building. These should be analyzed for 'total viable count' (TVC) in colony-forming units (cfu) per m^3 for air samples and per $10\ cm^2$ for surface samples. CIBSE quotes acceptable and unacceptable ranges for each and recommends cleaning of internal surfaces if more than 25 per cent of results are unacceptable. If the results for the room air only are high, this is indicative of contamination in the room. This is unlikely to occur very often since fungal or bacterial growth within a room should generally be visible or create a readily identifiable odour.

A number of different methods are used to clean ductwork and the internal surfaces of air-handling plant, depending on how firmly lodged the contamination is and how accessible the surfaces. These include vacuum, steam, compressed air and rotary brushes. Usually some combination of these will be required, although a primary requirement is that the method employed must not simply redistribute the contamination, and measures must be employed to prevent break-out of liberated material into the occupied space. Disinfection through biocidal fogging will only be required if cleaning alone will not remove the microbial contamination, and only after follow-through sampling has demonstrated its presence. Disinfection must never be used as a substitute for mechanical cleaning since the biocide will only work on the surface layer of dust and other detritus.

4.6
Reducing vehicle use

Introduction

In Chapter 3.7 we considered what could be done to reduce transport impacts through refurbishment of existing buildings. In this chapter we are going to look at how someone responsible for a medium to large workforce can encourage people to use alternatives to their cars for commuting, or at least share vehicles, as well as managing buildings to promote an active lifestyle.

We will also be looking at the management of car parking facilities to cater for car clubs and improve safety and security.

Travel plan

The Department for Transport (2008) defines a sustainable travel plan as

> a strategy for managing the travel generated by your organisation, with the aim of reducing its environmental impact. Travel plans typically combine measures to support walking, cycling, public transport and car sharing. These are reinforced with promotion and incentives and by the management of workplace parking. Travel plans also include action to reduce the need to travel, such as teleconferencing. They can focus on both commuter and business travel.

In their guidance for setting up a travel plan, Strathclyde Partnership for Transport (SPT) has set out a ten-step procedure as follows:[1]

1 Secure senior management support.
2 Appoint a travel plan coordinator.
3 Form a travel plan committee.
4 Undertake a site travel audit.
5 Undertake a staff travel survey.
6 Review relevant company policy.
7 Establish focus/working groups.
8 Establish vision, objectives, targets and key performance indicators.
9 Develop and implement action plan.
10 Ongoing monitoring and review.

Securing the support of senior management will usually require the development of a business case which should include evidence of the following advantages:

- A green travel plan would strengthen corporate image, with a direct impact on business capacity for attracting new business, boosting sales and gaining trust from shareholders.
- Teleconferencing provides a cost-effective means of communicating while saving on time and travel costs, particularly for overseas business, thus potentially improving the reach and efficiency of the business.
- Improving accessibility and parking availability at the site should enable more customers to enter the site.
- Incorporating statistics on sustainable travel performance would strengthen corporate sustainability reporting (CSR) and the environmental management system (EMS).[2]

A site audit is likely to address the following questions (Step 4 of SPT procedure):

- Pedestrian access: Identify pedestrian crossings and footpaths to the site: are they safe, well maintained, well lit and free from obstruction?
- Cycle infrastructure and facilities: Are routes on and off the site safe, well-maintained and unobstructed? Is there secure and convenient cycle parking?
- Are there changing/shower facilities? Do staff have access to lockers? (See Chapter 3.7 for guidelines.)
- Public transport provision: Identify routes, nearest bus stops and railway stations, availability of timetables and information (see Chapter 3.7).
- Are pedestrian routes to main public transport nodes well signposted, safe and clean?
- How good are public transport services to residential areas popular with staff? Are travel times and costs off-putting?
- Are there missing links to reach public transport services or the local cycle network? For example, is there a nearby bus route that might divert to serve the site? Could a rear entrance to a nearby station reduce walking times, or might a poor link to a station be bridged by a shuttle bus service (DfT, 2008)?
- Vehicle access: Are there any congestion or access problems on or to the site?
- Car parking management: Identify the number of parking spaces, who uses them and how are they allocated? Are there busy periods in the car park? Is there space for dedicated car club parking spaces close to entrance?

It is important to understand the motivations and challenges that drive the decisions of people when choosing how to travel to work. Mode of transport and length of journey can seriously impact stress levels at the beginning of the day, and make inroads into productivity. The following gives some pointers on questions to include in a staff travel survey (Step 5):

- By what mode do they travel to work?
- From where are they travelling, how long does the journey take and what factors influence their means of transport?
- What barriers exist to stop them from changing their travel behaviour?
- What would encourage them to travel to work more actively?
- Do they have any suggestions on how facilities could be improved for non-car users?

- What would encourage single-occupancy drivers to travel using sustainable modes?

A sample staff travel questionnaire is provided in the Department for Transport guidance (DfT, 2008).

In developing the travel plan it is important to look at existing policies and gauge potential resistance or challenges in implementing more sustainable measures. The following are some suggestions adapted from the SPT procedure (Step 6):

- Staff business travel: Policies for pool cars or pool bikes, travel to other sites, use of own vehicles for business and number and cost of business miles claimed.
- Are staff required to justify travel to meetings and use teleconferencing where possible?
- Visitor travel: For example, do visitors have to book a space in advance?
- Impacts of street parking and disturbance to the local community.
- Fleet management arrangements.
- Company policies which influence travel choice: What is the car business mileage rate? Are cycle mileage or other incentives available?
- Are there any staff public transport incentives?
- Can staff work flexible working hours to avoid commuting during the rush hour? Are there any home working initiatives?

For large organizations the above exercises should be carried out for each site.

Many organizations will have processes already in place from which useful baseline data can be gleaned, such as staff claims on car mileage and fuel used for the car fleet. The sustainability in facilities management guidance suggests that the following indicators be estimated in order to augment this baseline:

- the miles travelled per staff member to work using public transport;
- the number of staff members cycling or walking to work;
- the environmental impact as a result of the transport of goods and staff to and from the organization, including flights.[3]

It recommends using an online carbon calculator to provide a metric against which future performance can be compared (see Chapter 1.3).

Depending on the size of the organization, targets can be set at national, regional, office, department and individual team levels. It may be appropriate to integrate them with other carbon-based and environmental targets and introduce an element of competition between teams, offices, departments, etc.

Targets should be kept simple, measurable, achievable, relevant and time-based (SMART). For example, a reduction in overall carbon emissions or business mileage, or an increase in numbers using alternatives to cars for commuting. Like all targets, they should be continually reviewed and updated as necessary.

Provision for cyclists

Apart from the provision of cycle parking, showers, changing facilities and lockers discussed in Chapter 3.7, there are a number of incentives that are worth considering to encourage staff to cycle to work. The UK Department for Transport (DfT, 2008) suggests the following actions:

- Improve cycle routes to (and on) the site (Figure 4.6.1).
- Make available maps and other information about local cycle routes.
- Provide, or pay for, bike maintenance.
- Facilitate the purchase of cut-price or free staff bikes.
- Offer training for those who are not confident cyclists.
- Instigate a staff bicycle user group (BUG).
- Develop incentives to cycle.
- Organize events to encourage cycling.
- Purchase pool bikes for business miles.

At the time of writing, the UK Government's 'Bike2Work' Scheme offers significant tax incentives for the purchase of bicycles for work.[4] Some companies have developed financial incentive schemes for those who use alternative means for travelling to work based on the cost of providing car parking spaces. This scheme also rewards those who walk, use public transport or share car space.

Figure 4.6.1 *Dedicated cycle route, Ipswich*
Source: Peter Ito.

Car parking and clubs

According the DfT guidance:

> Management of car parking is a vital part of a travel plan. If you provide plentiful free car parking, there will be a built-in incentive to drive to work, and indeed each driver will be receiving a transport subsidy from the company running to hundreds or even thousands of pounds per year. Where firms have taken action to manage parking as part of their travel plan, there has been a greater reduction in car driving.
>
> (DfT, 2008)

In practice, parking stress and congestion are already acute issues for many sites. Constraining parking or introducing charges for parking may be one of the most contentious aspects of a travel plan. Zero parking is generally only an option for central locations where public transport is very good. If there are only a very few parking bays, these should as a priority be available to staff or visitors with mobility difficulties rather than to senior staff.

A needs-based permit system is a fair way to allocate parking. For example, the criteria for permits might be based on the following hierarchy:

1   those with personal mobility difficulties;
2   car sharing and car club cars;
3   those with out-of-hours work responsibilities;
4   those with caring responsibilities that cannot be fulfilled without a car on the journey to or from work;
5   those who live too far to walk to the office or from public transport routes to the site.

Car clubs and pools

Car clubs provide members with access to a pre-booked car parked in a designated bay in their neighbourhood using a swipe card (Figure 4.6.2). In the UK, there is a mix of commercial and community car clubs.[5] In the USA, they are available in many major cities and university campuses. Car pools, on the other hand, comprise cars that are purchased by the organization and are available for booking by staff for business use.

The downside of a car pool is the sunk cost of buying pool vehicles or committing to contract hire agreements, along with the administrative burden of a pool booking system and vehicle maintenance. For companies that do not already operate vehicles and smaller companies in particular this can be a major challenge. One option is to team up with other local firms to create a pool. However, the widespread availability of commercial car clubs offers an innovative solution for an increasing number of locations. Corporate membership of a car club can give cost-effective access to vehicles on a pay-as-you-go basis.

Some car club companies offer to set up conveniently located dedicated parking bays for organizations exceeding a specified demand requirement. As well as local journeys, there may be the option to travel to other cities by public transport and pick up a car club vehicle there. Modern car clubs that operate

Figure 4.6.2 *Dedicated car club parking*
Source: David Hawgood.

nationally offer a similar service to that provided by car hire companies, providing a range of vehicle types, including low-emission cars that are exempt from the London congestion charge, for example. Bookings can be made online or over the phone. Once a car is booked out, it is remotely programmed to be accessible only to that user by matching the vehicle's magnetic card-reader to the user's smart card.

Safer parking

In Chapter 3.7 we discussed the design requirements for the British Safer Parking Scheme. Although intended to support the Park Mark® award and mostly applied to public car parks, the principles can be applied to any car park where there may be security issues. In the guidance for the scheme the following issues are applicable to the management of the facility:[6]

• Security is a particular issue for car parks that are nominally open for only part of the time but allow vehicles to remain parked during closed times, but with significantly reduced security, while also allowing uncontrolled access by the public. Signage should be provided that warns people not to leave valuables in their vehicles and that security is reduced during out-of-hours periods.
• Even if car parks are unmanned, there should be a means for contacting readily available staff during opening hours.

- For car parks bordered by soft landscaping, shrubs and trees should be trimmed to ensure lines of sight from neighbouring buildings and sites are not interrupted.
- Dirty and badly maintained car parks are more likely to be vandalized and feel threatening to users. In particular, graffiti should be removed as quickly as possible.

Active occupancy

As well as the environmental benefits of walking, running and cycling to work, there are also potential health advantages to a more active lifestyle.

According to official statistics, just under one third of the US adult population is obese, that is having a body mass index (BMI) of more than 30 kg/m^2. The figure for the UK for 2008 was 24.5 per cent of those over 16 years of age. The proportion of the adult population of the USA that is obese has more than doubled since the early 1960s. Although this is in part due to diet, activity levels also make a significant contribution. There is incontrovertible evidence that active people are less prone to a whole range of illnesses. Regular physical activity contributes to the prevention and management of over 20 conditions including coronary heart disease, diabetes, certain types of cancer and obesity. Strokes cost the British National Health Service around £2.8 billion a year, while studies indicate that physical activity reduces the risk of having a stroke by one third.

With this in mind, a Federal programme has been launched in the USA called the National Physical Activity Plan, while in New York City a multi-departmental initiative fronted by the Department of Design and Construction has introduced the Active Design Guidelines (NYC, 2010). As one might expect, the New York Guidelines are tailored for high-density inner-city development and cover neighbourhood issues, urban design and architecture. They incorporate some useful suggestions for operating buildings as follows:

- Increase stair use among the able-bodied by posting motivational signage to encourage stair use.
- Reorganize building functions to encourage brief bouts of walking to shared spaces such as mail and lunch rooms, provide appealing, supportive walking routes within buildings.

One innovative scheme from the UK, developed by the Smarter Travel Unit at Transport for London and Intelligent Health Ltd and known as Step2Get, encourages children to walk to school by offering incentives.[7] School pupils are issued with personal cards which they swipe at touch points along a designated walking route. They accumulate points for each walk and are rewarded with vouchers which they can use to obtain cinema tickets or clothing when they have reached a set target.

Intelligent Health uses near field communication (NFC) technology to monitor the walking route. The 'receivers' which act as the swipe points are designed and manufactured by the company. The scheme can also be used to direct children along specific routes for safety reasons or to reduce overcrowding on local public transport services.

This system is at the heart of the Wimbledon Schools Walking project, which was also designed to reduce congestion and dwell times of buses, and involved some 300 pupils at Wimbledon schools.

In the USA, Federal funding has been used to establish the National Center for Safe Routes to School which has been established to 'enable community leaders, schools and parents across the United States to improve safety and encourage more children to safely walk and bicycle to school'.[8] Funding is available for improving pedestrian and cycle routes, providing information, cycle racks and so forth.

4.7
Sustainable maintenance

Introduction

Regardless of how well a building and its services are designed, if they are badly maintained, then their performance will deteriorate and they will not be sustainable. On the other hand, it is possible to design a building to minimize the maintenance burden and hence reduce the risk of failure. For example, a naturally ventilated building avoids reliance on fans and air-conditioning plant, albeit with a potentially greater cleaning burden from dirt entering through open windows.

Like many aspects of sustainability when applied to the design, construction and operation of buildings, the term 'sustainable maintenance' is subject to many interpretations. In a recent survey of maintenance operatives involved in the social housing sector in the UK: 'their approach starts with energy efficiency and a desire to make best use of resources while providing value for money';[1] meanwhile, a study on sustainable maintenance at the University of Greenwich is focusing on minimizing waste.[2] In reality, all of these issues, along with those discussed in previous chapters, need to be brought into a sustainable maintenance strategy. The definition provided in the introduction to the 'Inspiring Sustainable Maintenance Conference' in April 2012 states: 'Sustainable maintenance of buildings is the practice of ensuring the building supports the core business with minimum impact on natural resources including energy.'

The Building Services and Engineering Association (BS&EA) provides a regularly updated on-line suite of standard maintenance specifications[3] covering:

- heating and pipework systems;
- ventilating and air conditioning;
- controls, including building and energy management systems;
- ancillaries, plumbing and sewerage systems;
- electrical services in buildings including power supplies and associated electrical equipment up to 415 V;
- water treatment and hygiene;
- sprinkler systems.

In this chapter we will be investigating how the operation and maintenance strategy can support the sustainability objectives of facilities management, supporting the principles set out in previous chapters dealing with the management of energy, water, waste, air and environmental quality, legionellosis prevention and hygiene.

Sustainable maintenance strategy

At the heart of any maintenance strategy must be the aim to 'prevent' problems before they happen. The only times when it is acceptable to allow plant or equipment to break down is when there is automatic standby in place or when it has become redundant.

The conventional approach to preventative maintenance is for actions to be 'carried out at predetermined intervals or corresponding to prescribed criteria and intended to reduce the probability of failure' (CIBSE, 2008). In many instances, maintenance intervals are prescribed in the manufacturer's operating and maintenance (O&M) instructions and deviation from these intervals can invalidate a warranty. However, it has been discovered that in many instances plant and equipment has been over-maintained, wasting resources and in some instances reducing its life. This has led to the development of reliability-centred maintenance and condition-based maintenance:

> A Preventative Maintenance (PM) program is based on the assumption of a fundamental cause-and-effect relationship between scheduled maintenance and operating reliability. This assumption was based on the intuitive belief that because mechanical parts wear out, the reliability of any equipment is directly related to operating age ... In fact, it was discovered that in many cases equipment greatly exceeded the perceived or stated design life.[4]

Reliability-centred maintenance is the optimum mix of preventative, condition-based and, where appropriate, reactive maintenance. Condition-based maintenance (CBM) is based on work being 'initiated by trends highlighted by routine or continuous monitoring of the condition of plant' (CIBSE, 2008). Sometimes these will triggered by exceptions to a trend, such as a sudden increase in motor-winding temperature or water consumption, indicating a failure; or when reaching a predetermined limit. CBM is pro-active and should be used to initiate 'failure-finding' strategies.[5] Reactive maintenance, on the other hand, should only be relied upon rarely, perhaps for certain small and non-critical items, not covered by warranty or O&M instructions.

The techniques employed for CBM include acoustic emissions monitoring, vibration analysis, thermography, power quality monitoring, lubricant analysis and ultrasonic testing (Pearson and Seaman, 2003).

- Acoustic emissions monitoring detects the high-frequency waves produced in materials under stress, caused by forces such as friction, impacts, cavitation and turbulence. It is particularly useful for identifying the condition of motor bearings and any degradation in lubrication. Instruments are available that are calibrated to enable bearing stress to be benchmarked against pre-programmed criteria. These are available as portable devices (see Figure 4.7.1) or for integrating into a multi-sensor monitoring system connected to a building energy management system (BEMS).
- Vibration analysis 'can provide effective condition forecasting for most machines with moving parts' (ibid.). As bearings degrade or become misaligned, vibrations increase and hence can give an indication of when action is required if compared with values when new. Monitoring uses relatively

Figure 4.7.1 *Typical acoustic emissions monitor*
Source: Acoustic Emissions Consulting; www.aeconsulting.com.

simple accelerometers that can be calibrated to provide readings of root mean square (rms) acceleration and velocity. Some instruments also provide dB (decibel) readings that can be used to monitor phenomena such as cavitation, within pumps and pipework, for example; and impulse shocks, within worn bearings, for example.

- Thermography, or thermal imaging, can be used to detect anomalous thermal conditions within plant and equipment. As well as enabling the identification of gaps in thermal insulation within building fabric, as we saw in Chapter 3.1, it can be used to detect overheating due to electrical faults, excessive friction in drives, defective pipe insulation, internal blockages and uneven heat distribution in pipework and heat exchangers.
- Power quality refers primarily to the wave distortions and harmonics that can occur with out-of-balance three phase electrical supplies. These occur typically with variable speed drives and fluorescent lamps, for example. In extreme cases, these can produce overheating of cables, motors and transformers, as well as potentially damaging vibration within busbars, and failure of power factor correction capacitors and circuit breakers. Furthermore, increases in harmonic frequency can cause fluctuations in voltage that may impact on neighbouring consumers. In these cases the Network Operating Company will require harmonic distortion to be reduced through the installation of 'active filters' to comply with Electricity Association Recommendation G5/4 (EA, 2001). Ongoing power quality monitoring will provide reassurance that existing protection is working, while identifying any problems arising from neighbouring consumers.

- Motor circuit analysis (MCA) techniques utilizing resistance, impedance, inductance, phase angle, current/frequency response and insulation resistance have been successfully applied to the detection of winding defects (shorts, resistive unbalances and insulation to ground), cable defects and rotor defects. They have also been found to be able to trend and estimate winding failures with a high degree of accuracy.[6]
- Fluid analysis includes the monitoring of microbiological and chemical quality required for legionellosis control, as discussed in Chapter 4.5. Where it is possible to draw off samples of oil from motor bearings, compressors, transformers and generators, lubricant analysis can give an indication of wear and/or contamination.
- Ultrasonic testing involves the generation of ultrasonic waves into a solid material of known characteristics to detect flaws and reductions in wall thickness, typically where corrosion is suspected.

Table 4.7.1 is extracted from the 2003 BSRIA guidance on CBM and provides some examples of building services plant and equipment that can be monitored for condition and faults via a link to a BEMS, indicating the parameter sensed (Pearson and Seaman, 2003).

Reliability-centred maintenance (RCM) strategies can be adapted to the risks associated with failure. For example, a different approach is required where failure could result in loss of life compared to inconvenience or discomfort. In general, RCM 'treats failure statistics in an actuarial manner (based on calculating) conditional probability of failure at specific ages' of plant and equipment.[7] Tasks are designed to reduce the probability of failure, and feedback is used to improve both future maintenance and design.

Table 4.7.1 *Building services process monitoring via BEMS*

Plant/equipment item	Fault source	Parameter
Air filtration	Air-side fouling	Volume air flow or differential pressure
Pipelines	Leakage or fouling	Flow rate or pressure
Heating and cooling coils	Leakage, scaling or water-side fouling Air-side fouling	Flow rate, pressure or temperatures Pressure drop or heat transfer
Chillers	Motors Valves Misalignment/unbalance Leakage Fouling or scaling	Electrical current Position Vibration, acoustic or temperature Flow rate or pressure Flow rate or pressure
Motor drives	Bearing or lubrication Misalignment/unbalance Windings or castings Burnout	Vibration, acoustic or temperature Electrical current Temperature
Humidifiers	Scaling or fouling	Flow rate or pressure
Boilers	Scaling or fouling Burner Flue	Heat transfer Combustion performance Flow rate
Cooling towers	Scaling or fouling	Flow rate or pressure

Maintenance and sustainable facilities management

Poorly maintained building services will perform badly in a number of ways. As well as running the risk of breakdown and catastrophe, there are also impacts on energy consumption, water use, waste, hygiene, emissions and indoor environment to consider.

Energy

Section 17.1 of *CIBSE Guide F* recommends that:

> Maintenance and energy policies should be coordinated with the support of top management. Maintenance work [should] include energy efficiency measures and checks, as appropriate. Maintenance and energy management have the common objectives of:
> - ensuring that a building and its services continue to function reliably, efficiently and effectively
> - ensuring the health, safety and comfort of occupants, protecting and enhancing the value of investment in a building and its equipment.
>
> (CIBSE, 2012)

Guide F also provides a comprehensive checklist of energy-related maintenance issues in Appendix 17.A1.

Water

Maintenance of water systems to minimize operational water consumption, control *Legionella* and mitigate against other hygiene problems is discussed in Chapters 4.2 and 4.5. Maintenance actions, such as cleaning and disinfecting water systems and testing sprinkler systems, consume significant amounts of water, as well as in some cases posing a health risk to maintenance personnel. Hence procedures must be introduced that reduce water use and exposure to *Legionella* or other biohazards during maintenance actions.

Potentially significant quantities of water are wasted during sprinkler testing. For example, a 'fact sheet' from the Victoria Government in Australia reported in 2008 that some 500 million litres of water were used in sprinkler testing in Melbourne alone.[8] It suggested that some 90 per cent could be saved by a combination of reducing pressures at which testing was carried out, increasing intervals between tests and recirculating test water, either to recharge the sprinkler system or as grey water for non-potable uses. It is interesting to note that in the UK some 9 billion litres of water are used each year for fighting fires in commercial premises alone, resulting in some 350,000 tonnes of CO_2 being emitted.[9] Most of this is used by fire brigades rather than sprinkler systems.

As we have seen, maintenance of cooling towers, domestic water systems, swimming pools and spa pools involves periodic cleaning and disinfection which not only consumes large quantities of water, but also requires the processing of water containing high concentrations of oxidizing biocides.

> Cooling towers should be taken off line for thorough cleaning including disassembly of the packing and thorough surface descaling and disinfection (typically) every 6 months . . . It is not recommended to use high-pressure hoses for the removal of surface deposits from cooling tower components because of the generation of aerosols which may contain bacteria.
>
> (Brown and Roper, 2000b)

Generally it will be acceptable to discharge water used for disinfection to the sewer provided the chlorine is neutralized with sodium thiosulphite or similar, as agreed with the authority responsible for the sewer.

Emissions

Emissions associated with maintenance tasks include discharges to atmosphere, sewers, earth and ground water.

The accidental emission of refrigerant gases can occur during maintenance of refrigeration plant. The responsibility of maintenance operatives in this regard is governed across the EU by the so-called 'F-gas Regulation' transposed into UK law in 2009 under the Fluorinated Greenhouse Gas Regulations.[10] This requires 'operators' of stationary refrigeration, air conditioning and heat pump equipment having a charge of 3 kg or more (or 6 kg if hermetically sealed) to do the following (CIBSE, 2008):

- Prevent leakage, and repair any leaks as soon as possible.
- Arrange proper refrigerant recovery by certified personnel during servicing and disposal.
- Carry out leak checks every 12 months for 3 kg charge or greater (or 6 kg hermetic), 6 months for 30 kg charge or greater, assuming equipment with >300 kg charge has leak detection as required by the Regulations.
- If a leak is detected, then a further check is required within 1 month following repair.
- Ensure that only certified competent personnel carry out work with refrigerants, including leakage detecting.
- Maintain records of refrigerant charge volumes, leakage testing, faults, repairs and servicing.

Leakage and discharges of fuel and oil from generators, motors and transformers can find their way into sewers and the ground, potentially polluting natural water sources. Hence any maintenance action that poses the risk of spillage of fuel or oil should be carried out within a bunded area having sufficient capacity to contain the maximum spillage possible. Any leakage or spills should be dealt with immediately and residual liquids disposed of as a hazardous waste (see Chapter 4.3) or for recycling if in a suitable condition. This includes oil/fuel collected from interceptors in vehicle workshops, garages and car parks.

Indoor environmental quality

As we saw in Chapter 4.4, it is important that the facility and maintenance management is able to respond to complaints and problems that arise with the building environment. In Chapter 4.5 we saw how the internal condition of ducted ventilation and air-conditioning systems can become contaminated, and the monitoring required to anticipate this and decide on a cleaning programme.

It is a fundamental responsibility of the facilities management and maintenance team to maintain the building services so that they maintain comfort conditions within the limits set by the designers. If the designers have got it wrong, then this may not be immediately apparent, hence monitoring of conditions inside and out over a long period is vital, augmented with occupant feedback where possible.

Waste minimization

The maintenance operation for a building must apply the same waste strategy as other operations within the building (see Chapter 4.4), in terms of minimizing waste, recycling and the safe disposal of hazardous substances.[11] Potentially there are numerous waste streams arising from maintenance activities and their management may be more akin to that for an industrial process or construction site. In fact, for a complex site having multiple buildings and a rolling programme of minor works and refurbishments, it is worth adopting a tailored 'site waste management plan' (SWMP) in accordance with the 2008 *SWMP Regulations* to cover all maintenance-related activities (see Chapter 4.3, in *Integrated Sustainable Design of Buildings*, Appleby, 2011a).

Health and safety of maintenance activities

We do not have the space here to go into every aspect of health and safety associated with maintenance of buildings and their services. There are indeed numerous hazards faced by maintenance personnel in a wide variety of workplaces. In its useful introduction to health and safety for those responsible for maintenance and small building projects in small businesses, the i4profit web site suggests that:

> It is easy to overlook these activities because they happen now and again, and it is often a contractor or service agency doing the work. Sometimes people are in places where no one normally goes, e.g. the roof or electrical switchboard. They may be fault finding, trying to repair something quickly – often outside the routine. Not surprisingly there are many accidents. Falls from heights, e.g. ladders, are the most common cause of serious injury.[12]

In the UK, maintenance work falls within the ambit of the 1974 Health & Safety at Work etc. Act and relevant Regulations. Some maintenance activities will be classified as construction work and hence the 1996 Construction (Health, Safety & Welfare) Regulations and the 2007 Construction (Design and Management) Regulations will apply, within the criteria set out in the legislation. Other work will have to comply with relevant clauses under the legislation listed in Box 4.7.1.

Box 4.7.1 UK legislation applicable to maintenance work

- Management of Health and Safety at Work Regulations 1999
- Workplace (Health, Safety & Welfare) Regulations 1992
- Work at Height Regulations 2005
- Lifting Operations and Lifting Equipment Regulations 1998
- Provision and Use of Work Equipment Regulations 1998
- The Personal Protective Equipment at Work Regulations 1992
- Confined Spaces Regulations 1997
- Control of Asbestos Regulations 2012
- Control of Substances Hazardous to Health Regulations 2002
- Control of Noise at Work Regulations 2005
- Electricity at Work Regulations 1989
- Supply of Machinery (Safety) Regulations 1992
- Pressure Systems Safety Regulations 2000
- Carriage of Dangerous Goods (Classification, Packaging and Labelling) and Use of Transportable Pressure Receptacles Regulations 1996
- Transportable Pressure Vessels Regulations 2001
- Dangerous Substances and Explosive Atmospheres Regulations 2002
- Fire Precautions Act 1971
- Fire Precautions (Workplace) Regulations 1997 – as amended
- Health and Safety (First-Aid) Regulations 1981
- Reporting of Injuries, Diseases and Dangerous Occurrences Regulations 1995

4.8
Sustainable purchasing and soft facilities management

Introduction

In this chapter we are going to look at the sustainable purchasing of non-engineering items such as office supplies, food and consumables in general, and the management of 'soft services' such as cleaning.

In Chapter 3.2, we discussed the issues surrounding the sustainability of lamps and office equipment, while in Chapter 3.8 we covered 'responsible sourcing and sustainable procurement' of materials for refurbishment. Many of the same issues apply to the purchase of consumable items. Indeed, every product or service purchased has an impact on the environment. Sustainable purchasing is an approach to buying that can help reduce the impact of these goods and services on the environment, human health and social conditions. This means purchasers making better choices about what is bought, how often and who to buy from, which in some cases may also help save money.

A product or service has environmental impacts throughout its life cycle from the raw materials and energy used to manufacture or supply it, to the way it is recycled or managed at the end of its life (cradle to grave). Purchases may also have social impacts, which may be negative, for example, when goods or services are purchased from organizations that have poor working conditions or pay a low wage. On the other hand, a contribution can be made to growing businesses, creating jobs and improving economic performance.

Sustainable purchasing

The approach required to sustainable purchasing or procurement of products and services will depend to a great extent on the size and purchasing power of an organization. In the UK, as elsewhere, the public sector has the ability to purchase on a massive scale and is thus able to control the marketplace to a much greater extent than any private business. The UK Government established the Sustainable Procurement Task Force in 2005 which came up with the following definition:[1]

> Sustainable Procurement is a process whereby organisations meet their needs for goods, services, works and utilities in a way that achieves value for money on a whole-life basis in terms of generating benefits not only to the organisation, but also to society and the economy, whilst minimizing damage to the

environment. Sustainable Procurement should consider the environmental, social and economic consequences of: design; non-renewable material use; manufacture and production methods; logistics; service delivery; use; operation; maintenance; reuse; recycling options; disposal; and suppliers' capabilities to address these consequences throughout the supply chain.

Following this initiative, the UK Government has been responsible for the development of a comprehensive suite of guidance and specifications for public sector procurement, including:

- Government Buying Standards, which provide 'official specifications that all government buyers must follow when procuring a range of products';[2]
- the National Sustainable Public Procurement Programme (NSPP), which is 'a national approach to sustainable public purchasing by developing training materials and training trainers for anyone with an interest or role in sustainable procurement including local authorities and the NHS' co-ordinated by DEFRA;[3]
- the Flexible Framework, which 'is a . . . self-assessment mechanism developed by the business-led Sustainable Procurement Task Force, which allows organizations to measure and monitor their progress on sustainable procurement over time';[4] the framework allows organizations to develop their processes from 'Foundation' (Level 1) through to becoming exemplars in the field (Lead – Level 5), while identifying the key stages in the process: from staffing though developing policy, strategy, communication and process to engaging suppliers and measuring performance;
- the Office of Government Commerce (OGC) Sustainable Procurement Cupboard,[5] which provides a platform for 'procurement professionals . . . to share ways of implementing sustainable procurement practice in their organisations';
- Business Link 'Buying Sustainable Goods and Services',[6] which provides online guidance to businesses on how to select sustainable goods and suppliers;
- Forum for the Future BEST (Benefitting Economy and Society Through) Procurement programme;[7] this includes a sustainable procurement toolkit, which 'reviews demand, procurement actions & whole-life costs to improve social & environmental performance'.

The European Commission has been driving 'green public procurement (GPP)' across the European Union[8] and has produced a GPP Training toolkit with modules covering strategic, legal and operational matters, including technical information on sustainability criteria for a wide range of products.

Public sector sustainable procurement in the USA comes under the jurisdiction of the Environmental Protection Agency (EPA) which uses the term 'Environmentally Preferable Purchasing'[9] covering

> products or services that have a lesser or reduced effect on human health and the environment when compared with competing products or services that serve the same purpose. This comparison may consider raw materials acquisition, production, manufacturing, packaging, distribution, reuse, operation, main-tenance or disposal of the product or service.

The EPA publishes comprehensive online guidance that provides:

- information about green products and services;
- federal green buying requirements;
- tools for evaluating costs and benefits of purchasing choices;
- tools for managing the green purchasing process.

Taking the example of paper for feeding printers and photocopiers, there is a wealth of information on these websites to support the purchasing process.

The UK Government Buying Standard sets a mandatory specification for all paper as follows:

> Copying and graphic paper must have 100% recycled content, to include only genuine recovered fibre (i.e. no 'mill broke'), in accordance with NAPM (National Association of Paper Manufacturers) definition.[10]
>
> The recycling process must be elemental chlorine free (ECF), with adsorbable organic halogenated compound (AOX) emissions from the production of each pulp used below 0.25kg per air-dried tonne (ADT), or process chlorine free (PCF). NB AOXs are hazardous chlorinated compounds which result from the bleaching of pulp with chlorine or chlorine-based chemicals. Therefore, this standard will not apply to products derived from pulp which is not bleached or where bleaching is performed with chlorine free substances.[11]

In addition, those wanting to meet 'best practice' standards should specify that the paper meet EU Ecolabel requirements. It should be noted that globally there are at least 80 labelling schemes that cover paper and forest products.[12]

The detailed technical criteria for compliance with the EU Ecolabel, set out in an EC Decision from 2011,[13] cover emissions to water and air, energy use, sustainable forest management, hazardous chemical substances, waste management and fitness for use.

The US EPA's guidance to 'procuring agencies' is less specific, with no mandatory requirements, although the aim is clearly to encourage agencies to specify a high recycled content and that paper should be suitable for post-consumer recycling.[14]

It is worth noting that it is not possible to recycle the same paper indefinitely:

> In order to produce recycled paper, paper based on virgin fibre needs to be produced. Both types of paper are part of the same production chain. In fact, it is possible to recycle high-quality paper, such as graphic paper, several times for either the same, or lower-quality uses, reducing the need for virgin fibre.
>
> Both types of paper need to be purchased, as the amount of recycled paper cannot cover the total paper demand in Europe, and as there would not be recycled paper without having paper made from virgin fibres. The key issue is recyclability, not the recycled origin of fibres.[15]

Sustainable food

Purchasing of food is dependent upon a much more complex supply chain than is the case for paper for copying and printing. According to an EC report on green public procurement of food and catering services:

> The impacts of industrial farming and food production are highlighted and recognized as having a massive environmental impact in a (2006) EU study (on the environmental impact of products – EIPRO), where this area of consumption is considered responsible for 20–30% of the environmental impacts of total consumption, and in the case of eutrophication for more than 50%. Within this area of consumption, meat and meat products (including meat, poultry, sausages or similar) have the greatest environmental impact, followed by dairy products.[16]

The way in which food is currently produced and distributed is unsustainable. A selection of statistics from DEFRA[17] and One Planet Living (BioRegional/WWF, 2006) illustrates this:

- In 2009 115 million tonnes of CO_{2eq} /greenhouse gas emissions were associated with 'domestic food chain activity'.
- Household food waste totals 7.2 million tonnes annually, with some 4.4 million tonnes being avoidable.

Figure 4.8.1 *Locally grown produce at a farmers' market*
Source: Joe Mabel.

- More energy is required for packaging food than in its production.
- CO_{2eq} emissions associated with air freighting of food are ten times greater per mile than by road and 50 times greater than by sea.
- Air freighting of food into the UK has more than trebled since 1990.
- Air freighting strawberries from North Africa involves the emission of 370 times as much greenhouse gas as growing and supplying them locally.
- 50 per cent of food consumed in the UK is imported.
- Typically the UK imports 100 million litres of milk per year from the Netherlands and exports twice this amount to the same country.
- 70 per cent of UK freshwater consumption is associated with food production.
- Production of one kilogram of beef requires 15,000 litres of water.
- Organic food requires 40 per cent less energy than conventional methods, with significantly lower impacts to land and water courses.

The main areas of concern in food production, processing and consumption include:

- use of pesticides and fertilizers;
- soil degradation, forest destruction and loss of biodiversity;
- intensive husbandry, fishing and aquaculture;
- energy and water consumption in processing;
- waste in processing, handling, preparation, serving and packaging;
- additives in processed food.

The EU GPP product report proposes:

- procurement of organic food and livestock products;
- procurement of food produced under 'integrated production systems' (see below);
- procurement of sustainably produced or caught aquaculture and marine products;
- procurement of livestock products with high welfare standards;
- procurement in bulk or in packaging that has a high recycled content;
- use of reusable cutlery, crockery, glassware and tablecloths;
- use of environmentally friendly paper products;
- selective waste collection and staff training;
- minimization of the use of hazardous chemicals in food processing and the use of environmentally friendly cleaning and dishwashing products;
- procurement of water- and energy-efficient kitchen appliances;
- improvement of transport routes and energy efficiency and emissions of vehicles used in the catering service.

The following definition of integrated food production is taken from an IOBC/WPRS Bulletin from 2004 on Integrated Production:[18]

> Integrated Production/Farming is a farming system that produces high-quality food and other products by using natural resources and regulating mechanisms to replace polluting inputs and to secure sustainable farming.

Emphasis is placed:

- on a holistic systems approach involving the entire farm as the basic unit;
- on the central role of agro-ecosystems;
- on balanced nutrient cycles;
- on the welfare of all species in animal husbandry.

The preservation and improvement of soil fertility, of a diversified environment and the observation of ethical and social criteria are essential components. Biological, technical and chemical methods are balanced carefully taking into account the protection of the environment, profitability and social requirements.

In the UK, the Public Sector Sustainable Food Procurement Initiative was launched in 2003 with the following objectives:

- Raise production and process standards.
- Increase tenders from small and local producers.
- Increase the consumption of healthy and nutritious food.
- Reduce the adverse environmental impacts of production and supply.
- Increase the capacity of small and local suppliers to meet demand.

These have since been modified and in 2011 were incorporated into the Government's Good Buying Standards,[19] applicable to England only and excluding catering provision in schools. In the guidance to these Standards, the Government defines a sustainable 'food system' in which:

Consumers are informed, can choose and afford healthy, sustainable food. This demand is met by profitable, competitive, highly skilled and resilient farming, fishing and food businesses, supported by first-class research and development.

Food is produced, processed, and distributed, to feed a growing global population in ways which:
- use global natural resources sustainably;
- enable the continuing provision of the benefits and services a healthy natural environment provides;
- promote high standards of animal health and welfare;
- protect food safety;
- make a significant contribution to rural communities;
- allow [the UK] to show global leadership on food sustainability.

Food security is ensured through strong UK agriculture, and food sectors and international trade links with the EU and global partners support developing economies.

The UK has a low-carbon food system which is efficient with resources – any waste is reused, recycled or used for energy generation.

The 'Good Buying Standards' specification[20] is too detailed to reproduce here, but provides some useful pointers to anybody responsible for purchasing food for catering or for procuring catering services.

Soft facilities management

Soft facilities management includes such functions as catering, cleaning, mail room operation and landscape maintenance. In this section we will be focusing on the example of cleaning, whereas sustainable landscape management will be dealt with in Chapter 4.9.

The University of Toronto has developed a 'Green Cleaning Program' which it has defined as follows:

> Green (sustainable) cleaning is defined as a cleaning program designed with the health of building occupants, caretaking staff, and the environment as a primary concern when selecting cleaning products, and determining cleaning procedures. A Green Cleaning Program is designed around products, equipment, and procedures that are chosen with the specific intent of minimizing toxicity in the environment, and minimizing the consumption of natural resources, ultimately leaving the smallest ecological footprint possible during the cleaning process.[21]

Many cleaning products emit volatile organic compounds (VOCs) at concentrations that are detectable by humans. Some of these can go through antagonistic chemical reactions in the occupied space, for example, when combined with ozone to create formaldehyde. Exposure to some of these chemicals can cause irritation of eyes and mucosal membranes and induce asthma in sensitized individuals (see Chapter 4.4).

When disposed of in sufficient quantities, some chemicals in cleaning products contribute to the toxic waste stream. 'Chemicals such as alkyphenol ethoxylates are endocrine disruptors that are slow to biodegrade and have shown up in the endocrine systems of fish, birds, and mammals. Other chemicals cause algal blooms in water bodies, which in turn kills aquatic life.'[22]

In the UK, DEFRA has produced a guide for users of professional cleaning products[23] that sets out 'three key steps which are required to optimise sustainability'. These are:

1   Choose products that are designed for sustainability as well as safety.
2   Work with suppliers so that they responsibly manage their manufacturing impacts.
3   Minimize the environmental impacts that arise during . . . operations.

The AISE Charter for Sustainable Cleaning is a scheme that has been set up by the cleaning products industry in Europe which has 'the aim. . . . to encourage the whole industry to undertake continual improvement in terms of sustainability and also to encourage consumers to adopt more sustainable ways of doing their washing, cleaning and household maintenance'.[24] In order to gain certification and be able to display the appropriate label, the scheme requires products to go through a life cycle analysis and achieve performance standards relating to human and environmental safety, eco-efficiency, occupational health and safety and resource use.

These criteria apply to Green Public Procurement of cleaning products and services in Europe[25] and the UK Government Buying Standard[26] as well as the qualification for the appropriate EC Ecolabel scheme.

Cleaning operations in buildings can also involve facing hazards such as working at height, operating equipment such as extendable platforms and window cleaning hoists, or abseiling. In the UK, the 2005 Work from Heights Regulations incorporate a simple hierarchy of measures required to minimize the risk of accidents:[27]

- avoid work at height where they can;
- use work equipment or other measures to prevent falls where they cannot avoid working at height; and
- where they cannot eliminate the risk of a fall, use work equipment or other measures to minimize the distance and consequences of a fall should one occur.

4.9
Ecological management

Introduction

Ecological management of soft landscaping and green roofs or walls requires the nurturing of the flora and fauna that grow and frequent the site through sustainable landscape maintenance. This should be reflected in a site Biodiversity Action Plan (BAP) that links with the neighbouring ecosystems and the local BAP. In the USA, the Northeast Organic Farming Association (NOFA) has developed standards that have been recognized internationally as setting a benchmark for 'organic land care', which it defines as

> a sustainable ecological landscaping system that promotes and enhances biodiversity, biological cycles, and soil biological activity. It is based on minimal use of off-site inputs and on management practices that restore, maintain, and enhance ecological harmony and beauty in urban and suburban landscapes and gardens. 'Organic' means landscaping with no synthetic pesticides of any kind (insecticides, herbicides, fungicides, etc.) and with no synthetic fertilizers or soil amendments.[1]

In this chapter we are going to look at how these principles can be used to shape BAPs and sustainable maintenance of landscaping, green roofs and green walls, building on the strategies proposed in Chapter 3.9 for enhancing ecological value through refurbishment.

Development of BAPs for business and site

In the UK, the term 'Biodiversity Action Plan' is used to describe a framework for managing biodiversity at national, local, business and site level. For facility managers and those that manage buildings and campuses which host flora and fauna, the government's Business Lines service provides guidance on development of BAPs at business and site level.[2]

Companies and organizations are encouraged to develop organization-wide BAPs through an award scheme developed by the Wildlife Trusts known as the Biodiversity Benchmark.[3] This requires the organization to develop a biodiversity policy that has received high-level commitment to:

- comply with legal requirements relevant to biodiversity;
- biodiversity protection and enhancement;
- be fully documented, implemented, maintained and communicated.

This would normally be embedded into an environmental management system (EMS) in compliance with ISO 14001 or EMAS standards (see Chapter 1.3), including communication strategy, targets and reporting methodology. Company BAPs can be lodged on the Biodiversity Action Reporting System (BARS) website.[4]

The company/organization BAP should incorporate commitments to:

- assess biodiversity impacts associated with the business and associated processes;
- put pressure on each member of the supply chain to develop its own BAPs where not already in place;
- enter into relationships with other companies in the same sector to reinforce pressure on supply chains.

Each site will require a site BAP using an extended Phase 1 habitat survey for an area defined by a 2 km radius from the centre of the site. This should ideally be conducted in the spring or summer and identify key plant species for each habitat type (see Chapter 3.9), noting rare plants and animals, special habitats, including those that have a statutory classification, such as sites of special scientific interest (SSSIs). Each site must be seen within the local context, hence it is important to engage with local Biodiversity Plan Partnerships, as well as other stakeholders that are impacted by the management of the site ecosystems.

Each site will require a tailored biodiversity management system, in which all those involved in sustainable landscape maintenance should demonstrate an appropriate level of competence.

Sustainable landscape maintenance

Most sites are not comprised of pristine biodiverse landscapes, but incorporate a mixture of car parking, trees, shrubs, flower beds and lawns, frequently designed to minimize maintenance. Hence implementation of a biodiversity management system will normally be integrated into a sustainable landscape plan. According to a North American book on sustainable landscaping dating from 2010:

> The maintenance plan should be developed by a team including the facility manager, the landscape architect or designer, and the account manager of the landscape maintenance firm. The plan should be a long-term, 10-year document outlining the desired outcome as a result of implementing the plan. More specifically, the plan should include the following:
> - Scaled site plan
> - Inventory of existing vegetation
> - Skill level required to complete specified tasks and training requirements
> - Schedule for each maintenance practice for each season; (and requirements for:)
>   - Plant and soil stewardship
>   - Invasive species management
>   - Organic plant materials management
>   - Management of irrigation, water use, storm water, snow and ice

- Hardscape and structure management
- Recyclable material and waste management
- Equipment use and maintenance
- Fertilizer, mulching and composting practices.

(Gustafson *et al.*, 2010)

The UK Government has produced Buying Standards for the public procurement of horticultural and park services through Defra.[5] This includes requirements for purchasing soil improvers and dealing with non-native invasive species[6] (see also Chapter 3.9), with a ban on the purchase of products based on peat or sewage sludge, while promoting products that meet EU Ecolabel requirements[7] and compost that meets the 2011 version of British Standard PAS 100.[8]

It also requires packaging for ornamental plants to be reusable, recyclable or biodegradable; for irrigation to be timed, zoned and adjustable, with zones isolated under the dictates of soil humidity sensors; and for machinery to meet specified fuel and noise requirements. The US Environmental Protection Agency (EPA) has developed a 'GreenScapes Tip Sheet' for those managing 'landscaping and grounds keeping operations'.[9] It claims that: 'The economic and environmental cost of waste materials, water, pesticides, fuels, and oils from landscaping and grounds keeping operations can easily be reduced or eliminated with updated landscaping methods.'

The tips are bracketed under the headings of Waste, Water, Energy and Fertilizers & Pesticides; with sub-headings of 'Reduce, Reuse, Recycle and Rebuy', where 'Recycle' refers to recycling on site, whereas 'Rebuy' refers to using post-consumer recycled products.

We referred in the Introduction above to the definition of organic landscaping prohibiting the use of synthetic chemicals for fertilizers and pesticides. In the USA, the concept of 'integrated pest management' has been developed as

> an effective and environmentally sensitive approach to pest management that relies on a combination of common-sense practices [and] current, comprehensive information on the life cycles of pests and their interaction with the environment. This information, in combination with available pest control methods, is used to manage pest damage by the most economical means, and with the least possible hazard to people, property, and the environment.[10]

This approach does not prohibit the use of synthetic pesticides but minimizes the quantities required through management of 'the crop, lawn, or indoor space to prevent pests from becoming a threat'.

Maintenance of green roofs and walls

Green roofs and walls are widely thought to be maintenance-free. However, it is important to understand the implications of allowing a green roof to develop without intervention. The following extract from the livingroofs.org website explains the implications:

Extensive green roofs [are] generally . . . low maintenance. However, low maintenance does not mean no maintenance. Depending on the type of green roof there may need to be a degree of post-installation maintenance in terms of watering/ fertilizing. This is particularly true of sedum plugged or hydro seeded roofs. Mat type systems may need more maintenance as time goes on as they develop to grass quickly.

In Germany, there is a rule of thumb that states '... one year sedums, two years sedums some grass, three years grass some sedums, four years grass...'.

It is quite common to encounter extensive green roofs on the continent that have changed to dry grass roofs. This is because building managers cancel maintenance packages offered by the suppliers and allow the roof to do its own thing.

The important point is that as long as all drainage elements and shingle perimeters are kept free of vegetation, a roof left to its own devices will not harm the integrity of the building.

Another perceived barrier is the cost of maintaining a green roof. This cost though is relative to what kind of green roof is installed and how the owner wishes it to be used. Intensive green roofs can generally be considered as elevated parks and therefore require similar maintenance. Extensive green roofs require less maintenance and in general this can add only [a small amount to] the cost of maintaining a standard roof.

However, it is worth noting that in Germany most companies stop green roof manufacturers' recommended maintenance regimes after a number of years as they have fulfilled the planning criteria and have let the roofs go 'wild'. They merely visit the roof once a year to ensure that problematical shrubs and trees that could impact on the membranes have not colonised. This is generally a safety precaution, as green roofs are installed with root membranes and as they have shallow growing mediums, such plants would wither in time.

In general, therefore, extensive green roofs should be reasonably self-maintaining unless the client requires the roofs to look manicured.[11]

The UK-based Green Roof Organization (GRO) produced a Green Roof Code in 2011 that recommends the following ongoing maintenance actions for an established biodiverse extensive green roof:

- *Irrigation*: this is typically not required.
- *Fertilization*: this is generally not required, particularly where indigenous species are being encouraged to replicate native habitats. While a low vegetative density is common, zero vegetation is generally undesirable.
- *Plant management*: a maintenance programme should be drawn up to follow the biodiversity hypothesis, ensuring that no materials are removed from the roof that may adversely affect the biodiversity potential of the roof.
- *General*: drainage outlets (with inspection chambers) and gravel/shingle perimeters should be inspected twice yearly and cleared of any living or dead vegetation.

See also Chapter 3.9 for a discussion on the composition of intensive green roofs.

4.10
Case histories for sustainable facilities management

Crystal Peaks Shopping Centre, near Sheffield, run by Hermes Real Estate

The following case history has been adapted from a Better Buildings Partnership case study.

Crystal Peaks Shopping Centre, owned by Hermes, is located in 40 acres of green surroundings, seven miles from Sheffield. Attracting 13 million visits each year, it offers a pleasant community environment, with high-street names, alongside services including a library, medical centre and health club.

Initiatives introduced by Hermes and implemented by its property manager have resulted in a 44 per cent reduction in energy use between 2008 and 2011 as part of the company's comprehensive approach to responsible property investment. These have also resulted in a significant reduction in crime incidents on site and the introduction of a number of successful biodiversity initiatives.

Energy, water and waste

Energy use in common parts in 2011 was 44 per cent lower than in 2008, corresponding to a reduction in energy consumption of 6.6 million kWh and almost 1,500 tonnes of CO_2 emissions.

In 2011, the Centre sent zero waste to landfill, with 32 per cent segregated on site for recycling and the remainder sent to a materials recycling facility where residual waste goes for incineration. Since 2008, the Centre's waste strategy has resulted in 2150 tonnes of waste being diverted directly away from landfill.

These achievements have been brought about by a combination of the following actions:

- bespoke environmental training for the majority of staff and Chartered Institute of Environmental Health training for key staff;
- phased lighting replacement programme across the whole site, including LEDs;
- motion sensors and timers on lighting circuits in back-of-house areas, and daylight sensors and timers in car parks;
- improved monitoring processes, which lead to lower temperature settings for heating and reduced plant running times, for instance so that air-handling

Figure 4.10.1 *Crystal Peaks Shopping Centre main entrance*
Source: Hermes Real Estate.

units are only on for a few hours in the morning and afternoon, rather than all day;

- sub-metering of energy consumption has been introduced for each tenant so that this can be measured, with further sub-metering for large items of equipment planned in the future.
- recycling of cardboard, plastic, wood and organic waste;
- online water monitoring, with weekly checks for leaks.

Community security

A six-month pilot project with South Yorkshire Police saw a full-time officer join the team. This was so successful that the position was made permanent, helping the team to:

- establish links with local resident associations and community safety groups;
- increase communication with store managers on security issues, and improve the protocol for reporting and responding to incidents;
- host customer security awareness events and poster campaigns;
- provide additional training to all security staff;
- support projects with young people;

- share information with the police and Sheffield homes, so offenders could be deterred with the threat of eviction from council properties;
- the six-month pilot, compared to the previous six months, resulted in:
  - 44 per cent less criminal damage
  - 56 per cent less anti-social behaviour
  - 99 per cent less auto-related crime
  - 60 per cent fewer violent or public-order-related incidents.

These results were achieved despite more incidents being reported due to the better relationships between the police and retail store managers.

The police have found that the Centre provides the ideal setting for meeting with local people to discuss issues.

Community biodiversity

Crystal Peaks naturally lends itself to biodiversity initiatives. However, knowing what to focus on can be quite complex. The team worked with local experts and volunteers from Sheffield's Sorby Natural History Society to identify species and habitats present on the 40-acre site. They also consulted the local Planning Office and the local BAP for South Sheffield. This resulted in the following actions:

- site biodiversity surveys and the development of a biodiversity management plan;
- the installation of beehives, home to 50,000 bees, and introduction of more bee-friendly plants;
- the installation of bird boxes, and insect habitats made by local children;
- meetings with local environmental groups, supporting their projects and putting up a noticeboard where they can promote events;
- development of a 'stumpery', an area like a rockery but made from parts of dead trees, to provide habitats for invertebrates and create a point of customer interest;
- creation of a wildflower meadow;
- mulching vegetative waste for re-use on site, to encourage invertebrates;
- cleaning a brook near to the centre and helping with haymaking as part of a local project.

Cost implications

Most of the initiatives were carried out at little or no cost:

- bee hives: £700 to install two colonised bee hives and £300 to maintain them each year;
- security: £20,000 each year to part-fund a full-time police officer on site and part-time Police Community Support Officer;
- energy: £2,000 for motion sensors and daylight sensors.

Figure 4.10.2 *Wild flower planting at Crystal Peaks Shopping Centre*
Source: Hermes Real Estate.

Since 2008, Crystal Peaks has achieved:

*   £166,000 energy cost savings (based on £0.08 per kWh for electricity and £0.02 per kWh for gas);
*   £45,000 averted in direct landfill tax costs.

British Land head office, York House, London

York House is a multi-tenanted office building in West London with around 9,000 m^2 of office space, 4,000 m^2 of which forms the head office of British Land.[1, 2, 3] There is also some 1,000 m^2 of retail space and 22 apartments within its envelope.

Following the formation of a green building management group (GBMG) by British Land with the occupiers and managing agent at York House in 2008, the following improvements in environmental performance have been reported:

*   Total building energy use fell in 2010 by 1.1 million kWh compared to the previous year, cutting CO_2 emissions by 416 tonnes and saving an estimated £63,000. British Land-controlled energy use reduced by 32 per cent and occupier-controlled energy use by 9 per cent. This trend continued in 2011,

Figure 4.10.3 *York House front elevation*
Source: © British Land.

Figure 4.10.4 *York House typical open-plan office space*
Source: © British Land.

with 20 per cent less energy use per person, corresponding to 1,920 kWh per person in 2011, compared with 2,410 kWh in 2010, cutting carbon emissions by 32 tonnes for British Land-controlled energy use.

- This was achieved through a combination of fitting a weather compensation system that made sure that the boiler would not activate when outside temperatures were above 15°C, and installing a new energy management system and ongoing monitoring service that optimizes the operation of central plant for heating and cooling.
- Initiatives from tenants included fitting power-saving software to computers and replacing traditional lamps with energy-saving alternatives.
- The proportion of waste recycled also increased from 40 per cent in 2009 to 70 per cent in 2010 and 85 per cent in 2011. The percentage diverted from landfill was 98 per cent in 2010, some 19 tonnes; while in 2011 all waste that could not be recycled was incinerated with energy recovery, diverting 34 tonnes from landfill in 12 months and averting almost £1,900 in landfill tax costs.
- In 2011, water consumption fell by around 24 per cent: i.e. to 7,770 litres per person, compared with 10,220 litres in 2010.

Waste recycling

Software has been installed that measures printing more precisely, so that British Land can provide monthly usage information to each Head of Department, highlighting whether their team's consumption is reducing or increasing.

A project team was established to support people in reducing their paper consumption, with Heads of Department allocating Waste Reduction Champions to work within individual teams.

This initiative evolved from a campaign which significantly increased recycling, from 70 per cent during the first quarter of 2010 to 83 per cent in the final quarter. This was largely thanks to a new food composting scheme and to the efforts of a Staff Environmental Working Group to raise awareness of recycling facilities.

Other initiatives that British Land has introduced at its head office include providing a home for some 40,000 bees in two hives located on the roof of York House and replacing paper hand towels with electric hand dryers to reduce waste.

Notes

1.1 Introduction and scope

1 www.ons.gov.uk/ons/rel/npp/national-population-projections/2008-based-reference-volume—series-pp2/index.html.
2 www.roadmap2050.eu/attachments/files/Volume1_fullreport_PressPack.pdf.
3 www.decc.gov.uk/en/content/cms/tackling/2050/2050.aspx.
4 www.parliament.uk/documents/post/postpn_371-housing_health_h.pdf.
5 www.unepfi.org/fileadmin/documents/greenbuildings.pdf.
6 www.whitehouse.gov/assets/documents/Recovery_Through_Retrofit_Final_Report.pdf.
7 www.portal.hud.gov/huddoc/psstandards.pdf.

1.2 Policy and legislation

1 www.kyotoprotocol.com/.
2 www.unep.org/PDF/FinalMTSGCSS-X-8.pdf.
3 www.worldenergy.org/.
4 www.worldgbc.org/site2/.
5 www.usgbc.org/DisplayPage.aspx?CategoryID=19.
6 www.usgbc.org/ShowFile.aspx?DocumentID=10338.
7 http://ec.europa.eu/publications/booklets/others/84/en.pdf.
8 http://epp.eurostat.ec.europa.eu/portal/page/portal/product_details/publication?p_product_code=KS-31-11-224.
9 http://ec.europa.eu/clima/policies/eccp/index_en.htm.
10 http://ec.europa.eu/environment/consultations/pdf/background_water_efficiency.pdf.
11 http://osha.europa.eu/en/legislation/directives.
12 http://ec.europa.eu/environment/nature/legislation/habitatsdirective/index_en.htm.
13 www.iema.net/ems/emas.
14 www.microgenerationcertification.org/.
15 www.environment-agency.gov.uk/business/topics/permitting/32320.aspx.
16 http://webarchive.nationalarchives.gov.uk/+/http://www.communities.gov.uk/housing/rentingandletting/housinghealth/.
17 http://soundadvice.info/.
18 www.epa.gov/osw/laws-regs/rcrahistory.htm.
19 www.energystar.gov/index.cfm?fuseaction=find_a_product.
20 http://www1.eere.energy.gov/femp/index.html.
21 http://www1.eere.energy.gov/buildings/betterbuildings/.
22 http://portal.hud.gov/hudportal/HUD?src=/program_offices/housing/sfh/title/ti_home.
23 www.energystar.gov/index.cfm?fuseaction=find_a_product.
24 www.epa.gov/iaq/pubs/sbs.html.
25 www.epa.gov/osw/laws-regs/rcrahistory.htm.
26 www.osha.gov/SLTC/pel/.

1.3 Assessment tools

1 www.breeam.org/page.jsp?id=228.
2 www.rics.org/site/scripts/documents.aspx?categoryID=575.

3 http://www.bre.co.uk/sustainableshopfit/page.jsp?id=14.
4 http://www.regreenprogram.org/docs/regreen_guidelines.pdf.
5 www.breeam.org/page.jsp?id=373.
6 www.usgbc.org/DisplayPage.aspx?CMSPageID=221.
7 http://www.thegbi.org/green-globes/continual-improvement-for-existing-buildings.asp.
8 www.greenglobes.com/existing/homeuk.asp.
9 www.greenglobes.com/existing/homeuk.asp
10 www.ecomapping.org/en/index.html.
11 http://en.wikipedia.org/wiki/Ecological_footprint.
12 www.footprintnetwork.org/en/index.php/GFN/page/ecological_wealth_of_nations_en.
13 www.oneplanetcommunities.org/about-2/approach/the-environmental-challenge/ecological-footprinting.
14 www.footprintnetwork.org/images/uploads/Ecological_Footprint_Standards_2009.pdf.
15 www.carbontrust.co.uk/cut-carbon-reduce-costs/calculate/carbon-footprinting/pages/carbon-footprinting.aspx.
16 http://envirowise.wrap.org.uk/uk/Our-Services/Tools/Envirowise-Indicator.249257.html.
17 http://www.breeam.org/filelibrary/Technical%20Manuals/SD5073_BREEAM_2011_New_Construction_Technical_Guide_ISSUE_2_0.pdf.
18 www.rics.org/site/scripts/documents.aspx?categoryID=575.
19 www.greenbooklive.com/.
20 www.usgbc.org/DisplayPage.aspx?CMSPageID=220.
21 www.greenglobes.com/fitup/Flash/index.htm.
22 www.breeam.org/extranet/loginexb.jsp.
23 www.usgbc.org/DisplayPage.aspx?CMSPageID=2278.
24 http://www.thegbi.org/green-globes/continual-improvement-for-existing-buildings.asp
25 www.ecomapping.org/en/index.html.
26 http://eur-lex.europa.eu/LexUriServ/LexUriServ.do?uri=OJ:L:2009:342:0001:0045:EN:PDF.
27 www.globalreporting.org/resourcelibrary/G3.1-Sustainability-Reporting-Guidelines.pdf.
28 www.ecologicalfootprint.com/.
29 www.footprintexpert.com/Toolkit/Pages/ModelFramework.aspx.
30 www.cleanmetrics.com/html/building_carbon_footprints.htm.
31 www.ghgprotocol.org/calculation-tools/service-sector.

2.1 Reasons to retrofit

1 www.communities.gov.uk/documents/statistics/pdf/1133593.pdf.
2 www.gva.co.uk/WorkArea/DownloadAsset.aspx?id=2147488375.
3 www.bre.co.uk/filelibrary/pdf/rpts/waste/ConstructionWasteReport240906.pdf.
4 www.bre.co.uk/greenguide/podpage.jsp?id=2126.
5 www.jiscinfonet.ac.uk/infokits/learning-space-design/implementation/forward/refurb-or-build.
6 www.pie-mag.com/articles/1707/german-retail-investment-chances-tip-toward-refurbishment/.
7 http://emptyhomes.com/wp-content/uploads/2011/06/New-Tricks-With-Old-Bricks-final-12-03-081.pdf.
8 www.bsria.co.uk/news/low-carbon-refurb/.
9 www.passivhaus.org.uk/standard.jsp?id=20.

10   www.carbontrust.co.uk/emerging-technologies/current-focus-areas/buildings/pages/
      buildings.aspx.

2.2 Post-occupancy evaluation

1   www.bre.co.uk/page.jsp?id=1623.
2   www.usablebuildings.co.uk/Probe/ProbePDFs/BRI1.pdf.
3   www.wbdg.org/resources/fpe.php.
4   www.excellence.dgs.ca.gov/AssetManagement/S6_6-4.htm.
5   www.gsa.gov/graphics/pbs/GSA_SevenStrategies_090327screen.pdf.
6   www.gsa.gov/graphics/pbs/GSA_SevenStrategies_090327screen.pdf.
7   This is an edited version of an article written by the author for the *Building Services
     Journal* in November 1989, based on work carried out for the European Commission
     in Brussels (Appleby, 1989).
8   Having been the subject of a number of takeovers and name changes, Bryan
     Colquhoun & Partners are now within URS Scott Wilson.

2.3 The cost of sustainable refurbishment and management

1   Index of *Building Magazine* cost models from 2000 onwards (subscription required
     to access): http://t35ts1t32010.uat.building.co.uk/data/costs/cost-model.
2   www.davislangdon.com/EME/Research/.
3   www.reeep.org/130/esco-model.htm.
4   http://ec.europa.eu/enterprise/sectors/construction/files/compet/life_cycle_costing/
     guidance__case_study_en.pdf.
5   www.bcis.co.uk/ordb.
6   www1.eere.energy.gov/femp/program/lifecycle.html.
7   This is an extract from the Guidance to *A Common European Methodology for Life
     Cycle Costing (LCC)* for the European Commission in 2007, reproduced here with
     the permission of Davis Langdon, an AECOM Company. Available at: http://ec.
     europa.eu/enterprise/sectors/construction/files/compet/life_cycle_costing/guidance__
     case_study_en.pdf.

2.4 Carbon reduction strategy

1   www.ecologicalbuildingsystems.com/workspace/downloads/proclimaRoof
     RenovationStudy2011.pdf,
2   This an extract from a briefing paper produced by the UK Highly Distributed Energy
     Future Consortium (HiDEF). For references given in the extract, refer to the original
     paper, available at: www.supergen-hidef.org/Publications/Documents/Papers/
     Briefing%20Papers/The%20Energy%20Characteristics%20of%20Low%20and%
     20Zero-Carbon%20Dwellings%20and%20the%20Implications%20for%20
     Future%20Energy%20Systems.pdf.

2.5 Community energy and infrastructure

1   www.decc.gov.uk/en/content/cms/tackling/2050/2050.aspx.
2   http://realtimecarbon.org/.
3   http://lightbucket.wordpress.com/2008/10/22/carbon-emissions-from-electricity-
     generation-by-country/.
4   http://ceo.decc.gov.uk/en/ceol/cms/process/stage_3/plan/governance_str/governance
     _str.aspx.
5   www.communitypathways.org.uk/approach/community-energy-services-company.
6   www.planningforclimatechange.org.uk/case-studies/uk/.

7   www.planlocal.org.uk/pages/about.
8   www.lr.org/sectors/utilities/schemes/murs.aspx.
9   www.environment-agency.gov.uk/research/library/publications/115938.aspx.
10 www.sustrans.org.uk/.
11 www.ctc.org.uk/DesktopDefault.aspx?TabID=4923.
12 www.livingstreets.org.uk/about/our-mission1/.

2.6 Sustainable facilities management strategy

1   www.unglobalcompact.org/docs/news_events/8.1/UN_Global_Compact_Annual_Review_2010.pdf.
2   www.environment-agency.gov.uk/business/topics/pollution/113738.aspx.
3   www.bifm.org.uk/bifm/knowledge/resources/goodpracticeguides.
4   For the typical contents of a Building User Manual, refer to Box 4.1 in Chapter 4.6 of *Integrated Sustainable Design of Buildings* (Appleby, 2011a).
5   All in compliance with Reporting of Injuries, Diseases & Dangerous Occurrences Regulations (RIDDOR) 1995. See: http://www.hse.gov.uk/riddor/.
6   Based on communication dated 28 February 2011 from Julie Hogarth, Director of FM, Regent Street Direct.
7   For information on Home User Guides, see Chapter 4.6 of *Integrated Sustainable Design of Buildings* (Appleby, 2011a, pp. 404, 405).
8   See note 6.

2.7 Retrofit as part of sustainable facilities management

1   http://refurbprojects-online.com/2012/01/refurbishing-a-national-asset/.
2   When in order to heat its home to an adequate standard of warmth, a household is in fuel poverty when it needs to spend more than 10 per cent of its income.
3   www.bizjournals.com/nashville/print-edition/2011/04/15/downsizing-office-space-empty-restack.html?page=all.

3.1 Renovation of building fabric

1   www.passivhaus.org.uk/standard.jsp?id=20.
2   www.passivhaus.org.uk/filelibrary/Passivhaus%20Standards/PH_Certification_Criteria_-_non-domestic.pdf.
3   www.carbonlite.org.uk/carbonlite/energystandards.php.
4   Where water activity is the equilibrium, percentage saturation (%sat) of the material and condensation occurs at 100%sat.
5   www.passiv.de/07_eng/index_e.html.
6   www.passivhaus.org.uk/filelibrary/Passivhaus%20Standards/PH_Certification_Criteria_-_non-domestic.pdf.
7   www.energysavingtrust.org.uk/Insulation/Cavity-wall-insulation.
8   www.energysavingtrust.org.uk/Insulation/Solid-wall-insulation.
9   www.greenspec.co.uk/insulated-render.php.
10 www.bfrc.org/.
11 www.energystar.gov/index.cfm?c=home_sealing.hm_improvement_insulation_table.
12 http://bere.co.uk/projects/mayville-community-centre-passivhaus-retrofit.
13 www.greenbuildingstore.co.uk/page—grove-cottage-first-uk-enerphit.html.
14 www.esbnyc.com/documents/sustainability/ESBPlacematFINAL2.pdf.
15 This an extract from an article by the author in *Sustainable Buildings* (Appleby, 2011b).

3.2 Retrofit of building services and controls

1 www.aecb.net/PDFs/9Jan2009_MVHR_Final-2.pdf.
2 www.greenspec.co.uk/whole-house-ventilation.php.
3 Operative temperature is approximately equal to the average of air and mean radiant temperatures (CIBSE, 2006c).
4 www.sap-appendixq.org.uk/documents/MVHR_Installation_Guide_Final_11.02.11.pdf.
5 www.sphc.co.uk/domestic-hot-water-solar-thermal.
6 http://eartheasy.com/live_led_bulbs_comparison.html.
7 http://apps1.eere.energy.gov/buildings/publications/pdfs/ssl/energy_efficiency_white_leds.pdf.
8 www.direct.gov.uk/en/Environmentandgreenerliving/Greenerhomeandgarden/Greenerlabelsandclaims/DG_064872?CID=EGL&PLA=url_mon&CRE=energy_label.
9 www.topten.info/uploads/File/039_Barbara_Josephy_final_Washing.pdf.
10 www.bco.org.uk/news/detail.cfm?rid=118.
11 www.luxmagazine.co.uk/2011/05/when-to-take-the-tube/.
12 www.eu-energystar.org/en/index.html.
13 www.opengatedata.com/technical-resources/12-chiller-plant-improvement/.
14 www.energyactiondevon.org.uk/uploads/documents/brochure.pdf.
15 http://retrofitforthefuture.org/.
16 http://retrofitdepot.org/EnergyCarbonFinanceAnalysis.

3.3 Retrofitting renewable technologies

1 http://info.cat.org.uk/questions/pv/what-energy-and-carbon-payback-time-pv-panels-uk
2 www.greenspec.co.uk/retrofit-electrical-power.php
3 www.quietrevolution.com/faqs-technical.htm.
4 www.micro-hydro-power.com/micro-hydro-power-Estimating-Head-and-Flow.htm.
5 www.greenspec.co.uk/solar-hot-water-heating.php.
6 http://www.elle-kilde.dk/altener-combi/dwload.html.
7 http://uk-air.defra.gov.uk/reports/cat18/0806261519_methods.pdf
8 www.icax.co.uk/Suffolk_One_College.html .
9 www.inbalance-energy.co.uk/case_studies/residential_care_home_west_london.html.

3.4 Indoor environment and hygiene issues

1 http://ntp.niehs.nih.gov/ntp/htdocs/Chem_Background/ExSumPdf/Infrasound.pdf.
2 www.carpet-rug.org/commercial-customers/green-building-and-the-environment/green-label-plus/index.cfm.
3 www.blauer-engel.de/en/company/index.php.
4 www.ecologo.org/common/assets//CCD-174_Printing_Services_Draft_2.pdf.
5 www.hpa.org.uk/hpr/archives/Infections/2012/respiratory12.htm.

3.5 Water-saving measures

1 www.oecd.org/dataoecd/42/27/34416097.pdf .
2 www.data360.org/dsg.aspx?Data_Set_Group_Id=757.
3 http://envirowise.wrap.org.uk/uk/Press-Office/Press-Releases/Wales/Spending-a-penny-could-be-costing-companies-in-pounds.html.
4 www.anglianwater.co.uk/_assets/media/Water-Efficiency-Self-Assessment.pdf.

5   uk-air.defra.gov.uk/reports/cat07/0709180907_DA_GHGI_report_2005.pdf.
6   www.elementalsolutions.co.uk/wp-content/uploads/2012/08/wcs.pdf.
7   www.environment-agency.gov.uk/static/documents/Research/variable_flush_report_
    1165589.pdf.
8   http://wtl.defra.gov.uk/criteria.asp?technology=00030012&sub-technology=00030
    0120001&partner=&section=2&submit_=Search&tech=000300120001.
9   www.waterwise.org.uk/pages/indoors.html#5.
10 http://wtl.defra.gov.uk/criteria.asp?technology=00030014&sub-technology=000
    300140001&partner=&section=2&submit_=Search&tech=000300140001.
11 http://www.allianceforwaterefficiency.org/commercial_dishwash_intro.aspx.
12 http://sd.defra.gov.uk/advice/public/buying/products/electrical/dishwashers/
    standards/.
13 www.energystar.gov/index.cfm?c=comm_dishwashers.pr_crit_comm_dishwashers.
14 www.rainwaterharvesting.co.uk/rainwaterharvesting-swimming-pools.php.
15 http://publications.environment-agency.gov.uk/PDF/PMHO0307BMDX-E-E.pdf.
16 http://www.ukrha.org/content.php?t=12&page=press.
17 http://wtl.defra.gov.uk/technology.asp?technology=00030010&sub-
    technology=000300100002&partner=&section=66&submit_=Search&tech=00030
    0100002.

3.6 Measures to reduce and recycle waste

1   www.defra.gov.uk/environment/waste/.
2   www.epa.gov/climatechange/wycd/waste/measureghg.html.
3   www.defra.gov.uk/environment/waste/.
4   www.recycle-more.co.uk/nav/page688.aspx.
5   www.theneweconomy.com/energy/utilities/the-future-of-trash-collection.

3.7 Catering for sustainable transport strategies

1   www.decc.gov.uk/en/content/cms/statistics/climate_stats/gg_emissions/intro/intro.
    aspx.
2   www.fiafoundation.org/publications/Documents/auto_society_exec_summary.pdf.
3   www.acea.be/news/news_detail/vehicles_in_use/.
4   www.securedbydesign.com/pdfs/New-Build-Car-Park-Guidelines.pdf.
5   www.securedbydesign.com/pdfs/New-Build-Car-Park-Guidelines.pdf.

3.8 Material impacts in refurbishment

1   http://envest2.bre.co.uk/detailsLCA.jsp.
2   BEES is the Building Environmental and Economic Sustainability LCA model developed
    by the National Institution of Standards and Technology (NIST). See www.bfrl.nist.gov/
    oae/software/bees/bees.html.
3   www.bre.co.uk/greenguide/podpage.jsp?id=2126.
4   www.bre.co.uk/greenguide/podpage.jsp?id=2126.
5   www.bre.co.uk/greenguide/podpage.jsp?id=2126.
6   www.constructionresources.com/.
7   www.greenbuildingstore.co.uk/.
8   www.greenspec.co.uk/html/products/productscontent.html.
9   www.wbdg.org/design/greenspec.php.
10 www.ecbcs.org/docs/Annex_39_Report_Subtask-B.pdf.
11 www.kingspaninsulation.co.uk/Products/Optim-R/Optim-R/Overview.aspx.
12 www.instagroup.co.uk/media/5753/instaclad_brochure_screen.pdf.
13 http://selector.com/au/suppliers/aerogels-australia/products/spaceloft-insulation.

14 www.cabot-corp.com/wcm/download/en-us/ae/LUMIRA_BRO_0511_final.pdf.
15 www.breeam.org/filelibrary/Technical%20Manuals/SD5073_BREEAM_2011_
    New_Construction_Technical_Guide_ISSUE_2_0.pdf.

3.9 Enhancing ecology by refurbishment

1 www.gigl.org.uk/Resources/Habitats/tabid/107/Default.aspx.
2 www.nhm.ac.uk/nature-online/life/plants-fungi/postcode-plants/.
3 http://www.gisp.org/publications/brochures/globalstrategy.pdf/.
4 http://www.ciria.org.uk/suds/faqs.htm#cheaper.
5 http://www.sierraclub.org/sierra/201009/coolschools/default.aspx.
6 www.greeninfrastructure.net/gi_case_studies.
7 www.sustainableschoolswales.org/examples/short_examples/sustainable_drainage_
    systems.php.

4.1 Energy management

1 www.abricon.com/BSISO16001v2.asp.
2 www.cibse.org/pdfs/newOOMtable1.pdf.
3 'Code 5' refers to the *Code of Practice for the Metering of Energy Transfers with a
    Maximum Demand of up to (and Including) 1MW for Settlement Purposes.* Issue 6,
    Version 10, 2010. Available at: www.elexon.co.uk/wp-content/uploads/2012/01/
    bsc_cop5_issue6_v10.0.pdf .
4 www.thermalimageuk.com/page6.htm.
5 www.ior.org.uk/ior_/images/pdf/general/REI-G3%20Operational%20Improvements
    %20-%20Final%20Jul-07.pdf.
6 www.cibse.org/pdfs/newOOMtable1.pdf.
7 See note 6.
8 See note 6.
9 www.carbontrust.com/resources/reports/advice/sector-specific-publications.
10 www.energystar.gov/index.cfm?c=guidelines.guidelines_index.
11 www.buyingsolutions.gov.uk/categories/Utilities.

4.2 Water management

1 www.environment-agency.gov.uk/business/topics/water/34866.aspx.
2 www.businesslink.gov.uk/bdotg/action/detail?itemId=1082902691&type=
    RESOURCES.
3 www.allianceforwaterefficiency.org/commercial_dishwash_intro.aspx.
4 www.energystar.gov/index.cfm?c=comm_dishwashers.pr_crit_comm_dishwashers.
5 www.wrap.org.uk/content/rippleffect-water-efficiency-businesses.
6 www.wrap.org.uk/content/free-advice-help-businesses-save-water-and-money.
7 www.wrap.org.uk/content/rippleffect-water-efficiency-businesses.

4.3 Waste management

1 http://portal.acs.org/portal/fileFetch/C/WPCP_012290/pdf/WPCP_012290.pdf.
2 www.articlegrandeur.com/articles/green-electronics-60.html.
3 http://ec.europa.eu/environment/waste/weee/index_en.htm.
4 http://ec.europa.eu/environment/waste/weee/index_en.htm.
5 www.businesslink.gov.uk/bdotg/action/detail?itemId=1081275138&r.l1=10790
    68363&r.l2=1086048456&r.l3=1081267120&r.s=sc&type=RESOURCES.
6 http://europa.eu/rapid/pressReleasesAction.do?reference=MEMO/11/598.
7 http://sd.defra.gov.uk/advice/public/buying/products/food/standards/.

8   http://publications.environment-agency.gov.uk/PDF/GEHO0411BTQZ-E-E.pdf.
9   www.environment-agency.gov.uk/static/documents/Business/low_guide_v1.2_
    1397222.pdf.
10 http://publications.environment-agency.gov.uk/PDF/GEHO0411BTQZ-E-E.pdf.
11 http://wastehierarchy.wrap.org.uk/wraptool.
12 www.cdph.ca.gov/certlic/medicalwaste/Documents/MedicalWaste/HospitalP2
    Strategies.pdf.

4.5 Legionellosis prevention and hygiene

1   www.ncbi.nlm.nih.gov/pubmed/18448198.
2   www.hindawi.com/journals/jeph/2009/812829/.
3   www.cdc.gov/MMWR/PREVIEW/MMWRHTML/00045365.htm.
4   www.jstor.org/discover/10.2307/30112106?uid=3738032&uid=2129&uid=2&
    uid=70&uid=4&sid=56147942193.
5   www.hse.gov.uk/pubns/spalegion.pdf.

4.6 Reducing vehicle use

1   www.rutland.gov.uk/pdf/Step%20by%20Step%20guide%20to%20travel%20
    planning.PDF.
2   www.sustainabilityinfm.org.uk/resources/view/24 (requires registration and log-in).
3   www.sustainabilityinfm.org.uk/resources/view/24.
4   www.bike2workscheme.co.uk/?utm_source=google&utm_medium=cpc&utm_
    term=cycle%2Bto%2Bwork%2Bscheme&utm_campaign=Bike%2B2%2BWork%2
    BScheme.
5   www.carclubs.org.uk.
6   www.britishparking.co.uk/write/Documents/safer%20parking/Park%20Mark%
    20LifeCarePlansLeaflet%202011%20-%20page%20for%20web%20-%20small
    %20version.pdf.
7   www.intelligenthealth.co.uk/step2get/.
8   www.saferoutesinfo.org/.

4.7 Sustainable maintenance

1   www.sust.org/pdf/Maintenance%20Report/SDOY-Maintenance_Summary.pdf.
2   www.gre.ac.uk/schools/arc/research__consulting__partnerships/sustainable_building
    _research_group/projects/project_profiles/sustainable_building_maintenance
3   http://www.sfg20.com/.
4   www.wbdg.org/resources/rcm.php?r=sustainableom.
5   www.wbdg.org/resources/rcm.php?r=sustainableom.
6   www.reliabilityweb.com/art04/Motor%20Circuit%20Analysis%20Concept%20
    and%20Principle.pdf.
7   www.wbdg.org/resources/rcm.php?r=sustainableom.
8   www.pic.vic.gov.au/resources/documents/Fact_Sheet_-_Options_for_cutting_water_
    use_in_fire_sprinkler_maintenance.pdf.
9   www.business-sprinkler-alliance.org/uk-wastes-9-billion-litres-of-water-a-year-
    fighting-business-fires-reveals-new-report/.
10 www.legislation.gov.uk/uksi/2009/261/pdfs/uksi_20090261_en.pdf.
11 http://www.ehs.ufl.edu/HMM/shop.htm.
12 www.is4profit.com/business-advice/employment/health-and-safety-introduction/
    maintenance-and-building-work.html.

4.8 Sustainable purchasing and soft facilities management

1   http://archive.defra.gov.uk/sustainable/government/documents/full-document.pdf.
2   http://sd.defra.gov.uk/advice/public/buying/.
3   www.defra.gov.uk/environment/economy/purchasing.
4   www.defra.gov.uk/publications/2011/03/28/pb13423-flexible-framework-guidance/.
5   www.procurementcupboard.org/AboutUs.aspx.
6   www.businesslink.gov.uk/bdotg/action/layer?topicId=1086751281.
7   www.forumforthefuture.org/project/buying-better-world-sustainable-procurement/overview.
8   http://ec.europa.eu/environment/gpp/toolkit_en.htm.
9   http://www.epa.gov/epp/.
10 www.napm.org.uk/recycled_mark.htm.
11 http://sd.defra.gov.uk/advice/public/buying/products/paper/paper/.
12 www.ecolabelindex.com/ecolabels/?st=category,forest_products_paper.
13 http://eur-lex.europa.eu/LexUriServ/LexUriServ.do?uri=OJ:L:2011:149:0012:0024:EN:PDF.
14 www.epa.gov/epawaste/conserve/tools/cpg/products/define.htm.
15 http://ec.europa.eu/environment/gpp/toolkit_en.htm.
16 http://ec.europa.eu/environment/gpp/pdf/toolkit/food_GPP_background_report.pdf.
17 www.defra.gov.uk/statistics/files/defra-stats-foodfarm-food-pocketbook-120402.pdf.
18 International Organization for Biological and Integrated Control of Noxious Animals and Plants, West Palearctic Regional Section. See: www.iobc.ch/iobc_bas.pdf.
19 http://sd.defra.gov.uk/advice/public/buying/products/food/.
20 http://sd.defra.gov.uk/advice/public/buying/products/food/.
21 www.fs.utoronto.ca/caretaking/green.htm.
22 www.fs.utoronto.ca/caretaking/green.htm.
23 www.sustainable-cleaning.com/en.home.orb.
24 www.sustainable-cleaning.com/en.home.orb.
25 http://ec.europa.eu/environment/gpp/pdf/toolkit/cleaning_GPP_product_sheet.pdf.
26 http://sd.defra.gov.uk/advice/public/buying/products/cleaning/.
27 www.hse.gov.uk/falls/regulations.htm.

4.9 Ecological management

1   www.organiclandcare.net/sites/default/files/upload/standards2011.pdf.
2   www.businesslink.gov.uk/bdotg/action/detail?itemId=1084076041&type=RESOURCES.
3   www.wildlifetrusts.org/how-you-can-help/working-business/biodiversity-benchmark/requirements.
4   http://ukbars.defra.gov.uk/.
5   http://sd.defra.gov.uk/documents/spec-horticulture-services.pdf.
6   https://secure.fera.defra.gov.uk/nonnativespecies/index.cfm?pageid=299.
7   http://eur-lex.europa.eu/LexUriServ/site/en/oj/2006/l_325/l_32520061124en00280034.pdf.
8   www.wrap.org.uk/content/bsi-pas-100-producing-quality-compost.
9   www.epa.gov/epawaste/conserve/rrr/greenscapes/pubs/tipsheet.pdf.
10 www.epa.gov/opp00001/factsheets/ipm.htm.
11 http://livingroofs.org/2010030887/perceived-barriers-to-green-roofs/maintgreenbarr.html.

4.10 Case histories for sustainable facilities management

1 http://www.britishland.com/files/pdf/occupier_updates/spring2011/spring2011_office_2.pdf.
2 http://www.britishland.com/index.asp?pageid=535&casestudy=72&category=3.
3 http://www.britishland.com/index.asp?pageid=535&casestudy=179&category=3.

Bibliography

Anderson, J. and Mills, K. (2002a) *IP9/02 Part 1: Refurbishment or Redevelopment of Office Buildings? Sustainability Comparisons*. Watford: Building Research Establishment.

Anderson, J. and Mills, K. (2002b) *IP9/02 Part 2: Refurbishment or Redevelopment of Office Buildings? Sustainability Case Histories*. Watford: Building Research Establishment.

ANSI/BIFMA (2007) M7.1-2007: *Standard Test Method for Determining VOC Emissions from Office Furniture Systems, Components and Seating*. Grand Rapids, USA: American National Standards Institute /Business and Institutional Furniture Manufacturers Association. Available at: www.bifma.org/standards/standards.html (accessed 14 February 2010).

Appleby, P. (1989) 'Indoor air quality in Brussels', *Building Services Journal*, November: 69–70.

Appleby, P. (2011a) *Integrated Sustainable Design of Buildings*. London: Earthscan.

Appleby, P. (2011b) 'Decarbonisation: the challenge of the old', *Sustainable Building Journal*, March: 18–19.

ASHRAE (2000) *Guideline 12-2000 ASHRAE STANDARD: Minimizing the Risk of Legionellosis Associated with Building Water Systems*. Atlanta, GA: American Society of Heating, Refrigeration and Air Conditioning Engineers.

ASTM (2012) *C1728-12 Standard Specification for Flexible Aerogel Insulation*. Penn, USA: American Society for Testing and Materials.

Baker, N. (2009) *Handbook of Sustainable Refurbishment*. London: Earthscan.

BBP (2009) *Green Leases Toolkit*. London: Better Buildings Partnership. Available at: http://www.betterbuildingspartnership.co.uk/working-groups/green-leases/green-lease-toolkit/ (accessed 15 April 2011).

BBP (2010a) *Low-Carbon Retrofit Toolkit*. London: Better Buildings Partnership. Available at: http://www.betterbuildingspartnership.co.uk/working-groups/sustainable-retrofit/ (accessed 20 September 2011).

BBP (2010b) *Green Building Management Toolkit*. London: Better Buildings Partnership. Available at http://www.betterbuildingspartnership.co.uk/working-groups/owner-occupier-partnerships/green-building-management-toolkit/ (accessed 31 January 2012).

BBP (2011) *Managing Agents Sustainability Toolkit*. London: Better Buildings Partnership. Available at: http://www.betterbuildingspartnership.co.uk/working-groups/property-agents/managing-agents-sustainability-toolkit/ (accessed 3 April 2011).

Bertoldi, P., Boza-Kiss, B. and Rezessy, S. (2007) *JRC Scientific and Technical Reports*. EUR 22927 EN-2007. *Latest Developments of Energy Service Companies across Europe*. Luxemburg: European Commission. Available at: http://publications.jrc.ec.europa.eu/repository/bitstream/111111111/7668/1/22827%20esco%20report-edition%20paper%20version%20.pdf (accessed 27 February 2012).

BioRegional/WWF (2006) *One Planet Living: A Guide to Enjoying Life on Our One Planet*. Bristol: Alastair Sawday.

BioRegional (2008) *Biomass for London*. London: BioRegional. Available at: http://www.lep.org.uk/uploads/LEP%20Biomass%20for%20London%20Wood%20Fuel%20Supply%20Chains%20(inc%20ISBN)%20Jan%202009%20FINAL.pdf (accessed 8 April 2012).

BRE (2000a) BRE Digest 446: *Assessing Environmental Impacts of Construction: Industry Consensus, BREEAM and UK Ecopoints*. Watford: Building Research Establishment.

BRE (2000b) *Energy Consumption Guide 19*. Watford: Building Research Establishment.

BRE (2009a) *Environmental and Sustainability Standard – BES 5058: Issue 1.1 BREEAM in Use*. Watford: Building Research Establishment.

BRE (2009b) *BES 6001: ISSUE 2.0: Framework Standard for the Responsible Sourcing of Construction Products*. Watford: Building Research Establishment. Available at: http://www.greenbooklive.com/filelibrary/responsible_sourcing/BES_6001_Issue2_Fin al.pdf (accessed 21 April 2012).

Brown, R. and Roper, M. (2000a) *Application Guide AG 20/2000: Guide to Legionellosis: Risk Assessment*. Bracknell: Building Services Research & Information Association.

Brown, R. and Roper, M. (2000b) *BSRIA Application Guide AG19/2000: Guide to Legionellosis: Operation & Maintenance*. Bracknell: Building Services Research & Information Association.

Brundrett, G. (1992) *Legionella and Building Services*. Oxford: Butterworth-Heinemann.

BSI (1992) *BS 5234-2: Partitions (Including Matching Linings): Specification for Performance Requirements for Strength and Robustness Including Methods of Test*. London: British Standards Institute.

BSI (2002) *BS EN 1279: 2002: European Harmonized Standard for Glass in Buildings – Insulated Glass Units (IGUs). Part 3: Critical Type Testing (for Gas Leakage Rate and for Gas Concentration Tolerances)*. London: British Standards Institution.

BSI (2003a) *BS 8555:2003: Environmental Management System. Guide to the Phased Implementation of an Environmental Management System Including the Use of Environmental Performance Evaluation*. London: British Standards Institute.

BSI (2003b) *BS 5489-1: 2003 + A2: 2008: Code of Practice for the Design of Road Lighting: Lighting of Roads and Public Amenity Areas*. London: British Standards Institute.

BSI (2005) *BS EN ISO 7730:2005: Ergonomics of the Thermal Environment. Analytical Determination and Interpretation of Thermal Comfort Using Calculation of the PMV and PPD Indices and Local Thermal Comfort Criteria*. London: British Standards Institute.

BSI (2007) *BS EN 12464-2:2007: Lighting of Work Places: Outdoor Work Places*. London: British Standards Institute

BSI (2008) *Standardized Method of Life Cycle Costing for Construction Procurement*. London: British Standards Institute.

BSI (2009) *BS EN 16001 Energy Management Systems*. London: British Standards Institute.

BSI (2011a) *PAS 2050: 2011: Specification for the Assessment of the Life Cycle Greenhouse Gas Emissions of Goods and Services*. London: British Standards Institute. Available at: http://www.bsigroup.com/en/sectorsandservices/Forms/PAS-2050-Form-page/Thank-you/ (accessed 29 January 2012).

BSI (2011b) *BS EN 12464-1:2011: Light and Lighting: Lighting of Work Places. Indoor Work Places*. London: British Standards.

BSI (2011c) *BS 5266-1: 2011: Emergency Lighting: Code of Practice for the Emergency Escape Lighting of Premises*. London: British Standards Institute.

BSI (2012a) *PAS 2030: Improving the Energy Efficiency of Buildings: Specification For Installation Process, Process Management and Service Provision*. London: British Standards Institute.

BSI (2012b) *PAS 2031: Certification of Energy Efficiency Measures (EEM) Installation Services*. London: British Standards Institute.

BSRIA (1998) *Report 78740: Draft Final Report: Evaluation of the CIBSE Draft Protocol for Building Health Checks*. Bracknell: Building Services Research & Information Association.

BSRIA (2007) *BG 1/2007: Handover, O&M Manuals and Project Feedback*. Bracknell: Building Services Research & Information Association.

Carbon Trust (2006) *CTV005: Office Equipment*. London: Carbon Trust. Available at: http://www.carbontrust.com/media/13113/ctv005_office_equipment.pdf (accessed 2 April 2012).

Carbon Trust (2007a) *CTV 027: Metering :Introducing the Techniques and Technology for Energy Data Management*. London: Carbon Trust. Available at: http://www.carbontrust.com/media/31679/ctv027_metering_technology_overview.pdf (accessed 26 April 2012).

Carbon Trust (2007b) *Degree Days for Energy Management: A Practical Introduction*. London: Carbon Trust. Available at: http://ew.ecocongregation.org/downloads/Degree_Days_carbon_trust_booklet.pdf (accessed 29 April 2012).

Carbon Trust (2008) *Management Guide CTV 038: Low-Carbon Refurbishment of Buildings: A Guide to Achieving Carbon Savings from Refurbishment of Non-Domestic Buildings*. London: Carbon Trust. Available at: www.carbontrust.co.uk/publications/pages/publicationdetail.aspx?id=ctv038 (accessed 5 February 2012).

Carbon Trust (2010) *CT161: How to Implement Lighting Controls*. London: Carbon Trust. Available at: www.carbontrust.com/media/31642/ctl161_how_to_implement_lighting_controls.pdf (accessed 2 April 2012).

Carbon Trust (2011a) *Power Play: Applying Renewable Energy Technologies to Existing Buildings*. London: Carbon Trust. Available at: http://www.carbontrust.co.uk/publications/pages/publicationdetail.aspx?id=ctg050 (accessed 5 February 2012).

Carbon Trust (2011b) *Energy Management: A Comprehensive Guide to Controlling Energy Use*. London: Carbon Trust. Available at: www.carbontrust.com/media/13187/ctg054_energy_management.pdf (accessed 25 April 2012).

Carbon Trust (2011c) *Energy Surveys: A Practical Guide to Identifying Energy Saving Opportunities*. London: Carbon Trust. Available at: http://www.carbontrust.com/media/7393/ctg055_energy_surveys.pdf (accessed 25 April 2012).

CIBSE (2000a) *TM23: Testing Buildings for Air Leakage*. London: Chartered Institution of Building Services Engineers.

CIBSE (2000b) *TM26: Hygienic Maintenance of Office Ventilation Ductwork*. London: Chartered Institution of Building Services Engineers.

CIBSE (2002) *TM13: 2000: Minimizing the Risk of Legionnaires' Disease*. London: Chartered Institution of Building Services Engineers.

CIBSE (2004) *Guide F: Energy Efficiency in Buildings*. London: Chartered Institution of Building Services Engineers.

CIBSE (2005) *Knowledge Series KS1: Reclaimed Water*. London: Chartered Institution of Building Services Engineers.

CIBSE (2006a) *TM22: Energy Assessment & Reporting*. London: Chartered Institution of Building Services Engineers.

CIBSE (2006b) *TM31: Building Log Book Toolkit*. London: Chartered Institution of Building Services Engineers.

CIBSE (2006c) *Section A3: Thermal Properties of Building Structures*. London: Chartered Institution of Building Services Engineers.

CIBSE (2006d) *Guide A: Environmental Design. Section A1: Environmental Criteria For Design*. London: Chartered Institution of Building Services Engineers.

CIBSE (2007) *Solar Heating Design and Installation Guide*. London: Chartered Institution of Building Services Engineers.

CIBSE (2008) *Guide M: Maintenance Engineering and Management*. London: Chartered Institution of Building Services Engineers.

CIBSE (2009) *Guide H: Building Control Systems*. London: Chartered Institution of Building Services Engineers.

CIBSE (2012) *Guide F: Energy Efficiency in Buildings*. London: Chartered Institution of Building Services Engineers.

CLG (2001) *Planning Policy Guidance 13: Transport*. London: Department for Communities and Local Government.

CLG (2006) *A Decent Home: Definition and Guidance for Implementation*. London: Department for Communities and Local Government. Available at: http://www. communities.gov.uk/publications/housing/decenthome (accessed 12 December 2011).

CLG (2011) *Draft National Planning Policy Framework*. London: Department for Communities and Local Government.

Concerted Action-EPB (2011) *Implementing the Energy Performance of Buildings Directive (EPBD)*. Brussels: CA-EPBD. Available at: http://www.epbd-ca.org/Medias/Downloads/CA_Book_Implementing_the_EPBD_Featuring_Country_Reports_2010.pdf (accessed 12 December 2011).

CPSL (2009) *Carbon Management: A Practical Guide for Suppliers*. Cambridge: University of Cambridge Programme for Sustainability Leadership.

CTC (2010) *Cycling: A Local Transport Solution – Guidance for Local Transport Plans*. Available at: http://www.ctc.org.uk/resources/Campaigns/100422_CTC_CALTS_Summary.pdf (accessed 28 February 2012).

Davis Langdon (2012) *Spon's Architects' and Builders' Price Book*. London: Spon Press.

DECC (2010) *Renewable Heat Incentive: Consultation on the Proposed RHI Financial Support Scheme*. London: Department of Energy & Climate Change.

DECC (2011a) *The Green Deal and Energy Company Obligation Consultation Document*. London: Department of Energy and Climate Change. Available at: http://www.decc.gov.uk/en/content/cms/consultations/green_deal/green_deal.aspx (accessed 25 November 2011).

DECC (2011b) *Draft DECC Green Deal Code of Practice*. London: Department of Energy and Climate Change. Available at: http://www.decc.gov.uk/en/content/cms/consultations/green_deal/green_deal.aspx (accessed 25 November 2011).

DECC (2011c) *Research Summary: Understanding Potential Consumer Response to the Green Deal*. London: Department of Energy & Climate Change.

DETR (1999) *ECG 19: Energy Consumption Guide 19 – Energy Use in Offices*. Watford: Building Research Establishment.

DfT (2008) *The Essential Guide to Travel Planning*. London: Department for Transport. Available at: http://ways2work.bitc.org.uk/pool/resources/essential-guide-to-travel-planning-final-mar-08.pdf (accessed 9 May 2012).

EA (Electricity Association) (2001) *ER G5/4: Planning Levels for Harmonic Voltage Distortion and Connection of Non-Linear Equipment to Transmission Systems and Distribution Networks in the UK*. London: Electricity Association.

EA (Environment Agency) (2006) *Managing Japanese Knotweed on Development Sites*: Bristol: Environment Agency. Available at: www.environment-agency.gov.uk/static/documents/Leisure/Knotweed_CoP.pdf (accessed 23 April 2012).

EA (Environment Agency) (2007a) *Conserving Water in Buildings*. Bristol: Environment Agency. Available at: www.environment-agency.gov.uk/static/documents/Leisure/geho1107bnjree_1934318.pdf (accessed 21 March 2010).

EA (Environment Agency) (2007b) *SC060024: Cost-benefit of SUDS Retrofit in Urban Areas*. Bristol, UK: Environment Agency. Available at: http://publications.environment-agency.gov.uk/PDF/SCHO0408BNXZ-E-E.pdf (accessed 24 April 2012).

EA (Environment Agency) (2008) *Sustainable Drainage Systems (SUDS)*. Bristol: Environment Agency.

EA (Environment Agency) (2009) *Resource Efficiency Science Programme. Science report SC070016/SR3: The Impact of Household Water Metering in South East England*. Bristol: Environment Agency. Available at: http://publications.environment-agency.gov.uk/PDF/SCHO0709BQSO-E-E.pdf (accessed 14 April 2012).

EA (Environment Agency) (2010) *Hydropower: A Guide for You and Your Community*. Bristol: Environment Agency. Available at: www.energysavingtrust.org.uk/Publications

2/Generate-your-own-energy/Hydropower-A-guide-for-you-and-your-community (accessed 8 April 2012).

EC (2006) *Energy Services Directive 2006/32/EC*. Available at: http://eur-lex. europa.eu/LexUriServ/LexUriServ.do?uri=OJ:L:2006:114:0064:0064:en:pdf (accessed 2 November 2011).

EC (2009a) *Mainstreaming Sustainable Development into EU Policies: Review of the European Union Strategy for Sustainable Development*. COM(2009) 400. Available at: http://eur-lex.europa.eu/LexUriServ/LexUriServ.do?uri=COM:2009:0400:FIN:EN: PDF (accessed 11 December 2011).

EC (2009b) *White Paper: Adapting to Climate Change: Towards a European Framework for Action*. COM(2009) 147. Available at: http://eur-lex.europa.eu/LexUriServ/LexUri Serv.do?uri=COM:2009:0147:FIN:EN:PDF (accessed 11 December 2011).

EC (2009c) *Regulation No 1221/2009 of the European Parliament and of the Council of 25 November 2009 on the Voluntary Participation by Organisations in a Community Eco-Management and Audit Scheme (EMAS)*. Available at: http://eur-lex.europa. eu/LexUriServ/LexUriServ.do?uri=OJ:L:2009:342:0001:0045:EN:PDF (accessed 17 January 2012).

EC (2009d) *Directive 2009/125/EC of the European Parliament and of the Council of 21 October 2009 Establishing a Framework for the Setting of Ecodesign Requirements for Energy-Related Products (Recast)*. Brussels: European Commission. Available at: http://eur-lex.europa.eu/LexUriServ/LexUriServ.do?uri=OJ:L:2009:285:0010:0035:en: PDF (accessed 9 April 2012).

EC (2009e) *EC 2009/894/EC. Commission Decision of 30 November 2009 on Establishing the Ecological Criteria for the Award of the Community Eco-Label for Wooden Furniture*. Brussels: European Commission. Available at: http://ec.europa.eu/ environment/ecolabel/about_ecolabel/pdf/ep_proposal.pdf. (accessed 19 March 2010).

EC (2010a) *Directive 2010/31/EC of 19 May 2010 on the Energy Performance of Buildings (Recast)*. Brussels: Official Journal of the European Union. Available at http://eur-lex.europa.eu/LexUriServ/LexUriServ.do?uri=OJ:L:2010:153:0013: 0035:EN:PDF. (accessed 19 October 2011).

EC (2010b) *Directive 2010/30/EC on the Indication by Labelling and Standard Product Information of the Consumption of Energy and Other Resources by Energy-Related Products (Recast)*. Brussels: European Commission. Available at: http://ec.europa.eu/ energy/efficiency/labelling/labelling_en.htm (accessed 29 March 2012).

EC (2011a) *COM(2011) 109: Energy Efficiency Plan*. Available at: http://eur-lex.europa. eu/LexUriServ/LexUriServ.do?uri=COM:2011:0109:FIN:EN:PDF (accessed 2 November 2011).

EC (2011b) *COM(2011) 571: Roadmap to a Resource Efficient Europe*. Available at: http://ec.europa.eu/environment/resource_efficiency/pdf/com2011_571.pdf (accessed 11 December 2011).

EC (2011c) *COM(2011)681: A Renewed European Union Strategy 2011–14 for Corporate Sustainability Reporting*. Brussels: European Commission. Available at: http://ec.europa.eu/enterprise/policies/sustainable-business/files/csr/new-csr/act_en.pdf (accessed 2 March 2012).

Envirowise (2002) *Green Efficiency: Running a Cost Effective Environmentally Aware Office*. Available at: http://envirowise.wrap.org.uk/cymru/Our-Services/Publications/ GG256-Green-Officiency-Running-a-cost-effective-environmentally-aware-office.html (accessed 14 April 2012).

EPA (Environmental Protection Agency) (2008) *Inventory of U.S. Greenhouse Gas Emissions and Sinks: 1990–2006*. Washington, DC: US Environmental Protection Agency. Available at: http://epa.gov/climatechange/emissions/downloads/08_CR.pdf (accessed 18 April 2012).

EPA (2011) *Healthy Indoor Environment Protocols for Home Energy Upgrades*. Washington, DC: Environmental Protection Agency. Available at: www.epa.gov/iaq/homes/retrofits.html (accessed 15 January 2012).

EST (2006a) *Energy Efficient Ventilation in Dwellings: A Guide to Specifiers*. London: Energy-Saving Trust.

EST (2006b) *CE131: Solar Hot Water Systems – Guidance for Professionals: Conventional Indirect Models*. London: Energy-Saving Trust. Available at: www.greenspec.co.uk/files/refurb/EST-solarWaterHeating.pdf (accessed 8 April 2012).

EST (2009) *Quantifying the Energy and Carbon Effects of Water Saving: Full Technical Report*. London: Energy-Saving Trust.

Federal Facilities Council (2001) *Learning from Our Buildings: Federal Facilities Council Technical Report No. 145: A State-of-the-Practice Summary of Post-Occupancy Evaluation*. Washington, DC: National Academy Press. Available at: www.nap.edu/openbook.php?record_id=10288&page=R1 (accessed 7 February 2012).

Federspiel, C. and Villafana, L. (2003) 'Design of an energy and maintenance system user interface for building occupants', *ASHRAE Transactions*, 109(2): 665–76. Available at: http://www.cbe.berkeley.edu/research/briefs-feedback.htm (accessed 4 May 2012).

GRO (2011) *The GRO Green Roof Code*. Sheffield: Groundwork. Available at http://livingroofs.org/images/stories/pdfs/GRO_CODE_2011.pdf (accessed 16 May 2012).

Gustafson, S., Zellers, R and Miller, K. (2010) *Sustainable Landscaping*. Houston, Texas: IFMA Foundation. Available at: http://www.groundskeeper.com/misc/IFMA_Sustainable%20Landscaping%20Guide_Final.pdf (accessed 15 May 2012).

HMG (2005a) *Housing Health Safety Rating System (HHSRS) Regulations*. Available at: http://www.legislation.gov.uk/uksi/2005/3208/pdfs/uksi_20053208_en.pdf (accessed 13 April 2012).

HMG (2005b) *Hazardous Waste (England & Wales) Regulations, As Amended*. Available at: http://publications.environment-agency.gov.uk/PDF/GEHO0411BTQZ-E-E.pdf (accessed 3 May 2012).

HMG (2007) *Waste Electrical and Electronic Equipment (Amendment) Regulations*. Available at: http://www.legislation.gov.uk/uksi/2007/3454/pdfs/uksi_20073454_en.pdf (accessed 3 May 2012).

HMG (2010) *Building Regulations 2000 – Approved Document F1: Means of Ventilation*. London: RIBA. Available at: http://www.planningportal.gov.uk/uploads/br/BR_PDF_ADF_2010.pdf (accessed 22 March 2012).

Hoggett, R. (2010) *Community-owned Renewable Energy Projects*. Cornwall: Community Energy Plus. Available at: http://www.communitypowercornwall.coop/downloads/community_renewables_-_richard_hoggett.pdf (accessed 28 February 2012).

Housing Forum (2009) *Interim Working Group Report: Sustainable Refurbishment of the Existing Housing Stock*. London: The Housing Forum. Available at: http://housingforum.org.uk/knowledge/publications/sustainable-refurbishment-existing-housing-stock (accessed 16 January 2012).

HSC (2002) *HSC-L8. Approved Code of Practice (ACOP) and Guidance: Legionella Bacteria in Water Systems*. Sudbury, Suffolk: Health & Safety Executive.

HSE (1992) *Health and Safety (Display Screen Equipment) Regulations*. Norwich: Her Majesty's Stationary Office.

HSE (1996) *Guidance Note EH38: Ozone: Health Hazards And Precautionary Measures*. Norwich: Her Majesty's Stationary Office.

HVCA (1998) *Cleanliness of Ventilation Systems Guide to Good Practice TR17*. London: Heating and Ventilating Contractors Association.

IEA (International Energy Agency) (2009) *World Energy Outlook*. Paris: OECD/IEA.

IEA (International Energy Agency) (2010) *Energy Technology Perspectives*. Paris: IEA.

Intelligent Energy Europe (2010) *E4: Energy Efficient Elevators and Escalators*. Portugal:

ISR University of Coimbra. Available at: www.e4project.eu/documenti/wp6/E4-WP6-Brochure.pdf (accessed 3 April 2012).

International Organization for Standardization (ISO) (1984) *ISO 7730: Moderate Thermal Environments: Determination of the PMV and PPD Indices and Specification of the Conditions for Thermal Comfort*. Geneva: ISO. (Most recent revision with modified title: 2005)

International Organization for Standardization (ISO) (1999) *ISO 14031: 1999: Environmental Management – Environmental Performance Evaluation – Guidelines*. Geneva: ISO.

International Organization for Standardization (ISO) (2006) *ISO 14044: 2006: Environmental Management – Life Cycle Assessment and Requirements – Guidelines*. Geneva: ISO.

International Organization for Standardization (ISO) (2008) *ISO 15686-5: 2008: Buildings and Constructed Assets – Service Life Planning. Part 5: Life Cycle Costing*. Geneva: ISO.

International Organization for Standardization (ISO) (2011) *ISO 50001: Energy Management Systems – Requirements with Guidance for Use*. Geneva: ISO.

Johnson, J., Counsell, J. and Strachan, P. (2011) *Trends in Office Internal Gains and the Impact on Space Heating and Cooling*. CIBSE Technical Symposium, DeMontfort University, Leicester UK, 6 and 7 September 2011. Available at: http://www.cibse.org/content/cibsesymposium2011/Paper074.pdf (accessed 2 April 2012).

King, M. and Shaw, R. (2010) *Community Energy: Planning, Development and Delivery*. UK: TCPA/CHPA/LDA Design. Available at: www.tcpa.org.uk/data/files/comm_energy_plandevdel.pdf (accessed 29 February 2012).

Kosny, J., Yarbrough, D., Miller, W., Petrie, T., Childs, P., Syed, A. and Leuthold, D. (2007) *Thermal Performance of PCM-Enhanced Building Envelope Systems*. Atlanta, GA: ASHRAE.

Kougoulis, J., Kaps, R. and Wolf, O. (2011) *Background Report Including Draft Criteria Proposal: Development of European Ecolabel and Green Public Procurement Criteria for Imaging Equipment*. Working Document for 2nd AHWG Meeting for the Development of Ecolabel Criteria for Imaging Equipment, November 2011. Available at: http://susproc.jrc.ec.europa.eu/imaging-equipment/docs/IMAGING%20EQUIPMENT_Background%20report.pdf (accessed 12 April 2012).

Leaman, A. (2010) 'Are buildings getting better?' *Arup Journal*. 45: 4–8.

Leaman, A., Stevenson, F. and Bordass, B. (2010) 'Building evaluation: practice and principles', *Building Research and Information*, 38(5): 564–77.

LEP (2004) *Integrating Renewable Energy into New Developments: Toolkit for Planners, Developers and Consultants*. London: London Energy Partnership. Available at: www.lep.org.uk/uploads/renewables_toolkit.pdf (accessed 14 February 2012).

Low-Carbon Construction Innovation and Growth Team (2010) *Final Report*. London: HM Government. Available at: www.bis.gov.uk/assets/biscore/business-sectors/docs/l/10-1266-low-carbon-construction-igt-final-report.pdf (accessed 19 October 2011).

Loyd, S. (1997) *Facilities Management Specification 1/97: Guidance and the Standard Specification for Ventilation Hygiene*. Bracknell: Building Services Research and Information Association.

LPCB (2010) *Loss Protection Standard LPS 1175: Issue 7: Requirements and Testing Procedures for the LPCB Approval and Listing of Intruder Resistant Building Components, Strongpoints, Security Enclosures and Free-Standing Barriers*. Watford: Building Research Establishment. Available at: http://www.thenbs.com/Publication Index/DocumentSummary.aspx?PubID=76&DocID=296151 (accessed on 20 April 2012).

Mesarovic, M. and Pestel, E. (1975) *Mankind at the Turning Point* (The Second Report to the Club of Rome). London: Hutchinson.

NADCA (1992) *Mechanical Cleaning of Non-Porous Air Conveyance System Components 1992-01*. Washington, DC: National Air Duct Cleaners Association.

NYC (2010) *New York City Active Design Guidelines: Promoting Physical Activity and Health in Design*. New York: NYC Department of Design and Construction. Available at: http://ddcftp.nyc.gov/adg/downloads/adguidelines.pdf (accessed 1 October 2010).

ODPM (2006) *Housing Health & Safety Rating System: Operating Guidance*. London: Office of the Deputy Prime Minister.

Pearson, A. (2011) 'Height of sustainability', *CIBSE Journal* 3(11): 29–33.

Pearson, C. and Seaman, A. (2003) *BSRIA Application Guide AG 1/2003: Condition-Based Maintenance Using Non-Destructive Testing*. Bracknell: Building Services Research & Information Association.

Pejtersen, J. *et al.* (1989) 'Air pollution sources in ventilation systems', in E. Kulic *et al.* (eds) *Proceedings of CLIMA 2000, Sarajevo: The Second World Congress on Heating, Ventilating, Refridgerating and Air Conditioning*. Sarajevo, 2000. Vol. 3, pp. 139–44.

Phillips, R., Blackmore, P., Anderson, J., Clift, M., Aguilo-Rullon, A. and Pester, S. (2007) *Micro Wind Turbines in Urban Environments*. (BRE Report FB17). Watford: Building Research Establishment.

Power, A. (2008) *Does Demolition Or Refurbishment of Old and Inefficient Homes Help to Increase Our Environmental, Social and Economic Viability?* London: Elsevier. Available at: http://www.bis.gov.uk/assets/bispartners/foresight/docs/energy/energy%20final/power%20paper-section%205.pdf (accessed 4 February 2012).

RIBA (2007) *Outline Plan of Work 2007*. London: Royal Institute of British Architects. Available at: http://www.architecture.com/Files/RIBAProfessionalServices/Practice/OutlinePlanofWork(revised).pdf (accessed 5 February 2012).

Ridley, I. (2009) 'Indoor air quality and ventilation modeling', in M.D. Mumovic and Santamouris (eds) *A Handbook of Sustainable Building Design & Engineering*. London: Earthscan.

Sherwood Burge, P. (1992) 'Bacteria, fungi and other micro-organisms', in G. Leslie and F. Lunau (eds) *Indoor Air Pollution: Problems and Priorities*. Cambridge: Cambridge University Press.

Shimmin, J. and Khoo, I. (2002) 'Web-based occupant feedback for building energy management systems', in S. Damiani *et al.* (eds) *Knowledge-based Intelligent Information Engineering Systems and Allied Technologies*. Amsterdam: IOS Press, pp. 214–19.

SLL (2009) *Lighting Handbook*. London: Society of Light and Lighting.

UN (1992) United Nations Conference on Environment & Development, Rio de Janeiro, Brazil, 3 to 14 June 1992: Agenda 21. Available at: http://www.un.org/esa/dsd/agenda21/index.shtml (accessed 10 April 2012).

UNEP (2011) *Towards a Green Economy*. Available at: http://www.unep.org/greeneconomy/Portals/88/documents/ger/GER_synthesis_en.pdf

Waters, M., Plimmer F. and Kenney, S. (2007) 'Developer strategies for sustainable development in the UK: redevelopment versus refurbishment and the sustainable communities plan', paper presented at Strategic Integration of Surveying Services conference, Hong Kong, 13–17 May 2007. Hong Kong: Hong Kong Institute of Surveyors. Available at: http://www.fig.net/pub/fig2007/papers/ts_4a/ts04a_04_waters_etal_1385.pdf (accessed 6 February 2012).

Waterwise (2009) *The Water and Energy Implications of Bathing and Showering Behaviours and Technologies*. Available at: http://www.waterwise.org.uk/data/resources/27/final-water-and-energy-implications-of-personal-bathing.pdf (accessed 15 April 2012).

Wilson, S. and Hedge, A. (1987) *The Office Environment Survey: A Study of Building Sickness*. London: Building Use Studies Ltd.

World Commission on Environment and Development (1987) *Our Common Future* (The Brundtland Report). Oxford: Oxford University Press.

World Energy Council (2010) *Energy Efficiency: A Recipe for Success*. London: WEC. Available at: http://www.worldenergy.org/documents/fdeneff_v2.pdf (accessed 27 October 2011).

ZCH (2012) *Mechanical Ventilation with Heat Recovery: Interim Report of Ventilation & Indoor Air Quality Task Group*. Milton Keynes: Zero-Carbon Hub. Available at: www.zerocarbonhub.org/resourcefiles/ViaqReport_web.pdf (accessed 28 March 2012).

Index